YOU'RE IN THE FRONT ROW

How to Kick Off Your Career in Sports

Even If You're Not a Star Athlete

By Glenn Capeloto

Facts on Demand Press

You're in the Front Row

How to Kick Off Your Career in Sports
Even If You're Not a Star Athlete

Copyright © 2012 by Glenn Capeloto
www.yourcareerinsports.com
GlennCapeloto@yahoo.com

Cover Design by: Robin Fox & Associates
All photographs appearing in this book are the property of the author or the author has
a permission statement on file to allowing reproduce herein.

ISBN: 978-1-889150-58-1
Published by: Facts on Demand Press
BRB Publication, Inc.
800-929-3811

Cataloging-in-Publication Data
(Provided by Quality Books, Inc.)

Capeloto, Glenn.
    You're in the front row : how to kick off your career
in sports even if you're not a star athlete / by Glenn
Capeloto.
      p. cm.
    ISBN-13: 978-1-889150-58-1
    ISBN-10: 1-889150-58-4

    1. Sports--Vocational guidance.   I. Title.

GV734.3.C37 2012   796.023
                          QBI11-600189

You're in the Front Row
How to Kick Off Your Career in Sports Even If You're Not a Star Athlete

By Glenn Capeloto

———————

Having a career in sports is a dream come true for many. I've been very fortunate to be involved in sports management for more than 40 years, having served as an Athletic Director, a coach, an NFL agent, a scout, and an author. As President and Founder of Sports Management WorldWide, our mission is to offer the best sports job training and curriculum available. We pride ourselves in being the global leader in sports business education and are always on the lookout for better ways to educate and prepare our students.

You're in the Front Row - How to Kick Off Your Career in Sports, Even if You're Not a Star Athlete, written by Glenn Capeloto, is a great first step toward achieving your goal to be part of this exhilarating industry. It's a fabulous and fresh introduction to dozens of occupations in sports, with constructive and candid advice from a variety of experts who have made it to the tops of their craft. The guidance and examples provided in Glenn's book are real life and motivating.

At Sports Management WorldWide, we have chosen *You're In the Front Row* as our required book for our Online Introduction to Sports Jobs Course. It is a must read if you are thinking about pursuing a livelihood in sports.

Even if you're just a sports junkie, you'll find it a highly entertaining read.

Dr. G. Lynn Lashbrook
President and Founder
Sports Management Worldwide
SportsManagementWorldWide.com

Table of Contents

Dedication

There are several I express thanks to

➤ To my wife Donna, and my children, Chad, Amy, and Ryan for supporting my sports endeavor throughout the years.

➤ To my parents, Bill and Jeanne Capeloto, for letting me attend so many Seattle SuperSonics and Seattle Totem games as a kid, and for all their love and support.

➤ To Steve Nasinec. Thanks for all the life lessons many moons ago.

➤ To the fortune teller in Hawaii, who in 1983, actually predicted I would "Write THE BOOK."

➤ To Sonicsgate.org for their efforts to get the Sonics and the NBA rightfully returned to the fans of Seattle.

➤ To Bob Blackburn (the original voice of the Sonics) and Pete Gross (the original voice of the Seahawks) for being such great mentors and providing me an opportunity as a young adult to break into an industry which has given me so many special moments to treasure.

Bob Blackburn, Known as *The Voice*
Starting in 1967, Bob broadcast
2,300+ Sonic games over 25 seasons.

-

Photo courtesy of Mrs. Pat Blackburn

Pete Gross, original voice of the Seahawks
Starting in 1976 Pete announced 331
Seahawk games over 17 seasons.

-

Photo provided with permission of the
Seattle Seahawks

Early in your existence, sports becomes part of your life

Soon after, it becomes a family affair

Now learn how it becomes your career!

Foreword

A FOREWORD PASS

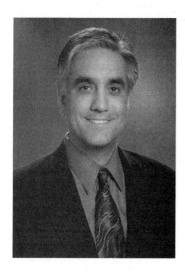

By Pedro Gomez

ESPN Reporter

There probably isn't a day that goes by when a sports fan doesn't wish they could work in sports. The first dream, of course, is to be hitting fastballs over the fence at Dodger Stadium, nailing down three-pointers at Madison Square Garden, or even throwing spirals down-field at Soldier Field. Of course, the great majority of us cannot come close to being the gifted few who can call themselves a professional athlete.

For the rest, there are paths that allow the dream of being associated with a sports team or somehow being linked in some form of sports that are achievable. After all, sports fans can never get enough of sports. We watch and read, trying to fill an appetite that seems endless. It's why ratings for NFL games routinely trounce the highest-rated weekly shows.

In *You're In the Front Row - How To Kick Off Your Career In Sports, Even Without Being A Star Athlete,* Glenn Capeloto delivers many of the trails to the treasure map to make your sports dream come true. No matter the route you desire - whether it's to become a radio play-by-play announcer, a sports writer, a statistician, a clubhouse attendant or any number of other jobs that can get you as close to the action as the millionaires who sit courtside or right behind home plate or in the luxury boxes - this book provides many of the necessary routes.

Glenn even gives you a roadmap toward becoming a team mascot (hey, it gets you into the arena or stadium).

Many of these messages are delivered through first-hand accounts from many of us who long-ago dreamed the dream and decided to jump head-first into the deep end of the swimming pool. Many times, that's exactly what it takes, the will to try something that seems so foreign and difficult to many of us. But if you have the desire and willingness to give it a go, you may find yourself years from now the same way I have for nearly 30 years since I first began answering phone calls at a small newspaper south of Miami, Florida.

A day hasn't gone by in my life where I've woken up in the morning and dreaded going to work. It has never been a drag. The greatest joy in life is enjoying what you do for a living. Over the years, I have been fortunate enough to call places like Fenway Park, Lambeau Field, Wrigley Field, the Staples Center and other great sports venues my office, if even for one night a year. But on those days and nights, there has never been a better place to be.

Don't go into this with the mindset of becoming financially rich. Go into it believing you will become emotionally wealthy beyond your belief. And sometimes, the money actually can come, as well.

Introduction

When Sports Sneeze, the Whole World Catches a Cold

Americans have an undeniable and insatiable appetite for athletics. Some are fulfilled by being pennant-waving fans in the stands. Then there are sports nuts that dress up every Saturday or Sunday in the Fall like it's Halloween, wearing face paint and donning a jersey of their favorite team as if *they* were about to take to the field and go into battle. Others break out every BBQ utensil they own while picnicking from dawn to dusk. Unless you're about to leave the stadium, tailgating is not driving too close to the car in front of you. It's the sports way of life and a weekend reward for millions of football crazies across the country. Where else do people so willingly spend money they don't have to party so hard? It makes no difference what age the fans are or what socioeconomic level they come from. Their team could be zero and ten, and they'd still drop hundreds to thousands of dollars weekly to be part of the action. How many fantasy leagues are there today? Sports enthusiasts can never get enough to satisfy their addiction to their favorite team.

This book is intended to help provide the recipe to achieve your dream to work in the sports industry. Whether it's a full-time career or a part-time situation you seek, there are a wide variety of occupations available that can present you an association with the sports world, provide an excellent living, and perhaps a paid-for travel opportunity.

As a long-time professional sports statistician, I can't tell you how many times when I have shared with people what I've been fortunate enough to do over the years, they've said, "Wow, you're so lucky! How can I do that? Where can I get a press credential? Can you get me into the game?" There is clearly an unparalleled lust to be somehow close to the competition.

With sports now a multi-billion dollar commerce (the National Football League alone generates $9 billion dollars annually), the industry has become so vast several thousands of people are required to fill positions of all kinds. This book highlights dozens of them and features interviews with several who currently occupy these jobs.

What are *your* odds of landing one of these occupations? There are 92 NFL, MLB, and the NBA combined franchises alone which employ approximately 200-300 people each. That doesn't count the significant number of (non-athletic) people getting paid by 189 minor league baseball teams, nor the many thousands of people earning a sports-related living at 343 Division I universities, 287 Division II schools, 443 Division III colleges, or 286 NAIA campuses. ESPN's staff numbers near 6,000.

The great appeal about a sports career is it's a job you actually look forward to doing. Instead of, "I've got to go to work," it's, "I GET to go to work." So what job in sports do you want to call your own? Maybe you'll be a gifted TV producer or director. Perhaps you'd enjoy the gypsy life of a scout or a referee. Numerous job opportunities exist in management, broadcasting, and dozens of other front office positions that make coming to work exciting and satisfying. Perhaps you can combine your love for athletics with business and marketing savvy and be involved in sports media sales. Marketing departments, stadium managers, IT experts, sales consultants and electricians all are necessary to bring critical elements of a sports franchise's branding success to life. All that flashing neon signage requires someone to make it happen. That's a far cry from sports franchises of yesteryear which operated with a staff of five.

Getting started isn't as tough as you think. Begin your search with an academic institution and their sports information office. Maybe your try-out begins with an internship with one of the hundreds of major and minor league professional sports franchises to determine your niche. This book includes an extensive directory to make it easy. There is a multitude of behind-the-scenes freelance positions available too. So the prospects of an affiliation with sports may be much more possible than you think.

I've been experiencing and enjoying my dream hobby since I started college at the University of Washington in 1975. Unexpectedly, I launched my sports profession as a play-by-play announcer for a 10-watt student radio station. This led to a life-long affiliation with sports as a statistician. Rewardingly, I've been courtside for the NBA Finals, up in the press box during the World Series, in the broadcast booth for NFL and collegiate championship games and traveled throughout the country enjoying a number of stadiums from the broadcast booth.

Realistically, some sports careers can be financially and emotionally challenging. This industry is definitely a "who-you-know" business with job security a management change or a league lockout away. With many positions in sports, you may not make nearly enough money to achieve financial freedom. Maybe you'll earn just enough to cover your cost of living, unless you're one of the fortunate and talented few to reach upper management or gifted as a writer, sports agent or broadcaster. For many, the privilege of getting to sit courtside or up in the press box and get paid is reward enough.

In developing this book, I've spoken with a number of renowned, highly successful sports figures who were willing to share their story and offer recommendations on how you can proceed and succeed in a variety of sports-related endeavors. You will gain huge insight from some of the sports industry's most successful at their craft. Noteworthy sports announcers and sports executives had to start somewhere. One sport executive who shared his vast expertise with me guided the Redeem Team back to Olympic glory and proudly wears a World Series ring. Another that I'll showcase started out as a ball boy for an NBA team under Hall of Fame coach and player Lenny Wilkens. NBA Superstar Spencer Haywood refused to get in the team photo unless this ball boy was included in the team picture. Now, this former ball boy is one of the most respected sports executives in all of sports. How about someone who is a Hall-of-Fame basketball player who was the first woman to try out for an NBA team and is now the President of a women's professional basketball team and Vice President of an NBA team? Another contributor is a former sports agent turned team executive who successfully defended President Reagan's attempted assassin, John Hinckley, Jr., in court. Each of these flourishing individuals and many more share their perspective on the current state of sports and what you can do to make the team.

What are the evolving possibilities for women in the sports world? Do you know what the critical responsibilities of a TV Broadcast Associate are? How much does this person get paid? You'll be shocked. This book will explore how and where to get your foot in the door, just what it's like to be part of a sports TV broadcast, how to work side-by-side with a sportscaster while simultaneously communicating with a TV control truck, and so many more sports-associated professions.

You never know when opportunity knocks. One person I interviewed got his big break into professional sports while bidding at an auction for a pie. Bizarre but true! We'll cover many other career paths too.

One of the great things about sports is its rich tradition, so you'll also read how baseball, basketball, and football became so historically intertwined in our lives.

Best of all, this book will even provide you with an actual list of where to look for work and whom to contact, including web sites and phone numbers.

I wish there had been a book like this when I was a budding college student. The following chapters just might ignite your sports passion and create your lifetime ticket to future sporting events. Then your friends will be pestering you to get them a press pass.

Chapter 1

The Price of Admission

True sports fans possess a distinctive DNA. They just can't seem to get their fill of their favorite team(s). What if you could combine that insatiable passion with a paying career? Imagine being able to awaken in the morning and say: "I GET to go to work!" You'd no longer have to pay for those pricey season tickets. Parking at the stadium would be free. Not only would you cheer your favorite athletes up close, you might even meet them. At some stadiums, you'd even get fed for free, in the press box yet. A sports career might not be as farfetched as you think. This book will give you an overview of several job possibilities with practical advice from the experts. Just maybe *You're In The Front Row* might provide the elixir that re-directs your occupational aspirations.

A career in sports doesn't require that you run a 4.3 40, stand six-foot-ten, or can drill a 98-mile-per-hour fastball 425 feet. So how do you go from being one of millions who live for sports to employment in sports? If you're a committed individual with a lot of perseverance, the possibilities are nearly endless.

The *Wide World of Sports* is getting wider and wider, so much so it's become a vast ocean of career opportunities. The sports industry now requires a variety of skills and talents to accommodate the athletes, the teams, media, sponsors, the fans and so many more related industries. Whereas the front office of a sports franchise used to be five people wearing a host of hats, it now takes a small army to produce a sporting event. The Dallas Cowboys employ 6,000 people on game day.

Everything has become totally specialized. Marketing and salespeople, coaches, referees, event coordinators, web content experts, announcers, statistical experts, photographers, medical professionals; the list goes on and on. As most in the industry discovered for themselves, the career ladder to success requires getting your foot in the door and not being opposed to paying your dues. The exact order of your career's progression could take many different paths. This book will profile several.

Once upon a time, sport was mostly innocent and pure, a diversion for participants to channel their excess vitality. Sports used to be a hobby, something for recreation, not a career. It meant going to a ballgame with your dad, mitt in hand, and ordering peanuts or cracker jacks. Team logos proudly defined a city.

In today's sports industry, now it's mostly about the dash for cash, with several entities grabbing for the loot. Professional and collegiate teams, players and their representative unions, broadcast entities and advertisers have all contributed toward refining sports into one of the largest industries in the United States. Whereas players were once civic treasures, now they're a commodity. The gridiron has been overshadowed by greed-lock. Strike is no longer a term automatically associated with a baseball thrown over the plate. If you happen to be a sports team owner, your unborn great-great-great grandchildren are already multi-millionaires. Sports have become so over-commercialized, you can't even use the restroom without being pitched by some sponsoring plumbing company.

This racing engine called sports isn't going to slow down anytime soon, not with multi-billion dollar industries sitting behind the driver's seat. Oversaturated sports coverage through cable TV and the world-wide web won't allow it.

Front office administrators, broadcast executives, and advertisers know the world of sports is an absolute religion to some, an insatiable obsession that is constantly recycled by the hope that "this is the year" for their home team. Sports have always been a hand-me-down generational affliction and now it's a year-round mania. From the draft to free agent signings to pre-season to the regular season and hopefully the playoffs, there is no longer a downtime.

Success in sports used to be quantified by wins and losses and tabulation at the turnstiles. Today, that's just one contributing piece of the proceeds pie. Entertainment value has been superseded by corporate success. The measuring stick for accomplishment nowadays is gauged by the amount of generated revenue, state-of-the-art stadiums (generally at the tax-payer's expense), and the magnitude of broadcast and advertiser agreements. The new gladiators in sports are the marketers. In the first half of the 20th century, publicizing meant listing who the home team was playing that night on the stadium's exterior signs. Promotions meant bat or ball nights. Cross-pollinating every possible marketing dimension of your franchise now is essential to the survival of your city's team. Corporate suites have become vital profit centers for pro sports.

Many of today's athletes are overpaid and overhyped and no longer worthy of being deified. Many are no longer role models like our sports heroes of the past. Whereas Babe Ruth and Lou Gehrig were solid gold, today's steroid abusers are gold-plated. Players themselves are measured more by lengths and amounts of contracts than performance, with hefty multi-million dollar agreements the norm. Where athletes used to give their all, now they want all they can get.

Some referees are even paid more than the President of the United States. How did it come to all this?

Sports aren't just season-long now. It's an exaggerated 12-month industry. The economics of contemporary pro sports dictate that wherever there is a dollar to be made is a career opportunity for the whiz that can make it happen. If a sponsor name can be attached to something, anything, there's money to be made. Stadiums no longer adorn the name of some proud civic connection of a city. Because of naming rights, now its moniker is the name of a major corporation. Even uniforms are a moving advertisement now. Watch baseball on TV and behind the batter, you'll see a computer-generated ad on the backstop area. Even priority tail-gating has become a revenue source. Home Run derby and the Slam Dunk competition have taken on a life of their own. An All-Star Game has become a weekend of celebration and corporate opportunity. Old-Timers' days have evolved into retro uniform games, with old merchandise being repackaged as collectible throw-backs. Thankfully, sports still has some semblance of nostalgia.

Since athletic competition creates considerable hoopla and is such a significant player for the entertainment dollar (both professionally and collegiately), out of necessity, the current commerce of sports has become extremely departmentalized and requires specialists at many levels. As the essential needs for revenues to increase have grown, so have opportunities in sports careers. The more the money involved, the larger the number of positions required in the business. This is good news for career seekers who would love to combine their professional livelihood with their appetite for sports. This creates a multitude of employment prospects that just might put YOU in the front row.

Before you say: "That's the career for me," let's further illuminate this addictive industry that seems to attract job applicants like ants to a picnic.

Outsiders mostly see the glamour of sports careers – the massive salaries of athletes, the limelight, and the glorified lifestyle. The reality is this is an industry typically renowned for compensating its employees quite poorly. You can expect to be overworked and underpaid with a lot of grunt work your daily duty. On game-days, you'll work from sun-up to sun-down and 'overtime pay' does not exist. It's truly the school of hard knocks. Upward mobility is slow and challenging with supply and demand retarding your chances. Quickly, the magic becomes mundane and wears off for some who can't stick it out or afford it. A sports-related occupation can provide lots of nirvana, but it also delivers lots of challenges.

It's understandable why many people want to make the career sacrifice and have a burning passion to be an integral part of the action. For some, being just a paying fan isn't enough. To fans, the stadium is their sanctuary, a place to escape the challenges of the work week. Almost like a drug, it allows them to park the stresses of their lives and be carefree, if only for an afternoon. Now sports are like group therapy. Somewhere along the line, the tradition of faithfully cheering your city's team became tethered with a party hearty mentality and a corporate association. 'Game Days' are now an electric experience and viewed as significant social events. Attending a Super Bowl would be a sign of elite status. Wholesome family picnics have been replaced by tailgate parties at the stadium. TiVo must have been invented with sports addicts in mind. Sports are even a component of divorce settlements. "I get the season tickets," or "I own the Los Angeles Dodgers." "No, I do."

Even the athletes that fans admire eventually succumb to the one opponent they can't defeat – Father Time. Then even players themselves long for some kind of extension with sports, anything that will continue their connection with an athletic organization.

Sports teams are like a religion and the playing surface is the altar where fans gather to worship. Football has become an insatiable obsession in American society. Basketball and baseball have gone global. Soccer remains number one if you factor in international appeal. Sports have even created their own language to describe the action with expressions like "Web Gem" and "Getting Posterized."

Team employment opportunities come in many shapes throughout professional and collegiate levels. This book will explore many of them. Besides the 134 teams that exist in the NFL, NBA, WNBA, MLB, and NHL, there are hundreds of minor leagues needing positions filled. In baseball alone, there are 189 minor league franchises. The Canadian Football League has eight franchises. Major League Soccer provides 15 more teams to consider for employment. For those in college, it's imperative to get an internship. It will give you a reference point of what other jobs entail. Know that the wages are meager if not non-existent. You'll need to be dedicated, determined, persistent, patient, hungry, driven, and enthusiastic. Liken it to the Kentucky Derby. You'll start out of the gate in last place, but if you run the race hard, you'll find the finish line. An internship will allow you to learn skills, gain hands-on practical experience, and develop valuable networking contacts. It places you in actual work situations.

Once you gain entry into this coveted industry, go the extra step, prepare, and learn. Experience and attitude will carry you far. Make your mark because many companies will promote from within. Learn as you earn. Don't just count on sports executives to boost your network. Alumni provide key contacts, too. Paper resumes aren't nearly as valuable as a handshake and introduction. Make yourself memorable. Go to trade shows and job fairs. Attend events. When opportunity knocks, answer the door.

So how do you go about getting your foot in the door? What skills do you have or need to develop to join a sports organization? Sports management courses and journalism curriculum are being offered more and more throughout the country. The majority of tomorrow's sports administrators will benefit from a degree in sports management. You'll need to be well-rounded when facilitating the business office, the media sector, the coaches, the stadium supervisor, and so many more departments. More than 260 colleges and universities now offer sports administration courses.

With the ongoing labor disputes and lockouts that are so commonplace now in sports, you might want to strongly consider getting a legal degree or training in accounting. It isn't a coincidence that two of the major sports league's commissioners have legal backgrounds. In this day and age of collective bargaining agreements, lockouts, and anti-trust lawsuits, we might see a day where a lawyer might win the

MVP (most valuable performer). There's so much money at stake, an accountant might be voted the Sixth Man award. X's and O's have been replaced by $$$.

Your best launch-pad into the world of sports is through participation at the collegiate level. Interning with your Sports Information Office will provide invaluable hands-on experience.

Sport is an exciting industry that begs for creativity and talent. Create your own checklist and see if you excel at the following traits. Are you:

Organized

Creative

Passionate

Persistent

Persuasive

Willing to pay your dues!

Hunger for sports won't distinguish you. Are reduced wages and the long hours worthwhile? You may need to be flexible with the position you accept, geographically flexible too. Now that you've had a splash of sports reality, put down the foam finger, set aside the face paint; let's examine dozens of livelihoods that could become your future.

Pitcher Randy Johnson once got a birdie, but he wasn't golfing at the time. During a 2001 Spring Training game against the Giants, Johnson uncorked a 95 MPH fastball toward the plate. A dove chose an inopportune time to do a fly-by, and the Big Unit's pitch exploded the bird into a cloud of feathers. I'm guessing Johnson didn't yell FORE, so the bird didn't have time to duck. The umpire ruled the pitch a "fowl" ball.

Chapter 2

Getting Started - The Tryout

A proving ground for many with a sports career aspiration starts at their own high school or college campus. For some, it's the student paper. For me, it was the student radio station. For many, it's through a college Sports Information Office.

Where to Begin - Internships

Acquiring an internship in the sport industry is a crucial first stepping stone in your career path and serves many important purposes. It places you in actual work situations that allow you to learn skills, gain hands-on practical experience, and develop invaluable networking contacts. It also allows you to test-drive the industry. Is this what you really want to do?

The job description for interns looking to break into the sport industry is pretty basic. Work for free for long hours. If you want to advance your career, there's no shortcut. The key is to get your foot in the door.

Where you get started depends on where you are in your schooling or career. If you're still in high school, volunteer for the student newspaper or work at the school's athletic events. Maybe you'll keep stats for a football or basketball game. Perhaps you'll be the public address announcer at the stadium or gym. Your school's athletic director likely will have key contacts at the next level or provide a valuable recommendation. Treat this as the equivalent to earning a scholarship. Any undertaking on your part shows initiative and desire to learn, plus the practical experience will benefit you as you seek the succeeding opportunity.

The next level up is your university or college. Try securing an internship with a College Sports Information office. Every Division One school has one, and D-II, D-III and NAIA-level schools likely do too. Know that as the size of the university or college gets smaller, so does the extent of their staffing needs. Get started right away. My son Chad didn't even wait until he started attending college. He began volunteering his time at Arizona State University sporting events while he was still a junior in high school. They were pleased to utilize him during game-day operations, and it opened an important career opportunity for him as he began attending ASU.

Sports Information Office interns are asked to perform a wide variety of duties. You may assist in promotions, preparation of game-day operations for the press box, write media releases or pre-game notes, facilitate the media during a game, and interview players after the contest. There are dozens of details you'll be asked to help with, and the hours are long. Expect to be the first to arrive and last to leave. While you're interning, develop a portfolio of your work and achievements.

If you live in a major market, professional teams typically have a working relationship with local colleges and utilize these schools like a sports farm system. They get free labor in exchange for providing practical experience. You get a multi-faceted inside look at the working environment of a professional team. Everyone wins. There are some internship opportunities that do provide compensation. Your career counselors will post internship opportunities with these professional teams throughout the school year in an ongoing basis. It's your responsibility to apply for the internship, and if you are accepted, give it all you've got during this try-out process.

If you're talented, some teams will hire you upon graduation, so get your foot in the door, perform at a higher level than your peers, learn all you can during your audition, and develop your network while becoming indispensable.

Campus Collaboration
The College Sports Information Office

Imagine an octopus that can juggle. That's the multi-tasking job description of a college Sports Information Director. The SID's responsibility is to the Athletic Director and President of the school. For many SID's, this job usually becomes a long career. They handle anything that has to do with publicizing the team and the players while handling all game operations. The duties are innumerable and ongoing. Unlike the professional ranks, colleges have several sports teams to promote and represent.

On games days, it probably feels like game daze with so many components to handle and so many staffers to oversee. The SID's day starts early and ends very late. You're processing media credentials, handling seating assignments, making sure telephone lines are properly installed for broadcasters, managing press conferences, and maintaining up-to-date statistics for the NCAA and the media. This job is hard to come by. Writing ability is a key, and you certainly can't be shy.

On non-game days, the SID will compose media releases, develop the press guide, attend practices and arrange for press conferences. It helps for the SID to have a positive relationship with sports writers and editors. An extension of the sports information office is the home broadcast team, so the SID is also closely involved with their radio announcers. The national web site for SID's is:

College Sports Information Directors of America - www.cosida.com.

Doug Tammaro is the Sports Information Director at Arizona State University, elevating his sports career there in 1993. Doug's sports passion grew from his upbringing in the Steel City as a fan of the Steelers during their 1970's glory days. Even by age 10, he would watch games and then write stories about them, just like a beat reporter. Throughout high school, he would serve as official scorekeeper for softball games in Ellwood City, Pennsylvania (North Pittsburgh), usually doing as many as 10 games a week for $5 a game and a free hot dog from the concession stand.

After graduating from Baldwin-Wallace College in Ohio, he spent a year interning at the University of Cincinnati, then another year at Notre Dame. "I was at Notre Dame the year they filmed Rudy," says Doug. "In June 1993, an opening for a sports information office position was posted by Arizona State University. I had just visited Arizona during a Notre Dame baseball team road trip there, and I fell in love with the area. I knew I wanted to live there." As career fortunes go, Tammaro applied and got the job.

Tammaro's responsibilities as Sports Information Director are varied, acting as a liaison between his various teams on the one hand and the news media on the other. He'll prepare press guides, manage media credentials, assign parking, author a weekly press release, arrange and provide information for interviews, host events, handle seating charts, conduct post-game press conferences, and then update post-game statistics. "After the game ends, I'll still be working for another two to three hours," says Doug. Then there are media days at which athletes and coaches make themselves available to reporters, photographers, and the broadcast media. When there's a road trip, Tammaro travels with the team.

Doug Tammaro

In describing his other duties, Tammaro explains it as "being in charge of anything to do with the program 'as people see it.' A good SID can provide thoughtful material. Even when the team isn't winning, you make sure others consider all sides of things. It could be the media, alumni, fans, I'm constantly educating about all aspects of the program. I take pride in finding positives. The duties involve a lot of reacting, though."

In some respects, Tammaro says the position includes a responsibility for ticket sales. "Winning is the ultimate cure."

With the evolution of social media, Tammaro says the position has forced him to be more aggressive. "You tweet information now. It wasn't long ago we'd fax the box score after the game. Now, the post-game information is just uploaded. We don't communicate as much. You don't get the chance to say 'let me explain that.' In an e-mail, you can't tell the 'tone' in their message. It's become much more depersonalized."

A job like Tammaro's requires a strong support staff. Much of that support comes in the way of interns. This is a great platform to launch your sports career. You learn to deal with media, gain writing skills, and experience game-day operations. It just might be the door-opener you're looking for.

Tammaro says this is a great first step for any job in sports, no matter what you want to do. Whether your dreams are to be a broadcaster, a coach, or some other position, nothing will benefit you as much as working in the sports information office. "You have to get a broad sense of what's going on. You're a part of so many things and grow up fast. Communicating in media relations, you're forced to become a good communicator." The tasks may seem menial. You'll look for typos, call people on the phone once in a while. "Coaches could benefit from working in media relations, setting up press conferences, learning how to write a release."

Tammaro likens his duty to watching a sporting event without the audio and no announcers to inform you. "Then where will the information come from? Announcers can't help but listen to you."

Tammaro's says there are a lot of proving grounds available for high school kids. "Social media platforms are good. Public speaking classes are beneficial too. If you want people to listen to you, you need to be able to talk. Being a journalist is good for understanding both sides, so work at the school newspaper."

If you get a job in the SID office, be ready to learn about sports you may not have had an interest in. Be ready to do the job, not get thanked, and not get recognition. "People who get no PR are the ones best at doing it," says Tammaro. "Be ready to help out. The answer is never 'I don't know;' always offer to find out."

Working alongside Doug Tammaro is Randy Policar, who works as an Assistant Sports Information Director at Arizona State University. Like many kids growing up, Randy had dreams of being involved in the sports world. At the age of 13, Randy went to sportscasting camp. By 16, he was interning at KJR, a sports radio station in Seattle. His duties included being a board operator, a position he was hired for a year later. Along the way, he worked at the sportscasting camp he'd attended earlier.

In 1998, Policar left Seattle to attend Arizona State University where he was introduced to Mark Brand, ASU's Sports Information Director. For four years, Randy volunteered his time to work at all different kinds of Sun Devil sporting events. There was some financial reward. At the time, if recommended by the Sports Information Office, Arizona State offered a half scholarship to volunteers from their sophomore year on. Randy immersed himself in other avenues too. He edited sound bites (interviews) at a local TV station and was a radio producer at KGME Sports Talk. Randy also had fortunate timing with his 2001 internship with the Arizona Diamondbacks, working with their TV department. The Diamondbacks won the World Series that year.

Upon graduation in 2002, Policar was hired by the Arizona Rattlers Arena Football team, doing everything you can imagine. These duties even included being Public Address announcer for home games and serving as radio color analyst for road games. By his second season with the Rattlers, Randy earned a promotion to become the team's Public Relations Director, a position he held for two more years. The Arena Football League fell on tough financial times, so in 2005, Policar rejoined the

Arizona State Sports Information Office, but this time as a paid employee. Randy currently assists for Sun Devil football games, writing press releases among his numerous weekly duties. He is also responsible for all media relations for the nationally acclaimed Sun Devil baseball team, traveling with them for away games and doing radio commentary on the road.

Policar has experienced a lot in a short period of time. His advice for those with (non-playing) sports aspirations: "Get involved and volunteer. Whether it's at your high school or university, be around. Join your school's newspaper or radio station. At the college level, you'll learn how to deal with the coaches, the athletes, and their egos."

As this book has strongly noted, the sports industry does NOT pay the majority of non-athletes well, especially for entry-level positions. Even as the Rattler's Public Relations Director, Policar made only $25,000 a year. Entry level opportunities in college sports information offices (at least at ASU) earn about $30,000. That's IF you can get hired. Policar says he was very fortunate to start at a Division One upper level school like ASU, simply because they already knew him. "Relationships mean everything. The odds are tough breaking in at this level. The competition is keen. You'll probably need to work at a smaller school." In Policar's opinion, he says the odds are tougher to become a PR Director or play-by-play announcer than to become an athlete. "Just do the math. There is one PR Director per team, and maybe a few announcers. How many players are on a football or baseball team?" One thing for sure, we certainly know who's getting the better end of the pay scale.

Making the Pros - Media Relations

The Media Relations office for a professional sports franchise or a college team is vital. No department affects the image of a franchise more than this one. Media Relations plays an important role, not only in the coverage and popularity of their respective teams, but they also serve as a liaison between media outlets and the coaches and players they represent. Whatever it takes to maximize positive coverage, this branding extension provides an integral resource. The media relation department's primary function is to provide local, national, and international media with up-to-date, accurate, and timely information that hopefully puts an encouraging spin on their team. This all contributes to fan perception, which ultimately leads to the stimulus of ticket and merchandise sales. Of course, a winning team certainly helps their ultimate cause of filling stadiums and promoting their players and coaches.

The day-to-day tasks are very similar to an SID. It's a demanding, usually low-paid position with typical work days during the season that start early in the morning and last till midnight. The one obvious difference is that pro teams play a much longer and more frequent schedule. For example, during a baseball home-stand, this grueling game-day process will repeat itself for up to 10 nights in a row. As many media departments have been known to utter: "Finally, the team is on the road!"

If you're looking to kick-start your sports career, the media relations department is a great place to accomplish it. Such was the case for Vince Kozar. Kozar is a Phoenix-area native. Like many kids, he grew up with his favorite sports allegiances, and the Suns were his. Kozar always felt he had a head for sports, players, and teams. Yet, he went to school to become a journalist.

Kozar worked in the student media in high school and at Arizona State University. One day, at ASU's Walter Cronkite School of Journalism, he noticed a posting for an internship opportunity with the Suns. He applied and was accepted. The opportunity re-directed his life.

Kozar has since graduated from intern to Basketball Communications Manager for his favorite NBA team, a position he has held since 2007. Prior to that, he was given the lead media responsibilities of the Phoenix Mercury WNBA team for two seasons, which was his testing ground.

Now, Kozar is the go-to guy for all Suns home games. He travels to about 20-percent of the Suns road games as well.

When you watch a basketball game on TV, you can't help but notice along the sideline, all the announcers and their broadcast crews, the reporters, the stats crew, the players, and camera operators. And that's just courtside.

Kozar's job is to coordinate preparation for these game-day operations and a whole lot more. It's an amazing feat if you think about it. There are so many behind-the-scenes preparations required.

In no particular order, this branch of media relations must tend to players, coaches, and their families and also coordinate credentials for the attending press and broadcast coverage, and handle the official stats crew. Then there are hospitality responsibilities. There is a media room, a guest room, and a family room. These each require catering and possibly even babysitting. Then there's the ticket distribution to the players and coaches. Don't forget parking arrangements. It's a constant trouble-shooting job. Then there will be pre- and post-game interviews and press conferences to tend to.

Prior to all this, Kozar and his staff have to write press releases, do research, make sure game notes are up-to-date with all the current stats, provide starting lineups, report to the league who will be working the official stats crew each night, and distribute pre-game notes.

Asked if he even gets to watch the game, he says, "maybe 50-75 percent of it." Otherwise, he's busy making sure the press table is ready for occupancy, that everyone has tickets, that the stat computers are functional, and that the shot clock works. During the game, it's also Kozar's job to keep an eye for a team or individual record that might be broken, just in case he needs to write and distribute a media note while the game is progressing. Don't forget the fourth-quarter and post-game notes; the on-court, post-game broadcast interviews; and locker room post-game interviews.

Two hours after the game, Kozar probably will be in his office updating the stats and game notes. When there are back-to-back games, it can be a sleep-depriving nightmare, because you have to be ready to do it all again the next day. In between, the very next morning, there are team practices to attend to also.

Kozar's recommendation to those that share his aspirations: "Don't get discouraged. Be willing to start at the bottom. For the Suns organization, they like to promote from within." If you prove yourself, so will other organizations.

There are only 30 NBA teams, only 30 Major League Baseball teams, and 32 NFL teams. Show the ambition, take the initiative. Get your foot in the door somehow. Along the way, you'll find your niche and get noticed.

Every now and then, a Herculean accomplishment occurs on the world's biggest stage.

In the 1996 Atlanta Olympics, the U.S. women's gymnastics team needed Kerri Strug to complete a near-perfect landing in the vault to earn the team a Gold Medal. She was their final performer. It was all on the line. In her first attempt, Strug badly injured her ankle. Now Strug had to do it with what turned out to be a third-degree lateral sprain and tendon damage. Summoning up unbelievable strength and courage, Strug etched a vision in Olympic history forever, landing on one foot before collapsing in pain. The completed vault received a score of 9.712, guaranteeing the Americans the gold medal.

In one of the most emotional Olympics scenes ever, Strug's coach, Bela Karolyi carried her onto the medals podium to join her team, after which she was treated at a hospital.

Chapter 3

Sports Announcing

How many times have you watched your favorite sporting event, be it in person or on television, and asked yourself, "How did those guys get to sit courtside or in the so-called exalted press box?"

"Boy, I'm never going to be a Vin Scully, Al Michaels, or Bob Costas, and I'm not a professional athlete-turned sports announcer, but wouldn't it be great to have the same vantage point they do?" Not to mention, GET PAID to have that seat.

To many, national sportscasters have a dream job. They generally are well-compensated. They receive great public exposure, especially on the TV side. Many sportscasters receive as much attention as the players.   They get paid to travel around the country and get all their expenses covered. Some are treated like Rock Stars with limos taking them to their deluxe hotel and to the stadium. Sportscasters also rub elbows with the athletes, coaches, and other celebrities and sports hot shots!

Although Sportscasters will all tell you how fortunate they are to be in their position, it's not all fun and glory. It's a highly stressful job with long hours and grinding travel schedules. Preparation for a broadcast doesn't just start when they arrive at the stadium. When they're not broadcasting, they are researching and preparing. Otherwise, they're hopping on a plane or bus and living out of a suitcase. There are irregular and often unpredictable hours, work pressures, and disrupted personal lives.

The Microphone Has No Eraser

There are especially challenges for beginning broadcasters. Employers want people with experience, but without the opportunity, where you do get that experience?   Announcers are often required to complete long-term, on-the-job training, which can be accomplished at campus radio or TV facilities and at commercial stations while students serve as interns. Work experience at college or high school radio or TV stations is very valuable.

As the saying goes, timing is everything. It's particularly true in broadcasting. A day after leaving my News Director job in Walla Walla, I got hired in Spokane, Washington on a Friday. I was expected to report to work on Monday. I hadn't even packed yet. Needless to say, it was a busy weekend for me.

Novice broadcasters usually start at small stations for low pay. My first job in Walla Walla paid just $900 a month.   Announcers at small markets will be asked to wear multiple hats too, with many off-air duties as well. They may operate the control board, monitor the transmitter, sell commercial time to advertisers, keep a log of the station's daily programming, and produce advertisements and other recorded material. In today's market, individuals with advanced computer skills may have an advantage. Sometimes the duties get bizarre. As a small radio market news reporter, I had to go up in a hot air balloon. (It was actually pretty cool). Another time, I toured a state penitentiary with the warden, unescorted by security, as we walked among the inmates. Before entering the facility, I was required to sign a waiver stating that if I was "captured, killed, maimed, or dismembered, the State of Washington was not responsible." How comforting. From then on, I received frequent phone calls from inmates pleading their case, as if I could announce something that would get them out of prison.

If sports announcing is the career you strive for, know that the competition is substantial. You'll need an excellent speaking voice, writing skills, and a keen knowledge of sports. You'll likely end up gaining experience at some small-market station with duties that have nothing to do with sports. Be forewarned that sports announcing can be a merciless career. Even talented broadcasters are often faced with circumstances out of their control when it comes to job security. There are many moving parts that can throw a monkey wrench into things. Changes in station or network ownership, format, and ratings frequently cause periods of unemployment for many. Also, consolidation among broadcast companies causes disruption. In some cases, announcers leave the field because they cannot advance to better paying jobs.

To get started, you might consider a broadcasting school. If your college doesn't have a student station to develop your skills, get yourself a tape recorder and sit in front of your TV and call the action.

Gary Bender
National Network Sportscaster

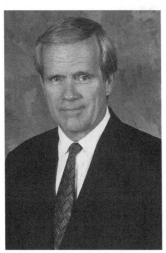

Gary Bender (picture to the left) is a nationally renowned and long-time respected sportscaster who has seen and done it all. Bender's book, *Call of the Game*, shares excellent tips on how to prepare to get into the broadcast business, how to become a better announcer, and so much more. If you have aspirations to be a sports announcer, his book is a must read.

Bender began his sports career broadcasting the University of Kansas football and basketball games in the 1960's. In the early 1970's, he was the radio voice for the Green Bay Packers and the 1975 TV voice for the Seattle Pilots, er, Milwaukee Brewers. Sorry, I still carry a grudge for Bud Selig taking away my hometown Pilots.

For over a decade (1975-1986), CBS Sports was the primary home for Bender. His first two years at CBS, Bender was paired up with pro football Hall of Famer Johnny Unitas. Bender also teamed with a couple other pro football Hall of Famers, John Madden and Sonny Jurgensen, among many others. CBS also used Bender for college football and basketball. In addition, Bender called the 1981 NBA Finals between Houston and Boston. Another pair of pro basketball Hall of Famers, Bill Russell and Rick Barry, worked as his color commentators.

If you survive in the business as long as Bender has, there will certainly be some epic moments that will highlight and perhaps define your career. For world-renowned sportscaster Al Michaels, no one can forget his signature phrase *"Do You Believe in Miracles?"* when finishing the call of the classic 1980 Olympics hockey clash between the U.S. and Russia. For Bender, it came while announcing for CBS in back-to-back NCAA basketball championships in 1982 and 1983. In '82, Bender had the call of the game-winning left-corner jump-shot by then-North Carolina freshman Michael Jordan with but 17 seconds left that beat Georgetown 63 to 62. As if that weren't enough drama, Bender was again at the microphone the following year when he announced what became known as "the shot heard round the world," when North Carolina State's Lorenzo Charles rebounded a misguided, 30-foot desperation heave and memorably dunked the ball into the basket on a last split-second slam to stun Houston's Cougars. The University of Houston's power-dunking lineup that year, known as Phi Slama Jama, included perennial future NBA All-Stars Hakeem Olajuwon and Clyde Drexler, making this collegiate championship upset accomplishment all the more legendary over time. Who can visually forget NC State Coach Jim Valvano ecstatically running around the court looking for anyone to hug after his Cardiac Pack won this buzzer beater for the NCAA brass ring, 54-52. One's broadcasting career doesn't get any better than this. Another memorable announcing moment for Bender came in 1975 during his first year broadcasting the NFL for CBS. "Teamed with Johnny Unitas, we were announcing a December game at the old Bloomington Stadium. Roger Staubach threw a famous 'Hail Mary' pass to Drew Pearson to rally the Cowboys to a late victory. The real tragedy was what happened after that pass. With only 18 seconds remaining, QB Fran Tarkenton furiously tried to rally his Vikings to victory, starting at their own 15-yard line. On the next play, Tarkenton thought he had gotten rid of the ball in time to avoid a substantial loss. The referee disagreed and ruled it a 14-yard sack back at the one. Tarkenton was so upset he ripped off his helmet and slammed it across the field. Tarkenton's father and two brothers were watching CBS' broadcast from Georgia. Bender later learned it was at this point Tarkenton's father suffered a heart attack and died. "I realized for the first time what an immense responsibility a broadcaster has," said Bender.

College Football also enjoyed Bender's smooth broadcasting style (1987-1992), where he teamed with Dick Vermiel for ABC Sports, while at the same time, doing radio play-by-play for the NFL Phoenix Cardinals (1988-1991).

Always busy and in demand, Bender also did play-by-play for Major League baseball, serving as the number two broadcaster (behind Al Michaels) for the 1987 and 1988 seasons. Bender teamed with Joe Morgan and Reggie Jackson for the 1988 American League Championship Series in which Oakland defeated Boston. Through his career, Bender has covered 27 different sports, including the Olympics as well. Bender has wound down his career as the TV play-by-play announcer for the Phoenix Suns, working alongside NBA sharp-shooter Eddie Johnson and Scott Williams. As for his future, he's returning to his roots at the University of Kansas, serving as a spokesman for his alma mater.

Successful broadcasters all have a unique and interesting story where their career took flight. For Gary Bender, it began as a 7th grader, while riding a tractor growing up on his family's farm in Kansas. "To pass the time while plowing the fields, I would simulate a game in my mind, and 'call the action.' That's where I first started developing my skills," says Bender. Since there was no one to emulate, I developed my own style and learned timing." The story gets betters. "I even sang the national anthem, and voiced commercials like Gillette razors, 'look sharp, be sharp' and other TV ads of the day. When I did my first game, I felt like I'd done this before."

Bender got his first professional announcing job at a 1000 watt station in Hutchinson, Kansas. "At a small market, you can make a lot of mistakes, where no one knows," says Bender. "Everyone needs to start where someone believes in you." Bender served his apprenticeship wearing a number of hats. "I was a DJ, did my own sports show, announced the news, and on Saturday nights, hosted a country/western show. I was 'Big Ben', and along with Ed the Red Head, we did our show from the studio. All these people would come down to the station. We ate like champions! When my career advanced, I was prepared for it."

His first big break came with WIBW TV in Topeka. "I got to announce Kansas and Kansas State games. While there, I got to broadcast for WIBW Radio in the 1967 NCAA tournament in Louisville, (which included eventual champion UCLA's sophomore sensation, Lew Alcindor [Kareem Abdul Jabbar]).

If there was a poster boy for preparation, Bender would be the example. "I can remember when Bob Costas and I worked together at KMOX radio in St. Louis. I'd come with pages of research, and Costas would show up with a couple notes scratched onto a napkin. Costas has always had a photographic memory. That's what makes him so uniquely outstanding. That's one reason why Costas was able to professionally transition directly from Syracuse University to a major market."

If he had to do it all over again, Bender says he would try to start as a sports voice at a university. "Radio is your likely first step. Expand your skills and some relationships. Develop your style and get comfortable. Repetition is important. There are no shortcuts. In my case, each career phase was necessary. I could have never gone without the intermediate steps. There will always be disappointments, but steps that happen along the way serve a purpose. You have to believe; that's what drives you. Always do your best. Preparation is the one element YOU can control. You never know who'll be listening. There could be some network executive passing through town who discovers you. Be ready!"

The broadcast industry has certainly evolved in a huge way since Bender started his career. "When ESPN came along in 1979, we at CBS laughed at them. We didn't view them as credible competition nor think they could sustain their 'all sports, all the time' innovation. Boy, were we wrong. They are the most remarkable success story our business has ever seen. Whatever ESPN wants, they get," says Bender.

For today's aspiring sportscasters, Bender says it's much harder to get into the business than in his early days. "Back then, maybe five applied for a particular opening. Now you'll get heavy competition from all over the country. Granted, there are far more sports announcing jobs, but there are also many more qualified candidates. There are so many capable young people today where it's not for lack of ability, but a lack of opportunity," Bender said. "Today, you've got to be better. Sports fans are so 'in the know.' Today's broadcasters have so many resources I never had, internet, 24-hour sports networks. The fan is far more sophisticated today. You've got to be exceptional. That's a challenge."

Bender says he doesn't believe in luck. "Luck is a residue of design; it's something you've nurtured along the way. It goes back to preparation."

If you want to be a sportscaster, Bender says to be honest about why? "What's your motivation? Is it because of money or prestige? Or is it because it's really what you want to do?" Bender refers to this as "total tunnel vision." "For me, it was because there was nothing else I wanted to do more."

For those who are committed to their sports endeavors, that is great advice for all.

Bob Rondeau
University of Washington
Radio Play-By-Play Voice

I refer to Bob Rondeau as my successor as "The Voice" of Washington Husky sports, but that would be a BIG stretch of the truth as he just happened to start his brilliant Husky announcing career shortly after I concluded mine (as an amateur student announcer for a 10-watt blowtorch student station at Washington).

Bob Rondeau is an eight-time award winner as Washington State Sportscaster of the Year. A Denver native and alum from the University of Colorado in 1972, Rondeau began

Bob Rondeau on left and Author

his announcing career as a newscaster for KVFC radio, located in the four corners town of Cortez, Colorado. A year later, he graduated to a news reporter assignment at KLAK in Denver, covering the legislature. In 1975, Rondeau made the trek to Phoenix, Arizona, becoming the News Director for (now defunct) KRUX AM 1360. Two years later, that station went under (not an uncommon occurrence in radio), and it was time to pass the resume around again. Rondeau heard from a Denver acquaintance, Lee Rogers, who was now in Seattle. KOMO Radio needed a full-time sports announcer, now that Seattle had recently added the Seahawks and Mariners to the SuperSonics as hometown professional teams.

"Up until then, I had never really thought about sports. I was ready for a change of scenery," says Rondeau. "I auditioned for the job and got it. I worked split shifts, providing the morning announcing duties from home on occasion. Since I worked late nights covering games, the station actually installed an Associated Press teletype into a closet in my home."

In 1978, KOMO radio acquired the broadcast rights to the Washington Huskies, with popular local sports icon Bruce King initially handling the play-by-play. Rondeau served as King's analyst. In 1980, King took a TV sports anchor job in New York City and Rondeau took on the play-by-play duties. Except for 1986-1988, when another station briefly garnered the Husky radio rights, Rondeau has been synonymous with University of Washington sports ever since.

Who in broadcasting keeps the same job for 28 years? Says Rondeau, "This is beyond my wildest dreams; I never could have envisioned with the transient nature of broadcasting, to still be in Seattle this long."

I can personally attest to why Rondeau has outlasted the industry norm. Besides being a wonderful and likeable person, Rondeau is one of the most equipped, professional broadcasters there is. "You're only as good as your preparation," he says. "You try to avoid surprises on game day."

Rondeau says he's really fortunate to have covered the Huskies during their glory years in the 1980's and 1990's. Interestingly, Washington's 2008 football season, when they went 0-12, professionally sticks out in Rondeau's mind. "There was such a toxic atmosphere around Husky football. With the drudgery, our work was really cut out for us. It may have been some of our best effort."

Rondeau knows from experience that it pays to be a well-rounded broadcaster. "Even in sports, we're all just reporters. I'm thankful for my news background. It pays to be broad-based. Be worldly. You'll better relate to all in your audience."

Like many success stories, Rondeau was in the right place at the right time. "Many times, who you know is better than what you know." He suggests you separate yourself from the masses, "and don't be shy. It's infinitely more competitive now. There is more opportunity nowadays, but the job pool is bigger. With the proliferation of media, it's an appealing career."

All these many years later, I recently sat side-by-side with Bob, doing stats for him at a Husky-Sun Devil basketball game in Tempe, Arizona. With a wink in his eye, Bob surprised me by doing an on-air shout-out back to Seattle, thanking me for doing stats and acknowledging me as the 'former voice of Husky sports.' I guess the legacy lives on.

Sports Analysts – Adding Some Color

An analyst for sports broadcasts typically gets hired from the players' or coach's pool. Sometimes there are rare national exceptions, like Howard Cosell, Dennis Miller, and Tony Kornheiser.

Earnings are relatively low, except for announcers who work for large market stations or networks. TV pays higher than radio.

Some successful TV sports announcers start their careers as a sports writer. A son of Cuban refugees, Pedro Gomez was born 20 days after his parents arrived in America, just two months before the U.S. missile crisis in October 1962. A Miami native, Gomez pursued his initial professional journalism career in Miami, then San Diego, and eventually the San Francisco Bay area. He became a full-time baseball beat writer in 1992, covering the Oakland A's for the San Jose Mercury News and the Sacramento Bee until 1997. His sports writing career then took him to Phoenix, where he was a general sports columnist for the Arizona Republic for six years.

In 2002, ESPN recruited Gomez, thus starting an electronic media chapter in his sports reporting career. As a regular TV reporter for SportsCenter since 2003, Gomez's primary ESPN responsibility is as a correspondent for baseball, also for Baseball Tonight. Gomez has covered 15 World Series and more than 10 All-Star games.

Gomez says he doesn't consider himself an announcer, rather a reporter. "If you take a look at the ESPN roster of experts, almost all the reporters had a print background."

Gomez remembers when he got drafted by ESPN. "When I got a call from Bristol [ESPN's home-base], I said I don't have a TV background. They responded by saying we can make a reporter into a TV person, but we can't make a TV person into a reporter."

As you've read throughout this book, it was through the benefit of a professional connection that Gomez caught this break. "ESPN was looking for a reporter with a foundation in print, preferably bilingual. An old boss of mine, the sports editor for the San Jose Mercury News, recommended me. You never know who you know that will advance your career." Gomez's lengthy qualifications certainly fit ESPN's criterion.

Gomez's recommendations for aspiring journalists (electronic or print) are to have a foundation in print. "With print, there is no safety net, no TV producer. You have no choice but to learn." Gomez views many of today's writers as nothing more than bloggers. "They're sitting home, sharing their opinions, but they need to get out there and do research. That's one of the biggest deficiencies I see with today's so-called reporters. This job is not an opinion. There's more to it. Can they write a real story?" To launch your journalistic career, Gomez suggests you learn how to be a reporter. "Join your school paper." As for the trend of newspapers becoming a fading dinosaur of an industry, Gomez believes: "there will still be opportunities, maybe just not as many."

One other bit of advice from Gomez: "Do it because you love it! If you have the passion for what you do, the BIG money may follow.

From Athletes to Announcers

If you are a well-spoken, accomplished athlete, you've got a definite advantage in getting your foot in the door as a sports broadcaster, especially if you were a colorful athlete with a magnetic personality. Deion Sanders comes to mind. His bravado has led to a successful career as an NFL Network commentator. Michael Irvin is another NFL Hall of Famer not known for being bashful who is now a nationwide radio talk show host for ESPN and analyst for NFL radio broadcasts. Irvin has also been cast in movies.

A number of players use broadcasting as their tether to the game once their playing days are through. As a star player, just your name or reputation alone might get you an audition. Keeping the position is another matter. Working in the broadcast booth at several NFL games, I've seen many retired "name" players (and coaches) who just don't have what it takes as a game analyst. They struggle mightily. Color commentary like: "Wow, what a play," or "Incredible!" doesn't add a thing for the listener.

I think it also depends on the type of sport former players try to transition to after their playing days are through. For example, a basketball broadcast has so little stoppage of play, there's less time for the analyst to comment. With baseball and football, there can be thirty seconds or so between plays or pitches, so there's plenty more room and need for the analyst to share expertise.

Here are some examples of accomplished athletes turned broadcasters who have found success and carved out their own niche in their post-playing careers.

Ed Cunningham
ESPN/ABC Analyst

Ed Cunningham is one of the best football color analysts I've ever worked with, describing the game in a strategic way, while still in layman's terms for the fans to enjoy. Cunningham's athletic accomplishment was achieved in a low-profile position, as a center and team captain for the 1991 National Champion Washington Huskies football team. He graduated with a business finance degree. A third round draft choice in 1992, his NFL career lasted five seasons, representing the Arizona Cardinals and Seattle Seahawks.

Ed Cunningham

If you saw him today, Ed would have a hard time convincing you he was once an offensive lineman, having dropped 70 pounds from his playing weight of 295. He looks more like a wide receiver now. Back then, he described himself as a "glorified bodyguard, doing hand-to-hand combat with the likes of Lawrence Taylor and Reggie White."

Broadcasting became somewhat of a hobby for Cunningham while he was still a senior at Washington. "It took a few years of broadcasting before I decided this is what I wanted to do for a career," said Ed. While still playing in the NFL, Cunningham became a football analyst for Arena Football for WB 61 in Phoenix. Ed considered this a great training ground. "For one thing, the amount of teams and players per team was manageable from a homework perspective. I was also fortunate that WB 61's professional TV crew took me under their wings and really taught me about broadcasting, the nuances of the industry and the patterns of the game. Because I was so interested in learning, they were very helpful. You can't just show up and tell stories about your playing days and consider yourself a good analyst."

Cunningham likens broadcasting to cramming for a weekly final or doing a term paper. "Research and preparation are the biggest keys. Thankfully, we have direct access to coaches and players. However you need to know 'what' to ask. Don't just ask questions that allow for 'coach-speak' responses. Develop stories about players, regarding their lives both on and off the field. In other words, prepare, do your homework."

Cunningham said being an athlete doesn't mean you'll be a good announcer. "You have a base knowledge about a complex game few people have, but that's not enough. You're going from a mostly physical preparation as a player to one that is all mental."

I asked Cunningham what he considers a good color analyst. "Someone who is friendly in audience terms, that gives not only the what, but the why things are unfolding during the game. Hopefully you've done a good job of setting it up before it happens." Having worked beside him during a BCS game between Boise State and Oklahoma, I can attest that no one does a better job at this than Ed Cunningham. I enjoyed the game even more because of Ed's commentary. He definitely explains the "why'" when so many so-called "color" commentators do not or cannot.

It's this outstanding preparation and ability to communicate the game to fans that led Cunningham to announce NCAA football for CBS, then ABC. Cunningham joined ESPN/ABC in 2006, and in 2008 also became an in-studio analyst on College Football Live. "The sooner you make the decision this is what you want to do for a career, then you can get serious about the work," he says.

Like many athletes turned announcers, Cunningham feels very fortunate he still gets to attend the game he loves and be around the action. His advice if you want to get into sports announcing: "Be dedicated and practice your craft. Attend a high school contest and announce the game, even as a podcast. Sit up in the stands with a tape player like it's a real broadcast. Record it, listen back, critique it, and do it again. Find your style, who you really are. Be honest. Praise the players; don't always look for the negative, but critique when necessary."

This is certainly sage advice. Just look where Ed Cunningham's broadcasting career is now, traveling all around the country for ESPN/ABC TV as an expert football analyst. As I call it, "Living the Dream."

Ron Wolfley

NFL Analyst and Sports Talk Show Host

Just ask former NFL linebacker Brian Bosworth who Ron Wolfley is. While a fullback for the Arizona Cardinals, it was Wolfley who laid the lumber on "the Boz" and ended Bosworth's NFL career. A fourth round 1985 draft pick of the St Louis Cardinals, Wolfley was a four-time Pro Bowl selection (1986-1989) as a fearless special teams player. He is the answer to the trivia question: "Who was the only NFL player to play in St Louis for both the Cardinals and Rams?"

These days, Wolfley does double duty, serving as a afternoon sports radio talk show co-host for Sports 620 KTAR in Phoenix, and as the colorful radio analyst for the Arizona Cardinals. Maybe it's the multiple concussions he experienced as an All-Pro special teams player and fullback, but Wolfley seems to describe things with an off-the-wall excitement and distinctive style that almost emulates John Madden.

Ron Wolfley
With permission of Ron Wolfley and the Arizona Cardinals

Wolfley became convinced to enter the broadcasting world because people kept telling him as a player that he was a good quote. "In 1991, I served as an analyst for Arena Football and loved it. When I finished playing in 1995, I thought I'd give it a full-time go," he said. In 1997, Phoenix launched a new sports talk station, KMVP, and I got hired to do a two-hour evening talk show."

Having played for so many NFL seasons, Wolfley really knows his stuff. "Being an NFL analyst is also a great way to remain connected to the game. Other than coaching, it's the next best thing; being around the guys, the coaches, the players."

Wolfley now spends his afternoons hosting a sports talk show and weekends from August through January as an NFL radio analyst. "I consider it a blessing to be able to broadcast games. It's a rush, calling it as it happens. That's the exciting part I'll always tap into."

Wolfley earned his Pro Bowls as a standout special teams player, though he refers to this position that segues between offense and defense as a "transitional technician." He loves doing radio and prefers it over TV. "It's a combination of information and entertainment; it's truly theater-of-the-mind." But how does he draw the line when it comes to perhaps criticizing a call or a player's performance from the home team? "Coaches and players will respect you for the fact you've played the game," says Wolfley. "I have great regard for those in the line of fire, but I will never make it sound like the game is simple. You have to remember that on every play, someone is trying keep the opponent from doing their job. The coaching staff can have the best play called, but if someone fails to execute, it won't work. That's football. I will share my honest opinion."

Wolfley says he would relish the chance to coach in the NFL, but he says it's way too late. "I do love to help players develop." Wolfley did give the coaching profession a professional try at Phoenix College in 2004 and 2005. "I was the worst head coach in Junior College history." He also coached with the Rattlers the same two seasons.

So Wolfley stays connected to the game behind the microphone. As an NFL analyst, his perspective is to "expand the vision of the game." "The play-by-play announcer's job is to follow the ball and describe 'what' happened, which Dave Pasch does a great job of doing. My job is to explain the 'why.' I like to call the game 'inside out' and see the whole field. What formation is a team in? What is the personnel group or the configuration of the secondary? That comes from expertise from playing the game. That's the advantage a former player has in serving as a color commentator."

Asked to compare today's players to ones from his era or before, Wolfley wryly says "They're certainly a lot wealthier. Back when I played and even before my era, the attitude was 'I' owe the game, the game doesn't owe 'me.' Players today seem to have a sense of entitlement, that the game owes them."

It's that unselfish attitude, raw emotion, and appreciation for his job that plows Wolfley's successful announcing career, just the way he used to generate openings for his return specialists as a Pro Bowling "transitional technician" wedge-buster during his NFL playing days.

Steve Raible
TV News Anchor and
NFL Play-by-Play Announcer

Steve Raible

Steve Raible is truly a jack of all trades, currently serving as the long-time award-winning News Anchor for KIRO TV in Seattle, and as an outstanding play-by-play radio announcer for the Seattle Seahawks. I can personally confirm this from being his 'road game' statistician. Free time is not an affliction for Raible, especially during the NFL season.

Raible was a pioneer member of the Seattle Seahawks franchise as a 1976 second round draft choice out of Georgia Tech. "Raibs" ran his speedy routes opposite Hall-of-Fame receiver Steve Largent for six seasons. Then in 1982, Steve joined KIRO TV, covering everything from Olympic Games to Presidential elections.

For nearly three decades now, Raible has been part of the Seahawks radio crew. He was encouraged to join his new team as an analyst by then play-by-play announcer Pete Gross. "Pete gave me a call in June 1982 to let me know his current color commentator, ex-Husky and 49er Don Heinrich, was leaving to join the San Francisco broadcasting crew, and suggested I give it a go," says Raible. "I was out of town, so Pete did the sales pitch on my wife Sharon, telling her, 'your husband is never going to be a Steve Largent; he should really consider this, but he's got to quit football to do it.' Sharon then convinced me to look at the big picture and hang up the cleats. That's what led to my retirement from the NFL. The Seahawks tried to talk me out of it, but it was the right time and the right decision. Then-Seahawks special teams coach Rusty Tillman told me his one regret was that he didn't make the decision when to call it quits, that the team did it for him. Personally, I'm glad I got to make that career decision. I had prepared for this transition. The rest is history."

A true gentleman and friend to Raible, Pete Gross continued serving in the play-by-play capacity for the Seahawks' first 17 seasons, with Steve now serving as his expert commentator. Pete was sadly forced to give up the microphone because of cancer. In 2004, Raible's Seahawk analyst responsibilities shifted to play-by-play duties with NFL Hall-of-Fame quarterback Warren Moon as his wing man.

Raible actually started his transition into a broadcast career during his second year in the league. "I voiced some public service announcements for KIRO TV and participated in their Variety Club fundraisers. Then I was afforded more duties like an overnight shift and doing commercials, and by my third year in the NFL, I was also doing fill-in work for KIRO radio's renowned Wayne Cody for his three-hour SportsLine talk show on Saturday nights. By 1978, I knew this was the career direction I'd take after my NFL playing days," says Raible.

By 1980, it was all falling into place for Raible. "I got to know the local TV executives and the sports guys in Seattle. KING TV asked me to do some work on their 'Seattle Today' show and then asked me back as a two-week substitute host. That was great fun and invaluable experience in front of the camera."

Raible has grown his broadcast career far beyond a football analyst role. He's also known as Seattle's most recognized TV news anchor. Asked which media career he prefers better, Raible responded with "That's like asking which kid do you like more. Seahawks play-by-play has kept me connected with the organization.   Players always change, coaches come and go, but I'll always appreciate the ongoing relationships with front office guys like Gary Wright and Dave Pearson. You can't properly prepare to do my job without that bond. If the coaches and assistant coaches know you've played,

Steve Raible and Warren Moon
With Permission of the Seattle Seahawks

have been through the NFL wars, and are fair and honest, they'll talk to you and share with you. They have all been very kind and open to me. You can't do this job without this rapport with the coaches."

Raible refers to his broadcast partner, Hall of Famer Warren Moon, as amazing. "There's nothing Moon hasn't seen or experienced in his lengthy football career. As a former quarterback, he's so knowledgeable. When he walks through any stadium, everyone wants to say hi to him.   Coaches love him; he's a wealth of information. We have a great chemistry in the booth."

As an announcer, Raible says he works harder to prepare for a game than when he was a player. "Playing the game was a great teacher for me; it helped me to scout opponents, which is a huge asset when preparing for broadcasts." As for objectivity, Raible humbly says he was never good enough as a player to now judge other players as an announcer. "I won't single out a player if he messes up. I won't question a coach's calls. If the offense isn't moving, Warren and I will acknowledge that, and perhaps offer suggestions. You can still tell the story without being overly critical and singling someone out."

Raible's famed mustache has gone by the wayside, the result of a dictate from his TV station when they went to high definition in 2008. Steve's enthusiastic play-by-play career for the Seahawks continues to soar.

Mychal Thompson

Mychal Thompson
Lakers Radio Analyst

Like many retired athletes, Mychal Thompson's post-playing career took him behind the microphone.

A Bahaman native, Thompson had a decorated NBA career as a power forward and center. He was drafted by Portland as the number one pick in the 1978 draft, the first foreign-born player to be selected at that position. Thompson was a Trailblazer fixture for eight seasons. After a half-season pit stop in San Antonio, Thompson joined the Lakers in 1987, backing up Kareem Abdul-Jabbar, while earning back-to-back championships in Los Angeles.

Upon retirement in 1991, Thompson got into broadcasting right away, starting in Seattle with the Sonics' Kevin Calabro. Thompson became an NBA broadcasting nomad, going to Portland, back to Seattle, on to the Grizzlies, the T-Wolves, back to the Blazers, and now with the Lakers. Along the way, he has also co-hosted several sports radio talk shows.

Thompson is a kick to work with and still has zest for the game. To him, becoming a broadcaster was not a tough adjustment. "It's still just basketball. It doesn't have to be more complicated than it is. Some retired players go into coaching. I knew before I retired, this was something I wanted to do."

Thompsons' most fun is during the playoffs. "Nothing compares!" His favorite announcer, "Seattle's Kevin Calabro. He's the best I ever worked with!"

For those with similar aspirations, Thompson says, "You don't have to be a former player. If you understand the game, you'll do fine. Start anywhere, take anything and work your way up. Be patient and build your portfolio."

Eddie Johnson
Suns TV Analyst

Eddie Johnson is a 17-year veteran of the hardwoods, playing nearly 1,200 games in the NBA. One of the game's greatest sharpshooters, Johnson played for six teams in the league, starting with the Kansas City Kings in 1981. Johnson holds the distinction of being the NBA's all-time leading scorer for players who were never chosen or named to an All Star team, draining 19,202 career points. When he retired in 1999, Johnson ranked 22nd overall in league scoring.

Johnson strongly considered coaching toward the end of his lengthy NBA career, but as a player, he'd spent enough time away from the family, so he gravitated to announcing. "I still loved basketball, and I love to debate, so I combined the two and came up with broadcasting," said Johnson. "I figured it was better than being a politician, though in college I did want to be a lawyer, but I didn't think I could go into a courtroom and be believable." Next to a basketball court is a different story for Eddie.

Eddie Johnson

Johnson started preparing himself to be part of the media even before his playing days were over. "Even as a player, I practiced for this career by doing interviews and giving thorough answers. About my 14th year in the league while playing in Seattle, I did a blog for the *Seattle Post-Intelligencer* newspaper, and also did a radio show for the NBA. This led to a radio show during my days in Houston, and followed with being part of a TV staff while playing in Charlotte. One summer, Kurt Rambis and I did some studio stuff for the NBA on a weekly basis. That really signaled the beginning of my broadcast career. TNT and NBC then started using me for some in-studio duties."

After Johnson hung up his sneakers, the Phoenix Suns' Jerry Colangelo hired him as a TV analyst for Phoenix Mercury WNBA games. That led to another TV opportunity for Johnson as Tom Dillon's sidekick for Arizona State University men's basketball. "The Phoenix Suns then hired me as an analyst, and I've been with them ever since," said Johnson. That association is now going on 12 years.

Johnson's success as a broadcaster comes from being a true student of the game. "I've spent 26 years in organized sports. That's worth three times a doctorate. I'm always on top of the game," says Johnson. "It's like being in college when studying for a final exam. You can't just study that last hour and succeed. I watch games every night and am an ESPN junkie. The computer is my close companion. I have always studied my craft non-stop. Who's playing well, who's injured or struggling? I will always be informed and prepared."

It's because Johnson does understand the game so well that he excels as a commentator. "Guys who haven't played the game can certainly summarize, but Doug Collins and Steve Kerr are great at their craft because they can talk about the game in depth. It's definitely a tougher road for a non-athlete," says Johnson.

Johnson says today's current players even come to him for advice on how to prepare for a post-playing days career in broadcasting. "Amare Stoudemire, Jared Dudley, Grant Hill and others have all approached me on how to train to be an announcer. I tell them to give respect to the interviewer and be cognizant. Be willing to pay your dues, study, observe and work at your craft."

With his wealth of basketball knowledge, Johnson has still not ruled out the possibility of coaching on the hardwoods. "I have been interviewed, but the right circumstance hasn't presented itself yet," says Johnson. If and when it does, Johnson will certainly know what to say to those who will listen and want to learn.

On June 18, 1993, the Phoenix Suns and Chicago Bulls squared off for Game 5 of the NBA championship. The Bulls had captured the first three of four games in the series and were poised to win the title on their home court. Certain his Michael Jordan-led Bulls would be victorious, the mayor of Chicago, Richard M. Daley implored his citizens to not trash downtown in celebration. The Suns spoiled the pending party with a 108-98 road victory. As he left the playing court, Phoenix's Charles Barkley was heard screaming, "We Saved Chicago, We Saved Chicago!"

Chapter 4

Sports Reporting

Imagine being the conduit between fans and their favorite sports teams. Like the home team broadcaster, you become high profile and synonymous with the event. Sports reporting is an occupation that has its glory and certainly has its stress. You're also in the Front Row. If you can communicate concisely and creatively, don't like working in an office, like to travel extensively, and don't mind low or average pay, this is a possible career for you.

In today's heavily saturated sports world, there are a number of occupations you might consider to be a sports reporter.

In my career as a sports statistician, I cross paths with numerous sports writers. With the recent extinction of so many newspapers across the country, I ask various beat writers what they'd recommend to aspiring sports journalists. The prevalent response: "Run, Forrest, run," the catch-phrase from the hit movie *Forrest Gump*.

The future of a sports writer as we've known it is a changing breed, yet nearly all cities and communities large and small, have a Sports Section. That means at least one staff writer is needed to cover the beat for thousands of daily and weekly papers. If your career escalates to a major league city, you'll be assigned to cover all the games and travel with the team you're covering. You'll write features, plus interview players and team management.

Though the traditional landscape has changed, there will always be a need for a sports reporter.

Sportswriters and Journalists

If you aspire to be a sports writer, it is essential to have a strong writing ability and a strong sense of the sports you cover. You need to be able to write in an entertaining way. Remember the term, "Deadline." Typically, the conclusion of an evening game is very near the strict deadline for tomorrow's paper. Your duties will entail attending many sporting events and cultivating relationships with team members directly. Reporters still want to be first, but foremost, factual. Then you have to personalize your stories with your own unique slant. Sometimes, your story may be controversial, so as a reporter, you'll be challenged to weigh the balance of perceived truth versus the relationships it may cost you. Objectivity is a must.

Here's your typical day. First of all, forget about this being a Nine-to-Five job. Since most sporting events occur in the evening, you'll probably get to the office in the late morning or early afternoon. You'll write stories, call your sources for possible stories, and go over ideas with your editor. You'll possibly attend a news conference and keep an ear for breaking news. Hopefully, you're the one breaking it first. Then you'll attend the game, writing your story as the game unfolds, so you can meet deadline.

Like many sports careers, you do it for the passion, not the pay. If you're the top of your field, sports writing can be lucrative.

Besides the ability to write, it's important to creatively distinguish yourself. This can be assisted by working as part of a sports organization. Stand out by developing your portfolio. Gain valuable experience by covering events for your high school or college publication. With so many experienced writers having recently lost their jobs, there will always be a number of interested competitors for the job.

Paul Coro is the beat writer for the Phoenix Suns. He is passionate about his job. Coro says a sports writer is the bridge between the athlete and the fan. "You need to understand what the sports fans want and serve them. A sports writer has the access to provide this. You can take them into the locker room; provide them insights they don't have access to. Be it courtside or through interviews, you are their microphone."

Coro knew what he wanted to do since junior high school. He was good in English, so he pursued his dream working for his high school paper. In college, he majored in journalism and did what internships he could. "My first job was in news, which later served me well for sports. I covered crime and finance stories, along with the police and fire beats."

San Antonio provided Coro his first professional news reporter job. Two years later, he took an entry level job in Kansas City to get on his sports track, primarily covering high school events while occasionally doing college and pro events on a fill-in basis. Since he was five-foot-ten, he knew his only path to the NBA was through his writing skills. In 1997, Coro managed to get home to Phoenix area, joining the *Arizona Republic*. Once again, he took a career step back, covering the lead high school games. His position eventually graduated to reporting Arizona State University games for three years. In 2003, Coro achieved his dream, getting the assignment of being the *Republic's* beat writer for the Suns.

Coro describes the position as "living this surreal life around the rich and famous. You have your work in the paper on a daily basis, and the environment is exhilarating stuff. The fun part is being around the players. You're in the mix."

It's not all glory though. "There's competitive pressure; you work morning and night all week, with few nights off. There are zero nights off during the NBA's eight-month season. The offseason isn't really an offseason, since the draft, free agency, management changes, and summer leagues always offer something of interest." With the web, there is now a 24-hour news cycle, and there's a lot more informational demand. Factor in odd-hour commercial flights following the team around, and it can get exhausting. "Deadlines have gotten worse over time." Imagine the grind of being a writer for pro baseball. MLB teams play 162 games, with 81 road games a year, but they typically get at least a few days in each city. In the NBA, there are 41 away games, all just a brief one game pit stop before moving on to the next destination.

Another challenge is the journalistic fine line every reporter faces, when to write that critical story that a team or player may not appreciate. "You sometimes have to write difficult things and still have to go in the next day. That's the only way we keep respect. For the most part, athletes are their own worst critics, not the reporter," says Coro.

Sports writers need to be geographically mobile if they want to advance their career. You have to be willing to relocate from one city to the next, especially with some newspapers closing. The market is ever-changing.

To get started as a sports writer, get involved in your high school or college paper. The more experience you have, the better the chance to climb the ladder. A journalism degree is a typical college degree. Sports information offices are a great proving ground too. Upon graduation, you'll probably start at a small town paper.

For employment, check out the Associated Press Sports Editors job site, also ESPN.com and sportsline.com.

Average salaries range from $25,000 to $45,000, depending on your experience level and the size of the market you work in. Veterans in larger markets will certainly earn more.

One extension for a talented sports writer is to author sports-related books. Sports columnists and beat writers have the benefit of a front-row relationship with many sports celebrities. Since they are the pros of prose, they are a natural to tell the in-depth story of the athletes and teams.

Another salary-supplementing position for sports writers is serving a dual role as sports talk show hosts. These sports specialists broadcast during the day and cover their teams at night or on weekends. It provides great credibility for the TV or radio station being able to promote themselves as the station with the top experts.

Blogger

It's not just a newspaper that needs sportswriters. Bloggers now have a major presence on pro and collegiate team websites. There are also league sites that employ sports writers as bloggers. Check out MLB.com, NFL.com, and NBA.com, along with many other professional and collegiate teams.

A blog is a type of interactive website or part of a website, usually maintained by an individual with regular entries of commentary, descriptions of events, or other graphic or video material. Since blogs are interactive and allow visitors to leave comments, this distinguishes itself from other static websites.

Imagine the interactive possibilities related to the sports world with blogging. With so many local newspapers becoming extinct, blogging has extended the careers of many sportswriters who have lost their jobs as columnists and reporters.

As a blogger, you may work for a team directly, and follow them on the road like Clare Farnsworth does for the NFL Seattle Seahawks. Farnsworth calls himself a Digital Media Writer. Formerly, he was a veteran sports writer for the *Seattle Post Intelligencer*, a morning paper that after 100+ years of existence, stopped publishing in March 2009. Despite 22 years on the staff, Farnsworth was suddenly unemployed. This is why many of the sports writers I've spoken to suggest against a career such as theirs. "It's a dying breed." Many are now freelancing their way to the finish line of their career.

Says Farnsworth, "It's great that I can continue what I was doing for 32 years as the Seahawks' beat writer. I no longer have the huge newspaper deadline."

Working directly with the team, Farnsworth has closer player access. "You still travel with the team; get to go in the lunch room with the players. It is still the same type of duty, but I don't have to chase things as much. The information comes to me officially. It creates a different and better personal lifestyle."

Farnsworth says he feels like less of a reporter and more like a writer. "No more life-interrupting 9p.m. phone calls when there's a breaking story. Now I have time to delve into stuff and do proper research."

Pay-wise, Farnsworth says it's fairly close to his old job, "though I lost all my freelance stuff. The great thing is, I have really good FREE health care coverage, and now I'm on full-time salary."

For Farnsworth, it was his technical destiny. His advice: "Embrace what the industry has become. For a sports writer, the duty has become more blogging, tweeting and websites. The newspaper stuff has almost become an afterthought."

After covering the Seahawks for 32 years, Farnsworth has captured some special memories. "I covered NFL strikes in 1982 and 1987, Ken Behring trying to move the Seattle franchise to Southern California, the Super Bowl run in 2005, and the 2011 monumental playoff upset when Seattle out-sainted defending champion New Orleans."

While technological advancement has taken away his original media career, it can't take away Farnsworth's memoirs.

Stringer

This is a free-lance position that will get you into most sporting events. A radio reporter or sports announcing background is a must. The stringer will broadcast live game-day updates both during and after a sporting event. These live updates are 45 to 60 seconds in length. A couple examples of companies that do this are the Sporting News Radio Network and the Associated Press Network. Both will pay $50 per game, with the need for three game updates per hour. Sometimes, you'll do a live feed with each score in football and baseball. Sporting News will also pay an additional $25 for an end-of-game live guest interview. This gives you the potential of $125 per game if you're handling both networks simultaneously. You'll probably have your key game notes jotted down and will be winging it during your report. Contacts are a key to break into this position. A radio station connection would help to get you your credential.

Photographer

Maybe your penchant for sports is on the photography or video side. This will definitely put you close to the action and is an expanding field. With digital technology, now you don't have to be a darkroom dynamo.

Whatever the sport, football, basketball, baseball, and many, many more, there will always be plenty of photographers required to visually record the games. Look along the baseline during a basketball game and there will be several photographers on duty. During the playoffs, they're stacked in there like sardines, representing countries throughout the world.

The sports photographer needs to possess an instinctive ability to know when something noteworthy is a click away. Someone doesn't get "posterized" without a photographer capturing the moment. You never know when you might visually capture that one great play that will withstand the test of time.

Pro sports photographers fall into one of three categories: Staff members, Freelancers, and Contracted photographers.

Newspapers and other sports-specific publications like magazines, wire services, and photo agencies have always employed photographers. Even more opportunities are now available for talented photographers, with the internet providing almost an instantaneous platform to sporting events. Video is a valuable tool for the teams too.

Visually recording games has also become an important preparation tool for coaches before, during, and after competition. NFL Films became an empire, producing highlight videos for the league and the teams. Recruitment videos are another career avenue that has proliferated.

Some photographers have travel positions and do very well financially. Collegiate teams also have photographers on salary.

Personally, I wouldn't want Shaq landing on top of me while he's chasing a loose ball or getting stepped on by his size 22EEE shoes. The view is great, but sometimes dangerous.

Here are some suggestions to help zoom in on that sports photo career. Read technical manuals on cameras and photography. Learn about lighting, exposure, and digital technologies. Enroll in basic, intermediate, and advanced photography courses. These are available at your local community colleges or technical institutes. Build your portfolio. Be passionate.

Nationally acclaimed sports announcer Gary Bender has spent his entire career trying to achieve that perfect broadcast. Similarly, photo journalists are always in search of the one-to-die-for shot.

Like many sports occupations, the competition is keen, especially for the upper echelon photo journalists. It can be monetarily lucrative. Perhaps more importantly, it can be creatively rewarding.

From the Press Box

One of the great things about sports is the camaraderie, the opportunity to be part of the action, to have a place to hang out. The players and coaches use the locker room and the playing field or court as their inner sanctum. For the media, their locker room is the press box.

The press box is set up in a special section of a sports stadium for the media to report about a given event, generally on the level where the luxury boxes are. While it primarily serves as a working area mostly for announcers and writers, in many ways it also serves as a fun gathering place where media professionals share their opinions, their career challenges, and in general, serves as their home away from home. It's sort of like a private country club. These are not necessarily the best seats in the house. Sometimes a press box is so far from the field, the playing surface seems like a different zip code. It's like a fraternity, except that sorority sisters are now included on the invitation list.

The press box can be situated as several adjacent rooms, connected in the back by a long hallway. One large area with multiple rows serving as side-by-side workstations is available for the working press with several TV's simultaneously broadcasting other games from around the country. Then there'll be a series of independent broadcast rooms for the various announcing crews. Another room houses the official stats crew, while other booths will be manned by the coaching staffs, the instant replay crew, and the public address announcer. In stadiums that aren't enclosed, there is even access to the roof above the press box, where many photographers and camera operators visually record the game. As a statistician, I've even worked on a few roofs, because there weren't enough broadcast booths to go around. The wind almost blew my stat sheets into the crowd below.

Nowadays, many press boxes aren't the envied vantage point to watch the game they used to be. Many of the press boxes in today's stadiums are located in the corner or end zone, so the sideline views (goal line to the goal line) can be sold as more expensive luxury suites. Only the national TV network broadcasts are guaranteed a mid-field view. It's all about the revenue. Try announcing a game or doing stats from the end zone. It's not easy. Thank goodness for the free food and a good pair of binoculars.

Basketball arenas have a different press setup, as much of the media working area is courtside, closely surrounded by the fans, while other members of the media or stats crews can be positioned in mini press areas in the stands, surrounded by fans. Some announcing crews are courtside, while others are located midway up in the stadium. The work area is not nearly as private, except in the press room where meals are served and where writers and reporters do their thing. With swirling lights, rotating and flashing advertising, and the non-stop, earsplitting music, the environment itself is almost a sensory overload, with the game being a distraction. What happened to the days when you could still hear the screeching sneakers as players made their moves on court?

Though a member of the media may be partial to the team they cover, cheering in the press area is strictly forbidden. There is a professional creed of impartiality. Security personnel are there to eject violators, though I've never seen it happen. This mostly applies to the writer's section, as announcers for the teams are generally separated in their own broadcast booth, and allowed to express their emotions as they're expected to do.

Members of the media do get VIP treatment, as there's usually a great food spread in most stadiums and arenas. Most teams provide this pre-game meal as a complimentary service. Other teams have started to charge for the food.

Depending on the city and the stadium, the food is generally a real indulgence. It can include an array of roast beef, BBQ brisket, turkey, ham, or fried chicken, along with a green salad, a variety of veggies, rolls, and brownies, pies, cobblers, and cookies for dessert. You definitely won't go hungry. Forget about counting calories.

Once the game starts, everyone gets down to business.

By the age of 12, Bobby Jones was already a golf prodigy, having shot two rounds of 70. By age 14, Jones entered his first major tournament. At age 21, he won the U.S. Open at Inwood Country Club in New York. Six years later, Jones had already won nine majors. In 1930, Jones achieved the ultimate, winning all four majors in a single calendar year. It became known as golf's Grand Slam. It's never been done before or since. By age 28, Jones retired from the game.

Chapter 5

Controlled Chaos

Televising sports, especially on location, takes a tremendous amount of equipment, manpower, and planning. The Control Truck is the heartbeat and brain of the broadcast. Inside the truck, it's essentially controlled chaos. Here are some of the key positions.

What it is Like Working in the 'Truck'

The TV Producer:

The broadcast starts with the Producer, who's responsible for preparing and executing all elements of covering a sporting event. Even before the jump ball happens, or the football referee swings his arm to indicate the start of the game, the Producer is well into his duties. During the game, which replays air and when? When do promos run? When are timeouts taken...or not? The producer has the final say.

Renowned network broadcaster Gary Bender says producers need to have three common characteristics: organized, cool under pressure, and support and respect for the broadcast team. "The producer will offer ideas into the announcer's headsets, and it helps to be on the same wavelength as the talent. Throughout the broadcast, they keep everything together."

I've experienced the control truck, and it gets emotional. Some producers are calm and collected. Others are screamers. You can't have sensitive ears. I've seen people get fired during a broadcast. The hours are long, and you can expect to work weekends. You'll have NO life of your own. You don't have to be a stat geek or in a fantasy league, but you must have a good depth of sports knowledge, be organized, and creative. Oh, and you have to be perfect.

There's always the possibility of a catastrophe for a producer. Maybe it's a technical disaster, the mikes or headsets don't work, a monitor goes on the fritz, or maybe the analyst's telestrator malfunctions. Expect the unexpected, and then calmly deal with it.

Inside the truck (or multiple trucks), you have several positions besides Producer. There's the Director and the Technical Director (T.D., also known as the Switcher; they punch up the camera shots as directed), the Video Engineer, Chyron (inserts the graphics), Tape Operators (though now they don't use tape), and an Audio Mixer (the A-1 blends the different sound sources available).

The Director:

The Director is the ultimate choreographer, constantly rattling off rapid-fire commands throughout the broadcast. Directors serve like a traffic cop and implement the mechanical view of the broadcast. "Give me a camera shot of the coach, go to Camera three, I need a zoom-in on the huddle." They also maintain order among the staff in the control room(s). Every cameraman follows the director's positioning lead. The decision of the director ultimately decides what makes it on the air. There's little room for error.

As you can imagine, the director really needs to know the sport and be in synch with the announcers on which shots they have up on the screen. It's not just which shot to use, but the rhythm and pace to the change of camera shots.

Switcher:

The switcher is the director's right hand man. (Their official term is Technical Director). They actually physically edit all that is visually available to them in 'real time.' They switch from camera shot to camera shot, overlay graphics and dissolve to visual special effects. While the director is thinking of what to display next, the switcher is almost simultaneously doing it. The director usually gives a warning command (a standby command) then the execute command throughout the show.

Video Engineer:

The Video Engineer makes sure the pictures are properly shaded and the right color. Shading means exposure and contrast. Because each camera has subtle variations, the video engineer will compensate for those color differences. It can get tough when it's an afternoon ball game and the sun affects a stadium's shadows.

Chryon:

The chyron position is an in-the-truck job. The chyron keys (types) in important information (i.e., stats) that is graphically displayed on your TV screen. For many professional sports broadcasts, this can be a traveling position. Local freelancers are hired for this position too. For an NFL telecast, the graphics person will get flown around the country on a Friday, spend Saturday with the Broadcast Associate pre-loading information throughout the day, and of course be more than busy on Sunday loading in-the-game action. Monday, they fly home. They'll have their travel costs covered, get housed in a luxury hotel, and receive about a $50 daily per diem. They'll also receive about $40 an hour for their time, based on about a 28-hour work week over three-and-one-half days. That's about $1,100 a week. A good place to get your feet wet for this computer position would be at local stadiums for their in-house production shows. An example is working at a baseball or football stadium and inputting the graphics that might get displayed on the scoreboard.

Another form of graphics input is what FOX calls their fox box. It's also referred to in the industry as the "bug" or the "gumby" (ESPN slang). The bug will also note the score or how much time is left and is usually connected to the stadium's scoreboard computer. This position involves inputting things like strikes, balls, and outs for a baseball broadcast. While the chyron information is historical and biographical, the bug is describing what's happening right at that moment. The bug is also sold for sponsorship and can do special graphics and animations.

Official Stats for the Network:

All major networks and many regional ones will utilize an official stats person. This position afforded me the chance to work for FOX during the memorable 2001 World Series. This is different from the official stats crew, although you do work in conjunction with them during a football or basketball telecast.

For a baseball broadcast, you'll be in the press box within view of the Official Scorer. The network wants to know as soon as possible if a play was a hit or an error. (The official scorer will give a thumbs up or a thumbs down). You'll be asked to keep an eye for all substitutions. Is there a pinch-hitter coming up? Is there action in the bullpen? Which bases have runners? What's the line score on the scoreboard? You'll also assist the talent stats person, who will occasionally ask you to verify certain information. Most official stats people don't bother, but I also keep pitch counts, document the at-bats, strikeouts, walks, 2-out runs scored, runners in scoring position, and whether the lead-off batter reaches. Sometimes the network's talent stats guy takes offense at your providing more information than he does and tell you to speak when spoken to. My observation of this (and I've experienced it many times) is that they're insecure about being shown up. They don't want anyone taking away their position.

For a football broadcast, the official stats person is in the same room as the official stats crew. Primarily, the network and talent stats person need to know ASAP what the official yardage is at the end of a play. The official crew will make that call, and the official stats person (who is on a headset to talent stats and the truck) will immediately relay the information. "Four yard pick-up, 2nd and six." Official distance of punts, field goals, penalties, along with totals from ongoing drives, first downs, individual player and team stats will be input into a computer in the control truck. In the NFL, the announcers (and talent stats) will have a monitor of all these tabulations as the game goes on.

For a basketball official stats person, duties are much the same. You'll typically be situated courtside (sometimes up on the sidelines) and communicating on a headset with talent stats and the graphics people in the control truck. You'll have your own monitor to see what the statistical totals are for an individual player or team. You'll also serve as an extra set of eyes to see whom the officials might call a foul on or if a shot attempt is a three or a two. A good official stats person will think third-dimensionally and offer statistical reasons why a game is unfolding the way it is.

Maybe it is turnover differential. Perhaps there's a disparity of offensive rebounds, resulting in one team getting lot of second chance points. It could be dozens of things. It boils down to WHY is a team winning or losing? Contribute those reasons to the graphics person, and you'll be a star. It helps considerably to keep the scoring runs, too. When is a basket made and with what time showing on the clock, i.e., the Suns have outscored the Magic 12-3 in the last 2:48.

Camera Operators:

Televised games require several camera operators. These are the unsung heroes of a broadcast. Without their pictures, it's just radio. It's critical that they catch the moment. (For the 2009 Super Bowl, NBC used 52 high definition cameras). In football and baseball, they'll be strategically scattered throughout the stadium to cover all the angles possible. NFL games will also have a camera running along a guide wire running the length of the stadium above the playing field. This is robotically controlled, so someone still is required to operate it. Another interesting camera position is the one that sits perched on a mobile lift. This vehicle goes back and forth between the 20's depending on where the ball is spotted. It gives you a lower level sideline view. Basketball requires fewer camera operators. Because of the more intimate, close-up nature of basketball broadcasts, some camera operators get to sit sideline. Beware of flying bodies.

Camera operators are responsible for securing their assigned equipment and taking it to their location to set up and shoot the event.

John James, a veteran video engineer (he prefers video colorist) , says "It's a hurry-up-and-wait position while they pass the time for the director to choose the camera view and/or receive orders what to do. The director says "Get me a medium shot, go wider." The director constantly guides camera operators to secure the visual story."

Camera operators are allowed to be somewhat creative, showing the directors something they maybe didn't expect. "I like that Camera 5, let's take Camera 5." A veteran of this craft is Ralph Kelso. Kelso says you have to have quick reactions. "You need to know sports and like sports. You also need to be able to follow orders and have situation awareness. You need to be two steps ahead of the game. Something like that comes with experience and knowledge of the game."

After the game, the camera operator has to return the camera equipment for inventory and properly stow it away. Everyone helps pack the truck, which includes putting everything that was deployed away: the cables, lenses, cameras, tri-pods, microphones, monitors, lighting equipment, and telestrators. The camera operator's job isn't done until this is all complete. This might take an hour or two after a broadcast is over.

Camera operators also have to be ready for any kind of weather conditions, whether it's sunny, snowy, or rainy. Mother Nature can sometimes be harsh to a camera person. You also have to be physically fit to move the heavy equipment. Even the hand-held camera operators are putting 15-30 pounds on their shoulder throughout the long broadcast. The new 3-D cameras are actually two cameras-in-one, so that doubles the weight load. It can be physically demanding. On average, you also have to be on-site six hours before the game.

A-1's (Audio Mixer) and A-2's:

Sound for a sportscast is divided into two elements, setup for the broadcast, and the audio mixing of it. The overall purpose is to capture the live sound of the game. To start with, the A-1 is responsible to make sure the internal communications between everyone are functioning properly. There can be no broadcast without everyone in the truck talking to each other.

The A-1's are like the Wizard of Oz behind the curtain, directing the sound and all the effects. They're like the sound commander. The A-1 tells A-2's where the sound effect microphones are placed throughout the stadium to capture the sound of the game, so it doesn't sound hollow, i.e., the sound of shoes screeching on the basketball court, or the bounce of the ball off the rim. Microphones are also hidden near the team's benches so they can pick up comments from the coach. The A-1's usually remain inside the truck.

The A-2's duties are outside the truck. A-2's run the audio cables and positions the mics. That's the set-up phase. Then there's the show phase, where the A-2's stay in the field, functioning like an emergency doctor in the broadcast room. They need to be a little bit of an electrician. Maybe the announcer has a microphone that fails. The A-2 needs to replace that immediately, so something may have to be swapped out instantaneously to keep the show happening. If the headset quits working, the equipment needs a quick replacement. Maybe it's a TV monitor or telestrator that needs a quick fix or substitution. The A-2's , the silent contributors of the broadcast, get these things done.

Floor Director/Stage Manager:

The floor director is utilized for football, baseball, and basketball broadcasts (as well as other sports). This person is on a headset in direct communication with the control truck throughout the broadcast. The primary duty is to coordinate communication between the truck and the announcers. The floor director will cue the broadcasters per the director and producer. During the game, when a commercial break is coming or concluding, the floor director will give the announcer countdowns on when to cease and to recommence with the broadcast. During the broadcast, the floor director will also hand the announcer index cards containing live commercial reads at an appropriate time. Good floor directors also make sure the broadcast crew in the booth has things like water and snacks.

Doris Shanahan's entree to a position as a floor director didn't go the usual broadcast school route. Hers came through a varied background, beginning with theatre and working as coordinator for an ad agency. "After that I was a freelancer for commercial and industrial shoots in film and video, including a couple feature films, initially working as a production assistant."

She began doing sports on the side. "They needed spare hands. I learned more technical aspects of sports broadcasting." Over time, Doris began working her way up to production manager.

"Eventually, I figured out it was easier to work regularly scheduled games rather than tying up weeks and months on film productions. You still get to call your own shots; however, the hours are better."

Shanahan describes her job as, "keeping the announcers happy, and keeping the production truck happy. My position used to be strictly freelance, now we are under contracts for most work locally."

Shanahan explains a typical day for a floor director. "This is really a multi-tasking position. You speak with the producer and associate producer to coordinate times when you are needed and where exactly you need to be before, during, and after the game, including pre-game and post-game interviews, studio, news, and web hits. You make certain other members of the crew are aware of when and where they are needed. In the past I've been known to wear four headsets at one time, but things are getting more specialized all the time."

The broadcast booth requires that all the setup is indeed properly set up. Play-by-play equipment is on this side, color announcer that side, stats headset over there. Monitors need to be where they're supposed to be. Is there enough water for the announcers so they have "spit to speak?" It's also the floor manager's job to provide cues to the talent. "I make sure they know when they're on camera and, when they're off, let them know how much time they have coming and going on air." As floor manager, Shanahan also bears the responsibility of making sure the announcers look good. "Are the ear pieces and wiring hidden, is the lint off their coat, are the ties straight."

The compensation for this position varies from place to place and with experience. Local rate is sometimes set by contract, a collective bargaining agreement, whether or not one is a union member, or one may simply be hired directly by a non-contracted entity. With contracts there are health insurance, pension, and other benefits previously paid for by the freelancer, if the freelancer had benefits at all.

Most times, a stage manager gets hired on a local level rather than traveling one by visiting broadcasters as a cost-saving measure.

Shanahan describes this position often as a possible career stepping stone for eventual producers or directors. "Most floor directors don't want to stay in this position forever."

Broadcast Engineer:

This occupation might be described as a troubleshooter position. As a broadcast engineer during a sports event, you'll enjoy the same great court-side or press box view as the announcers you're working with. The rank of this job is so important, professional teams for baseball and football travel this position. Except for keeping voice levels consistent during the broadcast, you may not be asked to do a whole lot more. Yet if the equipment malfunctions, you become the most valuable member of the broadcast crew. Without a functioning microphone, Bob Costas might as well be Marcel Marceau, the legendary mime. In many ways, the engineers are an insurance policy, earning their wage when things aren't working. If the ISDN line (phone line) won't connect, you're needed to mend the problem.

This occupation might not be as hard as you think, according to Tom Brown, a 30-year veteran in the broadcast world. Brown has done every job in radio, from programming, to production, to sales, to announcing. He's also been a Sales Manager and General Manager. Brown began his board operator career without any training.

"I had just received my radio license in 1980. Back then, it only required paperwork to get one. I walked into a radio station in my home town of Pryor, Oklahoma and boldly asked 'What do I do next?' The Program Director and Production Manager looked at each other and said: 'What are you doing Friday night?' They needed a board operator for the local high school football broadcast. 'Want to run the game?' Though he had no experience, Brown accepted. "This is what you need to do," he says. "Be a sore thumb. Be willing to do anything and everything. Learn on the job. Practical experience is everything."

Brown says audio and visual equipment training is something you can start to get at a high school or college. "Another approach is to do a promotion internship for a radio station. You'll start by doing on-site station events. From that, you'll learn some engineering by setting up for remote broadcasts. Technically, you're now doing what a courtside engineer does." There are also trade schools that teach engineering.

As an engineer, part of your job is to make the announcer comfortable and sound good. If the microphone works properly, the broadcaster is at ease.

Another part of the job is to make sure the microphone is off at the right time. Some announcers can get colorful or emotional during timeouts, and inappropriate foul language has been known to slip out. A good engineer just might save the career of a sportscaster by sparing this embarrassment.

Brown shared the experience of his baseball engineering debut broadcast. "I was working with the Milwaukee Brewers crew with legendary Hall-of-Fame announcer Bob Uecker. Later in the broadcast, MLB Commissioner Bud Selig joins us for a couple innings. It doesn't get any better than that."

Another time, Brown was engineering for the Miami Heat Spanish Radio broadcast. It couldn't have been too exciting a contest, because Brown said, "The statistician actually fell asleep during the game." I wonder if he got paid.

Runner:

A runner is essentially a freelance gofer position that networks hire for a day's worth of odd jobs and is a wonderful way to break into the biz. This is how CBS sportscaster Jim Nantz got his first TV job. It doesn't require experience, just a connection with the network or perhaps the media relations department of a university or college. Typically, college interns will get an assignment like this. Your duty is to make sure the broadcasters have everything they need, water, snacks, etc. Before halftime, you make sure there's a platter full of hot dogs (and all the condiments), so when the announcers take their break, they don't have to waste time standing in the long chow line with the attending media. You might even be assigned to shadow sideline reporters and be at their beckon call.

The Competitiveness of Getting a Job in the "Truck"

People who want to get into the production side of sports start at the bottom, and even that is competitive. ESPN gets 900 job applications a year for production assistant spots. Approximately 20-percent of those who get interviews get into the network's seven month internship program. A production assistant will graduate to associate producer and then to a producer, if the person has what it takes to multi-task.

Another route into sports television is through a research job. NBC chose just three researchers for the 1996 Olympics from 800 applicants.

Networking, Connections and Travel

Imagine sitting next to Al Michaels, with a center-of-the-field view, in the press box as his personal "information specialist." I guarantee others like legendary announcer Keith (Whoa, Nellie!) Jackson had it in their contract too, to have a designated person of their choice that is paid to travel as "their" statistician. The national television networks cover all your expenses, provide deluxe hotel accommodations, and excellent meals too. And of course, you get paid a negotiated amount (most get told this is what you get) for your time.

Sadly, the same opportunity does not exist with local collegiate broadcasters. There are 343 Division One Schools in the NCAA. Be it football or basketball, nearly all have an announcer that should at least want a home stats guy. Unfortunately, economics dictate otherwise. Arizona State's play-by-play man, Tim Healy, wasn't allowed a budget for a football statistician until just a few years ago. Healy then was allowed $75 a game and offered the position to me. In basketball, he relies strictly on a stats screen (A TV which displays up-to-date statistics of the game). Many times, when I've been working a game for FOX TV, my seat was adjacent to Healy's, and when I'd pass my game note along to Barry Tompkins, I'd kindly repeat the process and hand it over to Healy. He'd immediately share the tidbit with Devil-land, "The Devils are on an 11-2 run," and then wink a thank you over to me. There was never a question if my note was accurate. Tim trusted that I was correct. It was gestures like this that caused Healy to offer me the football stats slot that one season. Healy and analyst and former Sun Devil quarterback, Jeff Van Raaphorst, would also throw my name over the air after providing them a noteworthy stat. Healy would consider utilizing me more, but he never had a budget, and he knew I'd be passing up paid jobs to work for him. He understood we all have to pay the bills.

A former co-worker of mine, Chris Visser, gave me a big assist in breaking into the NFL FOX TV arena. Chris was Program Director of Phoenix's KGME, one of the radio stations I sold advertising for. ESPN's Mike Golic, a former NFL lineman, got his start in broadcasting there too. If you recognize Chris' last name, his sister is nationally revered sportscaster, Lesley Visser, one of the pioneers for women sportscasters. Lesley is married to long-time sportscaster, Dick Stockton. Dick uses Chris as his personal spotter every NFL Sunday in the fall. Chris Visser is an excellent spotter and really knows his stuff. He's also well-connected in the sports world. Being affiliated with FOX TV, Chris gave me a call in the mid-90's and asked if I'd like to work official stats for their upcoming Arizona NFL broadcast in Tempe. Sun Devil stadium was still the Cardinal's home until August of 2006.

"Work an NFL game? Sure!"

As previously noted, the "Official" statistician for a network is different from a team's league-required official stat crew. For professional or college football television broadcasts, the network's "official stats" position is actually assigned in the team's official stat area, making sure that the stats tabulated for the league match what is being said or graphically shown to TV viewers. Most league stat crews don't like the arrangement because the network guy is typically an affordable local hire without much experience that tends to ask a lot of questions. "How long was that last drive?" "How many plays were there?" "What are the third down conversions today?" The network's official stats person can be a nuisance to the league crew. When working this position, I always keep my own manual charts, and don't need to bother the official crew nearly as much. Most times, it was a question about a play, like, 'Was that officially a 3-yard rush or 4?' TV Networks want to be exactly right. That's where their official statistician would come in handy. You are their conduit to the league's official crew. Quickness is the key. "Hurry up, hurry up, was that 3 or 4?" the talents' stats guy will often bellow. "Need it now!" Third down was about to happen and was it third and five or third and six? The announcer has to be correct! And fast!

Don't just bring your stat sheets, drive charts, and sharpened pencils to the game. Bring a thick skin with you too. Most guys working network official stats are treated like a real peon. Usually it gets intense at times. Matter of fact, it happens quite frequently.

A Travel Position in Sports

There is nothing like being flown to another city to work a sporting event. You see stadiums on TV all the time and fantasize about what it would be like to walk across that field before the game, what it would be like to sit in that stadium's press box.

Just watch a TV broadcast from University of Washington Husky Stadium in Seattle. The cameras will inevitably show the breathtaking waterfront view of Lake Washington that leads right up to the stadium and the yachts that line the docks filled with tail-gate parties, aqua style.

Who can't get into experiencing that pageantry that dominates college football Fall Saturday's across the country? I once asked legendary announcer Keith Jackson, who has called historic college football games throughout the country for decades, which college stadium he considered the most beautiful setting across the land. Washington's Husky Stadium was his choice. It should be noted that Michigan Stadium (known as the Big House because it holds 109,901 fans) was his favorite to announce a game from.

The debate of which football stadium is the best is obviously subjective and deeply biased by the home fans. Is it a Pro Football stadium or a College Football venue? Sometimes, the same stadium provides the home field for both pro and college. Up through 2005, Arizona State's Sun Devil Stadium served as home for both Arizona State University and the NFL's Arizona Cardinals. Come New Year's and the Bowl season, some of these stadiums take on an elite status.

Going to the Superdome

After working an NFL game for FOX, I was now in their database. Little did I realize what would occur after this initial introduction with FOX TV; an experience of a lifetime.

For the 2000 NFL season, I was fortunate enough to be one of only 15 stat guys working on Sundays. Late that August, as the NFL preseason was winding down, I got a call from FOX TV out of Los Angeles. The regular season was just a week-and-a-half away. FOX had gotten my name from some television producer I'd recently worked with out of California. The talent statistician they had arrangements with for their "seventh crew" couldn't fulfill the obligation, and they wanted to know if I was interested.

"Are you kidding?"

Yeah, we'll need you to work in New Orleans' Superdome in 10 days. Can you make it?" It took about half a second to accept.

The Superdome in New Orleans

(Photos used with permission from the New Orleans Saints and the New Orleans Superdome)

For FOX, the seventh crew was like an audition crew. Typically, the pecking order for FOX's NFL broadcasts start with their top announcing and production team. Currently, that team is Joe Buck and Troy Aikman. These guys get assigned the marquee matchup of the week.

The so-called seventh crew sometimes uses up-and-coming announcers and production personnel that were still getting experience under their belt. Based on the NFL schedule, the seventh crew was only needed to cover about six games over the whole season. That was fine by me. As I came to learn, the travel was grueling, especially when you're already working another full-time job. You fly out on a Friday night, and don't get home until very late Sunday. Since I flew out of Phoenix, this usually meant longer flights too.

Friday, you check into your (deluxe) hotel late. Then you spend a large portion of a Saturday helping the B.A. (broadcast associate) with pre-game research and have dinner with the announcers and production team to go over Sunday's schedule. Then on game-day, you're on-site at the stadium about five hours early just in case anything else came up. That usually meant a lot of free time to eat complimentary catered stadium food (breakfast and lunch) provided for the broadcast crew.

Through all the years, I've never been nervous doing stats at a game. Not until I worked my first game as a talent statistician for NFL FOX on the road. My knees were literally shaking. Most games, I settle into a rhythm right away. Not this day! This was the BIG TIME and I was getting a case of the nerves. I was sitting in the press box of the Superdome, host venue of five previous Super Bowls. About half way through the first quarter, I was confident I was doing a capable job and finally relaxed. Even during the 2001 World Series, I can't remember getting nervous like I was that day in New Orleans.

That season, I also got to visit Denver, Charlotte (twice), and Atlanta. Just wish I could have worked even more games and seen more cities and stadiums. It was memorable. It will be for you too.

From this point on, whenever FOX TV came to Phoenix, I usually got a call. Not just in football. "Do you do baseball, too?" With my fingers crossed, I replied: "I sure do." FOX TV started using me as their "official stats" guy in Phoenix for major league baseball. When the 2001 National League playoffs rolled around, I was the one who got the call.

Curt Schilling and Randy Johnson led the Diamondback's charge that season with a combined 43 victories in the regular season. Luis Gonzales slugged a (still) team-record 57 home runs and knocked in 142 RBI's.

Round One in the N.L. Division series, St Louis came calling. Tony Womack's walk-off hit eliminated the Cardinals, three games to two. Now it was on to round two, with the Diamondbacks and Atlanta Braves battling for the National League championship. Schilling was masterful, and Arizona advanced in five games.

Next up, it was the 2001 World Series. "I guess you'll be bringing in the 'A' Team now, huh?"

"Nope, Glenn, you're the 'A' Team."

Arizona would host Games 1, 2, 6 and 7, and I was still the one they relied on. I can still proudly remember in Game 2 when I mentioned that the Yankees had yet to have a leadoff batter reach base, and it was now 13 innings into the Series. This was relevant stuff. Even FOX's lead stats guy for Joe Buck hadn't come up with that one. On my headset, I could hear the directors in the truck screaming: "Is that true? Is the official stats guy correct? Check it out." It was true, and immediately, Buck and analyst Tim McCarver were talking about "my stat" as a contributing reason the Yankees lost Game 1 and were losing in Game 2. Arizona won Game 1 by a score of 9-1. Game 2 was a 4-0 Diamondbacks shutout of the Yanks.

This was the World Series, and in a small way, I had influenced this world-wide broadcast. When you've provided some information that the announcers immediately use, you know you're doing your job.

It only takes just one announcer, or one strategic connection to hook you up, and you've got your foot in the door. That's the recipe. No position is too small or menial. You'll hear me (and others) state this over and over, because you never know whom you will meet that can boost your career.

Gotta See It For Myself

In 2009, I was working a national radio NFL broadcast in Glendale, Arizona, and the radio analyst that day was James Lofton who grew up with Warren Moon and is a 2003 NFL Hall of Fame inductee. Lofton and I were sitting in the press box in the corner of the Cardinal's home stadium.

Lofton said, "Glenn, see the scoreboard over our shoulder? Look at it through your binoculars."

Through binoculars, it obviously looked massive. He said, "That's what the scoreboard in the new Cowboys Stadium looks like in person."

That's all it took. I had to go experience that for myself. I called the Seahawks, and said, "I can make the Seattle road game at Dallas in November, if you can use me."

"Come on down, Glenn," said their radio producer, Brian O'Connell.

It's said they grow everything BIG in Texas. There is nothing I could eloquently write that would give description of the new Cowboys Stadium proper justice. Imagine standing on the field before the game, looking up at those massive video screens, viewing the pageantry and religion that is Cowboys football on a Sunday afternoon. This is all part of the nirvana of being involved in the sports world.

The gem that is now the Dallas Cowboys home field is a cathedral, and the largest domed stadium in the world. It took 1.2 billion dollars to erect this palace. Seating capacity for football is 80,000, with a maximum capacity for other events around 110,000. The two sideline high-definition TV screens run from the 20 yard line to the 20 yard line, measuring 160-feet by 72-feet. These monitors alone make it almost unnecessary to watch the actual game. The video board is actually larger than the court used during the 2010 NBA All-Star game hosted in this stadium.

As I came to experience, you can get lost in Dallas Stadium. I'd never missed a kickoff or shown up late for a broadcast until I worked that game with Seattle in Dallas. I had my stats sheets all ready and grabbed my camera to go down to the field to check the stadium out. (Of course, this included a close-up view of the famed Cowboy Cheerleaders).

It was getting close to kick off time, so I started my trek back up to the radio booth, except, I got lost in this massive shrine. Panicking, I started asking ushers for directions. No one knew where to send me. I was still running around with no clue where I was going. The coin flip was now done, and the teams were heading out on the field for the opening kickoff.

I imagine Seahawk play-by-play voice Steve Raible, analyst Warren Moon and Brian, the radio producer who hired me, were wondering where the heck I was. Two plays into the game, I finally found my way and sheepishly walked into the radio booth. Thankfully, I'd worked a number of games with Steve and Warren, and they were very cool about it. Each couldn't help but give me a mischievous grin.

Said Moon with a smile, "I just knew when you headed down to the field before kickoff it was going to be trouble." He was right. It's all part of the experience of visiting stadiums throughout the country.

Curve Balls

Expect the unexpected when working on a sports broadcast crew. You never know what could happen or go haywire during the course of a sporting event.

The seemingly easy stuff to rectify is technical issues. Your stats monitor (if you have one) goes on the blink. Your headset isn't working, so you can't hear the control truck, or they can't hear you. Maybe the official stats crew is correcting something they input after a play has been reviewed and overturned, so they momentarily get behind and aren't current with what they're providing. And they aren't the ones who get an earful from the TV truck, it's you.

"What's wrong with the stats? Why are they three plays behind? Get on them!" Meanwhile, the official stats crew in basketball is in another part of the stadium. It's not exactly convenient for you to communicate with them, let alone tell them, while they're scrambling to catch up, how to do their job.

Maybe there isn't a place for you to sit, so you have to stand up for the entire four-hour broadcast. This happened to me during the 2001 World Series. To be a part of that, I certainly didn't mind.

Most collegiate press boxes in which I've worked, as well as many professional stadiums offer very cramped working space. You're rubbing shoulders with the announcers with minimal room to tabulate your stats on. If you're a spotter, you're usually standing to the side, or behind the announcers, leaning in only to point out who made the play, then stepping back.

I've had a wind gust through the football broadcast booth nearly blow my night's efforts down to the fans below. In 2007, I flew to Green Bay to work the Seahawks – Packers playoff game at Lambeau Field. What a thrill to work at this historic stadium, let alone during a playoff encounter. Imagine January in Green Bay, with near blizzard conditions. A day earlier, 300 members of the Packers' ever-ready faithful answered the team's 'Shovel Advisory' and showed up to clear the seats and aisles for $8 an hour.

Nearly all announcers will open the windows to their booth so they can get a clearer view of the field. Seahawks play-by-play announcer Steve Raible, analyst Warren Moon, and the rest of our broadcast crew were in for a COLD day. There was no snow on the ground at kickoff; however, another snow storm was predicted. The weatherman was right. By the time the fourth quarter rolled around, around five inches of snow had fallen on the frozen tundra known as Lambeau Field. Throughout the game, the playing field just kept getting more obscure. Sidelines and yard stripes were permanently disappearing with every non-melting flake that fell to the ground.

Eventually, all you could see was a white surface. With swirling winds, our broadcast booth was not exempt from the snowy conditions. At one point of the broadcast, Warren Moon said, "I feel sorry for our statistician, Glenn. His stat sheets are getting covered up with snow." At this point in the game, the Packers were winning handily, and the final result was no longer in question; however, I still had a job to do. For the entire fourth quarter, I had to rely on the scoreboard to tell me the down and distance. Otherwise, it would have just been a complete guess. Imagine if it had been a close finish.

I can only imagine how the famed voice of the NFL, John Facenda, must have described the glacial action during the infamous NFL Championship Ice Bowl in 1967 in Green Bay. That game was for the privilege to represent the NFL in the first-ever Super Bowl against the upstart AFL. At game-time, the mercury registered at minus 15 degrees (not Celsius). With the wind chill factor, the temperature said 40 below.

"It was a gray, frosty afternoon in Packer-land, a day like no other. Bundled only in shoulder pads, long johns, and their flannel uniforms, the combatants performed on a cast-iron field, trying to skate their way down the frozen tundra known as Lambeau Field. Winter's numbing chill was their teammate. Biting winds served as their blanket, howling like a coyote ready to conquer its next prey. Who would keep their cool? Would it be Green Bay's tandem of Starr and Nitschke, or Dallas' Meredith and Lilly that would survive the arctic onslaught and endure this mind-numbing New Year's Eve frigid fallout? Even the marching band received no mercy from Mother Nature. The conductor used an icicle for a baton. Some of the band ended up on injured reserve, with the frozen woodwinds used for firewood, and the brass players' mouthpieces needing to be de-iced before they could be removed from their blue, lifeless lips."

In actuality, the University of Wisconsin–La Crosse Marching Chiefs band was scheduled to perform the pre-game and half-time shows. However, it was so brutally frigid that their performance was cancelled and seven members of the band were transported to local hospitals for hypothermia. The Packers ultimately rewarded their frozen faithful, prevailing 21-17.

In basketball, you are sometimes provided a non-enviable view of the game. I was working a basketball game in a baseball stadium, where Arizona State was hosting powerhouse Tennessee in an NCAA women's matchup at Chase Field, home of the Arizona Diamondbacks. With the layout of the basketball court across the infield, someone forgot to consider that the scoreboard was behind the TV announcer, Ted Robinson. Robinson was an experienced broadcaster, but he had never encountered a setup like this. Nor had I. Instead of primarily focusing on typical game stats I'd keep, first, I had to write down the score after every point so Robinson knew what to tell the viewers. It was a challenging night.

Even in controlled environments, sight lines can be a challenge. Before being shifted to Sun Devil Stadium in 2006, the Insight Bowl was played at Chase Field too. One end zone was situated in the infield area, and the other was in left/center field. Right field comprised the stands along one sideline. Since baseball press boxes are geared around home plate, our broadcast booth was essentially behind the end zone. It wasn't too bad when a team was approaching your end of the field; however, trying to gauge how many yards a player just ran or passed for was extremely challenging. Was that a 14-yard gain, or 19-yards? You had no sideline perspective. Gauging punting distance was also difficult.

Arizona State hosted the Fighting Irish of Notre Dame in 1998. ABC was broadcasting it as its Game of the Week, which meant hall-of-fame announcer Keith Jackson was in town. I was hired to do official stats that day, but it was not the job I ended up doing. Sun Devil Stadium suffered a power outage in the first quarter. The power was never restored for the rest of the game. In a situation like this, the official on the field is responsible for the game clock. ABC nominated me to do my best guesstimate on keeping them honest about how many minutes there were at any given point of the game. When it was said and done (with the help of the official crew), we managed to stay within about thirty seconds of the time of the official referee. The Fighting Irish won the game, 28-9.

Whether working for a broadcaster, or for the stats crew, there's occasionally some interesting drama. One game, in which the Sonics pummeled Utah, one of the Jazz players came out to the press table after the game. He had already showered and the official crew was wrapping up their night's duty. This player had seen the final box score in the locker room, and was furious. He came out to argue that (in a blow-out loss), he had "four rebounds, not three!!!" This player was not even a starting player at this point in his career. It made you wonder how much that extra rebound was worth to his contract.

Announcers will sometimes get into the act with the stats crew. One season, Milwaukee's radio play-by-play announcer almost came to blows with a member of the Sonics' official crew -- during the game. The Bucks' announcer argued there should have been a re-set on the 24-second clock and demanded it. I don't imagine legendary referee Earl Strom would have taken kindly to any announcer circumventing or criticizing his responsibility as lead official. The announcer wouldn't let up, the discussion got heated, and the 24-second clock operator finally told the announcer to "SIT DOWN AND SHUT UP!" They nearly had to be separated.

Even courtside statisticians are not exempt from getting dragged into the action. Bob Blackburn's son Dave was keeping radio stats for his dad the night in Seattle the Philadelphia 76ers were in town to battle the SuperSonics, battle being the operative word, because the action was very physical on the court. Sonics power forward Lonnie Shelton had just manhandled the rugged George McGinnis, and no call was made. As the younger Blackburn recalled, "McGinnis went down court and greeted referee Jess Kersey with a forearm and knocked him out." Kersey had to be taken to the hospital. As a witness to the altercation, Dave had to file a written report to the NBA and almost got flown to New York to give testimony. It can get interesting along press row.

Sometimes as a statistician, you get to throw the announcers a curve ball. Such was the case with Los Angeles-based sportscaster Jim Watson. Watson is just a character with a never-ending smile, a genuinely fun guy to be around. I first worked with Watson for a Pac-10 volleyball FOX broadcast. I had never even attended a volleyball game, let alone done stats for one. I had no clue what a dig, kill, or spike was. When T R O Productions hired me, I initially declined, telling them there had to be someone qualified to do it. T R O insisted they had faith in me, so I relented.

"Just don't tell them you've never done a volleyball match before," they said. When I got to the stadium, I was introduced to Watson and the first thing he asked me was: "Have you ever done a volleyball game?"

I wasn't very convincing, so he proceeded to give me a crash course on the rules. "If you don't know the answer, just make one up," Watson said.

Throughout the first game, I did my best, but knew I was out of my comfort zone. By the second game, I was getting the hang of it. Watson congratulated me for surviving the broadcast. I promised him if we ever paired up for basketball, I'd be much better equipped.

Later that winter, FOX TV hired me to do a Pac-10 basketball game in Tucson. Watson would be there. With Watson being an easy-going guy, we had a great time. Watson soon realized I was substantially better at basketball stats and was soon using all the game notes I was passing along to him. It was time to have a little fun. As we were coming out of a timeout, I handed Watson a note just as he was about to go back on the air. It read:

"Three kills, five spikes, and 10 digs." Watson was about to announce this, when he realized my prank. He barely managed to contain himself, he was laughing so hard. I just smiled. I've worked with Watson a number of times since, and each game, it's become our ritual for me to slip him a volleyball stat, reminding him of our first encounter. He never knows when it's coming, but Watson laughs every time.

As I've previously noted, former Seahawk wide receiver Steve Raible is the radio play-by-play announcer for the Seattle Seahawks. Prior to that position, Steve was the color commentator and did post-game analysis. Raible once shared with me that on the way to the locker room after a game, he got stuck in the elevator, and escape wasn't going to happen anytime soon. Raible proceeded to do his post-game show from the elevator via a cell phone. The show must go on!

To me, the main thrill of traveling to do stats is the chance to see other cities and stadiums across the country, especially since my expenses are usually getting covered. Give me a broadcast booth, any booth, and I'm excited to be there. Well, most of the time anyway. ESPN flew me to my hometown of Seattle to work a national high school game of the week. I get a paid-for trip back home? Accommodations paid for, and car too? You bet! The visiting California team included three players with pretty famous fathers, Wayne Gretzky, Joe Montana, and Wil Smith. All three were in attendance. But this was still a high school game, with a press box not much larger than a long closet. The game kicked off around 6 p.m., so poor lighting was also a challenge. The trip did have its other benefits. The next day, my Uncle Ron treated me to the Washington Husky – USC game. My (under) Dawgs upset Southern Cal on a thrilling last-second field goal. It was a good weekend.

If you asked various sports announcers about some memorable moments in their broadcast career, or strange venue they broadcast from, there would be a long list of crazy stories. Greg Schulte is the play-by-play announcer for the Arizona Diamondbacks. Earlier in his career, he once announced a game from the back of a pickup truck.

Sonics announcer Bob Blackburn was once calling a junior college championship football game in California early in his sportscasting career. The evening got very foggy; trying to call the action from the press box became visibly impossible. Bob had to move the broadcast up to the field and run up and down the sideline with a long mike cord trailing behind him just to call the game. At one point, Bob got nailed on the sideline and went tumbling one way, while the microphone went flying the other direction. If you're going to be a sideline victim and get sent sprawling, at least Bob got hit by one of the best. Turns out, the player who ran Bob over was Joe Perry, who ended up in the NFL Hall-of-Fame as the (current) all-time leading running back for the San Francisco 49ers. I don't think the refs threw a penalty flag for roughing.

Most pro football stadiums now don't offer much of a vantage point either, and the determining factor is revenue. A majority of press box views for the NFL are in the corner near the end zone. The better sideline views are reserved for the suites, which are occupied by the owners and their guests, high-paying season ticket holders, the coaches, and the national TV broadcast crew. Even the official stats crew, which is responsible for tabulating the game's historical records on behalf of the NFL, gets a challenging sightline from the corner. In Chicago's Soldier Field, you get a 40 yard-line view, but the overhanging section from above obscures your view when there's a sky-high punt. You temporarily lose sight of the ball. There are still some dual-purpose stadiums like Oakland's Coliseum, where the pro football and baseball team share the facility. Converted baseball stadiums don't make for the best football field configurations, however.

Where to Look For Work on a Local Level

When considering how to break into sports, it's quite likely your hometown's University or College provides at least radio broadcast coverage. Depending on market size or location, television is a strong possibility, too. TV will require many behind-the-scenes free-lance positions, including a home statistician for football broadcasts. Usually, TV wants an official stats person too. They're unlikely to budget for a traveling position, unless you're an announcer, producer, or director.

If you're interested in a travel position at the college sports level, working within a University's Sports Information Office might provide your best opportunity.

Another way to go about getting hired to work at sporting events is through local production companies. Regional television companies understandably do their best to keep their overhead to a minimum. Clearly, there's no getting around traveling the announcers, the producer, and directors. Many times positions like audio and video technicians are traveled too. There are other travel positions that are also necessary to maintain the quality and continuity of their away-from-home broadcast. However, not all behind-the-scenes positions are flown in. That's where a local crewing company comes in. They serve as a broker to the networks to provide seasoned freelancers capable of filling duties like camera operators.

Amy and Scott Kelso operate T R O Productions in the Phoenix, Arizona, area. T R O facilitates brokerage-type partnerships with TNT, TBS, FOX Sports Net and many others, providing free-lance professionals ready to be hired at a moment's notice. This pool of free-lancers includes camera operators, floor directors, graphics specialists, tape operators, statisticians, spotters, runners, electricians, technicians, score box operators, and other control truck positions. There are examples of other T R O-type companies throughout the country.

Most of the time T R O will provide a month or two notice (sometimes longer) on positions needed. When I was hired to do stats for New York Yankees TV or Los Angeles Dodgers TV, I would pretty much know months in advance and could plan my schedule accordingly. Some positions like audio and video tech guys require a full-day commitment. Positions like a statistician need to report about an hour-and-a-half to two hours early.

T R O has been in operation for 30 years, handling all different types of sports, usually for TV, but radio positions as well. They've even asked me to work Volleyball, Lacrosse, and Gymnastics events. The commonality is that each of the broadcast requirements for most of these positions involves essentially the same duty, regardless of the sport. The graphics people still pre-load essential statistics, the floor director still guides the announcers. The camera operators probably have one of the biggest adjustments, based on the nature of the sport and their position they're shooting from. A football or baseball stadium shoot is obviously far different from a close-up basketball court vantage point. The playing surface is much more widespread for baseball and football, thus requiring many more camera operators. This in return, creates many more decisions for the producer and director in the truck, thus making them the ultimate multi-taskers. Picture an octopus with each arm a different set of eyes, simultaneously watching several rows of small TV's, needing to direct the switcher to which camera provides the best view available at that moment. "Go to Camera 5...now!" "Camera 3, get me a sideline shot of the head coach."

At the same time, the director is constantly directing the cameramen what shots to capture instead. The camera operators even have photos of all the team's coaches taped to their camera, just in case they're asked to locate a defensive coordinator for example. The camera operators are expected to be real sports fans too. It's a necessary part of the job because they also need to think like a director and find interesting camera shots for the director and producer.

Save for broadcast coverage of the extensive Olympics, here is an extreme example of what NBC's TV coverage was like for the 2009 Super Bowl.

The number of cameras used and the miles of cable used amassed some interesting totals:

450- Number of people which were part of the NBC production, technical, administrative and support crews

93- Microphones (including 12 on-field parabolic microphones)

52- High Definition Cameras (2 SD Cameras for Game Clock and Play Clock)

50- Miles of Camera and Microphone cable (this could connect San Francisco with San Jose)

45- Vehicles (control trucks, mobile units, office trailers, Horse Trailer)

24- Digital Video Replay Sources

22- Hard Cameras (including 2 Super Slo-Mo's and three "X-Mo's)

20- Hand-held Cameras (including two Steady Cams)

10- NEP Supershooter Trailers in the TV Compound

8- Digital Post-Production Facility (5 Avid Suites, 3 Final Cut Pro Suites)

5- Robotic Cameras (including two fixed on the Field Goal posts)

2- RF Hand-held cameras

1- "Cable-Cam" camera suspended above the playing field

1- Hard Camera for scenic views of Tampa Bay

On a local level, a company like T R O would typically be hired to crew about 12-15 positions for football, baseball, and basketball broadcasts, depending on their partnerships, so getting to know a local production company could provide you many opportunities for free-lance employment.

For certain primary positions, like floor director, camera operator, and tape operators, you can pretty much count on enough steady work to consider this your prime employment. As a statistician or spotter, you're still doing this as a hobby.

The first testicular guard, the "Cup," was manufactured in 1874, and the first protective helmet in the National Hockey League was regularly used in 1928. It still took until 1979 before the NHL made it mandatory for players to wear a protective helmet. That means it only took 105 years for men to realize that their brain is also important.

Chapter 6

Sports Statistics

You know you're a sports whiz if you're glued to the TV year round to watch the NCAA, NFL, MLB, NHL, MLB, NBA, NBDL, and WNBA; every AB, BB, RBI, HR, SB, CS, SF, and K; every IP so you can calculate the ERA, the number of WP's, IBB's, HBP's, and CG's; every KO, PR, or INT of your favorite football team in the Fall; including every TD, SK, YPG, FUM, REC, or XPA, and FGM; where BS in basketball is a good thing, along with a STL or AST, where GB is determined by W's or L's, where 3PM doesn't stand for a Star Wars character or the time of day, a TO (not Terrell Owens) is something you don't want, and ATM is not where you take money out of the bank; and you hope your favorite PF or SG can make the clutch FT or FG, or isn't on the DL or MIA, or DNP because of a coach's decision; that the VP or GM doesn't waive your QB, WR, RB, PG, or PH; and especially that the NBA won't go AWOL and the season won't be DQ'd because there's no CBA.

With the way sports statistics are tabulated today via computers and the worldwide web, yesteryear's methods now seem almost primitive.

The graduation from pencils and paper to use of a calculator was considered big stuff. Even in the early 1980's, basketball and football official stats crews still kept everything manually. I used to use a baseball book of averages that did the math for you (8 divided by 13 = 62%) to calculate percentages. Copies of the official box score were originally reproduced on carbon paper. Then a ditto machine was able to crank out copies faster, but still only after each statistic was handwritten. Printing legibly was a must. So was the hustle of the runners and the copy crew. If they didn't get the information distributed quickly enough during the course of a game, the numbers became useless and stale, unless beat reporters used them to refer to for their story.

Copy machines soon provided mass-produced versions of the box score, allowing for much faster distribution and relatively immediate use by broadcasters.

I can still remember when the NBA transitioned to computer input of sports data around 1990. It was like certain members of the stats crew had to learn a foreign language with letters and numbers indicating who did what and where on the basketball court. Unlike baseball or football where you have 20 to 30 seconds between plays to document the stats, this was all taking place during the course of an almost nonstop, fast-paced game. It was quite a mind-boggling adjustment.

Today, official basketball and football statistics have their league's thumbprint all over it. The NFL in particular closely scrutinizes the stats crew as the game is going on. If there is an inaccurate data entry or the computer malfunctions, you'd think the sky was falling. The more the software evolves, the more statistics the teams want kept. As John Olson, head of the stats crews for the Arizona Cardinals and Arizona State Sun Devils says, "Arithmetic and penmanship have been replaced by computer savvy and typing skills."

Currently, each NBA team provides a monitor along the press row so broadcasters and their statisticians have up-to-date statistics as the game goes along, most of the time anyway. There have been many instances where I'm working a game, and the stats monitor seems to be taking a siesta. It may go several minutes before it catches up. That's why I've always kept my stats manually. Stat monitors don't provide information on scoring runs anyway, which announcers and networks love, i.e. Phoenix has outscored San Antonio 12-1 over the last 2:43. Through the years, I've observed many other so-called talent statisticians in action, and they think that showing up with a note pad and a pencil makes them prepared. When the stats monitor freezes, and it regularly does, they're useless to their announcer or the graphics person in the broadcast truck they're communicating with. A lot of guys want to be statisticians, but most of them rely strictly on the stats monitor as a crutch and can't operate without it. My method is old school, but I never get caught unprepared.

During football telecasts, there is usually an 'official stats' guy providing the talent stats guy back-up support. Official stats will have direct access with the official crew. When doing stats for a football radio broadcast, you won't have that luxury, so you need to be self-sufficient. Too many times, I've seen a person get assigned a stats job who simply can't do the task. Maybe it's an intern working for a professional team, or for a college sports information office. The P.R. Manager or Sports Information Director will get a request from visiting media for a statistician and offer the position to a student. Sadly, it's the announcer who suffers. The announcers aren't shy about sharing their displeasure, either. "That last guy we had was terrible!"

Statistics aren't just for the media anymore, or to keep league records. Sports agents have always used stats to leverage better contracts for their clients. Media departments will always need stats to update their game notes and media guides. Players themselves (particularly in baseball) now use computers to track the opposition right down to each of their at-bats against a particular pitcher.

Now coaches want more stats for tactical purposes. Trends are a big part of their game-planning. Does an NFL runner carry the ball up the gut of the defense, or does he have a tendency to break to the outside of the line? Does a basketball player prefer to go to his left or right? A head coach may track whether his team outscores an opponent or visa-versa while a certain player is on the floor. This is called plus/minus.

Anything the mind can conceive and that computer software can create will keep the task of keeping more stats an ongoing challenge and desire. Coaching staffs will always require more and more information to evaluate not only their team, but the opposition. The science of drafting players has gone well past personal and film evaluation. Even the term film now sounds archaic.

And with ongoing technological improvements, a reporter or fan can have immediate access and instant information of a team's action via all sorts of portable electronic devices.

Statistical data creates a huge domino effect in the sports world. The player's personal accomplishments play a huge part in determining who's going to get those multi-million dollar contracts. Team General Managers and Sports Agents toss around those stats to negotiate player contracts like a world championship ping pong match. The player's statistical numbers are used to validate worth. Worth equates to necessary revenue to justify that value. And somewhere in the process of generating revenue, the fans, the networks, and the advertising sponsors end up footing the tab. Statistical sports data reaches into all our pockets. Even if you're not a fan, your tax dollars are busy building new stadiums. It's an ongoing tidal wave you can't avoid.

Where is the recording and documentation of sports statistics all heading? Olson's theory is that professional sports will gravitate toward a central location to input all games. The local stat crew, as currently designed, will fade away. Information not visible on a TV screen will still need a live local person to relay that information. Interpretations of all plays will be handled by the central location. Instead of 32 crews for each of the 32 NFL cities, there might be seven stat teams housed in a single location.

One of the great things about sports is the opportunity to discuss and debate. Who's the best team or player? My belief is that the human element of sports will always keep the need of a stats crew necessary for the tabulation of that game's historical data. The task of a sports statistician isn't just physical. Too much of the game requires an interpretation and that interpretation requires an on-site visual of the action. TV cameras cannot cover every angle, especially in a sport with the pace of basketball. Olson agrees that the continuous warfare that is basketball wouldn't allow the opportunity to efficiently interpret the action. "There aren't enough stoppages in play or time for replays to do the job justice."

There's another thing I agree with Olson on. "In the world of sports statistics, evolution is necessary to keep up with the insatiable information demand."

Notable Rule Distinctions of College Football and the NFL

When it comes to American football, the rules are generally consistent, but there are several minor differences. If you're doing stats for college games or pro games, it's important to know what rules apply. Here are the main ones you'll need to know.

Pass Completions

In college, a receiver only needs to get one foot inbounds at the time of the catch.

For the NFL, the receiver has to have both feet down.

End of a Play

A play in college is considered over when any part of a player's body (other than his hands or feet) touches the ground, or until they go out of bounds. This also applies to offense and defense, since an interception or fumble resulting in a change of possession keeps the play alive too. The player with the ball doesn't even have to be tackled. He can slip and fall, play over. The sole exception is if you're the holder for the field goal or extra point attempts. In the 1978 Rose Bowl the Michigan punter took a low snap. He had to go to his knee to field the snap before the punt. Play over. Down right there, Washington's ball at the spot of the knee, as it was 4th down. This was a huge play and momentum changer that contributed to the Huskies 27-20 upset win over the Wolverines.

Conversely, an NFL player with the ball can touch the ground with other parts of his body, as long as he hasn't been tackled or forced down by the opponent (down by contact) and keeps going. There was one new NFL rule in 2010 that has been implemented for safety sake. If the player with the ball is running downfield and loses his helmet, the play is whistled dead at that spot on the field. No more advancing the ball. The league is really trying to address the issue of concussions.

Extra Point Tries

For college, the extra point is from the three yard line. In the NFL, the ball is placed at the two. Each successful kick counts as 1 point.

College and pro teams can also attempt a two-point conversion after a touchdown. The college offensive team lines up at the three-yard line. Again, the NFL starts at the two. A successful conversion is worth 2 points for each. If they fail, they get zero points.

Blocked Kicks

Here's another key difference between college and pro football. In college, the defensive team can score on a blocked kick, fumble, or interception on a point-after touchdown if they return it all the way. This is worth two points for the defense.

Conversely, if the collegiate defensive team gains possession on a point-after touchdown attempt, then moves backwards from the field of play into the end zone and is stopped, a 1 point safety is awarded to the offense. The offense will still have to kick off.

Again, the NFL does it differently. A conversion attempt ends when the defending team gains possession of the ball. They can no longer advance the ball for points.

Clock Stoppage

In college, the clock stops after the offense completes a first down. Once the referee declares the ball ready for play (chains moved, ball spotted), the clock will begin again. Then there are timeouts, as well. Also in college, an out-of-bounds play does not stop the clock, unless it's a first down.

For the NFL, a first down does not necessarily stop the clock. The clock could stop when a player runs out of bounds, is tackled out of bounds, or when a team calls timeouts.

A penalty will also stop the clock for both college and the NFL.

Overtimes

Ties in college football were eliminated in 1996 when overtime was introduced. When regulation time ends in a deadlocked score, each team is given one possession from the opponent's 25-yard line. Each team gets one time out. There is use of a play clock, but there is no game clock operating at this time. The team leading after both have had a possession is the winner. If the teams remain tied, the overtime continues. A coin flip determines who goes first. Starting with the third overtime, a one point PAT is no longer allowed. This forces teams to attempt a 2-point conversion following a touchdown. This could go on for several overtimes until the game is decided

It makes for great drama, as each play is critical. It also avoids that kissing your sister ending that teams and fans alike used to hate with ties.

Maybe college games should distribute Vuvuzellas (those obnoxious horns predominantly used during soccer games that sound like 100,000 buzzing bees) after the third overtime.

Overtimes began in the NFL in 1974. In the NFL overtime, a 15-minute sudden death quarter is played. If neither team scores within the 15 minutes, there is a tie.

With a new rule instituted in 2011, an NFL *playoff* game doesn't necessarily end if the team that wins the coin-flip scores first. If the team who starts with the ball goes down and scores a touchdown the game is over; however if they only get a field goal, the other team has one chance to answer back.

If the team with the ball first has to punt, or there is a turnover, the game goes straight to sudden-death. This gives teams more incentive to score a touchdown, and increases the odds both teams will have the ball.

Two-Minute Warning

College football will not automatically stop play at the two-minute warning.

NFL football will stop play once the clock winds down to two minutes (in the 4th quarter only) or once a play is completed after crossing the two minute time frame.

Instant Replay

College officials have the option of using instant replay when they deem necessary (primarily in Division I). Every play can be subject to booth review. The review can only be initiated by press box officials.

For NFL reviews, each team receives two challenges at the start of the game. If both of those challenges are correct, the team receives a third challenge that they can use. Inside the last two minutes of each half, challenges are automatic, and again, initiated only by press box officials.

If a head coach makes a challenge, and the officials overturn the play, that team is not charged a time out. Conversely, if a team makes a challenge, and the play stands, that team is charged a time out. Time outs are precious, especially in the second half of a close game. Coaches have to judiciously decide how critical that play is versus the value of preserving the clock down the stretch.

There is high security for the press box booth designated for official review.

Kickoffs

In college, teams kick off from the 30-yard line. College kicked off from the 35 up until 2007.

NFL, teams now kick off from the 35-yard line.

With kickoffs that end up out of bounds before reaching the end zone, a college or NFL team can take the ball at the 40-yard line, at the spot where the ball went out of bounds, or demand a re-kick.

Missed Field Goal Attempts – Ball Placement

Where a team attempts a field goal is a big part of strategy, as it affects where the opposition may take over if the field goal is missed.

In both college and the NFL, if a field goal attempt is missed, the ball is placed at the spot where it was placed down. If the line of scrimmage is the 30-yard line, and the ball is snapped back to the 37, if the field goal attempt fails, the other team takes over at the 37-yard line.

You Score That How?

One of the charms of American football is the bizarre way various plays can unfold. With the shape of a football, when it gets loose, anything can happen and does.

When you're keeping stats, be it officially, or for a broadcast crew, there are a number of nuances that can really throw you off. That's why TV crews utilize an official stats person, to make sure their control truck and talent stats guy has a direct link to the official stat crew for the accurate call. They don't want to be showing inaccurate graphics on TV.

Here are some crazy examples.

Quarterback Yardage

In college, when a quarterback gets tackled behind the line of scrimmage, it is the discretion of the official stats crew if they deem it a passing or rushing attempt. If it is a rush, it counts as negative rushing yards against the QB. If they call it a passing attempt, then it's a sack.

In the NFL, let's apply the same situation. The QB gets tackled behind the line of scrimmage. Plain and simple, it's a sack. It will count against that team's passing yardage, but NOT against the quarterback's individual passing yardage. In the box score, it shows up as a net team loss.

First Downs

Collegiately, a first down is awarded each time the ball advances past the first down stick. If a team has first and goal inside the 10-yard line, no more first downs can be achieved on that possession.

The NFL has a different standard. A team can also get a first down, even when a first down begins inside the ten yard line. It can be first and goal from the one and a touchdown will also result in another first down.

Fumbles

If a fumble takes place in a college game, the amount of yardage (plus or minus) will be based on where the ball is recovered. The yardage will be credited to the individual stats of the fumbler.

Example 1: A runner gets past the line of scrimmage and gains 10 yards before he gets tackled and loses the ball. The ball squirts forward for 7 more yards. The runner gets credit for a 17 yard gain.

Example 2: A runner is hit 5 yards behind the line of scrimmage and fumbles. The ball gets batted around and is finally recovered 35 yards behind the line of scrimmage. That runner receives minus 35 yards for that carry.

The NFL rules are a bit more sympathetic. The yardage applied after a fumble is at the point of the fumble, unless the ball is recovered behind the point of the fumble.

More Fumbles

If the exchange between the center and the QB gets fumbled, college rules dictate that it counts as negative yardage against the quarterback's individual rushing total.

The NFL simply calls it an aborted play.

Another bizarre example of an aborted play in the NFL is when it's not clear who's responsible for the play going haywire.

Example: The quarterback takes the handoff and pitches the ball back to the running back, but misses him. The ball is loose and eventually recovered by the offense for a 21-yard loss. The official call: An aborted play. It counts in the stat column as 1 rush for zero yards.

Here's another strange one.

A collegiate quarterback is at his own 10-yard line, first and ten. He passed to a receiver at their 15. The receiver then runs sideways and fumbles. A mad scramble ensues, and the ball ends up at the 50 yard line. What's the call?

The receiver gets credit for a plus 40-yard reception. The quarterback ends up with a plus 40 yard pass completion.

In the pros, the same play will net the receiver and the quarterback just the 5 yards to the initial reception point.

In Arizona, the official stats crew for Arizona State University games and the NFL Arizona Cardinals is one in the same. It may be that way in other major markets too. Head of the stats crew, John Olson, says input of NFL official football statistics has become more complex because of what the league wants kept.

In some ways, the use of computers for football makes it more difficult for stats crews. Not only does it require a certain order of input, the amount of data kept has increased.

In 2008, NFL official stats crews had to also add "where" the receiver caught the ball. Was it the left, center, or right part of the field? They also added yards after the catch (YAC). I find yards after catch an interesting stat because it properly credits the receiver for adding yards to the reception mostly on his own (save for some nice blocks downfield).

Though the league required "spot of the catch" and "yards after catch", this also helped the teams in their scouting of opponents. It gave teams an indication of tendencies, such as where a receiver generally catches the ball on the field.

The bottom line is this. Stats in football will always be kept the same. The difference will be whether information is written down, or input into a machine, or both. It depends on who you're working for.

Don't Count On It

In this day and age of Super Stadiums, certain facilities require certain rules. Baseball has always had to deal with customized stadium rules based on the fact that their facilities aren't cookie-cutter designs. The height of the outfield walls, the playing area behind home plate, and dimensions to the outfield vary from park to park. Boston's Green Monster with its infamous thirty-seven-foot, two-inch left field wall in the park, only 305–315 feet to home plate is an historical example. Every baseball stadium is different from the rest. That's why the umpiring crew goes over that stadium's particular rules during the pregame exchange of lineup cards with each team's representative. "If a fly ball hits that guide wire or hanging speaker, the ball is still in play." If the ball gets lost in the ivy wall at Chicago's Wrigley Field outfield wall, an outfielder will signal that a ball is lost by raising his hands. When this occurs, the umpires will call time and rule the play a ground-rule double.

Dallas' new football stadium was immediately put to the test when a Tennessee Titan punter kicked the ball so high, it hit the monstrous (Jerry-Tron) video screen 90 feet above it. The NFL had to implement a rule that if a punted ball hits the video screen, the play doesn't count, and the ball must be re-kicked.

The NFL has another set of policies that apply to just four of their 32 stadiums. It's the NFL's policy regarding Retractable Roofs that was developed by the NFL Competition Committee. The only four stadiums this applies to are the University of Phoenix Stadium near Phoenix, Reliant Stadium in Houston, Lucas Oil Stadium in Indianapolis, and Cowboys Stadium in Dallas.

It's up to the home team to decide whether the roof will be open or closed 90 minutes before kickoff.

If the game starts with the roof closed, it must remain in closed position for the duration of the game.

If the game begins with the roof open, it can still be closed, but only if it begins to rain or hazardous conditions develop or are anticipated. Once the game has gotten to the five minute mark, the roof cannot be closed for rain at any time (including overtime). If there are hazardous situations that can affect the welfare of players or spectators, i.e. lightning storm, severe winds, the roof can be closed at any time. At that point, it cannot be re-opened. It's up to the game Referee to signal to the Stadium Manager whether to close the roof. Play may continue while the roof is being closed, except in emergency situations.

Another accommodating element the NFL instituted in 2006 was Flex Scheduling. It was implemented in conjunction with their contract with NBC so Sunday Night Football can feature the best match-ups to fans during the final seven weeks of the season. This makes it possible (12 days before each of these games) to move any game to an NBC Sunday night game. The only exemptions are previously scheduled Monday night games and late-season Saturday games. This of course greatly affects FOX and CBS, so their broadcast schedule plans for the last seven weeks of the NFL season must remain liquid.

Automatic First Down - Awarded to offensive team on all defensive fouls with these exceptions:

1. Offside.
2. Encroachment.
3. Delay of game.
4. Illegal substitution.
5. Excessive time out(s).
6. Incidental grasp of facemask.
7. Neutral zone infraction.
8. Running into the kicker.
9. More than 11 players on the field at the snap.

Five Yards

1. Defensive holding or illegal use of hands (automatic first down).
2. Delay of game on offense or defense.
3. Delay of kickoff.
4. Encroachment.
5. Excessive time out(s).
6. False start.
7. Illegal formation.
8. Illegal shift.
9. Illegal motion.
10. Illegal substitution.
11. First onside kick-off out of bounds between goal lines and untouched or last touched by kicker.
12. Invalid fair catch signal.
13. More than 11 players on the field at snap for either team.
14. Less than seven men on offensive line at snap.
15. Offside.
16. Failure to pause one second after shift or huddle.
17. Running into kicker.
18. More than one man in motion at snap.
19. Grasping facemask of the ball carrier or quarterback.
20. Player out of bounds at snap.
21. Ineligible member(s) of kicking team going beyond line of scrimmage before ball is kicked.
22. Illegal return.
23. Failure to report change of eligibility.

24. Neutral zone infraction.
25. Loss of team time out(s) or five-yard penalty on the defense for excessive crowd noise.
26. Ineligible player downfield during passing down.
27. Second forward pass behind the line.
28. Forward pass is first touched by eligible receiver who has gone out of bounds and returned.
29. Forward pass touches or is caught by an ineligible receiver on or behind line.
30. Forward pass thrown from behind line of scrimmage after ball once crossed the line.
31. Kicking team player voluntarily out of bounds during a punt.
32. Twelve (12) men in the huddle.

10 Yards

1. Offensive pass interference.
2. Holding, illegal use of hands, arms, or body by offense.
3. Tripping by a member of either team.
4. Helping the runner.
5. Deliberately batting or punching a loose ball.
6. Deliberately kicking a loose ball.
7. Illegal block above the waist.

15 Yards

1. Chop block.
2. Clipping below the waist.
3. Fair catch interference.
4. Illegal crack back block by offense.
5. Piling on.
6. Roughing the kicker.
7. Roughing the passer.
8. Twisting, turning, or pulling an opponent by the facemask.
9. Unnecessary roughness.
10. Unsportsmanlike conduct.
11. Delay of game at start of either half.
12. Illegal low block.
13. A tackler using his helmet to butt, spear or ram an opponent.
14. Any player who uses the top of his helmet unnecessarily.
15. A punter, placekicker, or holder who simulates being roughed by a defensive player.
16. Leaping.
17. Leverage.
18. Any player who removes his helmet after a play while on the field.
19. Taunting.

Five Yards and Loss of Down (Combination Penalty)

Forward pass thrown from beyond line of scrimmage.

10 Yards and Loss of Down (Combination Penalty)

Intentional grounding of forward pass (safety if passer is in own end zone). If foul occurs more than 10 yards behind line, play results in loss of down at spot of foul.

15 Yards and Loss of Coin Toss Option

1. Team's late arrival on the field prior to scheduled kickoff.
2. Captains not appearing for coin toss.

15 Yards (and disqualification if flagrant)

1. Striking opponent with fist.
2. Kicking or kneeing opponent.
3. Striking opponent on head or neck with forearm, elbow, or hands whether or not the initial contact is made below the neck area.
4. Roughing kicker.
5. Roughing passer.
6. Malicious unnecessary roughness.
7. Unsportsmanlike conduct.
8. Palpably unfair act. (Distance penalty determined by the Referee after consultation with other officials.)

15 Yards and Automatic Disqualification

1. Using a helmet (not worn) as a weapon.
2. Striking or purposely shoving a game official.

The Meaning of It All

If you're involved in a sports broadcast or a member of the media, you'll need to know your acronyms and abbreviations. You'll never use all of these during a broadcast, but it's best to understand the majority of them, especially to read the box score.

Acronyms for Basketball

G	Games Played		3PM	Three Pointers Made*
GB	Games Back (standings related)		3PA	Three Pointers Attempted*
W	Won		3PP	Three Point Percentage*
L	Lost		REB	Total Rebounds
DNP	Did not Play		OFF	Offensive Rebounds
Min	Minutes Played		RPG	Rebounds per Game
MPG	Minutes per Game		AST	Total Assists
Pts	Total Points		APG	Assists per Game
PPG	Points per Game		STL	Steals**
FGM	Field Goals Made		BLK	Blocks**
FGA	Field Goals Attempted		TO	Turnovers**
FGP	Field Goal Percentage		OT	Overtime
FTM	Free Throws Made		EFF	Efficiency
FTA	Free Throws Attempted		PF	Total Personal Fouls
FTP	Free Throw Percentage		Last 10 games (won-loss record)	
PCT	Percent			

* = The NBA did not have three point shots until 1979

** = Steals, Blocks and Turnovers were not recorded in the NBA until 1973

Basketball Positions

SF	Small Forward
PF	Power Forward
C	Center
SG	Shooting Guard
PG	Point Guard

Note: On the NBA stats computer, the starting positions will be listed in numerical order, in the order of forwards, center, then guards.

On a collegiate stats computer, the player's names will appear in numerical order, once they've made an appearance in the game.

Acronyms for Football

This list is a great resource for the types of stats you should tabulate. You will use the majority of these during the course of a broadcast.

Passing

CMP or CP	Completions
ATT or AT	Attempts
PCT or CMP%	Percentage of completed passes (*Completions divided by pass attempts*)
YDS	Passing Yards
YPA	Yards Per Attempt
LNG	Longest Pass Play
TD	Touchdown Passes
TD%	Touchdown percentage (*Touchdown Passes divided by pass attempts*)
INT	Interceptions Thrown
INT%	Interception percentage (*Interceptions thrown divided by pass attempts*)
SK	Sacks
SYD	Sacked Yards Lost
RAT	Passer (QB) Rating

Rating Formula:

Step 1:   Complete passes divided by pass attempts. Subtract 0.3, then divide by 0.2

Step 2:   Passing yards divided by pass attempts. Subtract 3, then divide by 4.

Step 3:   Touchdown passes divided by pass attempts, then divide by .05.

Step 4:   Start with .095, and subtract interceptions divided by attempts. Divide the difference by.04.

The sum of each step cannot be greater than 2.375 or less than zero. Add the sum of the Steps 1 through 4, multiply by 100 and divide by 6.

Rushing

ATT	Rushing attempts
YDS	Total Rushing yards
YPG	Rushing yards per game
AVG	Average yards per carry (*Total Yards divided by attempts*)
LNG	Longest Run
TD	Rushing touchdowns
FUM	Total fumbles
LST	Fumbles lost

Receiving

REC	Total receptions
YDS	Total receiving yards
YPG	Receiving yards per game
AVG	Average yards per reception (*Total yards divided by reception*)
LNG	Longest Reception
TD	Receiving touchdowns
FUM	Total fumbles
LST	Fumbles lost

Yards From Scrimmage

YDS	Total yards from scrimmage – Rushing yards + Receiving yards
YDS/PG	Total yards from scrimmage per game
RUSH	Total rushing yards
RU/PG	Rushing yards per game
REC	Total receiving yards
REC/PG	Receiving yards per game

Return

ATT	Total attempts (kickoffs/punts)
YDS	Total yards returned
TD	Kick/punt returned for touchdowns
AVG	Average kickoff/punt yards per return (*Total yards divided by attempts*)
LNG	Longest return
FC	Fair catches

Kicking

XPM	Extra points made
XPA	Extra points attempted
XP %	Percentage of extra point made (*XPM divided by XPA*)
FGM	Field goals made (all distances)
FGA	Field goals attempted (all distances)
FG %	Percentage of field goals made (*FGM divided by FGA*)
PTS	Total points

Punting

PUNTS	Total punts, Net Punts plus Blocked punts
YDS	Gross punting yards
AVG	Gross punting average

LNG	Longest punt
IN 20	Punts inside the 20 yard line, a touchback is not an inside-20
IN 20%	Inside 20 punts divided by Net Punts
TB	Touchbacks
TB %	Touchback percentage
BP	Blocked punts
RET	Punts returned
YDS	Yards returned on punts
AVG	Average return yards on punts
NET	Net punting average
	(*Gross punting yards, minus Return Yards, minus 20 yards for every Touchback, divided by Total Punts*)

Defensive Misc.

TOT	Total tackles
SOLO	Unassisted tackles
AST	Assisted tackles
SACK	Total sacks
STF	Stuffs: see TLOSS
TLOSS	Tackles for Loss *(Does not include Sacks)*
FF	Forced fumbles
BK	Blocked kicks both punts and field goals attempts
INT	Passes intercepted
YDS	Intercepted returned yards
LNG	Longest interception return
TD	Interceptions returned for touchdowns
PD	Pass Defended
	(*Any pass that a defender, through contact with the football, causes to be incomplete*)

Acronyms for Baseball

Ichiro Suzuki had an historic year for the Seattle Mariners in 2004: 704 AB, 262 H (a league record), and his AVG was an American League-leading .372. What do all those abbreviations stand for?

Offensive Abbreviations

AB	At Bats		OBP	On Base Percentage
BB	Bases on Balls (walks)		R	Runs
AVG	Batting Average		RBI	Runs Batted In
CS	Caught Stealing		SF	Sacrifice Fly
2B	Double		SH	Sacrifice Hits (Bunts)
GIDP	Ground Into Double Plays		S	Singles
HBP	Hit By Pitch		SLG	Slugging Percentage
H	Hits		SB%	Stolen Base Percentage
HRR	Home Run Ratio		SB	Stolen Base
HR	Home runs		SO	Strike Outs
IBB	Intentional Bases on Balls (Walks)		TB	Total Bases
			3B	Triples
LOB	Left on Base			

Pitching Abbreviations

AO	Fly Outs (Air)		IP	Innings Pitched
BB	Walks (Bases on Balls)		IRA	Inherited Runs Allowed
BFP	Batter Facing Pitcher		IPS	Innings Per Start
BK	Balks		L	Losses
CBO	Combined Shutout		MB9	Base Runners Per 9 Innings
CG	Complete Games		OBA	Opponents' Batting Average
CGL	Complete Game Losses		PA	Plate Appearances
ER	Earned Runs		R	Runs
ERA	Earned Run Average		RPF	Relief Failures
GF	Games Finished		RW	Relief Wins
GO	Ground Outs		S/SHO	Shutouts
GOAO	Ground Outs / Fly Outs Ratio		SO	Strikeouts
GP	Games Played		SV	Saves
GS	Games Started		SVO	Save Opportunities
H	Hits		TB	Total Bases
HBP	Hit Batters		W	Wins
HR	Home Runs		WP	Wild Pitches
IBB	Intentional Walks			

Defensive Abbreviations

A	Assist
DP	Double Play
CS	Caught Stealing
E	Errors
GP	Games Played
OFA	Outfield Assists
PB	Passed Ball
PK	Pickoffs
PO	Put outs
SB	Stolen Bases
TC	Total Chances
TP	Triple Plays

Keeping Score

When you're a sports statistician, you'll need to develop your own score sheets. Today, some statisticians let a computer do the work; however, when the computer goes down, or it needs re-booting, they're at the mercy of cyberspace. It can happen at the most inopportune time.

Other statisticians I've observed through the years have a blank piece of paper handy and write a few things down. They're letting a stats monitor (at a basketball or football game) do the work. To me, that's lazy, ineffective, and doing a disservice to the announcers you're working with. When the stat monitor is getting updated, or goes down, guess who's scrambling and unprepared to do their job? That's why I've always kept stats the "old school" way, as Bob Blackburn of the Sonics taught me. I'm never caught with my pants down when the computer takes a siesta, and I'm much more in tune with looking for compelling story-lines of the game that really impress the announcers and enhance their broadcast.

Over the years, I've seen many examples and have customized ideas from the best I've seen into my own working sheets. Below are examples of scoring sheets I've developed for football, basketball, and baseball.

Football

I use this sheet to manually track yardage on both a team and an individual basis. At a moment's notice, I can hand the announcers a compelling, up-to-date statistic about that team or a player.

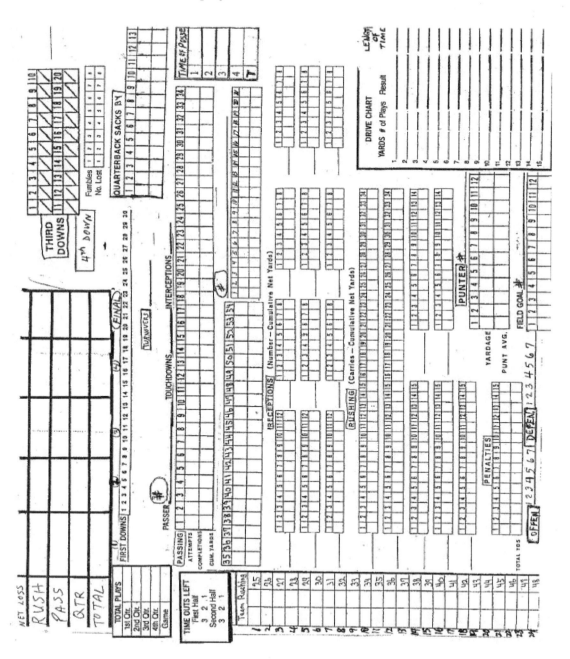

This sheet can be used to point to when trying to immediately communicate (non-verbally) with your play-by-play announcer about the length of a play during the football broadcast.

1 2 3 4 5 6 7 8 9 10
11 12 13 14 15 16 17 18 19 20
21 22 23 24 25 26 27 28 29 30
31 32 33 34 35 36 37 38 39 40
41 42 43 44 45 46 47 48 49 50
51 52 53 54 55 56 57 58 59 60
61 62 63 64 65 66 67 68 69 70
71 72 73 74 75 76 77 78 79 80
81 82 83 84 85 86 87 88 89 90
91 92 93 94 95 96 97 98 99 00

This is the sheet I use to track kickoff and punt return yardage. Sometimes, a player will generate a lot of additional all-purpose yardage. It's also used for tabulating drive charts in a football broadcast.

Number	1	2	3	4	5	Number	1	2	3	4	5
Yds						Yds					
T Yds						T Yds					
Avg						Avg					

PUNT RETURNER.   PUNT RETURNER:

Number	1	2	3	4	5	Number	1	2	3	4	5
Yds						Yds					
T Yds						T Yds					
Avg						Avg					

THIRD DOWN CONVERSIONS   FOURTH DOWN CONVERSIONS

0 1 2 3 4 5 6 7 8 9 10 11 12 13 14 15   0 1 2 3 4

  1 2 3 4 5 6 7 8 9 10 11 12 13 14 15 16   1 2 3 4

DRIVES:

#	1	2	3	4	5	6	7	8	9	10	11
Plays											
Yds											
Time											
Result											

I utilize these sheets to quickly hand the play-by-play announcer or analyst an in-game compelling story note as the football broadcast unfolds.

RECEPTIONS

RUSHES

_____ for _____

_____ yards

_____ TD

PASSING

_____ for _____

_____ yards

_____ TD

_____ Int.

SCORING DRIVE

_____ # OF PLAYS

_____ YARDS

_____ TIME OF DRIVE

SCORING PLAY

PUNT: _____ YARDS

RETURN: _____ YARDS

OF PREVIOUS PUNTS TODAY

_____

LONGEST _____

_____,_____,_____,_____,_____

_____,_____,_____,_____,_____

AVERAGE : _____

Here's the stat sheet I use for basketball.

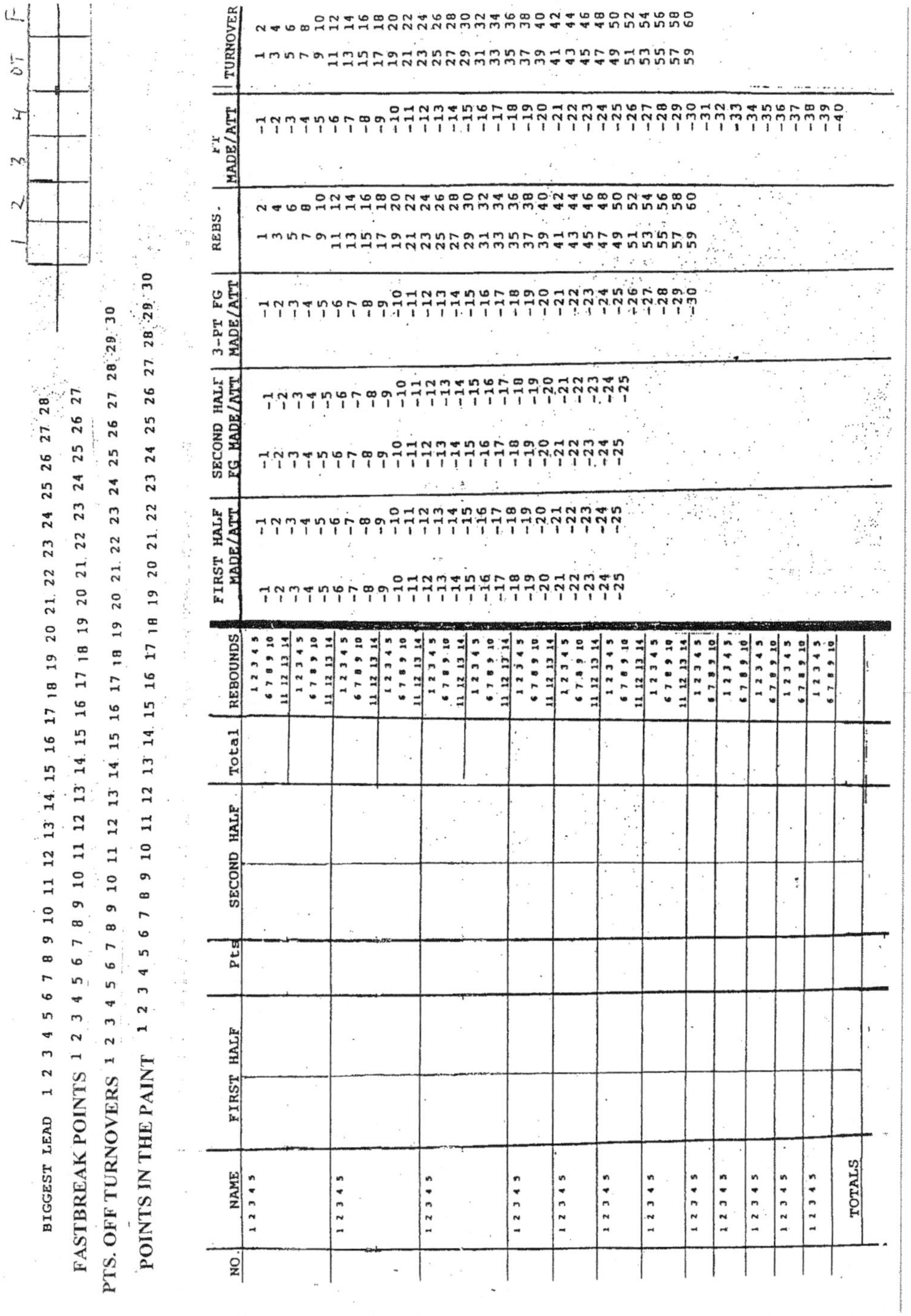

BIGGEST LEAD 1 2 3 4 5 6 7 8 9 10 11 12 13 14 15 16 17 18 19 20 21 22 23 24 25 26 27 28

FASTBREAK POINTS 1 2 3 4 5 6 7 8 9 10 11 12 13 14 15 16 17 18 19 20 21 22 23 24 25 26 27

PTS. OFF TURNOVERS 1 2 3 4 5 6 7 8 9 10 11 12 13 14 15 16 17 18 19 20 21 22 23 24 25 26 27 28 29 30

POINTS IN THE PAINT 1 2 3 4 5 6 7 8 9 10 11 12 13 14 15 16 17 18 19 20 21 22 23 24 25 26 27 28 29 30

1	2	3	4	OT	F

NO.	NAME	FIRST HALF	Pts	SECOND HALF	Total	REBOUNDS
	1 2 3 4 5					1 2 3 4 5 / 6 7 8 9 10 / 11 12 13 14 / 1 2 3 4 5 / 6 7 8 9 10 / 11 12 13 14
	1 2 3 4 5					1 2 3 4 5 / 6 7 8 9 10 / 11 12 13 14 / 1 2 3 4 5 / 6 7 8 9 10 / 11 12 13 14
	1 2 3 4 5					1 2 3 4 5 / 6 7 8 9 10 / 11 12 13 14 / 1 2 3 4 5 / 6 7 8 9 10 / 11 12 13 14
	1 2 3 4 5					1 2 3 4 5 / 6 7 8 9 10 / 11 12 13 14
	1 2 3 4 5					1 2 3 4 5 / 6 7 8 9 10 / 11 12 13 14
	1 2 3 4 5					1 2 3 4 5 / 6 7 8 9 10 / 11 12 13 14
	1 2 3 4 5					1 2 3 4 5 / 6 7 8 9 10 / 11 12 13 14
	1 2 3 4 5					1 2 3 4 5 / 6 7 8 9 10
	1 2 3 4 5					1 2 3 4 5 / 6 7 8 9 10
	1 2 3 4 5					1 2 3 4 5 / 6 7 8 9 10
	1 2 3 4 5					1 2 3 4 5 / 6 7 8 9 10
	1 2 3 4 5					1 2 3 4 5 / 6 7 8 9 10
	TOTALS					

FIRST HALF MADE/ATT		SECOND HALF FG MADE/ATT		3-PT FG MADE/ATT	REBS.		FT MADE/ATT	TURNOVER	
-1	-1	-1	-1	-1	1	2	-1	1	2
-2	-2	-2	-2	-2	3	4	-2	3	4
-3	-3	-3	-3	-3	5	6	-3	5	6
-4	-4	-4	-4	-4	7	8	-4	7	8
-5	-5	-5	-5	-5	9	10	-5	9	10
-6	-6	-6	-6	-6	11	12	-6	11	12
-7	-7	-7	-7	-7	13	14	-7	13	14
-8	-8	-8	-8	-8	15	16	-8	15	16
-9	-9	-9	-9	-9	17	18	-9	17	18
-10	-10	-10	-10	-10	19	20	-10	19	20
-11	-11	-11	-11	-11	21	22	-11	21	22
-12	-12	-12	-12	-12	23	24	-12	23	24
-13	-13	-13	-13	-13	25	26	-13	25	26
-14	-14	-14	-14	-14	27	28	-14	27	28
-15	-15	-15	-15	-15	29	30	-15	29	30
-16	-16	-16	-16	-16	31	32	-16	31	32
-17	-17	-17	-17	-17	33	34	-17	33	34
-18	-18	-18	-18	-18	35	36	-18	35	36
-19	-19	-19	-19	-19	37	38	-19	37	38
-20	-20	-20	-20	-20	39	40	-20	39	40
-21	-21	-21	-21	-21	41	42	-21	41	42
-22	-22	-22	-22	-22	43	44	-22	43	44
-23	-23	-23	-23	-23	45	46	-23	45	46
-24	-24	-24	-24	-24	47	48	-24	47	48
-25	-25	-25	-25	-25	49	50	-25	49	50
				-26	51	52	-26	51	52
				-27	53	54	-27	53	54
				-28	55	56	-28	55	56
				-29	57	58	-29	57	58
				-30	59	60	-30	59	60
							-31		
							-32		
							-33		
							-34		
							-35		
							-36		
							-37		
							-38		
							-39		
							-40		

This sheet comes in handy when tracking scoring runs by either basketball team.

RUNNING SCORE SHEET
First Half

Remaining Time	PLAY	HOME SCORER	SCORE	VISITORS' SCORER	PLAY

So I can quickly point out a pertinent stat as the game goes on, here's a sheet I keep in visual distance of the announcer.

POINTS:		/	TURNOVERS			
1	2	3	4	5	6	7
8	9	10	11	12	13	14
15	16	17	18	19	20	21
22	23	24	25	26	27	28
29	30	31	32	33	34	35
36	37	38	39	40	41	42

REBOUNDS:							
1	2	3	4	5	6	7	8
9	10	11	12	13	14	15	16
17	18	19	20	21	22	23	24

FOULS: TEAM/PERSONAL					
1	2	3	4	5	6

Your basic score sheet for a baseball game

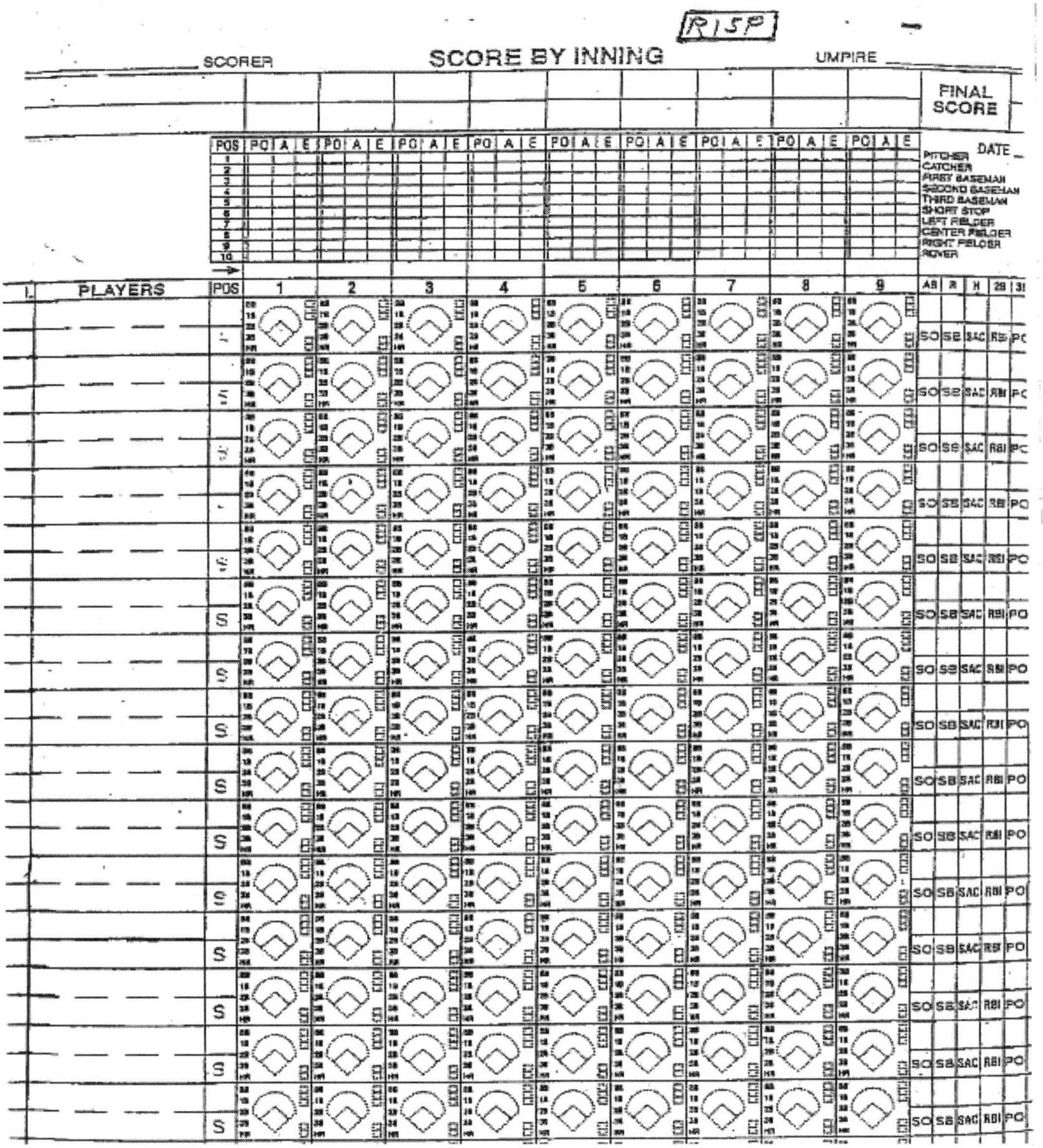

At the end of each inning, I hand the announcer a re-cap of how a starting pitcher is doing.

PITCHER_____

_____# of Pitches in _____ Inning
PITCHES
Thru_____Inning(s) = _____

_____Strikes_____Balls

_____Runs_____Earned Runs

_____ Strikeouts

_____ Walks

_____ Hits

_____ Runs   AFTER TWO OUTS

_____ Left on Base

___for_____ First Pitch Strikes

_____ # of Full Counts

_____ 1-2-3 INNINGS

Here's a sheet I use to keep pitch counts, and other pitching statistics

Pitcher	Pitches	Balls	Strikes	Hits	Runs	K's	Walks	LOB	Full Counts	1st Pitch Strikes Att #	Lead-off Batter On
	1 2 3 4 5 6 7 8 9 10 11 12 13 14 15 16 17 18 19 20 21 22 23 24 25 26 27 28 29 30	1 2 3 4 5 6 7 8 9 10 11 12 13 14 15 16 17 18 19 20	1 2 3 4 5 6 7 8 9 10 11 12 13 14 15 16 17 18 19 20								
	1 2 3 4 5 6 7 8 9 10 11 12 13 14 15 16 17 18 19 20 21 22 23 24 25 26 27 28 29 30	1 2 3 4 5 6 7 8 9 10 11 12 13 14 15 16 17 18 19 20	1 2 3 4 5 6 7 8 9 10 11 12 13 14 15 16 17 18 19 20								
	1 2 3 4 5 6 7 8 9 10 11 12 13 14 15 16 17 18 19 20 21 22 23 24 25 26 27 28 29 30	1 2 3 4 5 6 7 8 9 10 11 12 13 14 15 16 17 18 19 20	1 2 3 4 5 6 7 8 9 10 11 12 13 14 15 16 17 18 19 20								
	1 2 3 4 5 6 7 8 9 10 11 12 13 14 15 16 17 18 19 20 21 22 23 24 25 26 27 28 29 30	1 2 3 4 5 6 7 8 9 10 11 12 13 14 15 16 17 18 19 20	1 2 3 4 5 6 7 8 9 10 11 12 13 14 15 16 17 18 19 20								
	1 2 3 4 5 6 7 8 9 10 11 12 13 14 15 16 17 18 19 20 21 22 23 24 25 26 27 28 29 30	1 2 3 4 5 6 7 8 9 10 11 12 13 14 15 16 17 18 19 20	1 2 3 4 5 6 7 8 9 10 11 12 13 14 15 16 17 18 19 20								
	1 2 3 4 5 6 7 8 9 10 11 12 13 14 15 16 17 18 19 20 21 22 23 24 25 26 27 28 29 30	1 2 3 4 5 6 7 8 9 10 11 12 13 14 15 16 17 18 19 20	1 2 3 4 5 6 7 8 9 10 11 12 13 14 15 16 17 18 19 20								
	1 2 3 4 5 6 7 8 9 10 11 12 13 14 15 16 17 18 19 20 21 22 23 24 25 26 27 28 29 30	1 2 3 4 5 6 7 8 9 10 11 12 13 14 15 16 17 18 19 20	1 2 3 4 5 6 7 8 9 10 11 12 13 14 15 16 17 18 19 20								
	1 2 3 4 5 6 7 8 9 10 11 12 13 14 15 16 17 18 19 20 21 22 23 24 25 26 27 28 29 30	1 2 3 4 5 6 7 8 9 10 11 12 13 14 15 16 17 18 19 20	1 2 3 4 5 6 7 8 9 10 11 12 13 14 15 16 17 18 19 20								
	1 2 3 4 5 6 7 8 9 10 11 12 13 14 15 16 17 18 19 20 21 22 23 24 25 26 27 28 29 30	1 2 3 4 5 6 7 8 9 10 11 12 13 14 15 16 17 18 19 20	1 2 3 4 5 6 7 8 9 10 11 12 13 14 15 16 17 18 19 20								
	1 2 3 4 5 6 7 8 9 10 11 12 13 14 15 16 17 18 19 20 21 22 23 24 25 26 27 28 29 30	1 2 3 4 5 6 7 8 9 10 11 12 13 14 15 16 17 18 19 20	1 2 3 4 5 6 7 8 9 10 11 12 13 14 15 16 17 18 19 20								
	1 2 3 4 5 6 7 8 9 10 11 12 13 14 15 16 17 18 19 20 21 22 23 24 25 26 27 28 29 30	1 2 3 4 5 6 7 8 9 10 11 12 13 14 15 16 17 18 19 20	1 2 3 4 5 6 7 8 9 10 11 12 13 14 15 16 17 18 19 20								
	1 2 3 4 5 6 7 8 9 10 11 12 13 14 15 16 17 18 19 20 21 22 23 24 25 26 27 28 29 30	1 2 3 4 5 6 7 8 9 10 11 12 13 14 15 16 17 18 19 20	1 2 3 4 5 6 7 8 9 10 11 12 13 14 15 16 17 18 19 20								

Sports Statistical Resources

www.basketball-reference.com

www.baseball-reference.com

www.football-reference.com

www.pro-football-reference.com

www.mlb.com

www.nbcsports.msnbc.com/

www.ncaa.org

www.cbssports.com

www.nba.com

www.nfl.com

www.espn.com

www.foxsports.com

www.sportsillustrated.cnn.com/

www.sports.yahoo.com

www.dougstats.com

www.thesports100.com

www.workinsports.com

www.jobsinsports.com

www.thesportsking.com

Imagine having to complete a broadcast without your glasses. While announcing with John Madden, Gary Bender was left handicapped to finish announcing the game because Madden's demonstrative hand accidentally knocked the glasses off Bender from booth into the stands below.

Chapter 7

Front Office Careers

Operating a professional sports team on a day-to-day basis has become a massive undertaking, with many departmentalized specialists required to make it operate smoothly. When Jerry Colangelo created the front office for the expansion Phoenix Suns as their 28-year-old General Manager in 1968, the original staff was comprised of just five employees. Besides the G.M., it included a trainer, a secretary, a ticket manager, and marketing director.

These days, the positions in the front office of a professional team or a sports information office for a university or college are substantially more specific. Instead of just five spokes in the wheel, there are dozens required to support the tire and keep it rolling.

A constant adjustment for sports has been keeping up with innovation and technology. From outdoor stadiums to domed stadiums, from radio to TV, from natural grass to artificial turf, from general admission to catered, revenue-generating suites, from cable to digital television, and now social media and the advent of 3-D, there's always a new financial frontier to capitalize on.

With so many careers to choose from in the sports world, this affords a wide variety of possibilities for you to choose from. Visit the team's website or get hold of a media guide. The team directory of personnel positions is quite varied.

Here's a list of positions in one NBA team's Media Guide (the number of posts within that department is listed in parentheses):

Senior Management (13)
Administrative Staff / Executive Staff (7)
Coaching Staff (5)
Medical & Training Room Staff (8)
Player Personnel & Scouting (8)
Basketball Communications (5)
Marketing Partnerships (15)
Public Relations (3)
Charities (2)
Community Relations (9) – Includes the mascot
Game Entertainment (12)
Marketing (3)
Digital (9)
Production (8)
Television (5)

Radio (4)
Legal (1)
Information Services (5)
Finance (12)
Arena Operations (16)
Human Resources (6)
Game Night Personnel (21)

That is a total of 177 positions, and that's with just one NBA team (out of 30).

In the National Football League, there are 32 teams. Here's a list of another 145 possible positions in just one NFL team's Media Guide (the number of posts within that department is listed in parentheses). From General Manager to Scout to Head Athletic Trainer to Turf Manager, there are lots of positions that don't require supreme athletic skills.

Executive Staff (8)
Coaching Staff (18)
Football Operations (16)
Athletic Training/Medical (16)
Equipment (3)
Video (3)
Community Relations (5)
Finance (9)
Information Technology (4)
Media Relations (5)
Operation & Maintenance (8)
Player Development (1)
Marketing (11)
Broadcasting (8)
Scoreboard (3)
Business Development (8)
Box Office (10)
Ticket Sales & Service (7)
Security (1)
Administrative & Support Staff (1)

Major League Baseball, with its lengthy day-in, day-out schedule requires the most staff support. Considering there are about 30 spring training games and 162 regular season games over a period of seven months, time off is at a premium. Here's one team's staff list (the number of posts within that department is listed in parentheses).

Executive office (12)
Accounting (7)
Administration (7)
Baseball Operations (79)
    (Includes: Scouts, Team Travel, Athletic Trainers, Equipment Managers,
    Clubhouse Assistants, Bullpen Catcher, Video Coordinator)

Broadcasting (18)
(Includes: Announcers, Audio & Video Engineers, TV Graphics , Video Editor, Game Operations Coordinator)
Communications (4)
(Includes: Player and Media Relations)
Community Affairs (6)
Corporate Partnerships (11)
Facilities and Event Services (21)
(Includes: Security, Guest Services, Engineers, Groundskeepers, Housekeeping)
Special Projects and Fan Experience (9)
(Includes: Ballpark Attractions, Spring Training Groundskeepers, Outreach and Development)
Human Resources (3)
Information Technology (6)
Legal (2)
Marketing (9)
(Includes: Team Photographer, Creative Services, Ticket Sales, Publications, Promotions)
Ticket Sales (55)
(Includes: Account Executives, Group Sales, Suite Sales, Ticket Operations, Spring Training Box office Manager)
Travel Services (3)

According to my calculator, this MLB team alone employs 289 people. By multiplying that by 30 MLB teams, that's another 9,000 or so positions. That does not include concessionaires, ushers, vendors, maintenance, parking lot attendants, first aid stations, or personnel collecting tickets.

These are just totals for professional baseball, football and basketball. For each major league baseball team, there are several minor league affiliates. There are many other professional sports leagues to consider too (i.e. the NHL, Soccer, etc.).

Most major markets have up to four professional teams or more, (New York alone has 8 major professional teams), not to mention multiple nearby universities and colleges. That list of opportunities still doesn't even include a large number of free-lance jobs like camera crews, statisticians, floor directors, tape operators and other behind-the-scenes broadcast positions. Nor intern positions.

When you consider there are 343 Division One Universities, and 1,010 other (combined) Division II, Division III and NAIA colleges, there are a multitude of front office job capacities to jumpstart your sports career.

Just understand going in, that the compensation is low for most sports occupations. The hiring mentality is that people are SO into being a part of the sports industry candidates will take a low-paying position over financial security. Since there are probably 100 other people who would 'die' for any one position involved in sports, supply and demand massively favors the employer. It's just the way it is.

General Managers

The day-to-day responsibilities of a team's General Manager have grown tremendously in magnitude, and with it, so has their power and prestige. Part of the territory includes the pressure of handling multi-million dollar responsibility and the weight of your team's, fans', and city's dreams of a championship. Sometimes it can be a thankless job because for most teams, the only way their players will ever get a ring is to get married. If your team wins, the players are heroes; if your team loses, you're the goat.

The hours are long and so is the list of departments GM's oversee. Everything related to the organization has to run efficiently. On the field, they deal with the coaches and players. They will craft their team through trades, free-agent acquisition, and drafting. Off the field, they have to fill the stadiums and hopefully keep them sold out through myriad marketing scenarios. A GM will also negotiate their team's broadcast coverage on TV and radio and oversee advertising departments, promotions, stadium management, ticket takers, and ushers; the ascent of duties keeps getting steeper.

Jerry Colangelo
The Architect of Phoenix Sports

Phoenix media reverently refers to Jerry Colangelo as "The Godfather." That moniker might better apply to sports throughout the U.S. and beyond. If there was a Mount Rushmore of Arizona, Colangelo's mug would have to be on it for his vision, overall civic leadership, contributions, and generosity.

Jerry Colangelo

I couldn't think of a more qualified individual to include in this sports book than Jerry Colangelo. An accomplished athlete, he has served as a marketing director, a scout, a head coach, and a general manager. He operated professional franchises, has been an owner, and built a sports empire in Phoenix. Thankfully, he's observed me many times over the years in my sports endeavors and graciously allowed me some invaluable insights into his past as well as some recommendations for aspiring sports enthusiasts.

Without Colangelo's administration, the Phoenix Suns would not be one of the most consistent winning teams in NBA history. Phoenix would not have experienced their first major sports championship, which was accomplished by the Arizona Diamondbacks over the vaunted New York Yankees in the 2001 World Series after only four seasons of MLB existence. The Winnipeg Jets would not have relocated to the Valley to become the Phoenix Coyotes. The Phoenix Mercury WNBA team, the Arizona Rattlers Arena Football Team, and the Arizona Sandsharks of the Continental

Indoor Soccer League have all had Jerry's thumbprint on their Phoenix-area existence, too.

Most recently, U.S.A. basketball would not have recaptured their Olympic glory and international self-respect without Colangelo steering the ship as their national director, securing the gold medal in the 2008 Beijing Olympics.

Jerry Colangelo is a working-class guy, a self-made sports mogul, and an astute businessman. His reputation and word carry more weight than a signature on a contract. Colangelo arrived in Phoenix in 1968, after helping launch the Chicago Bulls franchise just two years earlier. Only 28 years old, he was hired as the first General Manager of the expansion Phoenix Suns. In his autobiography, he noted that when he moved his growing family to Phoenix, he only had $800 to his name. Even before then, Colangelo's always had the Midas touch, except when he lost the 1969 coin flip to the Milwaukee Bucks for the rights to UCLA phenom Lew Alcindor. Jerry even coached the Suns on two occasions. In 1987, Colangelo put together a group that purchased the Suns. Two years later, he was instrumental in putting together the group that built the Suns' current home stadium, U S Airways Center.

After attending a Cubs home game during a visit to his home town of Chicago, Colangelo became motivated to bring a major league baseball team to Phoenix. In 1994, Jerry put together a group of investors to buy a franchise. By 1995, Colangelo's group was granted a Major League Baseball expansion team: the Arizona Diamondbacks, with the team beginning play in 1998. Along the way, Colangelo was again directly involved in building another state-of-the-art stadium in downtown Phoenix, this one to host his new baseball team. Originally, the stadium was known as Bank One Ballpark, or for brevity sake, 'the BOB.'

Colangelo's remarkable recognition and reputation is global, and his effect on how the sports industry does business is significant. He has dined with Presidents and foreign leaders. Jerry has been named the NBA's Executive of the Year four times (1976, 1981, 1989, 1993). For all his many contributions and innovations to basketball, Colangelo was elected to the Naismith Basketball Hall of Fame in 2004. He is primarily responsible for turning Phoenix into a major league sports town.

Colangelo's long list of accomplishments is not restricted to sports. He has received several community awards, was behind the construction of the Dodge Theater in downtown Phoenix, a top performing arts venue in the American Southwest, and is currently spearheading numerous real estate ventures around Phoenix. The skyline of Phoenix would look a lot different if not for Jerry's influence and involvement.

Ask anyone who's worked for Colangelo on their opinion about the man, and a similar theme will be their response: he's very loyal to his people.

Colangelo's entree into the world of sports wasn't as much by design as it seems by destiny. Colangelo was a skillful basketball and baseball player. Jim Bouton, who later went on to a notable pitching career primarily with the New York

Yankees in the 1960's (Bouton became most famous for his 1969 tell-all best-seller *Ball Four*) pitched second string behind Colangelo on their high school team. As a Chicago-area basketball star, Colangelo's thirsty quest for a championship led him to sign with the University of Kansas. Jerry figured an NCAA Title was realistically attainable, since the Jayhawks had a fellow by the name of Wilt Chamberlain on their roster. But Colangelo's basketball career got a curve ball when Wilt left Kansas in 1958 to play for the Harlem Globetrotters for $50,000. Chamberlain wanted early entry into the NBA, but was denied as a junior in college, so he played a season with the Trotters instead of completing his senior season in college. Jerry shifted gears by returning to his home state to play for the University of Illinois.

Colangelo's time at the University of Illinois was well spent. "I gained an education and name recognition." He took courses that served him well in his future: "Sports psychology, accounting, economics, and business law. I gained experience as an athlete and became prepared to coach." These were all invaluable, fundamental essentials Colangelo would put into use by age 26, when Dick Klein asked Jerry to help launch the Chicago Bulls franchise in 1966. This would be quite the task. The Windy City had already failed twice in supporting a professional basketball team (the Stags and the Packers/Zephyrs). Colangelo was already working for Klein's incentive merchandising company, and when Klein's dream of owning an NBA team came to fruition, suddenly there was a career fork in the road for Jerry.

"A sports career was never a given for me," said Colangelo. "Klein asked me which side of his business I wanted to manage. I told him I'd perform wherever he needed me. Thankfully, he wanted me to develop the Bulls."

Imagine the priceless hands-on training Colangelo received. "Everything was new! We only had six employees that first year. Back then, the NBA league office only had a workforce of 16. I did all the managing, marketing, and scouting. I was a coach and an assistant coach. I would call other teams to learn about selling season tickets. In 1966, the Detroit Pistons season ticket total was only 93! Our ticket prices ranged from $2 to $5. You learn through other people's mistakes, too."

One of the most valuable things Colangelo said he learned in his early NBA days was perseverance. I asked him, "With all you've learned during four decades of sports management, if you could go through a time tunnel, what would you do differently?"

Colangelo's response tells you about the man. Says Jerry, "I would do it all the same, and wouldn't change a thing. You see, you learn in the trenches. You learn from your mistakes. You gain priceless lessons from going through that. I always was fortunate to have autonomy. You make mistakes and build through them. You grow as a person. Many people don't get that freedom."

Colangelo has been involved in professional sports for nearly 45 years, something he calls an eternity in today's day and age. "I'm a relic." He said he understands the growing desire to be affiliated with sports. "We live in that kind of society. I'm always being asked by athletes and non-athletes for job opportunities, career guidance, and recommendations." Jerry's preference is to bring in young, untainted people with no pre-conceived notions. "I receive stacks of resumes all the time from some very qualified individuals. I would rather train them and mold them."

Asked about today's pro sports operations, Colangelo said, "The industry appropriately operates with a split between the athletic or talent side and the front office or commerce side. Sports have become very sophisticated. It takes an organization, a team of people to succeed in business. When I started the Phoenix Suns, we had five employees. By the time the Diamondbacks came around too, the work staff eventually grew to more than 1,000. That bodes well for opportunities for those with sports career aspirations. You don't have to be an athlete to succeed."

When did sports become so sophisticated? When Colangelo started with the Bulls, he said he was initially amazed at how practices were run. "Coaches would sit around chatting and having a cigarette while the players randomly scrimmaged. There was no organization." That's why Colangelo went outside the mold and hired many college coaches early in his basketball managerial career. "I brought on coaches like Cotton Fitzsimmons, Bill Fitch, and John McLeod. All proved highly successful. I wanted teachers running my teams."

From a promotional perspective, Colangelo has many fond memories. "Everything was rudimentary back then." With the arrival of the Bulls in '66, he paraded a live bull down Chicago's Michigan Avenue to announce the new team in town. Jerry learned the hard way the first time he did his first ball night giveaway. "I made the mistake of distributing the balls before the game, rather than after it." During the Suns' infancy, Colangelo arranged a cross-promotion with Carnation Milk. He arranged for one side of the milk carton to have a bio of his players. Another side offered a special ticket offering. I remember when Bar S Bacon and hot dogs and the Seattle Sonics did something similar in the early 1970's. This actually ignited my passion for a sports career as a result. Colangelo referred to these promotions as 'Dealer Loader Programs,' or incentives to purchase. This was something he learned earlier in his sales career working for Dick Klein's incentive merchandising company. "Even the league's NBA Properties division was initially just T-shirts and caps. It took the league's leadership and innovation to bring rhyme and reason to what teams were individually doing."

Colangelo agreed with me that the evolution of sports really took off in the late 1970's, when access to information began to skyrocket. Perhaps not coincidentally, that's when ESPN evolved, and the cable revolution took off. "We've become more educated," said Colangelo. "There became additional sports exposure and information overnight, and with it the insatiable desire for even more sports coverage." The benefit is additional career opportunities for more people.

Sports run in cycles. Sometimes what worked once, or was the trendy thing to do, isn't as effective today, both from a playing and business side. Since Colangelo began his pro sports career in 1966, pro leagues have tripled in size. Free agency came about. So did the drafting of under-classmen, thanks to Spencer Haywood's (and Sonics' team owner Sam Schulman's) successful antitrust lawsuit against the NBA in 1970. Front office personnel massively grew and departmentalized. The technological revolution demanded even more transformation, challenges, and needs. There's increasingly more competition for the entertainment dollar in the sports industry than ever before, making it a moving target of business objectives and opportunities. If you're on the cutting edge, you can become invaluable. Imagine using the term, "Blog" in the 1960's? Someone would have thought you were an alien from Star Trek.

The history and heritage of the career Colangelo has devoted his life to has a special place in his heart. Said Colangelo in his book *How You Play the Game*, "We have to work hard to maintain the link that binds us to our past, that link between the past and present is what makes sports special."

As for the future in sports, "You can't turn back the clock," he says. "Once players got representation and unions, once collective bargaining happened, sports changed forever." Colangelo didn't view this was a bad thing, rather a necessary one. "Rewards became bigger, but so did the risks." With broadcast rights of TV and cable being so colossal, the economic ramifications are enormous.

The best teacher is experience, yet, with all the competition, it's hard to break into the sports world. Colangelo's sage advice: "Determine your goal, and recognize your strengths and weaknesses. Then go with your strengths. Are you a PR person? Is advertising or promotions your thing? Revenue producers always advance in marketing. Take inventory of what or who you know. Networking is critical. Get your foot in the door and be willing to accept any role. There are no guarantees, so prepare and pursue. Be enthusiastic! Most of all, be passionate!"

Few people start at the top in management. Jerry Colangelo was one of the extraordinary exceptions that did.

Coaching

There is no clear-cut path to a coaching career. Some coaches are former athletes that use this profession as an extension beyond their playing days. Some former professional athletes who weren't great players become outstanding coaches. Other times, great players try coaching but have a hard time managing their own expectations because other players don't possess the same ability or drive that they once did.

The great thing about coaching is you can participate early in your life and get as involved as you want. It may not be on a professional or collegiate level, but it can be very fulfilling. You don't have to measure success with wins and losses. Triumph can be defined by the positive influence you might have on a young athlete's life; perhaps forever.

Jack Lengyel will certainly not be remembered for the wins and losses he accumulated as a collegiate football coach. His overall record amounted to 32 victories and 55 defeats. His success and legacy is measured by character.

Lengyel began his head football coaching career collegiately at the College of Wooster in Ohio in 1966. He arrived late in the spring without the opportunity to recruit and went 1-8 in his first season at Wooster. Then, he turned a 1-8 team into an 8-1 team, compiling a remaining overall four-year record of 24-12. In 1971, he took on the unenviable task of resurrecting the football program of Marshall University in West Virginia. In November of 1970, a heartbreaking plane crash claimed 75 lives overall; 36 members of the varsity football team, 5 coaches, the athletic director, trainers, managers, 5 from the administrative staff, 24 boosters, and the flight crew members.

Marshall wasn't even sure they should re-build the football program. There was a strong sentiment by some faculty and alumni to just focus on their successful basketball program. In the previous 23 seasons, Marshall's football program had only achieved four winning seasons. This included a recent 27-game losing streak.

President Don Dedmon and the faculty were soon persuaded otherwise by the students, the grieving community, and the Big Green booster club. Operating like a fist, the heartbeat of their spirits prevailed. They wouldn't allow their fallen heroes to be forgotten. Resuming the football program was their way of honoring them.

At first, the position was offered to an assistant from Penn State, but he declined. Then a coach from Georgia Tech accepted the job, but resigned for personal reasons shortly after he took the helm.

At this time, Lengyel proactively pursued the position and was given the job. "I promised the State Governor and the University President I would stay at least four years and that I'd put the class structure back together," said Lengyel. "When I began, I thought I was just re-building a program. I didn't initially realize the magnitude of what I was about to take on. This catastrophe had devastated the university and the town. Everyone was about to learn what I believed is the greatest lesson in life and sports. That's to face adversity, get back up off the ground, and go onto success."

When Lengyel commenced his new position, there were only 31 days until spring practice. Lengyel had to immediately hire four new assistant coaches, trainers, and equipment managers. He inherited just 27 inexperienced freshman players, who weren't allowed by the NCAA to play varsity football as freshmen back then. Then there was the issue of recruiting while the wounds of the heartbreak were still fresh in everyone's mind. "Parents of many of the players we tried to recruit didn't want their son to play football for a school that had just had a plane crash," said Lengyel.

Athletic Director Joe McMullen petitioned the NCAA for an exemption to the freshman eligibility rule. Because of their unique and horrendous circumstances,

Marshall was allowed to offer recruits immediate permissibility to play. This reversed the course of their modest recruiting successes to that point. Since recruits could now play right away at Marshall, the rejections started turning into commitments. Lengyel and his assistants expanded their recruiting efforts to not only West Virginia, but also Kentucky, New York, Pennsylvania, and Ohio. "There's no doubt the selling point they could play immediately made a big difference to the players," said Lengyel. Ironically, the NCAA's rule that freshman could play varsity ball was given to all NCAA teams the following season. Says Lengyel, "If that same tragedy at Marshall occurred today, I doubt that any president given the circumstances would rebuild the football program."

Lengyel's towering task of raising a team from the ashes was still colossal. "For the spring game, we only had 48 players. This included three remaining varsity players that did not make the heartrending plane trip due to injury. It also included three varsity basketball players playing out their fifth year of eligibility; also walk-ons," says Lengyel. "We had ex-military, a fireman, and a policeman trying out. Without them, we couldn't scrimmage. We needed all the able bodies we could find. We even used coaches as stand-ins during practice. It was a real coaching challenge."

Finding their place-kicker was an interesting story in itself. Lengyel posted an ad in the school's paper, *The Parthenon*. It read: Room, board, books tuition and fees to anyone who could kick an extra point/field goal. "Sixteen players showed up to audition for the team. None were very accurate," remembers Lengyel. "Then this one hippie soccer player named Blake Smith was the last one to try out." After effectively showing he could split the uprights, Lengyel told him, "Get a haircut and a shave, you've got a scholarship, room, board, books, and fees." Blake would earn that scholarship soon.

With mentors like Ohio State's Woody Hayes, Michigan's Bo Schembechler, and Notre Dame's Ara Parseghian, Lengyel ran a power offense at the College of Wooster, but without experienced players on the offensive line, he elected to shift offensive strategies. "We didn't have the talent to do it," said Lengyel. "I called Bobby Bowden, who was coaching West Virginia that season. Bowden graciously invited me and my staff to observe their practices for three days. At that time, the Mountaineers were running an option offense called the Houston Veer. We'd watch them practice during the day and study their game films throughout the night. We only had three days to go before spring practice started to install the new Houston Veer offense at Marshall University. Talk about a speedy course in changing your offense. We were learning it and teaching it at the same time."

In the spring game, despite their obvious lack of depth, the Young Thundering Herd took on 68 varsity alumni and prevailed 26-0. "It gave us hope and was a starting point," said Lengyel. "We had to build the team backwards. Rather than using seniors as starters, and supporting them with the younger players, we had to begin with freshman. It was a difficult disadvantage to say the least."

As this untested Young Thundering Herd prepared for the upcoming season, the coaching staff emphasized conditioning, attitude, perseverance, and enthusiasm. Though they lacked experience, the squad was treated like a varsity team. Lengyel and his staff also devised unconventional ways to make the team competitive. "We were expected to do the unexpected, so we chose to do the unexpected," said Lengyel. "Because of our lack of depth and experience, we would have to compensate by always stunting our defense and throwing the football when they expected us to run. We chose to take risks."

In spite of a scrappy effort on the road against Morehead State, Marshall lost 29-6 in its season opener. The next game would be a highly emotional one; their home-field debut. The opponent, Xavier, would provide a major challenge. Marshall was deemed a four-touchdown underdog.

The game took on larger-than-life proportions, for both the team and the residents of Huntington, West Virginia. The town turned out en masse, not only to provide emotional support for their new football team, but to also pay tribute to the crash victims.

With the passionate community lifting them onto its fervent shoulders, Marshall responded, carving out a 3-0 halftime lead on the foot of their newly-added soccer player placekicker, Blake Smith. The second half was a back-and-forth affair with Xavier clinging to a 13-9 lead down the stretch. Only 1:18 remained as Marshall QB Reggie Oliver directed his team toward the opponent's end zone. With the clock ticking down to just one second left in the game, Oliver snapped the ball from the visitor's 13-yard line. Running a bootleg throw-back pass to Terry Gardner to the wide side of the field, and with Jack Crabtree getting the key block, Oliver completed a game-winning TD pass, giving the team and the demonstrative town an uplifting 15-13 win. Nearly two hours after game ended, the stadium's field and stands were still packed with supporters. No one had left. "They all had a friend, a teammate, a classmate, or a neighbor that died in the plane crash. No one wanted to leave," remembers Lengyel.

That same season also saw the Young Thundering Herd beat a then-undefeated Bowling Green team, which was on its way to the Citrus Bowl, 12-10 in the homecoming game. It was another noteworthy victory.

In spite of other offers, Lengyel fulfilled his promise and stayed on at Marshall for four seasons. The resurrected Thundering Herd managed four victories by their third season, losing two other games that year by a combined five points.

Overall, Lengyel guided Marshall to nine victories over four seasons. As he termed the experience: "From the Ashes to the Phoenix." Lengyel would follow that with a distinguished college administrative career, serving as the associate Athletic Director at Louisville and Athletic Director at Fresno State, Missouri, and the United States Naval Academy.

It took several coaches and 12 more seasons before the Thundering Herd would post a winning record. In the 1990's, Marshall was the winningest football program in the NCAA under head coach Bobby Pruett.

In 2006, Hollywood paid homage to this special tale, chronicling Lengyel and his 1971 team in the hit film, *We Are Marshall*. "It was a movie about a town, faith, hope, and perseverance," says Lengyel. "It's a story that needed to be told about the contributions of the university, community, coaching staff, and players that provided the foundation for re-building not only the football program, but the spirit of the town." Reprising Lengyel's coaching role was Matthew McConaughey. Not a bad way to be remembered.

Dave Griffin

Dave Griffin

There are many other great sports success stories. When I moved my family to Phoenix in 1994, I called the Suns organization to introduce myself and offer to do stats for visiting media. This is when I met Dave Griffin.

Griffin joined the Suns organization in 1993, a self-proclaimed fantasy nerd, and lifelong Suns fan. Beginning his dream job, Griffin started as a media relations intern, working his way onto their staff for four years. With his eye on an upper management position, Griffin quickly worked his way into a basketball operations position. This included draft and free agency information, video preparation, scouting reports, and statistical analysis.

Bryan Colangelo was the Suns General Manager at the time. He gave the persistently eager, hard-working Griffin increasing responsibilities. Griffin's list of titles grew to include assistant general manager of player personnel, director of player personnel, assistant director of player personnel, and basketball operations assistant with the Suns.

When Colangelo departed the organization to join the Toronto Raptors in 2006, Griffin was promoted to team vice president.

Until 2007, when Steve Kerr joined the Suns as their General Manager, Griffin essentially handled the GM duties. Coach Mike D'Antoni held the GM title, but he was already very busy with coaching duties during the season and as a U.S.A. Olympic Basketball assistant in the summer. Upon Kerr's arrival, Griffin was again promoted, this time to senior vice president.

While with the Suns, Griffin served as tournament director for the NIKE Desert Classic pre-draft camp and was an assistant coach at Scottsdale Community College. He was also part of the basketball press information team at the 1996 Olympic Games in Atlanta.

Following the 2009-2010 season Griffin left the Suns to become the Cleveland Cavaliers Vice President of Basketball Operations. Success well deserved.

Sports Agents

Although sports agents don't work in a team's front office or wear a uniform, their interaction with teams is undeniable, and for a sports career, this is one of the positions where "Show Me the Money" might actually occur. An effective sports agent can make huge money.

Sports agents and attorneys represent professional athletes and amateur athletes after they've (hopefully) used up their college eligibility. They also represent coaches, broadcasters, general managers, team owners and other sports executives.

Successful sports agents are characterized as aggressive but non-threatening with the ability to work under extreme pressure. Their day is rarely nine-to-five. Between meetings and negotiations, they spend extensive time socializing and schmoozing within the industry. Teams having to negotiate with a particular agent sometimes strikes fear into their organization and has great impact on which player they may draft or attempt to sign as free agents.

Besides negotiating salaries, obtaining media attention and providing career counseling are also characteristic duties. So is lining up endorsements for their clients. To be successful, you need to have outstanding interpersonal skills and a flexible schedule for this demanding job. In a career as a sports agent or sports attorney, you also need to be lucky and good. This field is highly competitive and can be more difficult than becoming a professional athlete.

A sport agent's many services also include investment and estate planning, and overall public relations of their clients. Today's agents have strong educational backgrounds in business and/or sports administration. Training in accounting and familiarity with contracts, legal issues, and tax implications are also essential. You may end up working for a company that specializes in representing athletes. Other specialists that work with or for a sports agency may include Financial Advisors, Insurance Agents, Marketing Executives, Real Estate Brokers, and Charity experts. Some sports agents will open their own firm and secure their own clients.

Most agents are paid on a percentage arrangement. Some agents (lawyers) charge a flat fee or by the hour. Sports agents like Scott Boras, Leigh Steinberg, and David Falk have built sports empires representing superstar athletes.

Most leagues require special certification to be an accepted sports agent. This is true in the NFL, NBA, MLB, and the NHL. Agents also pay dues to their respective leagues' players associations. This annual amount may range from $300 to $1500.

There is a limit as to what percentage an agent can receive on behalf of his client's contract. In the NFL, an agent's commission cannot exceed three percent. An agent representing an NBA player gets no more than four percent. Endorsement contracts allow higher commissions.

Here's an example of what a top player earns in yearly salary from their league and what the agent's fee amounts to:

SPORT		AGENT'S SALARY
NBA Salary	$25 Million	$750,000
NFL Salary	$18 Million	$540,000
MLB Salary	$20 Million	$600,000
NHL Salary	$10 Million	$300,000

Attorneys & Sports

Legal counsel and litigation in sports has become as common as the box scores of the sports page. With all the difficulties in labor relations going on in with the respective sports leagues and their players associations, one only needs to read today's sports page or watch *SportsCenter* to know that attorneys are an integral part of sports.

In some ways, an attorney's responsibilities are like that of a sports agent, since they might handle contractual matters. The attorney that is specialized in tax and business law, sports law, and copyright law definitely can carve out a career in sports. There are complex broadcasting contracts to negotiate. There are sponsorships, trademarks, and endorsements to protect.

An attorney might work for a team or might be employed by sports agents or sports-related promoters. Contracts are varied and complicated. Then there are the issues that arise when an athlete gets associated on the wrong side of the law.

As you can imagine, confidentiality, trust and discretion is very important with the sensitive information that attorneys are privy to.

Lon Babby

Lon Babby was a prominent MLB, NBA, and WNBA player agent for 15 years, and has led a varied professional life since graduating from Yale Law School in 1976. At age 29, Babby gained national notoriety as part of the defense team for John Hinckley, Jr., who attempted to assassinate President Ronald Reagan. "It was March 30 of 1981, and I was sitting in my office in Washington, D.C. Suddenly, I'm hearing sirens blaring everywhere outside. The whole city sounded like it was on high alert. Mind you, there weren't TV's around the office and no internet yet. My senior

Lon Babby

partner, William Fuller, calls me into his office and says 'we have a hot case.' We were asked to represent John Hinckley, Jr. This historical event took place just three blocks from my office. This case was my first significant exposure to the media," said Babby. Thanks to this four-man defense team from the Williams and Connolly law firm, Hinckley, Jr. was found not guilty by reason of insanity.

It was during his early years working for Williams and Connolly that Babby's strong sports interest took professional root. "I grew up in Long Island, a huge sports fan. My dad would take me to games at Ebbets Field, Madison Square Garden, and Yankee Stadium." In Babby's office, he proudly displays a picture of himself as a youth with the immortal boxer, Jack Dempsey. "Edward Bennett Williams was a great trial lawyer and very much a sportsman. Though my initial responsibilities for his firm focused on first amendment work and white collar criminal defense duties, Williams was part-owner of the Washington Redskins, and I was intrigued by his connection to pro sports. Soon Babby became intimately involved in the firm's representation of the Washington Redskins (1977-1980). "About 20-percent of my work soon became associated with the Redskins."

In 1979, Williams purchased the Baltimore Orioles. Now Babby added the responsibilities of being the O's Club Counsel and eventually General Counsel (1979-1994). "Now I was spending even more time in sports, doing player contract negotiations, preparing for salary arbitration cases with ballplayers, advertising and marketing contracts, labor issues, stadium concerns, including the construction and development of Oriole Park at Camden Yards, along with day-to-day general business management." Larry Lucchino (current President, CEO and part-owner of the Boston Red Sox) was a partner at Williams Connolly when Babby joined the firm in 1977. When cancer claimed Williams in 1988, Lucchino became President of the Orioles, and Babby became the team's General Counsel.

In 1994, Peter Angelos purchased the Orioles, and Lucchino left the organization. Babby also chose to resign that year. What next? The wheels of fate were turning. Baltimore native and retired NFL star Calvin Hill sought out Babby to represent his son Grant Hill, a graduating Duke basketball star.

"I didn't want to be a sports agent," remembers Babby. "I told Calvin Hill I'd represent his son, but as a lawyer. Unlike traditional sports agents, I only charged for my time. Grant Hill became my first player client. Over the years, this arrangement has saved Grant millions." This is how Babby distinguished himself from other agents. "I never did a percentage of income. The player created his value, not me. My niche was to work with quality athletes who are also quality people."

Grant Hill's NBA career began in 1994 as a first-round pick of the Detroit Pistons. "The first thing I did for Grant was negotiate his shoe contract. Then we worked on his Pistons' deal. Unlike today, there was no NBA rookie scale, so there was more for an agent to negotiate back then."

In 1997, Tim Duncan employed Babby as his agent. "I never thought of myself as a sports agent, rather as a player representative," said Babby. Future signees for Babby's services included Ray Allen, Shane Battier, and Luke Walton.

Currently the President of Basketball Operations for the Phoenix Suns, Babby says his career has undergone a poetic arc. "I started with the management side for 17 years, represented players for 15 years, now I'm back in management." Having been on both sides of the sports negotiating table, Babby finds that an enormous benefit. "I have a greater appreciation of what works and what doesn't work."

But why did he shift gears back to management? "The industry has become more problematic," says Babby. "My philosophy was to provide the best service possible at a reasonable price. Nowadays, kids go to college for a semester and then declare for the draft. They do not always choose agents based on the merits of the representation offered. I would go through proper channels with coaches and athletic departments, ethically playing by the rules. Other agents wouldn't wait. By abiding by the rules, it was often too late to secure a star player as a client."

Babby's advice if a career as a sports agent is the field you choose: "Be prepared in every respect. Understand the position of your adversary. Contemplate each move. Know the rules. It's like a chess match. I always had reasons for my position."

As a certified agent by the NBA and WNBA's Players Association, and MLB's Players Association, Babby also negotiated licensing and coordinated business structuring. There are more than 3,500 certified sports agents from 10 sports leagues in this country.

There is no set path to becoming a sports agent. Let's look at some of the knowledge and background this position will entail:

A law degree would be beneficial but is not a requisite to be a sports agent. You will need to be well-informed about contracts and legal agreements, so a strong educational background and studying law can only help.

With the massive escalation of player salaries, today's sports agents need to provide a wider array of personalized services for an athlete. Professional backgrounds like Financial Advisors, Insurance Agents, Marketing Executives, Real Estate Brokers, Trainers, Nutritionists, etc. can now be specialized offerings from a sports agency.

Understand the sport(s) you're looking to represent. Become the game's biggest fanatic. Know what any team's need might be. You never know when an injury may create an opportunity for the player you might represent. You need to be proactive and swift in capitalizing on a sudden possible opening for your client's services.

Every league has player unions and collective bargaining agreements. You'll need to comprehend every bit of these agreements in order to competently negotiate.

Like any social endeavor, effective networking skills are fundamental. So is a strong work ethic. Sports agents rack up the frequent flyer miles and are constantly burning up the phone lines, with hundreds of daily calls. Get ready for the grind. This is definitely not an 8 to 5 job.

Here are some other recommendations. Attend a college with an accredited business and/or sports management program. Learn everything you can about business and sports. You may want to consider a master's degree in business administration with a focus on sports management.

You will also want to research what are the requirements to be an agent within your sport of choice. To represent an athlete, you have to be certified. Different leagues have different stipulations. The NFL requires new agents to register with the NFL Players Association and pay yearly fees. You may also have to pay other fees and registrations, depending on which state you operate from. You must also become certified to represent athletes in a specific sport and maintain that certification as long as your representation continues.

You might consider joining a professional organization like the Association of Professional Sports Agents (APSA) to acquire valuable networking contacts and get access to possible job openings. Go online to websites like the Sports Agents Directory. It contains more than 3,500 Certified Sports Agents from 10 Sports Leagues. See www.sports-agent-directory.com

Here's a partial list of sports that agents might represent:

- MLB, Minor League Baseball
- NBA, WNBA, NBDL, CBA
- NFL, CFL, AFL
- NHL, AHL
- ATP
- FIFA, MLS
- PGA, LPGA
- Olympic Athletes
- U.S.A. Track & Field

Remember, it only took one client for Jerry Maguire to launch his solo career.

Rick Welts

Rick Welts

Someone I've known since 1975 actually began his career in sports as an NBA ball boy. Currently, Rick Welts is one of the most respected executives in all of sports. What a resume he created along the way.

Welts joined the Seattle SuperSonics in 1969 as a ball boy. If you look up an old team photo, he'll be right there alongside the early Sonics like Lenny Wilkens, Bob Rule, Dick Snyder, and Tom Meschery. Seattle had just been granted an NBA expansion team in 1967.

Welts worked his way up the Sonics chain, remaining with the team for 10 years in several different capacities. Along the way, he attended the University of Washington. Welts served as Public Relations Director during Seattle's back-to-back trips to the NBA finals in 1978 and 1979. The Sonics lone championship was in 1979.

In 1979, Welts joined Bob Walsh & Associates, one of the first sports marketing firms in the United States. As vice president, he was involved in creating the first sports subscription cable service (Sonics SuperChannel) as well as representing athletes in the NBA, MLB and NFL.

It was onward and upward for Welts. In 1982, David Stern (currently the NBA Commissioner), recruited Welts to the NBA League office in New York City, where he spent 17 innovative years. Along the way, Welts earned several career promotions and helped guide the revitalization of the league and its image through strong marketing initiated by the NBA. Welts is credited with the creation of the NBA All-Star Weekend concept in 1984. This has continued as a league highlight and a standard used in both the National Hockey League and Major League Baseball.

Welts also steered the 1992 Olympics "Dream Team" marketing program as the agent for U.S.A. Basketball. *Brandweek* magazine named Welts "Marketer of the Year" for his role in helping create and launch the WNBA in 1998.

During his tenure at the NBA office, Welts supervised league departments including corporate sponsorship and media sales, consumer products, media relations, community relations, team services, special events, creative services, and retail including the NBA Store. He was also responsible for the NBA's international business activities, from placing preseason games in foreign countries to opening the league's first international office in Australia to supervising six regional offices and 75 international employees in Asia, Europe, Australia, Mexico, and Canada .

When he departed in June 1999, Welts was the league's executive vice president, chief marketing officer, and president of NBA Properties.

Welts left the NBA to become president of FOX Sports Enterprises, a new entity that managed FOX interests in facilities and sports teams including the Los Angeles Dodgers, Dodger Stadium, STAPLES Center , the Los Angeles Kings, Madison Square Garden, the New York Knicks, and New York Rangers.

In June 2001, Welts became a partner in a sports consulting firm, ONSPORT. Prior to that start-up venture he served as president for one year of "First In Line," a joint venture between USA Network's Ticket Master & SFX.

One year later, Welts joined the Phoenix Suns organization as team president, enlisted to oversee all business operations of the Phoenix Suns and direct the club's interests in the management of US Airways Center and the Phoenix Mercury (WNBA). After nine seasons with the organization, the last two as the club's chief executive officer, Welts became a marketing free agent, resigning in September 2011 to pursue other interests. Welts wasn't unemployed long, as the Golden State Warriors snapped him up to be their President and Chief Operating Officer.

On May 16, 2011, in a front-page story in the *New York Times*, Welts publicly acknowledged that he is gay, becoming the first senior executive of a men's professional team sports organization to do so.

This stellar career all began while shagging rebounds and passing out towels for the Seattle SuperSonics.

Marketing Director

The primary challenges of the marketing director are to attract more people to the stadium and vend the team's merchandise. You're not only selling the games themselves, but the team's image, its players and their personalities, and licensed team products. With such fierce competition today for the entertainment dollar in a grieving economy, how do you successfully market a sports franchise?

A marketing person needs to possess media savvy, creativity, excellent communication and writing skills, tremendous energy, and the ability to multi-task. You will likely begin this profession as an intern.

In an ongoing effort to brand the team in such a fragmented market, the marketing director will work with several other internal departments; among them are public relations and promotions.

One key ingredient of success that certainly helps a marketing director is a winning team. This of course is not possible for every team; therefore, spectacular and popular ideas are the key ingredients to success.

What is the advertising strategy? What media will be utilized to implement that tactic? What contests, promotions, and giveaways will be done with the fans? How can social media facilitate the cause? What new wrinkles will be offered to those valuable sponsors to upsell or just retain their business? It's a never-ending challenge.

Promotion Director

Promotion Directors have the task of uniquely getting the attention of the paying public. Many times this will involve giveaways of team hats, T-shirts, or balls. Other times, it may entail working with charities and other nonprofit groups or arranging for appearances of the players. Celebrity games are always a crowd-pleaser.

Creativity can launch your livelihood. Although he wasn't employed at the time in a sports capacity, Drew Hedgcock forged career success by re-creating the euphoric scene that was Lake Placid where the 1980 U.S. Hockey team miraculously captured the 1980 Olympic gold medal. Drew was working for CBS TV as a page, assisting the Mike Douglas TV show in Los Angeles, when U.S. Head Coach Herb Brooks and team captain Mike Eruzione were the featured guests for that day's show. Drew took it upon himself to secure 300 mini American flags so that when Brooks and Eruzione were introduced on stage, the studio audience gave them a patriotic greeting of Olympic proportions. The crowd chanted "USA – USA – USA" with Brooks and Eruzione caught completely off-guard. The studio audience was awash with waving U.S. flags. Not even Mike Douglas knew about this mastermind idea. Drew was recognized on camera and eventually was hired by the Mike Douglas show because of his ingenuity.

Fresh out of college, I took a job selling season tickets for the Seattle Mariners.

The prior season, Seattle won only 67 games, one of the worst records in all of major league baseball. Maury Wills, former Dodger great, was the new Mariner manager, so optimism was high. At the very least, I figured I could get my foot in the door, and hopefully cultivate a full-time opportunity into the organization that way.

The Mariners didn't have a mascot yet, and, with the artistic help of my high school friend, Todd Dreyer, I'd even gone to the trouble of providing sketches of what the mascot could look like. Todd's conception of a Mariner mascot was an old Salty Sailor with a three-pronged pitchfork similar to the then-Mariners' logo on their hat.

Dan O'Brien was the team's President. I presented Todd's sketches to him. O'Brien admired the inventiveness, but it didn't help my cause of trying to get a permanent position with the team.

Four months and no (paid-for) commissions later, I was then told this was a seasonal position and that I wouldn't be retained.

What other mastermind branding ideas are out there which will create an institutional tradition? Someone made a mint creating a cheerleading mascot out of a chicken outfit. Some marketing executive deserves an A+ for somehow getting nearly every football team to celebrate their victory by dousing their head coach with Gatorade. Talk about major brand awareness.

Expect long hours and required attendance at all team games and events. If it will boost ticket sales and positive publicity, creativity will be your ticket to success in your organization.

Web Master

"Nothing but net" used to mean a swish in basketball. Now its translation is World Wide Web. Thankfully, the information highway has created an ocean of employment opportunities in the sports world, and the intellectual and creative person now has an important position on the team: Webmaster.

The internet has not only changed our lives, it has changed our way of doing business. Marketing sports is no exception. Effective web sites help promote the team, the athletes, and their games. The web has also become a valuable informational and selling resource. Web sites have become the team's address and phone number all in one, providing a great trickle-down effect. That's why it's URL (web address) is listed on all print ads, brochures, TV commercials, billboards, products, and stationery.

Websites have created additional revenue sources like advertising, site subscriptions, an electronic will call for game and season ticket sales, and licensed merchandise sales. Since it's quantifiable by "hits," the web has provided a valued marketing tool when teams approach advertisers. Now teams can provide a psychographic profile of the team's fans, a measureable asset the team can offer sponsors.

It's not just teams that offer sports products via the web. Sports merchandise, memorabilia, and tickets to games are available through other businesses too. TV and radio stations that offer sports also have their own popular links to the sports world.

Other strategies have evolved from web sites. Contests are now geared to enter online. Voting for the All Star game participants now occur through the web, creating quite a mailing list. Interactive questionnaires and surveys can be conducted. Web sites have also proven to be respected for their research and fundraising capabilities.

It's a microwave society now, so the webmaster is an important participant with both professional and collegiate teams. Fans want instant access and information. A good team site will keep them engaged. The web site needs to be user-friendly, and the content must be innovative and fresh. The web content person will provide statistical information, game photos, graphics, and videos. The web also provides fans efficient access to ticket purchase and team-branded merchandise. With ever-changing information, sports web sites need to be constantly maintained. If the content isn't frequently updated, it quickly becomes stale like old fish.

In some ways the content producers have the combined duty of a print journalist and editor. They'll be constantly researching and writing compelling stories and articles. They might be reporting breaking news. This has become the future for many sportswriters who have lost their career through the demise of newspapers. Now they call themselves "Team Bloggers." Other positions that have evolved from the internet are webcasts, podcasts, chats, twitter, and fan clubs.

There will always be some potholes on the internet highway. But that's where the IT Director comes in handy, handling the technical and security issues.

Scout

If you really want to be a gypsy and travel extensively, be a scout in professional sports. Scouts are the hidden heroes of a sports organization. It's their job to find talented players for their teams, so you'll be required to see players in action first-hand, be able to evaluate a player's skills, and recommend if that athlete has what is needed by your organization.

Whether recruiting for a college or employed for a professional organization, there is a great deal of traveling, sometimes all over the world. Being multi-lingual is an asset.

The scout will have a direct pipeline to the General Manager and the head coach or manager. How scouts go about finding these athletic gems will come from a variety of methods. Scouting duties may include observing other teams' players in anticipation of a trade. A scout will likely have established networks with coaches from high schools or colleges, even other scouts, so a promising prospect may come from word of mouth. Any relevant information is valuable. Will that player have the right stuff to become a star player? Is the prospect a good student, a solid citizen? Is there a history of injuries to consider? With the massive coverage of sports via television, a scout may uncover a gem worth pursuing watching TV.

Some scouts even negotiate and present contracts, so they need to be persuasive. The evaluation process is never-ending.

It's not just a team a scout might work for. There are scouting agencies that operate independently from teams as well as scouting pools.

There is a significant investment by teams towards scouting and a considerable financial responsibility by scouts to be correct. Any given player is a large investment for a team. The scout's recommendations determine whether or not to draft a prospect, and at what level to select a player. A scout's input also factors in on how much money to invest in a player through a signing bonus.

Many scouts are former coaches or retired players from the sport they work. Some scouts have made themselves experts through years of studying the game they love. You need to have a keen eye for talent. No matter your prior background, another trait of scouts is passion about their occupation.

If you're into social media and interested in scouting, you might consider developing a web site like Scout.com.

Some scouts focus on prospects; young players who are deemed worthy of the effort and expense of developing them for the potential that they'll pay off in the near term. Other scout's responsibilities are to watch existing professionals whose contractual rights might be coming to an end, and they may soon be available through free agency. Or they may be worth trading for. A team might have a need to fill a certain position. There's also the advance scout. This individual flies ahead to watch the teams their team is going to play in order to help their coaches strategize.

Then there's the Bird Dog scout. This scout is generally not on a team's employee list, but rather works for a service that sells their information to teams by suggesting young players worth evaluating. This position comes through a member of a network of contacts established by a full-time scout.

Scouting on the collegiate level includes watching high school talent. The responsibilities are typically handled by coaches with their team.

Human management is still the norm on determining which players an organization will draft, sign, or trade for, but talent evaluation might be a computer program away from altering how scouting is done at the professional level of all major sports. More and more, modern day scouts use computer programs to assist their evaluations and organize the collected data.

According to the United States Bureau of Labor Statistics, there are 217,000 people employed as scouts. (Note: coaching positions are included in this tabulation). Because many sports scouts work less than full-time, the salary averages are low, with the median salary earnings around $27,000. The top 10% of scouts earn more than $59,000 annually. Some earn much more.

If you're skilled at being a scout, it can mean a major difference in wins and losses and the overall success or failure of a team. An organization's financial success is directly affected by whether they've had a winning season or a losing one.

As a scout, you'll be mostly self-employed. Many scouts work part time in a particular region. If you build a successful track record, you might advance to a full-time position like scouting director for a team or perhaps to an administrative position like general manager. There is a high level of competition for the top scouting positions.

Advance Scout

An advance scout is one of the most invisible jobs in sports. Your job is to coach; however in this career you do it in writing and you'll rarely be advising your team in the same city. Such is the livelihood of Houston Rockets advance scout Pat Zipfel.

Zipfel is not your typical NBA advance scout. The NBA is an extremely who-you-know business. It's rare for a non-playing, non-related, and non-connected person to make it to the NBA. Most of the time, former players occupy this position, but truly a student of the game, Zipfel forged his way into the league through perseverance, dedication, and creativity. Zipfel did play college basketball at Cabrini (in Philadelphia) at a Division 3 school, "But I was a third-string point guard, and seeing me eventually shooting jump shots over Larry Bird or Michael Jordan was not a reality."

This did not deter Zipfel from somehow getting into the NBA. "My college coach, John Dzik, had a big influence on me. I decided I wanted to grow up and be like him and coach," so Zipfel started paying his dues. First, Zipfel was a Division 1 graduate assistant at The Citidel in Charleston, South Carolina. Then a head coach for Bucks County Community College in Pennsylvania. Next on the career ladder was Athletic Director and Head Coach for D-3 Centenary in New Jersey.

Along the way, Zipfel got connected to former Philadelphia 76ers executive John Nash, who was then the General Manager of the Portland Trail Blazers. "The Blazers were looking for an advance scout, and Nash recommended me to then-head coach Mo Cheeks."

"Maurice Cheeks, assistant coach Jim Lynam, and Nash gave three of us a blank scouting report and asked us to individually evaluate the game. We were given four hours to analyze and break down this game, and submit a report," said Zipfel. "The next morning, our reports were distributed to all those in the Blazer organization, and I got the job."

Zipfel stayed with Portland for five seasons, two with Cheeks, and three more with current head coach Nate McMillan. In 2007, Houston's Rick Adelman recruited him away to the Rockets' organization.

"This is a very 'behind-the-scenes' job," says Zipfel. "I learned X's and 0's strategy from perhaps the best basketball coach ever in my small college, Coach John Dzik. He taught me a foundation for the game. I learned the game inside and out; it prepared me to be a college head coach. I have a real passion for the game of basketball strategy. Five of my twelve players probably won't even know my name, but they remember my work! We're able to marry statistics and help the coach game-plan for the next opponent with a breakdown of that team. My position is unique because I'm not around the team or even at the games."

Pro basketball advance scout duties include filing an advance report to their coaching staff that is so detailed and so precise, a knowledgeable fan would be astounded at the preparation that goes into game-planning for an opponent.

The report tries to cover every tendency an opponent may have. Where a player gets his touches, whether an individual likes to drive left or right, whether a player looks to shoot first or pass the ball. Will a player pull up in transition for a jump shot or drive to the basket; what ranges does a player have? Where does a player like to receive a pass, where do the picks come from and at what angle, what are the isolation plays?

When it comes down to crunch time, which players are the weakest free-throw shooters, the best offensive rebounders, the best 3-point shooters? What are the suggested match-ups defensively; what is the isolation play run most often?

The report will also provide an analysis of every player on the team that's being scouted. Here's a random observation of one anonymous player's seasonal statistics and reputation:

7 ppg, 3 rebounds, 1 steal, 42% FG, 42% from 3, 89% FT

Advance: Slender, smooth, active forward who is an excellent stand still shooter and has been among the best in the NBA in 3 Point shooting percentage. A good runner who has some ball skills. Likes the spot-up shot who is not afraid to pull the trigger from 3 pt area. Finesse player who doesn't like contact. He is multi-dimensional who can play the 2-3 or 4 spots. Must be physical with him and make him put the ball on the floor - as he is an average ball handler. Strong right hand. Runs the lanes well and feeds off their guards in transition. Beware - he can shoot it! We need to close out on him! Capable of getting hot. Nice length. Average ball handler. Excellent FT shooter. He loves the deep corner shot and in transition spotting up.

Is almost exclusively a spot-up shooter: 88% of his attempts this season have been three-pointers. Has been a dangerous shooter over his career, and is shooting 70% FG over the last two seasons for his team (16% above average) – he is a 48% shooter on corner threes, which make up almost half of his attempts from the field this year. He is not a candidate to create off the dribble, and has only one attempt at the rim in the half-court this season. He will go left almost exclusively.

"This is a job a lot of former players go into without knowing the necessary work required to prepare every night," says Zipfel. "If your goal is to be in the forefront, this is not for you. You need to love the analysis of the game and not get caught up in the hype. It's a labor of love, and I love the strategy side of the game. At any given time, I can provide a written report of what any team has done their last five games. That's the goal, help my team win. If it comes down to what defense to run at the end of the game, and my team succeeds, great! You invest so much into every game, the magnitude is enormous, and you don't have a whole week to prepare like an NFL scout. I generally get just one day."

An advance scout will chart every single play a future opponent runs and note this written play-by-play sheet with terms like thumbs up, stack, slash, punch, box rip and floppy.

Here are some examples of sketched-out plays that will be included in the report:

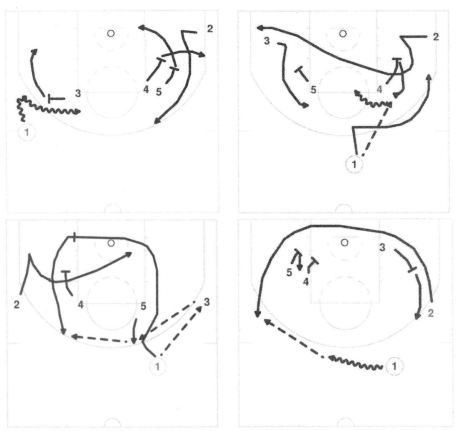

Zipfel still has aspirations to be a coach. "From Phil Jackson's triangle to Rick Adelman's system, I'd like to put it all together and put my own fingerprints on it. I'm sure it would probably be a college-level position. There are only 30 NBA head coaching jobs, but that's OK, I'd love to have a positive effect on students of the game."

Zipfel's story proves you don't have to be a former NBA player to make it in this profession. "There's no clear-cut path. Maybe start as a video coordinator like Cleveland Cavs top executive David Griffin did. Then graduate to advance scout. There's always a job out there, although college outlawed scouting positions in 1995." Zipfel said this was for budgetary reasons. "Work hard, find your passion, and be willing to sacrifice daily. There's a line out the door ready to replace you. Be willing to prove yourself every day!"

Zipfel kiddingly wishes he was paid by the hour. "I literally work as many hours as allowed in the day. That's the career and life I chose. For eight straight months, I hardly know what day it is, just who we play next. Eighty-percent of the time, I'm in a hotel somewhere. I may be in Toronto when the team beats Boston, but I celebrate the victories too. Win or lose, you feel it. There are a lot of highs and lows in a long season." Married with two children, Zipfel says it can be tough when the kids ask: "Daddy, when are you coming home?"

Traveling Secretary

This is a term primarily relating to a baseball position, but necessary in all professional sports. Pretend you're a Soccer Mom. You've got the big van and you have the responsibility to get the whole team to the game - out of town! On time!

As the team's road manager, you will book or charter for all team transportation and are responsible for getting the players to and from a stadium or hotel. Not only do traveling secretaries get the team to their destination, they arrange to get them fed. They're also responsible for getting the equipment there, too, in AOK condition. The traveling secretary has got to make sure the team's entire entourage keeps on schedule and knows the travel itinerary. In some ways, the traveling secretary is also the glorified bellhop, making sure the luggage also gets to its proper destination. This individual travels with the team to all road games and will frequently deal with players, management, and media, handling any travel-related issues.

Plan on being away from home for extended periods of time; more so with baseball or basketball than football. Football only has the one game per week, and roughly two road games per month. With basketball, you're constantly on the run with a series of one-night stays between games.

Here's an unforeseen wrinkle in their daily duties. The team just acquired a player through a trade. Now you have to help that athlete with the complications of relocating within two days. It's not just about getting a plane ticket. The traded player needs new living accommodations, help in selling the house, and assistance in packing up the family for an unexpected destination. Needless to say, a traveling secretary needs to be a trouble-shooter.

The life of a traveling secretary in professional baseball (and other sports) can sometimes be described as nightmarish. Baseball is the toughest because of so many uncertainties. A baseball travel party may include 60 or more people in the regular season. Teams play 81 regular season road games. With an average of three away games per each road series in a city, that's 27 different arrangements for just away flights, and about 15 return flights home. With baseball, you'll at least get a few nights in a row without having to pack your bags again.

Before commercial flights were available, this individual had to know train schedules to get the team from city to city. What if the last game of the series had a rain delay or went extra innings? Maybe there was a make-up game from a rainout plugged into the middle of the season. So much for all those previously handled arrangements. You have to be ready to make alternate plans on very short notice. You can't predict the weather. It's a constant game of What If? Did we factor in mechanical problems with planes? It happens. I wonder how many hotel cancellation fees each team accumulates during the year. This is a necessary cost of doing business.

Adding to their challenges, the traveling secretary is dealing with multi-million dollar athletes who are used to being pampered and require "suitable" lodging. Hard to believe, but some players have been known to be high maintenance. The traveling secretary also has to play ticket broker, handling each player's road requests.

Come postseason time, the challenge really grows. Who could have predicted that Game Three of the 1989 World Series would be postponed for ten days after an earthquake struck the Bay Area? After 9/11, all sporting events were postponed. There wasn't a baseball game played in New York for another 10 days, and the entire MLB 2001 postseason was delayed. So much for reserving all the October rooms the teams blocked out back in January.

In baseball's postseason, the traveling party increases to maybe 200, with families, front-office staff, sponsors, and increased media tagging along. Since you practically found out overnight who your first round opponent is, you have to be quick as a hiccup. You've had no notice where you're traveling to, which means more last-second arrangements for flights, acceptable hotels, buses to transport the team, trucks for the equipment, and food. Thank goodness for the charter planes most teams have today. Come playoff time, a team will need two to three planes, fueled and ready to go at a moment's notice.

Since you don't know if you'll advance in the playoffs, or who will advance in the other playoff series, you have to make arrangements for yet two more unknown cities. But starting when? You don't know how long your series or their series will last. Maybe you'll have to make a return trip to your current opponent's city. You might need more rooms, and "can you add Saturday night too – maybe?" The further the team advances in the playoffs, more of the unknown needs to be planned for. With so many yet-to-be-determined variables, you're in a constant reactive mode. Even start times for games are an unknown until the TV networks let you know. They're in the same uncertain wait-and-see-mode.

Winter months raise havoc for football, basketball, and hockey teams. This happened to me during a January NFL playoff game in Green Bay. Most traveled MLB team? With their Pacific Northwest starting point, it's the Seattle Mariners. In the NHL, the Los Angeles Kings travel the farthest with seasonal snow causing headaches traveling to the Northeast and Canada. The threatening effects of 9/11 have created increased responsibilities for traveling secretaries. Even charter passengers must submit to a no-fly list, and adding new names to a manifest at the last minute can create a delay.

This is typical of traveling managers of ALL professional sports. Baseball just happens to be the toughest, because of all the moving parts. I imagine when traveling secretaries take time off for vacation they want to just stay home. Taking another flight for them is like a letter carriers going for a walk on their day off. Yet it is all worthwhile to be the last team standing. And there isn't a travel manager of professional sports out there that would mind arranging for one last post-season trip. This is the journey that ends up in Washington, D.C. to receive the traditional congratulations from the President at the White House.

Equipment Manager

This is definitely a travel position for those wanting to be close to sports and one that is not gender specific.

The equipment managers face many challenges with their job. Since many sports are played outdoors, Mother Nature can be their ally or foe. It's like packing for a vacation and you don't know if the weather will be cold or warm, wet or dry. What kind of gear do you pack if the game is played under stormy conditions? If it's Green Bay in January, you've got a good idea about the elements. Conversely, what if it's a game played under extreme heat? That's when you make sure you make sure the athletic trainer doesn't miss the flight.

This position is not just handling and transporting the athletic equipment. This position involves maintaining (repairing) and cleaning an athlete's tools of the trade. Security of the equipment is another major responsibility. You'll attend all practices, games, and tournaments.

Marc St. Yves joined the Seattle SuperSonics as a ballboy in 1979, right after their NBA championship season in 1979. Since Sonics head trainer Frank Furtado had a five-year maximum rule for ball boys, St. Yves was forced to move on to other responsibilities in 1984. During that summer, St. Yves filled time by assisting the Sonics equipment manager at the Seattle Kingdome. Just two weeks before the season, the equipment manager resigned. Furtado was forced into hiring St. Yves because he was the only one who knew where all the gear was. Seemingly overnight, St. Yves had gone from ball boy to equipment manager.

Along the way, St. Yves has been front row with some of the game's biggest stars and experienced memories of a lifetime, at least one of which he wishes hadn't happened. Although he can laugh now, back in the latter stages of the 1989-90 season with the Sonics, this wasn't so funny. St. Yves was washing team uniforms at the Seattle Coliseum when a hot water valve got stuck open. All the mostly white uniforms turned lime green. Back then, players only had one set of uniforms and there was still one month left in the season. St. Yves took the uniforms to a dry cleaner to bleach out the mistake, but to no avail. For the remainder of the season, the home uniforms bore the color of a leprechaun and St. Yves' face was red with embarrassment. It did provide Shawn Kemp an extra souvenir to finish his rookie season.

In 1994, when the Sonics built the Furtado Center, a new team training facility, St. Yves added facility manager to his responsibilities.

Now thirty-two years after beginning his pro basketball association by folding uniforms and mopping up sweat-caused wet spots on the floor, St. Yves' sports career thrives as the director of team operations for the Oklahoma City Thunder. When the Seattle SuperSonics moved to Oklahoma City in 2007, St. Yves was brought along.

St. Yves' position can best be described as being the ultimate organizer. Duties include coordinating all team travel, organizing equipment, and overseeing the team's facilities. He's also involved in setting policy for the NBA's rules on uniform guidelines, handling special events, and overseeing the equipment department.

Perhaps St. Yves' biggest responsibility is making sure everything gets to where it needs to be in an efficient manner. This includes all players and coaches. He likens this to "herding cats." At least he's graduated from doing laundry.

MAJOR LEAGUE VIDEO COORDINATOR

Do you excel at video games? In a round-about way, Allen Campbell managed to forge his way into a professional sports career by contributing to a team's success via video scouting reports.

Campbell deserves an A for displaying a lot of sheer perseverance to earn his way into the big leagues. Like many amateur players, Campbell grew up with major league aspirations. An Arizona resident, Campbell played collegiately initially at a Junior College in Phoenix, then played Division One ball at Little Rock, Arkansas, as a pitcher. Campbell did earn a professional tryout with the Diamondbacks, but didn't receive a minor league offer. Undeterred, Campbell managed to get an audience with the Diamondback's front office.

Allen Campbell
Courtesy Arizona Diamondbacks

"I pestered the D-back's Human Resources department every other day. They finally added me as a staff assistant. I was a gofer, helping everybody including all the executives. I'd answer phones, pick up dry cleaning, anything and everything. This went on for four years. I really learned the business. It was also great exposure for me and allowed me face time with key executives. The powers-that-be started noticing me," said Campbell.

Team President Rich Dozier was one of those who observed Campbell's constant persistence and effort. Dozier asked Campbell what he wanted to do. "Within a week, General Manager Joe Garagiola, Jr. also called me in to his office and started taking an interest in my future," said Campbell. "My older brother Andy was a scout, and as a former player, I felt that was where my future was too."

The Diamondbacks sent Campbell to scout school, an MLB–sanctioned crash course to learn this component of the business. "You have to be sponsored to be included," says Campbell. "It's a huge honor. You really learn player evaluation; it was the best two weeks of my journey."

The Diamondbacks made Campbell an associate scout, giving him the responsibility of observing amateur games (high school and college). Then Campbell became an assistant coach for the Diamondbacks' scout team, which is composed of local high school kids in the Phoenix area who showed true potential. Essentially, the scout team is an invite team. This experience led Campbell to being offered the position of hitting coach in 2004 for a Rookie Ball A-Team in Missoula, Montana. "This was a bit of a risk because you only get a short-season contract (June – October) for $16,000. I took the job, but when the season was over, my contract didn't get renewed."

After three months of unemployment had elapsed, Campbell reached out again to Garagiola, Jr. "Within a week, I got a call back from Joe. He said he had something for me, a position as assistant video coordinator."

Video coordinator is a position that has evolved through technology. In the old days, ballplayers and coaches would simply go have a couple beers after the game to talk about what transpired out on the field. "Man, old 'Diz' was throwing a serious yacker tonight. He punched me out twice!" Now biomechanics and technology have allowed athletes to be true students of the game. Though the human element is still necessary, advance baseball scouting now relies heavily on video.

Once again, Campbell got a ground floor opportunity. "Jim Currigan was the head video coordinator. Starting in 2005, I spent three seasons under his tutelage. I worked my rear end off. Every day was a different challenge. I'd report for a 7 p.m. game by 11 a.m."

A major part of the job is charting pitches. When Campbell began his career as a video coordinator, video tape was used. Now it's all done digitally with teams using four high-definition cameras to capture all angles of every at-bat, which might change a bit when equipment on the road may differ. What was the location of the pitches, the velocity, the pitching count at the time? What happened during the at-bat? Was there a hit, and if so, where? Who fielded the ball? What was the defensive positioning? Was it a good play or bad? If it was a bunt play, how was the execution? Did the runner get advanced? The information that Campbell provides becomes teaching tools for the team. Campbell provides a complete individual breakdown for both pitching and hitting. When players complete their at-bat, they'll immediately go into the locker room to review what just transpired on the field, with Campbell's assistance.

Campbell has now become the Diamondbacks' head video coordinator and travels with the major league team. His film-study preparation is essential for the coaches and the players. His information, in conjunction with traditional scouting reports, provides vital insights. Before every game, the hitting coach will discuss with the players what tendencies they might expect from the opposing pitchers that night and their repertoire. Do they throw straight heat, or do they have a nasty curveball? What are their most common mistakes? Campbell will have video examples all ready to show the players during this hitter's pre-game meeting. Campbell says it takes him about four hours to prepare a five minute reel of video clips. "It's a long process, but one that pays dividends." Some players are more dedicated film-watchers than others. Hall of Famer Tony Gwynn was religious about his astute pre-game preparation, earning a nickname of "Captain Video." It's no secret why Gwynn was an eight-time batting champion. Over 20 seasons, he struck out only 434 times in 9,288 career at-bats, and never batted below .309 in any full season.

Here's a typical day for a major league baseball coordinator:

- Manage the equipment and video [if it's a road trip] on the getaway day.

- Set up player/coach viewer stations with that night's starting pitcher.

- Prepare and loop a video of that night's opposing starting pitcher to be seen on all clubhouse TV's.

- Prepare the advance video. Coordinate with the hitting coach and hold the advance meeting for the position players on the first day of each series. Included is a video of each arm in the opponent's bullpen and the starter. Each of their pitches will be spotlighted; what it looks like when getting hit on mistake pitches and what and when those were.

- Chart the game live once the game starts. Four angles of the game are digitally captured and are instantly accessible. Players and coaches can do an automatic review.

- Finalize game action post-game and complete the pitching chart and velocity sheets for the pitching coach to review.

- Attend to special requests. A coach or player may request a hitter DVD to review.

- Update and maintain player files. At season's end, the video coordinator is responsible for writing up an evaluation of each player.

Clearly, video coordination is a process that is very time-consuming, but one that is invaluable in a game that involves so much chess-like anticipation by the coaches and players. How will they go about attacking the opponent? The process serves as a confidence booster as much as a guideline for preparation. If you know what a foe does well as much as what they are weaker at, it might give you that little edge that leads to victory. You can appreciate why video pre-game and during-game review has become a dynamic cog of America's pastime.

The video coordinators work their tails off with routine responsibility, consisting of 10-14 hour days for 162 games, the equivalent of seven-plus consecutive months with rarely a day off. I don't imagine Allen Campbell spends his infrequent time off playing Wii.

Another well-known sports figure began his career as a basketball video coordinator. Erik Spoelstra now wanders the sidelines for Miami Heat as the head coach of LeBron James and Dwayne Wade.

Climbing the sports career ladder can be done. You just have to be like a human Swiss army knife. Show your versatility and become indispensable.

Administration

Administration is another area where women can make in-roads in the sports world. Such was the case for Susan Webner, currently the Manager for Minor League Administration for the Arizona Diamondbacks.

Webner grew up in Phoenix, but went across the country to attend the University of Pennsylvania where she majored in business. While in high school, she was very interested in sports, competing yearly in tennis and swimming. While at Penn, Webner accomplished two primary things related to sports, working as a photographer for the school's paper, *The Daily Pennsylvanian*, and functioning as a statistician for the student radio station's football and basketball broadcasts. She also pre-taped interviews with other Ivy League and non-conference coaches.

"It was about mid-way through college that I decided to pursue a career in sports," says Webner. "My first sports internship was in Philadelphia, working for the Comcast U.S. Indoor Men's Tennis Tournament. I even wore a mascot outfit, a giant tennis ball called 'Top Spin.' I got another break when a college friend who had gotten a job with the Phillies, asked me to also apply. I sent my resume and thankfully, the Phillies front office had a lot of University of Pennsylvania alumni. The Penn basketball head coach, Fran Dunphy, also lent an assist with a referral call."

Webner spent the 1996 season interning for the Phillies with "no guarantee for future employment." Her baseball duties included season ticket and group sales at then-Veterans Stadium, which also played home to the NFL's Eagles. "I then applied for an internship with the Eagles but was told I was over-qualified," says Webner. "The Eagles eventually offered me a full-time position in Penthouse Suite Operations, which meant I was now working every event at Veterans Stadium."

Webner had already been plotting a return to her native Arizona. "In 1995, while I was with the Phillies, the National League had awarded a franchise to Phoenix. My friend Felisa Israel, a Phoenix Suns employee, referred my resume to the

Diamondbacks sales department. Out of the blue, 18 months later the D-Backs gave me a call. I couldn't believe they kept my resume that long! Three weeks later, I accepted a position with them, selling season and group tickets again."

Webner's degree was in marketing, so when the D-backs started up their DiamondBackers Fan Loyalty program in 1999, she spearheaded the effort. Her success led to dual duty with the Phoenix Suns' Fans First version, as their two front offices then worked in conjunction with each other.

Heading into the 2001 season, Webner gravitated to the PR department, working in media relations. This magical D-backs season resulted in a World Series win and a lot of additional responsibility. "That was the season Gonzo (Luis Gonzalez) hit 57 home runs. I was editing the media guide and handling playoff credentials for major league baseball. It was something different every day for the next five years," said Webner.

Webner's organization skills didn't go unnoticed. She was drafted by director of player development A.J. Hinch in 2006 to work in his department, a position she has happily held ever since.

Webner's current tasks are varied. Amongst her many responsibilities, she handles player payroll for the minor leaguers not on the 40-man roster, visas for all foreign players, contracts for all minor league staff, and expense reports for roving instructors. Add to that flight and hotel arrangements, spring training coordination, and catering, "and lots of budgeting." It is Webner's job to make sure people are where they are supposed to be to start the season.

Webner is a great example of someone who carved out her own niche in sports and was willing to pay her dues. Her advice is to "widen your net." "You don't have to start your career at a major league-level or some other pro team. You have the minor leagues, the Olympics, ESPN; maybe it's working for Rawlings [baseball's glove company] or a sponsoring advertiser like Gatorade. You just never know what an internship or beginning position could lead to. I'm fortunate because I love what I do every day! When you do get an opportunity, be prepared and put some thought into it."

Community Relations

The community relations department designs and performs team activities with local agencies, civic groups, political, and governmental associations. It could be the Make-A-Wish Foundation, the Red Cross, children's charities, or other non-profit organizations. The goal is positive PR. Many times, a team's former star player will work in the community relations department, serving as a celebrity attraction to the kids whose lives they touch.

# # #

When trying to enter the world of professional sports, pay your dues any way you can. Someway, somehow, find a way to shoehorn yourself into the organization. As Jerry Colangelo says, "No position or opportunity is too small."

It's tough enough for a pitcher to hit the strike zone, but one that was just one-and-a-half inches? Such was the challenge for Tiger pitcher Bob Cain who on August 19, 1951, had to face St. Louis Brown's pinch hitter Eddie Gaedel, a vertically challenged player who stood 3 feet 7 inches tall. Gaedel's number was 1/8. After four high hard ones, Gaedel earned a walk and a standing ovation. On this day, Gaedel stood tall, but the American League office voided Gaedel's St. Louis contract the next day. That wasn't very big of them.

Chapter 8

$elling Sports

With this being the Era of Information, it's certainly a different period of challenge and constant adjustment for sports marketers to keep up with innovation and technology. From outdoor stadiums to domed stadiums; from radio to TV; from natural grass to artificial turf; from general admission to catered, revenue-generating suites; from cable to digital television; and now social media and the advent of 3-D, there's always a new financial frontier to capitalize on.

Out of necessity, sports have developed into a multi-billion-dollar industry and have become very sophisticated and departmentalized. That's why players require union representation and agents. That's why TV and radio networks financially compete so strongly for the privilege to control (or at least share) a league of their own. That's why team owners invest so heavily, just to have bragging rights and wear that diamond-laced ring on their finger that says Champion. Sports are a significant player for the entertainment dollar.

Show Me the Money

Games are no longer just a pair of tickets, two beers, and a couple hot dogs. Sporting events have become a total entertainment package, all intertwined to generate massive profits. Revenues for professional sports come in all shapes and forms. Most of the dollars come primarily from ticket sales (including suites) and broadcast rights. Other proceeds include signage, publications, merchandising, and concessions.

The new state-of-the-art Cowboy Stadium offers five levels of highly-decorated suites with a décor that offers leather walls, custom leather furniture, catered gourmet food, and your choice of three different color schemes. The Silver-level luxury box is the size of a small apartment at around 700-square feet and accommodates 18 people.

This suite life doesn't come cheap with prices ranging from $100,000 to $500,000 yearly. The expense doesn't stop there. The suite owners have access to all other non-Cowboy events, such as soccer matches, fights, concerts, and college football games, but they are required to purchase tickets to attend. If you want more suite tickets to Cowboy games, you can purchase up to five more. The suite attendees also can mingle in other private clubs in the stadium.

With 300 suites at an average of $300K yearly, that's at least an additional $90 million lining in Jerry Jones' pocket.

Someone who has been an integral marketing pioneer in the NBA for better than 35 years is Rick Welts, currently President and COO of the Golden State Warriors. He has contributed strongly to the NBA's progression in sports marketing with creation of the NBA All-Star Weekend among his many accomplishments.

It was in the early 1980's that Welts helped create the first subscription sports channel, the Sonics SuperChannel. "Originally, it was going to be without advertising at all. We designed a rate card predicated upon subscriptions."

With the advent of cable coverage and broadcast rights ever-soaring, things have certainly changed over the past three decades, and Welts says numerous teams are making the mistake of not adjusting with the times. "Too many teams are still trying to hold onto the past way of doing things. It's a mistake not to embrace where the customers are going. And that means changing with today's technology." Welts likened it to the record industry and the fight over file sharing and iTunes. "It will happen regardless."

In the NBA, selling tickets is still a team's biggest revenue source. Now there is the secondary marketing of tickets: companies that re-sell tickets. "Many teams have fought this, fearing it would de-value season tickets. Again, it will happen with or without you. It's better to embrace the change of media consumption; go with your customers," adds Welts.

It goes without saying that in business, monetizing your product or service is paramount, and as it goes in sports, just about everything is available for sponsorship. Interestingly, the NBA is the only league without a corporate logo. "This is not a moral or ethical issue, rather an economic decision," says Welts. "The rest of the sports world is already doing it. The NBA will eventually do it too. It's inevitable. Right now, it's just not at the right price."

That still leaves plenty of ways for a company to partner up with a sports franchise. Harvey Shank, a member of the Phoenix Suns front office for four decades, has seen it all and probably done it all when it comes to sports marketing and promotions.

Shank made it to the big leagues as a promising pitcher in the California Angels system. A 10th-round draft choice out of Stanford in 1968, Shank toiled in the minors for four seasons. Late in the 1970 season, Shank got called up to fill in for an Angel player who had to fulfill a military weekend in the reserves. Facing an Oakland A's lineup that included Reggie Jackson and Sal Bando, Shank made it into the major league record books with three innings of shutout ball in his one-and-only big league appearance.

While Shank was in Phoenix, a mutual friend introduced him to the bright new General Manager of the Phoenix Suns, Jerry Colangelo. Colangelo hired Shank as an intern in the marketing department for $100 a week. At a crossroads in his pitching career, Shank didn't know whether to keep pitching or stay with the Suns.

"Jerry stepped up to represent me in my next negotiation with the Angels," remembered Shank. "Few people know that this was Jerry's one and only attempt at being a sports agent. Jerry wrote the Angels, explaining to them how valuable I was. The Angels wrote back, saying: 'then you keep him,' thus beginning an ongoing 40-year career with the Suns." Even today, Colangelo and Shank have a good laugh over the less-than-successful negotiation with the Angels. "If only I had any talent to work with," teases Colangelo.

Shank started in sales with the promotion department under Ted Podleski; then worked his way up in the marketing department. "Then it was referred to as corporate sales. Now it's called marketing partnerships."

Working at a recent WNBA game, I thought it was the Bings playing the Life Locks. That's what the front of the jerseys said the team's names were. It was actually the Seattle Storm against the Phoenix Mercury. Everything is available for sponsorship.

"Sports marketing is a much bigger stage now," says Shank. "Many teams package their own media."

Stadium signage, display areas at the games, on-the-court or on-the-field events during time outs, via merchandising giveaway (i.e., T-shirts with logos or free french-fry coupons to exiting fans), vendor concessions (Coke-the official soft drink), Public Address and scoreboard announcements, stadium suites, and radio or TV advertising before, during, and after a game. Literally anything the marketing mind can conceive. Keep a watchful eye for parachuting products falling from the rafters. "Every game is a marketing-filled opportunity," says Shank. "Even timeouts are filled with sponsor-related possibilities."

In the NBA, about 25-percent of a team's revenue source comes from Network TV contracts, international business, and league merchandising. Of a team's remaining 75-percent of proceeds, two-thirds of that originates from season ticket and game ticket sales. The other one-third of a team's local revenue primarily comes from TV and radio ad sales. Depending on the market size of the team, one NBA home game alone equates to approximately one million dollars in revenue. For the playoffs, that figure goes up considerably. That's why revenue generated from playoff games can significantly affect a team's season-long bottom line. If fans want a regular season, sideline, front-row seat, on average they'll pay around $1,000 per seat, even more for some teams than others. You can understand why today's pro teams each employ 200-300 people. With a customer paying that much to attend a game, the fan experience has to be perfect.

If you are interested in selling sports media, the Phoenix Suns have their own in-house advertising sales department, and sell the commercials themselves. This is not necessarily the norm with all pro (or college) franchises. When it comes to broadcast rights, some teams accept a flat fee for the TV or radio rights to cover their games. When a team plays losing ball, the risk then falls on the TV or radio station, and the pressure is on those broadcast companies to recoup their costs with ad revenues. Good luck with that in a challenging economy and a sub-par team. Assuming a team plays well, this can work in your favor, but Welts says, "This arrangement also carries risk."

"Technology has certainly boosted the efforts of sports marketers in measuring the impact of sponsorships at games," adds Shank. "Now we do team surveys to help quantify advertisers' results; we can tell our sponsors what kind of reach and frequency they're achieving. It helps add value and is much more sophisticated."

Through four decades of service, Shank certainly remembers when marketing in sports wasn't so refined. "We had no video, no replays, and no electronic advertising. Marketing then consisted of hanging 10 banners in the rafters of the old Coliseum. It was real basic. The primary goal in the early days was to sell season tickets. We'd have a boy scout and girl scout night," remembers Shank. "Now it's geared towards how we can deliver their message in a unique setting; it's become a fan-affinity thing. Social media has become significant in sports marketing too."

Shank's advice if marketing is the area of sports you want to pursue, "Get an internship. Somehow, someway, get on a team's staff." Current Suns TV broadcaster Tom Leander began his affiliation with the Suns as their ballboy. "Most importantly, learn to write and communicate," says Shank. "You need to be able to think quickly on your feet."

If you have the desire and capability of Showing Them the Money, a sports franchise should manage to have room on their marketing staff for you.

Media Sales

It was once said that broadcasting is called a medium because it's not well done, but selling advertising in association with a professional or collegiate team is one avenue that can be lucrative while still scratching that sports career itch.

Since many professional and collegiate teams sell their broadcast rights to TV or radio networks, nationally and locally, every major city has TV or radio stations that carry sports and require effective media sales people.

As a sales representative for a TV or radio station that carries a team's broadcasts, there can be a lot of perks: tickets to the games your station covers, hospitality suites to entertain clients, and the occasional introduction and photo opportunity with star athletes.

This media alliance with your sports team also provides privileged inroads to advertisers, simply by association. You can offer a connection to the NFL, the NBA, or major league baseball. Other stations cannot. Much like you, advertisers want to be

What it looks like to work in a TV control truck

The switcher has to operate all of this at a split-second notice

The work stations for a Broadcast Associate and his/her crew are very cramped

Camera Operator –
End Zone Position

Being a sports statistician or football spotter provides a great view

In the Seahawk's booth with Steve Raible

Pointing out a stat to long-time Washington Husky announcer Bob Rondeau

Providing hand signals to Steve Raible

A sports career allows you to meet many superstar athletes and celebrities

Joe Namath – Super Bowl III MVP –
my favorite NFL QB as a youth

QB Terry Bradshaw –
Two-time Super Bowl MVP

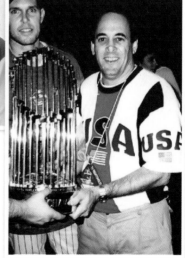

Super Bowl-winning coach Jon Gruden

Holding the 2001 World Series Trophy
with the Diamondbacks' Jay Bell

You'll also meet famous sports announcers

Bob Costas - One of the all-time
great sports announcers

Vin Scully – LA Dodgers announcer
for 62 straight seasons

In the Front Row
with baseball's funny
man Bob Uecker

Ernie Harwell – Hall-of-Fame
Tigers broadcaster

Pat Summerall provided
play-by-play for 16 Super Bowls

NY Knicks great Walt Frazier

Dr J – Julius Erving

NBA Hall-of-Fame
Coach Tom Heinsohn

Joe Morgan won the NL MVP
twice in 1975 and 1976

Twins slugger Harmon Killebrew
hit 573 Home Runs

Fred Lynn was the first to win the AL
Rookie-of-the-Year and MVP in '75

Mark Grace is doused with champagne
after 2001 World Series win

Lou Piniella

Cubs favorite Ron Santo

Phil's slugger Mike Schmidt –
3-time NL MVP hit 548 HR's

Muhammad Ali – the Greatest

Julia Ruth-Stevens –
Babe Ruth's daughter

Bob Feller WWII War hero
led AL in wins 6 times

Gaylord Perry – 314 wins

At the 2011 NBA playoffs
with a familiar face

The new Cowboy Stadium

Cowboy Stadium's video screen stretches 60 yards long

'part of the action' too. Marketing with a professional or collegiate team offers them a branding advantage.

Jessica Webb is a sales manager for Sports 620 KTAR Radio in Phoenix. As a Boston-area native and diehard Red Sox fan, Webb's career path always pointed toward sports. Her early athletic background included being a football manager for her high school team and volunteering for the NFL's "Air It Out" flag football tournament. "I liked the 'tribal' side of the game," said Webb, Webb also worked for the Arizona Diamondbacks during their inaugural 1998 season, interning in their marketing department. This helped her decide early on in her career not to work for a team. "Too many long hours and the compensation was way too low."

Undaunted to still be part of sports, Webb went to work for FOX Sports Arizona TV, selling sports-related advertising for two years. This experience and her sales success opened future doors in media for Webb, with her current position as sales manager for a highly successful sports talk radio station now serving as her ticket to the action.

In electronic media sales, most people either sell radio exclusively, or they stay on the TV side of the fence. There's generally not much crossover. I'm personally in my 26th year of selling radio advertising and really haven't had an itch to try TV sales. In some ways, it's just what you're used to. To me, I relish the creative aspect of the industry, getting to have more influence on cultivating and creating the critical elements of a media campaign. In TV, you wouldn't get to write commercials as I get to do.

When it comes to the Sports Radio format, Webb says there is a level of engagement second to none. "Whether a team is playing well, or losing, people still retain their affinity to teams."

That's the power of the spoken word in radio. Sports radio is a targeted format and provides an advertising access to high-level decision-makers. Part of this is the ego-driven association with sports by the marketing partners. Sports also provide inroads to larger sponsorship dollars not normally available to other media or broadcast formats. If you doubt this, count how many times Budweiser runs a thirty-second commercial during the Super Bowl every year. The current cost for a Super Bowl ad is approximately $3.5 million dollars a pop. That's $116-thousand dollars per second. Depending on which part of the country you live in, the median value of a home is less than 10-percent of this thirty second commercial. By comparison, a Super Bowl TV ad in 1967 sold for $40,000. The average cost of a house in '67 was $24,600. That comparison alone affirms the escalation and command of sports with advertisers.

Webb describes the fun side to selling sports radio as "sizzle, passion, and hospitality. There is a different relationship between the client and us. The fans are more tangible. There are many more marketing possibilities with today's media, too. Besides the traditional play-by-play involvement, there's digital media, with web,

Facebook, texting, and tweeting. You also have the grass-roots, on-site possibilities like a display area at the stadium for fan interaction and vital ties to important cause marketing efforts like Strike Out Breast Cancer fundraisers. That's a lot of tools in the belt to help our marketing partners connect the dots with the fans."

There are other perks and attractions. Players and coaches may attend client events. Advertisers are sometimes flown to road games and accorded sideline passes. "Other formats don't offer this kind of passion, engagement, and results," says Webb. "Not everyone can afford to name the stadium, but an advertiser can still own the brand and feel like they have a vested part of the team. Sports radio excels in providing a return on investment."

In many respects, selling media for Sports TV is very similar to radio. You're still selling the sizzle of association with a professional or collegiate sports team. As Ed Olsen, General Sales Manager for FOX Sports Arizona concurs, your advertising message in conjunction with sports is a big appeal for marketers. For example, if you're sponsoring a certain professional or collegiate team, there's more credibility to say "I'm a Husky" or whoever you call your team.

Olsen has paid his dues to achieve his current position with FOX TV. An Arizona native, he began his media career at a 10-watt music radio station with a dream to be an on-air personality. During college, he was guided to advertising sales. Cox Media was his first destination. "With the proliferation of cable at that time, I thought it would be a better choice than network TV," says Ed. Olsen started as an intern at Cox for a year and then moved along to traffic coordinator (the person who schedules the commercials) and sales assistant. By his third year, he was hired in sales, getting a territory that was 50 miles from Phoenix, a remote area called Casa Grande. Olsen spent a year pounding the pavement there before getting to shorten his commute and start selling in Phoenix for the next five years. Olsen was then promoted to Local Sales Manager, a position he held for six more years.

Olsen now guides his sales team in selling regional sports, including the Arizona Diamondbacks, the Phoenix Suns and the Arizona State Sun Devils. "I sold a lot of sports for Cox while there. My claim to fame was figuring out where to guide certain advertisers to place their commercials. For example, Monday morning on SportsCenter is the best time to be on ESPN in the fall. Sports fans will especially tune in then to see what happened in the NFL the previous day. It's the same thing with college game-day coverage. There is more of a point of emphasis by the fans to watch then." For Fox Arizona TV, their claim to fame is they are the LIVE LOCAL sports provider.

"The key words are live, local and watch," says Olsen. LIVE: The event doesn't get time-shifted; it will get seen when planned. Generally, there's no fast forwarding past your commercial, since most people view a sporting event when it's happening. LOCAL: In the case of many regional networks like FOX, Comcast, etc., they control where you can follow your favorite area teams. WATCH: "Sports is meant to be viewed," says Olsen. "That's the beauty of sports. Sports are inherently 'visual.' You get both audio and video, whereas with radio, you can only hear what's going on. There are some outstanding radio play-by-play announcers who can paint the picture, but would you rather watch a game, or hear it? Radio's mobility serves a great purpose, but if you're at home, you'll choose TV coverage over radio nearly every time." I must admit that I've been known to turn down the TV sound and listen to the radio announcer out of preference for their call of the action.

Olsen adds, "Certain sports translate better on TV than others. Hockey is tough to 'see' through a radio broadcast, football and basketball too. Baseball is probably the best sport radio can describe with its one-on-one matchups between batter and pitcher and the positioning of the runners at any given time. It's easier to 'see' the field.

"TV is also a better consumption environment for advertisers," says Olsen. "Look how much sport has added to TV, instant replay, TV replay reviews at critical moments of a game. Even radio announcers will use a TV monitor to be sure of a call. Televised sports are really a great way of capturing the viewer's attention."

TV Sports coverage is a different animal than network TV. "The selling of sports media requires a passion, for the game and for the team you represent. It's not sold as a commodity. It's more engaging. It sure beats trying to sell advertising on Judge Judy. Sports TV also lends well for association with on-air talent. A Vin Scully-endorsed commercial is a powerful testimonial. Just a commercial within a sports broadcast is an implied endorsement by the team alone; it's response inducing," says Olsen.

For the advertising buyer, Olsen agrees with his radio counterpart, that there is a tendency to respond more readily for sports than general market advertising inquiries.

Many of today's TV shows are now recorded on a digital video recorder (DVR). When viewers get around to watching that show, it's the advertising that gets fast-forwarded through. Not so likely with a sports broadcast.

Sports and Investments

Another money-related occupation associated with sport is the financial planner. With such massive dollars for athletes at stake and relatively short careers available for them to capitalize on, star athletes need economic protection. That's where a Wall Street whiz comes in handy.

Jimmy Walker is President for Walker and Associates, LLC, a highly successful Phoenix-based financial planning institution, but he is much better known for his constant philanthropic efforts.

Like many youths, Walker followed in his father's professional footsteps, selling life insurance policies. He sold his first policy at age 16. Walker also had sports in his blood, playing guard in the mid 1960's at Arizona State University. It was at ASU that a career-impacting relationship began. Walker developed a close bond with one of Arizona State's premier baseball players, a budding star named Reggie Jackson.

Jimmy Walker

When Jackson began his professional career with the Oakland Athletics, Walker sold Reggie a large life insurance policy. This connection led to introductions to many other pro ballplayers and more life insurance policy sales. Living in Phoenix, Walker's impressive and growing client list attracted local pro athletes to secure his financial services. First, Dick Van Arsdale, an original Suns All-Star signed on. Then newly appointed Suns General Manager Jerry Colangelo became a client. Always generous with his time and suggestions, Walker recommended to Colangelo that the expansion Phoenix Suns needed a booster club. Guess who Colangelo assigned to head the project. This was the beginning of a lifelong and mutually beneficial relationship between the two. One success followed another for Walker. In 1975, Walker and Reggie Jackson teamed up to buy a World Team Tennis franchise, calling it the Phoenix Racquets. Jackson soon lost interest, so Walker went it alone. Other renowned owners in Team Tennis included Bob Kraft (who now owns the New England Patriots), and Dr. Jerry Buss (owner of the Los Angeles Lakers). Walker's biggest coup was signing Chris Evert to headline his tennis team. Besides Reggie Jackson, Evert would be just one of several notable celebrities who would soon call Walker their close friend and confidant.

In 1983, Dr. Buss invited Walker to a function where Jimmy was introduced to Sammy Davis, Jr. and Muhammad Ali. It was then that Walker began a life-long friendship with the Champ. Relationships soon to follow included Kareem Abdul Jabbar and Magic Johnson.

In 1994, Walker charitably began a function that has blossomed into a massive fund-raiser. It was that year that the benevolent Fight Night began. Originally, it was set up so that Suns stars Charles Barkley and Dan Majerle would do a mock bout with four-time Jr. Flyweight boxing champion Michael Carbajal to raise donations for charity. The first year raised $180-thousand dollars. Soon, this even became known as Celebrity Fight Night. Regular attendees and close friends of Walker are a who's who of the rich and famous. Donald Trump, Muhammad Ali, Robin Williams, Billy Crystal, Bo Derek, Joe Montana, Barry Manilow, Kevin Costner, Reba McEntire, Rod Stewart, Michael J. Fox, Sharon Stone, and Jim Carrey, just to name a few. That's an all-star team of wealthy supporters. The event now raises $5-7 million dollars annually on behalf of Parkinson's research. Walker also created a support program in association with St. Vincent de Paul called Never Give Up, where celebrity friends donate their time and encouragement to those who are down and out.

Asked what route he might suggest for those interested in connecting with the sports world through financial planning, Walker recommends that you volunteer as an intern for a sports agency like International Management Group (IMG) or Fame. Walker described his professional route as unconventional, doing it the long and hard way. "Many of my relationships became clients because I went the extra mile, not because I went clubbing with them or hung out in the hotel lobby. When a Michael Jordan or Dr. J came to town, I'd have a car waiting for them at their hotel. You develop their trust and a relationship begins. You connect with them more genuinely that way."

Undeniably, Jimmy Walker has grown a solid association with the sports world through his thriving Wealth Management organization. His company represents more than 300 athletes and also a dozen celebrity actors. Walker's personal primary goal in life isn't financial though. Walker has earned his private reward by consistently proving that the more you give, the more you get.

Fund-raising for Athletic Departments

College athletics is certainly big business too. Generating revenue through ticket sales is only one component to keeping an athletic department solvent. TV broadcast rights have certainly made a huge difference to the bottom line; however, resource development to support intercollegiate sports programs through programs aimed at donors is crucial to a university or college's competitive success.

Athletes going through recruitment want to see state-of-the art stadiums and workout facilities. Just a scholarship offer isn't enough to attract the blue-chip prospects. Capital campaigns for new buildings and equipment require major financial support.

That's where your skill comes in. There will be many social events and meetings to promote financial support for the athletic programs. There are phone-a-thons to alumni to cultivate donations.

You'll be creating direct mail pieces, writing ad copy, and producing brochures, fliers, and invitations. Great people-skills, creativity, and excellent speaking and writing abilities will be necessary to succeed in this position.

This department needs people-power for many duties and functions. Interns and volunteers will be most welcome.

Isn't That Tweet – Cyberspace and Sports

Companies are always looking for new revenue streams and the sports industry is no different. Digital economy has become an important line item when budgeting, and the cyber world has become an important public relations tool. In today's ultra-competitive market for the entertainment dollar, anything that will garner the attention of sports fans and translate into increased ticket sales or marketing dollars makes a difference to the bottom line.

That's why online social networking sites have become integral mechanisms in which thousands of sports teams communicate. Blogs, Facebook, Twitter, LinkedIn, Myspace and other social networking tools have become important utensils for sports teams. They allow teams to personalize their relationship with their fans and consumers, while enhancing public image. It has also become a publicity challenge.

Because athletes are such public figures, occasional poor judgment can translate into public relations nightmares. How can you regulate these technologies? What legal liabilities may result? What about confidentiality?

Some colleges have discussed banning social networking sites altogether. So far, none of the major conferences have pulled the trigger. Out of concern for its image, the NBA and WNBA have instituted policies that restrict players and team personnel from using cell phones from two hours before a game to two hours after a game. Practices, meetings, and other team events, are left to the discretion of the individual teams.

Major League Baseball seems the most tolerant of the three major U.S. sports leagues. MLB has an iPhone application that has social media tools, and also maintains an active Twitter account. A number of players tweet regularly and the MLB actively promotes those players' Twitter accounts on its own website.

Real time reporting by the media is another matter. MLB does its best to restrict in-game reporting. This applies to blog posts, cell phone pictures and everything in between. Media can post no more than seven photographs from any game and audio/video is limited to two minutes with no streaming. No photo galleries allowed.

As part of its policing policies, the NFL (sometimes referred to as the No Fun League), has prohibited players, coaches, team personnel, and officials from any social media activity from 90 minutes before kickoff until 90 minutes after the game is over. Not even during halftime. NFL game officials and the officiating departments are prohibited from using social media at any time. Longstanding policies prohibiting play-by-play descriptions of NFL games in progress apply fully to Twitter and other social media platforms. Internet sites may not post detailed information that includes play-by-play during a game.

So what's next? Is the league going to crack down on the cheerleaders because the way they're swinging their pom poms might hand-signal the action? Is the way a beer vendor holds up his beverage tipping off a play? Maybe there will be a ban on licorice waving. No more twirling of the Terrible Towel? Sorry Pittsburgh Steeler fans; outlawed. No Cheese Heads allowed in Packer-land; you might be transmitting something from it.

Clearly, the NFL's social media policy is to protect its lucrative media contracts, particularly TV. DirecTV's NFL Sunday Ticket wouldn't control the same demand if the game's action was on Ustream. The media can't tweet the action, but what about Joe Fan? They can tweet to their heart's content. Do the media react by hiring citizen sports reporters from the stands? There's no way that the NFL will be able to control everything.

Instead, sports should be embracing the opportunities of social media as the players have, as long as the content isn't detrimental to the player, team or league's reputation or image. Teams don't need to react as if their corporate secrets are being exposed. To get star players to help interact with tens of thousands of fans on a nearly daily basis is huge. This social media 'thing' creates camaraderie. Usually, players want to be paid for any community or fan outreach. Now, however there's a powerful tool for organizations to interact directly with fans. As long as it's not bad PR, it further connects the teams with the fans. That can hopefully result in goodwill and enthusiasm. Teams need to let their prime assets, the players, provide an assist, rather than muzzle them. How better to enhance their fan base?

Some NFL teams are reportedly also using online information to keep a watchful eye on current and prospective players. Envision a Trojan Horse, a ghost profile if you will. Some teams are using the tactic of creating counterfeit profiles to link to Facebook and MySpace pages of potential draft picks. This investigative draft process offers teams a wealth of current information. Before social networking sites, teams had to rely upon feedback from college coaches regarding the character of a player. Always on the lookout for anything inflammatory, teams now use a network profile to aid background checks. It's become an important part of a team's process on making a final call on whether to draft players. They view it as an assist to possibly save them from making a big and expensive draft mistake.

Players need to be on the constant lookout for the general public, too. Whenever sports celebrities are out and about, cell phone cameras are a click away from sending their pictures to friends or posting them on blogs or networking sites. There's no escaping the public eye. Information leakage can be detrimental. 'Big Brother' is indeed watching.

Golden State Warriors President Rick Welts has been a close participant in the NBA's progression in sports media and marketing since the mid 1970's. As the Seattle SuperSonics' PR Director then, and a top executive and promotion guru for the NBA league office for 17 years, he has keenly observed and strongly contributed to the marketing and communication evolution in sports for more than thirty-five years. Credit Welts as the brainchild for All-Star Weekend in the NBA, involving the ever-popular 3-point competition and the slam dunk contest.

What does Welts think about today's player and media interaction with the fans versus 35 years ago? "Back then, I only had to deal with four area newspapers covering our Sonics games. There were so few media voices embracing the NBA in 1975. It was much easier to craft our team's identity then. Shaping our image now is so much more difficult with all the extensive media and fan scrutiny we get."

So where do you draw the line with the test that social media offers? On an NBA ticket, it states: No reproduction. But who owns the statistics data? "All the leagues will battle to retain control of this intellectual property; the video and audio, the statistics, and the photography," says Welts. Internationally, there are even different laws. What regulations apply when there's intercontinental competition? They don't govern our rules. We don't control theirs. "It's a moving target," he says.

The target also moves within the league. "The NBA is still trying to walk versus run first in sorting out the new media," Welts went on to say. "Teams are still wrestling with what the geographical limitation should be. The Los Angeles Lakers can't be promoting themselves within Phoenix, or visa-versa. What is the best business model? Where can web-ads appear? You can only regulate or contain it so far. From a revenue perspective, the NBA is still trying to figure that out, too. How does it help sell tickets? What are the sponsorship possibilities? Even Facebook hasn't figured out how to best monetize what they've got."

"Sports are highly scrutinized," he added. "Every hiccup that happens, all the powerful personalities; then there's a human factor to be considered. Yet, the implications and risks of this new media can't involve 'bad' news. The league and teams deserve to protect their brand and reputation."

So who controls what? Welts explains that, "a player has no right to a team's image or uniform, but there is some division between players and their team. Teams cannot dictate or restrict a player's persona outside his uniform." Upon arrival in Phoenix, "Shaquille O'Neal was the first noteworthy player to tweet to the public," Welts remembers.

I think it's only a matter of time before future collective bargaining agreements among players and their respective leagues more extensively define the do's and the don'ts of today's new and growing method of sports communication.

In an effort to level the competitive playing field, the NFL uses different footballs during the course of the game. This way, there's no funny business by the home team about the football put in play.

Each team on offense provides their own game balls (inflated to 14-15 oz.). The regulations go a step further. When there is a going to be a punt or field-goal attempt, yet another ball provided by the team on offense is put into use. It is even marked with a "K," so the officials can recognize it's the appropriately approved football for kicking situations only.

Chapter 9

Game Day Operations

There are a number of sports-related jobs that can put you in or near the action. These are not full-time careers, rather free-lance duties required for game-day operations. Here's a look at a number of key positions that might satisfy your sports itch.

Public Address Announcer

The Public Address Announcer is the game's emcee. The PA will introduce the team's starting lineup and announce official's calls and player substitutions.

In football, you'll also keep the crowd abreast of the current down and distance. Most PA announcers are hired on a part-time basis, and some work in multiple stadiums.

During basketball games, this is a great front-row seat. The PA is the game's maestro with everything scripted, right down to the national anthem and player introductions. They'll also emcee on-field or on-court entertainment and promotions.

I was once paid $6.00 per game to be the PA announcer for the Walla Walla Padres Class A team, all this for about four hours work. Even in 1982, $1.50 an hour was pathetic pay. Of course, that was 30 years ago. Actually, being a PA announcer for all sports is a pretty good position. Your voice is heard throughout the whole stadium.

Bob Sheppard recently passed away at the age of 99, just a couple days before iconic Yankee owner, George Steinbrenner, died. Sheppard was the stadium voice for the New York Yankees for 56 years, starting in 1951. "Now batting for the New York Yankees, Mickey Mantle!" Sheppard received national recognition when he passed, and he shared the spotlight with Steinbrenner, when both were remembered on the same evening at Yankee Stadium. A recording of Sheppard's voice will continue to be used to introduce Derek Jeter before his at-bats for as long as Jeter is a Yankee.

The First and Ten Guy

This football broadcast position is great—and easy, depending on which TV network you're working for. The duty of this person is to determine where that imaginary yellow line shows up on the field that gives the viewer a perspective where the first down line is. CBS uses a system called PVI, which stands for Princeton Video Imaging, the company that developed it. With CBS, you're hired as a freelancer to sit in the TV booth with the national announcers, with a mid-field view from the press box. Your job is to relay (via a headset) back to New York where to place that electronic line where the first down chain is spotted. Then you tell them where the line of scrimmage is after each play. "Left 42 – 2nd down." "Right 20 – 1st and ten." That's it! Your shining moment comes when there's a crucial measurement for a first down. You get paid around $125 to watch the game. Sweet!

FOX TV uses a different system called Sportvision. It accomplishes the same technological enhancement; however, FOX manages the system from inside the control truck with their vantage point coming from a tiny color TV monitor. With Sportvision, no person is necessary inside the press box to relay the information, essentially eliminating the position that CBS utilizes. Interestingly, FOX TV ends up paying far more to accomplish the same task. Where CBS hires a local freelancer to relay the information back to New York, FOX travels a person from city to city each week to handle this duty and pays $300 to $400 daily over three days. Their Sportvision person also gets housed in a luxury hotel, given a $50 daily per diem, and gets plane fare covered too. The drawback to that that position might be that this person is sitting in a control truck in the bowels of the stadium. You may as well be watching the game in a cave. I prefer to be up in the press box, feeling the action of the game.

Orange Sleeves Guy

If you look closely along the sidelines of a football game, you'll also see a person with long orange sleeves that extend to his elbows. This is not because this person is a Broncos fan. This person is the eyes and ears for the TV producer in the broadcast control truck. The orange sleeves guy works in conjunction with the network broadcasting the game, communicates with game officials when there is a TV timeout, and also tells the producer how much time is left, so they know when to finish a commercial and return to the game broadcast. The orange sleeves guy accomplishes all this by working in conjunction with the Green Hat guy. Both positions are strategically situated at the 25-yard line of the home team, so the referee knows exactly where to locate them.

Green Hat

The Green Hat position is the go-between with the NFL and the officials on the field. Each team has one, so there are only 32 NFL Green Hat positions in the country. They are essentially a game coordinator beside the field. In the last two minutes of each half, the up-in-the-booth referee can call for a replay without an on-field challenge being required. The Green Hat will communicate this to the on-field head official. Since the TV network provides video and audio for replay purposes, the Green Hat is also communicating with them too.

The Green Hat also controls TV commercials and the flow of the game. They make sure all commercials run and that the network doesn't abuse commercial breaks. There are only five commercial breaks per quarter and 20 for the game. The length of the commercial breaks is 1:50, and is timed with a stop watch. Sometimes there might be a couple times a game where the network gets a 10-second extension. The purpose is to ideally keep the length of the game to three hours. A game delay because of injury, does not mean the network gets additional commercial time.

The Green Hat works for the NFL, and gets paid $25 an hour. It's tough to get this position unless you know someone.

Sideline Chains

This person needs to be ready to avoid flying football players during sideline tackles. After a kickoff, you'll stand on the sideline holding the flagstick where the first down is commencing. Another person will stand where the first down destination is. Yet another person holds the flagstick where each down is spotted. Slowly but surely, you'll make your way down the field as the offense heads towards the end zone, unless the defense is having a good series and is moving the line of scrimmage backwards. Either way, stay alert or a lineman might be piling through you like a 330-pound bowling ball, along with four of his other NFL friends during a sideline gang tackle. You might want to be sure to have good health insurance if you land this job.

NFL Uniform Inspector

There is a certain aesthetic appearance the National Football League requires its teams to adhere to. As such, the NFL is not only particular about its team's uniforms, but their player's look of uniformity, too.

On any given game day, every home team will provide a team representative whose responsibility is to make sure that no player deviates from league policy regarding their dress code.

Greg Boyd is one of only 32 people who serve as an NFL Uniform Inspector or, as the players call them, the fashion police. Greg is certainly familiar with the player's point of view, having been a defensive end in the NFL for nine years. Boyd's specialty was as a stellar designated pass rusher achieving a career-high 10 sacks in 1980.

Boyd's sports career didn't end when he retired from the NFL in 1984. He went on to become a professional wrestler for seven years adorning the International Wrestling Association heavyweight belt for two years.

Boyd has spent the past 15 years as the NFL Uniform Inspector in Denver. "It's all about team image and NFL licensing on game day," says Boyd. "The NFL keeps a strict eye on everything, even what a player wears during a post-game TV interview. There can be no look of negativity or criminality." For TV interviews, the player must be in team-issued (Reebok) licensed apparel, or in street clothes.

Players have to be compliant in what helmets they wear (Riddell), their chin straps have to be white and snapped, and breathe-rite strips have to be white and contain no writing on them. Jerseys must be tucked in and the pants must cover the knee. The socks must have a certain look and color too. From the bend of the knee to the bottom of the calf, the socks must be team colors. From the calf to the shoe, the remaining color of the socks is all white. Gloves must be club-issued black or white (Under Armour brand). A team color accent on the gloves is allowed. There can be no individual look that disrupts the presentation.

Boyd works with a checklist that has every player's number noted. He'll spend the course of the game roaming both sidelines looking for offenders or in the press box with a pair of binoculars. "Some players will seek me out to ask if they're OK," says Boyd. "If a player is not in conformity to the uniform rules, they will get fined." The fine is exponentially more if the player is a repeat offender. Boyd could not disclose the fine amount.

The individual that serves as an NFL fashion cop is typically a player alumni of that club.

Official Stats Crew

Depending on which sport, there are usually several positions within an Official stats crew. Baseball has just one official scorer. Whether it's a hit, an error, a wild pitch, what have you, this person's call is gospel. Imagine having to make a crucial call that might determine a no-hitter or a perfect game.

John Olson heads both football and basketball official stats crews in Phoenix with mostly the same people. Olson has been doing this since the 1960's. He also helped form the original stat crew for Jerry Colangelo's expansion Phoenix Suns in 1968.

Olson points out that sports statistics involve five distinct stages:

- Input of the raw data based on the results of the action

- Calculation of the raw data

- Output of the data

- Duplication of the output

- Distribution to various outlets (media, broadcasters, etc.)

The Official Stat crew for a college football game is composed of:

- Computer Input – This person records the plays in a computer.

- A Caller – They determine what the play is about. Was it a 2-yard rush or 3?

- A Caller Recorder – This person writes down plays as they happen, in case the computer input gets bogged down, and they need to catch up later.

- Defensive Caller – This person reports defensive action, such as tackled by ..., sacked by..., intercepted by....

- Manual Statistician – This person keeps manual statistics in case of electronic failure.

- Participation – They note who started and who didn't, then who played and who didn't.

The Official Stat crew in the NFL includes one other position: Audit – this is a second computer position used only for review and correcting plays.

For basketball, positions have somewhat changed since the advent of the stats computer in the late-1980's. In a professional basketball game (NBA), there are seven key positions that comprise the official stats crew. Three people handle what's called IDS input. This is essentially electronic input of the game's statistics as they happen. They include everything you would see in a box score and more, like points, rebounds, assists, minutes, shots, etc., from a team and individual perspective for both the home and visiting teams. During the course of the game, this information is fed live to stat computers provided for visiting broadcast media along the press table. The TV control trucks receive this computer feed too. It is from this information and/or the in-the-stadium statisticians they've hired (official and talent stats people) that the graphics that get shown on your TV screen are formulated. For example, a player is stepping to the foul line, and the director of the broadcast wants to graphically show how many points and rebounds that player has to this moment (or some other pertinent stat). Via their computer feed, everyone has live up-to-date information for reference, EXCEPT when the computers go down. And this will happen. That's why I've always kept stats manually and used the stat monitor as my backup for information. The flip-side of this is that radio broadcasters have come to use stat monitors rather than statisticians. They might save $50 to $75 dollars a game, but they're stuck when the computer goes down. Good statisticians don't need the computer to survive. Average statisticians use it as a crutch, thinking they're doing their job by simply reading the stat monitor. They are in trouble when the computer goes on the fritz.

The stats computer misses a number of key elements of the game, too, certainly the stats that the TV crew seems to appreciate. Like scoring runs and when they started (i.e., the Suns are on an 18-4 run over the last 3:43) or how many shots a team has made or missed in a row.

The other key positions of the official stats crew in basketball are:

Official Scorer – What gets noted in this scorebook is gospel: Points, fouls, time-outs. If there is a discrepancy, the refs go to this person. Right or wrong, this is official.

Game Clock – This position can get dicey if it's down to the last second or two in a close game. Before the early 2000's, the game clock was strictly triggered by the person at the switch. Now, the human element has been supplemented. This was implemented by the NBA, in part to avoid the home team from showing any favoritism. Now, a game clock can be triggered by not only the game clock operator, but the officials too. Throughout the game, a referee's whistle can electronically stop the clock via a microphone on the shirt. A computer tells you if the ref or clock operator stopped the clock. Also, the refs now wear bell packs, with a switch that can start the clock. So at the closing moments of a tight game, there are now four people who can influence when the game clock commences. When it comes to the NBA playoffs, a stadium will be assigned a visiting clock operator from another NBA city. Usually it's a clock guy from a non-playoff team.

Shot Clock (the 24-second clock) – This is an especially crucial position when every late possession might mean the difference of a win or loss. Imagine if a team loses because they didn't get a shot off in time before the 24-second clock expires. Then this team misses the playoffs by just one game. Each home playoff game means about $1-million dollars in revenue to that team.

Scoreboard – Its accuracy is extremely important, especially when a shot is a three-pointer or two. In conjunction with the referees, it's also the official scorekeeper's job to be sure the scoreboard is correct. Other members of the official stats crew keep an eye on this too.

These front-row floor positions all work together to communicate with the referees when it comes to mandatory time-outs and substitutions.

The Official Stats crew always has alternates. Usually two or three for the data input positions (IDS), and a few extras for the on-floor positions. They must be league-approved with exams required prior to each season to make sure they're up-to-date on rules.

Official Timer

In Baseball, there is no time clock. The umpire is required to keep the game moving, such as when a manager or pitching coach visits the mound to strategize with his pitcher and infielders. Many times, the manager might be stalling to allow his bullpen pitcher time to warm up, so the ump makes his customary stroll to the mound to say "let's go."

For Basketball and Football, the clock operator is an important member of the officiating crew and game administration. Perhaps you've observed the Head Referee on the football field announce to the crowd, "Please reset the clock to 6:54." In basketball, the refs will just relay that along the press table. For basketball, there is also the 24-second shot clock operator, who is in ongoing visual contact with the referees throughout the game. If a pass gets tipped away, but maybe there wasn't a clear change of possession, it's up to the 24-second clock operator to decide whether to reset. On the court, the refs will use hand signals to sometimes affirm or override the decision of the 24-second clock operator.

The 24-second shot clock operator needs to have 100-percent focus. A change of possession could happen at any time. Did the last shot hit the rim, necessitating a reset? This I learned from experience. The SuperSonics asked me to man this position a couple times. One game was in the Tacoma Dome between Seattle and Don Nelson's Golden State Warriors. The ball was near mid court, so a shot wasn't about to happen. Someone on press row asked me a question, and I took my eyes off the action for a split second. I turned around and the ball was loose. I knee-jerked, and reset the 24-second clock. Ooops. No change of possession. The whistle blew and the referees, Don Nelson, and Sonics coach Bernie Bickerstaff were all walking toward me. The game had stopped and I was suddenly center stage. It felt like the whole stadium was glaring at me. The refs and coaches were cordial, but I felt like an idiot. In another game, I determined that a shot by the visiting team grazed the rim and I hit reset. Bernie Bickerstaff was furious. If looks could only kill! I was employed by the home team. How could I give the enemy another 24 seconds? Bernie looked at me like I was Benedict Arnold. At the next home game, a Sonics assistant coach approached me and said they reviewed film after the game. They said I clearly blew the call.

Being a 24-second clock operator will definitely put you into the front row and part of the action.

I T (Information Technology) Expert
Network Manager

Sometimes in the sports world, MVP's have the initials "I.T." If you're a computer expert with a passion for sports, there is a place and need for you. When there is a communication breakdown, be it the scoreboard malfunctioning during a special presentation, or when critical emails don't go through, the IT person is an invaluable member of the team.

IT covers an extensive array of areas, including computer processes, software, and hardware - essentially anything that renders data in a visual format.

In the world of sports, where rendering data, i.e., statistics and storylines, is imperative, computer systems going on the injured list is not an option. The game must go on. If you can install applications, design computer networks and information databases, and administer entire systems, teams may have a place for you in their lineup.

This is no longer a job that just requires keeping personal computers functioning properly. The responsibilities continue to spread. Michael McDonald has worked in the NBA for 16 years now. He is one of three IT experts on staff keeping nearly 180 people's communication tools from going on IR. McDonald says his job "entails everything and you never know from day to day what challenges you'll face. There're always a lot of help-desk issues."

McDonald got his early training from his dad, but like many, always had a passion for sports. A job placement agency called Sports Careers gave him an internship. Interestingly but not surprisingly, Sports Careers is owned by JD and Properties, owned by Jerry Colangelo. McDonald didn't start his sports career as an IT tech, though. As most sports enthusiasts do, he started simply by getting his foot in the door. Willing to do anything, McDonald took an arena job as suite attendant, a fancy name for an usher. The pay was $7.50 an hour. After one season, he steered his sports dreams through the ticket department. After a couple more years, McDonald caught a break and got hired in the IT department.

This is more than an 8 to 5 job. Besides being at the ready during the business day, he's required to be at all events at US Airways Center, just in case. This includes the Suns, the Mercury (WNBA), the Rattlers (Arena football), and numerous concerts. Entry-level pay is around $45 - $50 thousand a year. Emergencies can arise at any time. The league's official stats go into a data base. Breakdown is not an option, since the NBA sells this information to ESPN for their sports ticker. Another malfunction could be a sports writer's computer dying during the game.

Even with a required college degree, McDonald says "nothing can prepare you for our environment except on-the-job training." His best advice, "Do what you have to do. Be flexible and take chances. Stay with it and don't give up. Up to 200 people typically apply, so get your foot in the door to get noticed, because most companies hire from within. Volunteer for free if you have to. Go to the sports information office at your university and submit an application."

Stadium Manager

For this important position, you're essentially the ultimate sports landlord, and there's never a typical or predictable day.

This person is responsible for overseeing everything that goes on in a sports facility. Since many venues serve a multiple purpose, hosting concerts and other business events for as many nights and/or days possible, this individual is probably pulling late-night responsibilities most days of the week.

Your staff includes security, groundskeepers, electricians, ticket-takers, ushers, suite hosts, and concessionaires. Your interaction will include coordination with the marketing department to make sure pre-game and during-game promotions come off without a hitch.

If your facility is outdoors, there will be lawn service to manage. If there's inclement weather, you might have to get snow removed to make the playing surface functional or the stands useable. If issues arise, tag – you're it! It's your job to make sure the facility is maintained in good working condition and presentable.

Although he is far more famous for his professional exploits on a basketball court, these days former Suns superstar Alvan Adams feels more at home managing a multi-purpose stadium. Growing up in Oklahoma City, Adams was always interested in architecture. Thing is, Adams was too talented and tall to disregard his destiny as a basketball star. As a six-foot-nine All-American out of Oklahoma, Adams was a first round, fourth-overall draft choice of the Phoenix Suns in 1975. During his first NBA season, Adams garnered Rookie-of-the-Year honors and, along with Paul Westphal, led the Suns to an epic 1976 Finals matchup against the Boston Celtics. His decorated pro career lasted until 1988, culminating in having his #33 jersey retired by the team.

At a post-playing career crossroads that many pro athletes eventually have to face, Adams had to figure out what to do after basketball. Around this time, General Manager Jerry Colangelo had put together a financial group to purchase the Suns. Part of his modified direction for the team included a new stadium. Colangelo reached out to Adams to help develop and design the new stadium's locker room. As a recently retired player, Adams had a first-hand perspective on what worked and what didn't work for coach and player comfort and functionality. "I experienced some really bad locker rooms in the NBA," Adams recalled. "The old Boston Garden only had three shower heads, and two of them didn't even work. To compound that, the shower heads were installed at a standard height, not exactly conducive for tall guys."

It was simple insight like this that made Adams a valuable member of his new architecture team. "I developed higher shower heads and recommended more space between them. Where would the trainer's room be most functional? How much distance should there be from the lockers to the coach's chalk board. Is there space for a player to stretch his hamstrings on the locker room floor? It needed to be close enough to see strategy but far enough away to have room and comfort. Thinking spatially, I helped design every dimension."

The stadium opened in 1992. Since then, Adams has evolved into the role of Vice President of Facility Management, which entails just about everything you can imagine. Putting it simply, Adams says, "My job is to make sure the building is ready for everything it's supposed to be ready for."

It's a potpourri of duties. "You have to make sure the basketball rim is exactly ten-feet high, that the chairs are properly set, and that the building is properly staffed for events." There are about 180 ticketed events yearly, which equates to nearly every other night on average something is going on that Adams is responsible for.

He is in charge of ticket takers for events that range from pro basketball to arena football to concerts and other specialized public functions. Where he used to "clean the glass" for the Suns, he is now responsible for actual maintenance, dealing with engineers and the custodial crew. Guest relations and the parking garage staff report to him too.

When Bank One Ballpark opened in 1998 for the Arizona Diamondbacks, it included Adams' contribution, too, as did the prestigious Phoenix concert venue, the Dodge Theatre. Adams had now gone full circle to his original career aspirations. He was designing buildings. Future projects will include renovating the suites. Not a day goes by which doesn't include Adams' involvement. Nine months out, he's already working on the following year's budget for the stadium.

If all this organizational responsibility sounds like your thing, there are stadiums around the country that might utilize your skills. Just expect the unexpected when you report for work.

Groundskeeper

Imagine an occupation where you're part weatherman, part pharmacist, and part dietician. That's what a stadium groundskeeper is expected to be.

The head groundskeepers at the stadiums have many colorful nicknames. The Sultans of Sod. The Sodfather. Custodians of the Carpet. The Tenth Man.

Without these facilitators of the fertilizer, the tacklers of turf, the playing surface of your stadium would get pretty battered, especially after a football game where the field gets chewed up. The groundskeeper is always looking to make the playing surface look like a pool table. Since so many stadiums' playing surfaces are synthetic now, the duties have somewhat changed.

A baseball groundskeeper works with the team managers and the facilities managers while performing a variety of skilled tasks in connection with the year-round maintenance of stadium fields. This includes all aspects of keeping the diamond, infield, and outfield in top-notch condition regardless of what curve balls Mother Nature throws them.

Groundskeepers answer to the ballplayers as well, playing an integral role in keeping them safe from injury. Six of the nine defensive players stand on dirt, so it needs to be smoothed over just right. A bad hop can create terrible consequences. It's said that eighty percent of the game is played in the dirt. The infield is high maintenance and has to have the right amount of moisture.

Most groundskeepers hire their own staff and are responsible for training them. Typical equipment includes chemical applicators, irrigation systems, and aerators. Turf maintenance includes growing, mowing, cultivating, and fertilizing. If you work at Chicago's historical Wrigley Field, you might also deal with the pruning of their ivy-covered outfield walls, along with applying fungicides, herbicides and any another 'cides' you can think of. Some stadiums are decorated with shrubbery of various kinds, so you cannot have a black thumb. Note that there are federal, state, and local regulations with regards to the application of fertilizers, herbicides, or pesticides.

With baseball, you'll also mark the foul lines and batter's box, set bases and home plate in proper alignment, and construct the pitcher's mound to proper dimensions prior to the game. Just because the first pitch has been thrown, doesn't mean the grounds crew can then take a break. They may be asked to quickly repair the field during the game to keep the playing surface safe. It's imperative that the field is kept flat and free from any surface imperfections to avoid hazards for the players. One injury could mean the end to a multi-million dollar career so the stakes can be high. They are constantly scanning and dragging the field during the game for blemishes.

Cunning baseball managers have historically used groundskeepers to bend the rules. Some groundskeepers have become famous for grooming their stadium's field to the advantage of the home team. Emil Bossard was legendary as a groundskeeper for the Cleveland Indians in the 1920's. When the despised Yankees and Babe Ruth came to town, Bossard drew the batter's box a few inches closer to the pitching mound, lessening the Sultan of Swat's reaction time against Cleveland's pitchers. Another noted Bossard ploy was to adjust the bullpen mound three inches higher than the game mound. Another strategy for a visiting team that likes to bunt a lot, the baselines could be doctored to make the ball more likely to roll foul or fair.

The grass needs to be as flat as a buzz cut. A choppy outfield can result in a ball bouncing the wrong way or a player incurring an injury. Another tactic by some groundskeepers (with unofficial encouragement from their managers) is to allow the grass to grow a little taller for certain teams, hoping to slow down a few ground balls for their infielders.

Major League Baseball does its best to prevent a team from gaining a competitive advantage by checking each ballpark three times a year. It's sort of like drug testing, with two visits coming unannounced.

A typical day at the ballpark requires a crew of about 18 workers. You'll arrive about twelve hours before the first pitch and probably still be there an hour after the last out.

Many of the duties for a football field are the same, except you'll erect goal posts, measure and mark the yard lines, set up player benches, and set up communication devices and head sets for the coaches and game officials.

After enduring a day as a member of a grounds-keeping crew, being asked to mow the lawn when you were a kid will no longer seem like a punishing memory. This is one job where the grass really is greener.

Cheerleaders

There is a great deal of competition for this very visible position with every football and basketball team utilizing these performers. You'll have to audition against hundreds of applicants. If you make the squad, you'll have four-hour practices two or three times a week. Physical conditioning is a must.

With the visibility that comes with the job, some cheerleaders have gone on to fame and fortune. Paula Abdul was once a Laker girl. Others become actresses, TV celebrities, reality show participants, singers, or models.

Earnings are very low. You're likely doing this for exposure and love of sports. Training and experience in dance is a must. This is a position with a short lifespan and constant turnover.

Team Mascot

If you're not shy, are somewhat athletic, can entertain and dance, and don't mind sweating up a storm inside a goofy, 20-pound, boiling-hot outfit for hours at a time, being a sports mascot might be for you.

Team mascots have been associated with athletic competition nearly from the beginning of sports. With many teams nicknamed after wild animals, live beasts were often used to patrol the sidelines. But having lions and tigers and bears (oh my), proved dangerous for those fans attending the games. Even so, many collegiate teams still have a live mascot motivating the fans.

This is a physically demanding position and sometimes dangerous. With all the wild shenanigans pro mascots do to one-up each other, a broken limb does occasionally happen. The Mariner Moose once fractured his ankle riding a juiced-up quad around the Kingdome after it crashed into the outfield wall. The high-flying Phoenix Gorilla has broken his ankle (I assume it's a he), doing his crowd-pleasing slam dunks. In 1995, Wild Wing, the mascot for the Anaheim Mighty Ducks, nearly became a cooked goose while attempting to jump off a trampoline and over a wall of fire before the start of a hockey game. Unfortunately, his skate got stuck in the trampoline and poor Wild Wing caught on fire!

The most famous and financially successful crowd pleaser was the Chicken, formerly calling San Diego his home nest. The Chicken began flapping his antics in 1977 and makes appearances throughout the country.

The Gorilla earned his job when attending a Suns game in 1980 as an Eastern Onion singing telegram messenger. Security invited the Gorilla onto the court, where the Gorilla proceeded to put on an entertaining show for the rest of the basketball fans. His antics became such an instant hit with the crowd, the Suns hired him. The Gorilla is now a charter member of the Mascot Hall of Fame, inducted in 2005. Other initial 'team' inductees included the Phillie Phanatic, Mr. Met (the original MLB mascot), and Slider of the Indians.

There are four major league teams that still do not have a mascot: the New York Yankees, the Chicago Cubs, the Los Angeles Dodgers, and the Los Angeles Angels of Anaheim (although the Halos do have the rally monkey, a stuffed primate souvenir fans wave to get the team revved up). You get an A if you can name the only two teams with human mascots in North American sports. They are the Minnesota Vikings and the Boston Celtics (with Lucky).

Because the position sometimes requires acrobatic ability, having a gymnastic background is a plus. There are even some schools that offer training to people interested in starting a career as a mascot.

This occupation is a limited fraternity. If you figure there are only 1,100 colleges across the U.S. and about 300 professional franchises, that's slim pickings for an abbreviated career.

Usher

Ushers have always had a fond place in my heart, because if not for the Seattle Coliseum ushers letting me sneak down to the better seats as a kid, I might never have become involved in sports.

Normally, as an usher, your job is to keep people from standing in the aisles, going where they shouldn't go and from sitting in the wrong section, and also to keep an eye for unruly fans. Expect the occasional obscenity. If you're working at a baseball or football stadium, you'll also deal with Mother Nature's mess. An usher at a football game is sort of like being a postal worker, regardless of the weather your job must go on. The majority of stadiums are not domed. Freezing rain, snowy seats, and chill in December are as expected as taxes due in April.

One good thing about this position is that there are a large number of ushers needed at every stadium throughout the country. Occasionally, you even get to catch part of the action.

Vendor at the Stadium

Being a vendor at sporting events is a job that doesn't pay much money, but at least you're in the stadium. Whether you're a steward of sodas, the baron of beer, or a passer of peanuts or popcorn, you're always getting yelled at. It's either "Hey beer man," or it's "hot dog guy, sit down; you're blocking my view."

This is a job that requires skill, physical stamina and some zest. With a lot of pizzazz, you can become a celebrity. Growing up in Seattle, I had the pleasure of watching the evolution of two people who became noteworthy stadium celebrities.

Bill Scott was better known as "Bill the Beer Man." During the 1970's, 80's and early 90's, if you went to a Seahawks or Mariners game in Seattle, you couldn't help but get an earful of Bill Scott's famous shout-out to the fans: "Freeeze your teeth and give your tongue a sleigh ride." Bill wasn't just a vendor though. He was more of a cheerleader at the Kingdome, or as he called it, "a conductor of synergy."

The Beer Man's first sporting event was when Pele played an exhibition soccer game on April 9, 1976, in front of a sell-out crowd. Scott got year-round opportunity with the Sonics, Seahawks, and Sounders (North American Soccer League), calling the Kingdome home.

Scott always hawked beer, but in 1981, he also embarked on his cheerleading career and boy could he rev up a crowd. If the home team was playing flat, "Bill the Beer Man" would turn the crowd into a volcanic eruption. Seattle was already famous for inventing the wave. Scott would incite sections into competing across the stadium. It was like a ping pong reaction until you couldn't hear yourself think. His one-of-a-kind style endeared him to thousands of fans, and the fans became his addiction. Bill "the Beer Man" Scott didn't get wealthy while selling suds and serenading the crowd, but he sure enriched the experience for those who cheered Seattle sports.

Another Seattle-vending celebrity was the beloved Rick Kaminski, better known as "The Peanut Man." Sadly, Kaminski passed away in July, 2011. Kaminski had such a legion of fans, the Mariners actually recognized Kaminski's legacy by honoring him at Safeco Field.

At his peak, this patriarch of peanut vending could hurl goobers at 72 MPH, that according to a Mariners scout who actually clocked him with a radar gun. The Peanut Man's accuracy was uncanny. His repertoire included the over-the-head heave, the long hook shot, the football pass, and the behind-the-back line-drive. If you ordered a bag from Rick, you didn't dare take your peepers off the peanuts.

Rick could hurl a bag of peanuts across an entire section at a stadium and hit his intended target right on the money - throwing behind his back!

Kaminski actually warmed up before a game in his own private bullpen. His ritual included stretching and tossing about 30 bags at a target. In 1976, peanuts cost 45-cents. They're about $4.00 now, and the Peanut Man typically sold 200 to 300 bags in one afternoon.

Photo on left: Author switching roles with famous Seattle peanut vendor Rick Kaminski.

Hot dogs have seemingly always been associated with sports, but particularly baseball. According to the National Hot Dog and Sausage Council, a vendor's hot dog bin weighs about 40 pounds fully loaded. Imagine toting that 40-pound bin up and down stadium stairs for three hours. A vendor will typically cover four to five miles per game. And referees thought they got a workout. All officials have to carry is a whistle.

Since a vendor works on commissions and tips, they also have to move fast. A typical Daytona 500 crowd will consume about 10,000 pounds of wienies. Thankfully for the hot dog hawkers and other food vendors, you have a captured crowd. Legend has it Babe Ruth once consumed 12 hot dogs and eight bottles of soda between games of a doubleheader. In a poll, the Babe was also voted most likely to win a hot dog eating contest among current and former players. John Kruk came in second in the vote and Tommy Lasorda third.

If you've ever wondered why beer vendors remove the cap from the bottle before serving you, there are a few reasons. It forces the consumer to drink the beer before leaving the stadium; the stadium wants consumption on the premises only; and it also eliminates the possibility of a potential projectile weapon out of the hands of drunks.

Things to consider if you seek this kind of employment, it's seasonal and the job doesn't shell out much money unless you can sell peanuts with pizzazz.

Ticket Sales Come in Many Forms

The ticket department keeps track of all seats sold and facilitates group ticket sales. This position will also involve handling season tickets and special fan requests. You'll report to the business manager and general manager. Strong organizational skills are a must.

As a ticket taker or salesperson, fans can't get into the stadium without you. If this position interests you, you should apply directly to a sports arena. In the old days, you might have also been asked to turn in a tally sheet or tabulate tickets. Now that there are electronic scanners, counting tickets has become much more efficient.

There are other forms of ticket sales relating to sports. You might work for a ticket agency that acquires and re-sells tickets to the game and also concerts and other entertainment events.

There is also the army of hawkers who scalp tickets near the stadium. They're easy to spot. They hold a fistful of tickets above their head or hold up a sign saying: "Need tickets!" Scalpers look to buy cheap and sell high. A scalper's best chance at success is if the team is winning and/or the game is sold out. This is a very perishable product to vend. Once the game draws near, the value of the tickets drop significantly. After the game commences, the tickets become about as useable as a moldy strawberry. Be careful you understand how close to the stadium you can sell tickets. This may or may not be legal in your state, so know what the local laws are.

A nearby officer will be more than happy to tell you where you can sell game tickets without getting arrested. The most creative example I witnessed of a ticket scalper trying to avoid legal consequences was the one who told the arresting policeman: "I'm not scalping tickets, I'm selling a wallet. It just happens to have tickets to the game inside it."

Bat Boy, Ball Girl

This is truly a sports junkie kind of position and a great way to break into the sports world. Warriors President Rick Welts started out this way in 1969 with the Seattle SuperSonics. Interestingly, Wimbledon first introduced ball boys in 1920.

Imagine being a bellman at a hotel. In the NBA, every team has a staff of pimple-faced teenagers who handle all sorts of duties for their players, and it involves a whole lot more than fetching rebounds. In order to get a position like this, you'll either need to audition for it or be fortunate to have a friend or family member who works for the team.

You'll be expected to arrive about three hours before the game. You'll have grunt work for the team's training staff, like setting out towels, making a few ice bags, and setting out heat packs to keep the player's muscles warm. Once the players arrive, generally about two hours before tipoff, you'll run errands for the players. This may involve helping with ticket requests and game passes and fetching whatever pre-game request the players may have. You'll sit courtside with the players and tend to their needs. This may involve tending to the game uniforms or returning stuff to the locker room, like a jacket, or warm up outfit, things they don't need. Then these assistants will straighten up the locker room.

Some perks for ball boys can be interesting. Various locker room attendants might receive tips from the players for doing special tasks, this serving as their lifeblood. This could even include retrieving a phone number from an attractive lady in the stands on behalf of a player. If successful, that tip is usually pretty generous. The amount of the tips can vary greatly. Some players are just more charitable.

Andre Benavidez is 19 years old and is in his third and final year as a ball boy for the Phoenix Suns. Andre says there is a requirement to be at least 16, with a maximum age constraint of 19. Like other teenagers, Andre earns minimum wage for this job, and they receive no additional tickets. He got a lucky break to join the team through his mother's relationship with the Suns front office as a season ticket holder. After what Andre described as a simple interview process, (they asked two questions) he was hired. His responsibility is to help prepare fan giveaways like dozens of rolled up T-shirts, perhaps inflate noise-making devices, and place promotional flyers on seats. Sometimes he's involved in game operations stuff like helping set up for the Phoenix Gorilla's slam dunk performance.

In the pre-game, Andre and others will rebound for players and wait for the game to begin. During the game, he might find himself on the court cleaning up sweat from a sprawling player, or, right after a free throw attempt, wiping up where perspiring players just camped out along the key. "You have to wait until the players are at least past half court, in case there's a steal and change of possession. One time, the lightning-quick Leandro Barbosa almost trampled me on a fast break. Others said they'd never seen me run so fast." Another game, Andre almost experienced a Shaq attack. "Shaquille O'Neal (325 pounds) was diving for a loose ball and nearly landed on me. Although you get a great view, those end-of-the-court floor seats near the photographers aren't always the safest place to be." When Andre got to sit under the basket during the All Star game, he certainly didn't mind his vantage point.

When the players are finished with their post-game meeting, some ball boys will go in the locker room and pick up sweaty uniforms, socks, jocks, and underwear.

In baseball, duties of a batboy or batgirl include laying out equipment for the players. You might have to get your hands dirty by adding mud to the baseballs to be used in the game. In 2003, baseball formally adopted a minimum age of 14 for bat boys. This was in part the result of Dusty Baker's then three-year-old son Darren dutifully running out to retrieve a bat from the batting box during Game Five of the 2002 World Series, just before there was a decisive play at home plate. The Giant's J.T. Snow had just scored on a Kenny Lofton triple. Snow realized the collision that was about to happen near home plate and pulled the young Baker out of harm's way just in time.

You might also consider being a Water Boy and work the sidelines at a football game. You'll provide drinks to athletes and maybe even star in a hit movie like Adam Sandler. "You Can Do It!"

Game Production Manager

If you've got a love for music and consider yourself a silent cheerleader, this is a position for you. The Game Production Manager is the game's disc jockey. That job is to get the crowd involved and excited through motivating music and timely sound effects.

Pyrotechnics

This is also known as the special effects position. Remember how you were told not to play with matches as a kid. It doesn't apply here. If you like things that go BOOM, burst, or fall from the sky, here's your calling. From streamers to fireworks, to flames or snow, you can really make a bang at this job, and you don't have to wait until the 4th of July.

Johnny Most broadcast Boston Celtic games for 37 years and was behind the microphone for several championship seasons.

Renowned national broadcaster Gary Bender shared this fun tidbit about this legendary Celtic announcer. The raspy-voiced Most was having an ongoing problem with his hearing. After two months, he finally went to get the quandary medically checked out. Turns out, all this time, Most had forgotten he still had left his broadcast hearing piece inside his ear.

Chapter 10

Game Officials

Do you love the constant grind of travel? How about living out of a suitcase for weeks at a time? Do you have thick skin, and like getting told by 50-percent of the people you work around that you're a bum and incorrect at least half the time? Hopefully personal threats don't concern you, or flying objects thrown your way by complete strangers. Welcome to the unappreciated sports job called Referee or Umpire.

Officiating is a thankless occupation that requires extreme knowledge, instantaneous judgment, and the ability to keep the highly intense action under control. Daydreamers need not apply.

In some cases, the referees are part of the show business, less so than in former eras of sports. Game officials take verbal and occasionally physical abuse. The fans never seem satisfied, the coaches will ride them throughout the game, and players think they personally never make a mistake. The emotional control of an official is tested time and again throughout the contest. If you want to be a referee or umpire, you need the ability to keep your cool under pressure, forget the fans, and show unbending confidence. The proving ground will start at the amateur level, likely high school level competition.

Baseball Umpires

Becoming a major league umpire is not an easy path to travel, nor is there a plethora of positions available. The hours are long and the climate can sometimes be the antagonist. Sort of like being a postman with shin guards, a chest protector and a face mask, instead of avoiding vicious dogs, you're ducking fouled-off baseballs and foul-mouthed managers when a call doesn't go their way. Through rain, the cold, or extremely hot days, you're out there doing your duty. Besides the wearisome job and the abusive treatment, it's one long road trip to the Bigs.

In major league baseball, there are only 70 umpires (17 crews of four, with two rovers). Getting to The Show, as they call making the major leagues, is an arduous task and a lengthy process. Pay for a beginning major league umpire starts around $120,000, with senior umps earning up to $357,000 per season, obviously based on experience and tenure. Major League umpires receive a generous daily per-diem allowance of $340, but that covers all items; hotel, rental car, meals, tips, telephone, etc.

Be sure you have strong knees if you're umping home plate. Home plate umpires squat an estimated 620 times in a game. (No wonder catchers have bad knees). Umpires will officiate about 175 games a year, including preseason games, and more if they're assigned to work the playoffs.

Here are some of the perks for veteran umpires. A crew chief makes $10,000 extra. An All-Star game pays $10,000, a Division Series $12,000, League Championship $15,000, and World Series $20,000. You cannot work the League Championship and World Series in the same year. So a 26-year veteran crew chief "could" make $357,000 for the season, $10K for being crew chief, $10K for the All Star game, and up to $32K more for playoffs. That totals $409,000. Umpires also have four weeks of vacation now, so they only work about 135 games. But it takes them 7-15 years to make the majors.

Umpires are known to have careers that last decades, so there is little turnover. An umpire crew generally stays together all season, so you are part of a small family. You'll tote your own equipment, make your own travel and hotel arrangements, and are on the move twice a week. Then before every game, the home plate ump has to get dirty by rubbing up 60 balls with Lena Blackburne Baseball Rubbing Mud (it comes from an undisclosed site on the Delaware River in New Jersey).

If you're umpiring in the minors, you may not want to be married. The travel demand is seemingly unending, and the salaries are very poor. Professional Minor League umps begin at around $1,800 a month. Triple-A umpires might make $20,000 a year.

If you want to make the majors as an ump, you must attend a six-week umpire training school.

The Harry Wendelstedt Umpire School is renowned as the Harvard of umpiring. You'll learn how to improve all facets of umpiring - e.g., plate work, base work and positioning, rules interpretations, situation management, and mechanics for the two-umpire system, the system worked in the lower Minor Leagues. If you graduate from there, your umpire career is off and running. Having a big stomach is not a requirement to attend.

There are other umpire schools available. The Major League Baseball Umpire Camps assist umpires in furthering the advancement of their college, high school, and little league umpire careers. The camp also serves as a preparatory course to those considering a career as a Major or Minor League umpire.

MLBUC also features "Tips from the Athletic Trainer" to improve your physical well-being and prolong your career, provide nutritional counseling, and give safety presentations. There is even a Virtual Umpire Camp CD Rom.

Harry Wendelstedt Umpire School

88 South St. Andrews Drive

Ormond Beach, FL 32174

www.umpireschool.com

(800) 818-1690

Held Jan. 2-Feb 6 every year. Tuition cost : starts at $2,320

Jim Evans Academy of Professional Umpiring

200 S. Wilcox Street, #508

Castle Rock, CO 80104

(303) 290-7411

www.umpireacademy.com

Five-week professional course held in Florida. Tuition cost: starts at $2,250

Other camps held in Tucson, AZ and other international locations

Major League Baseball Umpire Camp

245 Park Avenue, 34th Floor

New York, NY 10167

(212) 931-7537

www.mlbuc.com

Week-long. Tuition Cost: Starts at $899

The Umpire School by Minor League Baseball

Vero Beach Sports Village

4003 26th Street

Vero Beach, FL 32960

877-799-UMPS

www.therightcall.net

Month-long. Early January to early February. Tuition Cost: starts at $2,250

You might find this historical timeline on umpires interesting:

1876 – William McLean, from Philadelphia, became the first professional umpire when he umpired the first game in National League history between Boston and Philadelphia on April 22.

1878 - The National League instructed home teams to pay umpires $5 per game.

1879 - National League president William A. Hulbert appointed a group of 20 men from which teams could choose an umpire, therefore becoming baseball's first umpiring staff. Umpires were also given the authority to impose fines for illegal acts.

1885 - Umpires began wearing chest protectors.

1901 - Thomas Connolly umpired the first game in the American League between Cleveland and Chicago on April 24.

1903 - Hank O'Day and Thomas Connolly worked the first modern World Series between the Boston Pilgrims and Pittsburgh Pirates.

1909 - The four-umpire system was employed for the first time in the World Series.

1921 - Umpires in both leagues began the practice of rubbing mud into the balls prior to each game in order to remove the gloss.

1947 - In the 1947 World Series, featuring the Brooklyn Dodgers and New York Yankees, the current six-man crew was established as an alternate umpire was stationed along each foul line.

1952 - The four-man umpiring crew was instituted for all regular season games.

1956 - Ed Rommel and Frank Umont broke a long-standing taboo by becoming the first umpires to wear eyeglasses on the field.

1966 - Emmett Ashford became the first black umpire in the major leagues when he reached the American League after 14 seasons in the minor leagues.

1970 - The first strike by umpires in major league history lasted one day during the League Championship Series. This action prompted both the American and National League presidents to recognize the newly-formed Major League Umpires Association and negotiate a labor contract with them.

1972 - Bernice Gera became the first woman to umpire a professional baseball game when she worked a Class A New York-Penn League game.

1973 - Art Williams became the first black umpire to reach the National League staff.

1974 - Armando Rodriguez became the first Hispanic umpire to work in the major leagues as he joined the American League staff.

1979 - Major league umpires went on strike for the third time in history from Opening Day until May 18. Replacement umpires were used during this strike.

2000 - On February 24, the World Umpires Association (WUA) was certified as the exclusive collective bargaining agent for all regular full-time major league umpires.

The evolution of the strike zone:

1876 - "The batsman, on taking his position, must call for 'high,' 'low,' or 'fair' pitch, and the umpire shall notify the pitcher to deliver the ball as required; such a call cannot be changed after the first pitch is delivered."

High - pitches over the plate between the batter's waist and shoulders

Low - pitches over the plate between the batter's waist and at least one foot from the ground.

Fair - pitches over the plate between the batter's shoulders and at least one foot from the ground.

1988 - "The Strike Zone is that area over home plate the upper limit of which is a horizontal line at the midpoint between the top of the shoulders and the top of the uniform pants, and the lower level is a line at the top of the knees. The Strike Zone shall be determined from the batter's stance as the batter is prepared to swing at a pitched ball."

1996 - The Strike Zone is expanded on the lower end, moving from the top of the knees to the bottom of the knees.

Football Officials

Unlike their basketball and baseball counterparts, football referees moonlight just once a week, generally on a weekend. That means 345 days off. The playing season is shorter with around four months to a season. Since their services are only required one day a week, most football referees also maintain full-time jobs.

With just a 20-game NFL season (currently including four preseason games), compensation ranges from $42,295 and $120,998 (top scale 20-year veteran) per season, more if assigned playoff duty. Be ready to do dozens of short sprints on the field. Typically, an NFL official has another prestigious job, i.e., lawyer, which allows the flexibility to travel on weekends. To these officials, this job is more likely a passion.

Pro and college football each use seven officials during the game. There's the head referee (positioned 10 yards behind the QB), the umpire (positioned five yards behind the D-Line), the head linesman (stands on the sideline), the line judge (stands on the opposite side of the line of scrimmage; also is the official timekeeper), the field judge, the backfield judge, and the side judge (all stand in the backfield area).

Unlike umpires in baseball, they don't rotate positions from game to game. Officials have a specific area on the field they're responsible for. There are 32 NFL teams, so with a maximum of 16 games a week (remember, there are bye weeks now), just 112 work on the field. There are booth officials, too. College football is certainly highly popular, and there are many more opportunities at this level for officials. Average annual compensation for college football refs is around $36,000.

You'll likely spend at least ten years refereeing college football before moving up in the ranks and being considered by the NFL. To get in the NFL, you'll also have a psychological test and take an examination on the rules after attending training sessions.

Football officials have all their games taped and reviewed by the league's officiating department.

When you've blown your last whistle or thrown your last penalty flag, retired officials sometimes become observers and scouts of future officiating candidates. The league is always scouting for the next candidate to join the referee ranks, observing colleges, the Canadian Football League, and the Arena Football League for nominees.

Study your sport. Get the rules mastered. Study other officials and how they handle themselves. Volunteer and get as much experience as you can.

Basketball Referees

The NBA is full-time employment but for a seven-month job. You can have another job during the offseason, but only with the permission of the NBA. There are only 60 positions at this level. The NBA officials can earn around $150,000 (entry level) to $550,000 for the most senior referees for an 82-game season. As an NBA official, you need to be in great physical condition, as you will run an estimated 5 to 7 miles per game. Off-court responsibilities include filing two email reports to the league, one immediately after the game, and another after watching a DVD of the game. Refs will get paid extra for working the playoffs. There is a playoff pool that is even broken down into non-workers getting a share. There are additional shares for working the first round, the second, the third, and then the Finals. There are 32 refs that work the first round and then it narrows to 12 for the Championship Round.

Rick Showers

Rick Showers has been a referee since he was 18. Rick played high school basketball and baseball, and began his referee career upon graduation. Thirty-four years later, he now officiates women's basketball for the Pacific 12 and Big West conferences. Initially, he signed up with the Arizona Interscholastic Association (AIA), which assigns all officials in the state. Talk about paying your dues, Rick started by refereeing high school basketball for 25 years. "Beginning pay was $15 for a freshman game, $25 for a varsity match. If you worked state tournaments, you got $45."

While still doing high school games, Rick applied to the Arizona Community College Athletic Association (ACCAC). "I went to a tryout camp, which requires invitation and was picked up on the women's side. For Junior College, I worked seven games my first year, getting paid $75 for each of those games. After working at this level for two years, I got invited to attend a Division 1 Pac-10 tryout scrimmage."

Rick was picked up by the then-Pac 10 (now Pac 12) and went to a summer camp for veterans "where we homed in on skills, movement, and had classroom studies." In July, he received a schedule for the upcoming Pac-10 women's season (November – March). His pay had now grown to $200 a game.

"Typically at the D-1 level, most refs work multiple conferences," he said. Since 2011, this was his third year with the Big West Conference, while still working with the Pac 12 too. "There are different game fees. I have my flight paid for and receive $220 a day per diem to cover hotel, meals, and a car rental." In the Pac 12,

Showers now gets paid $1,050 per game. The Big West pays him $750 per contest, plus airfare and per diem, which equals about another $400.

It's up to Showers to arrange for his own travel arrangements. He just has to make sure he's at the game one-and-one-half hours before tipoff. "I can fly or drive." Keeping taxes is a real chore, since he gets a 1099 form from each school.

It can be a grind, with travel the hardest part. "You get up early for the first flight out the next morning. You have to deal with security, parking, and waiting for planes. You work the game, get to bed many times at midnight, and start all over again. You learn how to sleep on a plane. Even if you get to your next destination early, some hotels won't let you check in until 3 p.m."

Showers said his vagabond career is tough on a marriage too. "When the season starts in November, my wife says 'I'll see you in March.' When the season is over, then you go through a withdrawal." For a spoof version of the challenge of an NBA referee's life, find the Billy Crystal movie *Forget Paris*.

Rick shared one of his wildest refereeing experiences. "I was officiating a women's game at Washington State, and the visiting team happened to be Arizona State. It was a close game, and with five minutes to go, ASU was mounting a comeback. After a WSU foul, their female head coach said to me: "Rick, do I have to wear a short skirt to get a call." Rick gave the coach a Technical Foul for the comment. Protocol at the end of the game is to call your supervisor to explain what the T was for. That must have been an interesting discussion.

One year later, Rick was assigned to referee a game in Tempe, and ironically, WSU and their same head coach were the visitors. Promising her best behavior, the WSU coach apologized to Rick.

Tommy Nuñez

Tommy Nuñez was tweeting long before this term became associated with social networking. Nuñez's career spanned five decades as a veteran referee of the NBA hardwoods, having spent 30 years officiating, and another five years as part of the NBA's management of referees. In 1973, Nuñez became the first and only Mexican American to officiate any major league sport in the history of U.S. sports. That distinction has now been duplicated by only one other individual - his son, Tommy Nuñez , Jr., who is a current seven-year veteran NBA referee.

After getting out of the marines, Nuñez had two cousins who encouraged him to be a referee. At age 21, Nuñez spent the next 12 years earning his shot at the pros. He first officiated high school and junior college basketball. "Back then, I earned $15 a game for JC ball. For high school, I earned $7.50 a game, and if you worked a junior varsity game, you made an extra five bucks."

Through amateur basketball, Nuñez got introduced to the expansion franchise Phoenix Suns in 1968. He worked a couple summer games for them and in 1972 was recommended to the NBA for consideration. "I was invited to an NBA referee camp in Buffalo, New York, resulting in working five preseason games that year. I signed my first contract in '73 for $12,000. There were no long-term agreements back then. We worked a year at a time. I worked 41 games that first season." The following year, Nuñez earned full-time status.

In 1973, there were 18 teams in NBA. Now there are 30 franchises. Nuñez was mentored by some of the greats back then. "Richie Powers (23 years), Earl Strom (29 years NBA, 3 years ABA), Darell Garretson (27 years), and Jake O'Donnell (28 years). These were the legends of NBA refs. Mendy Rudolph (22 years) was the best ever. He was in a class of his own," says Nuñez. Rudolph eventually became the NBA chief of staff. In his book, *Calling the Shots*, Strom described Rudolph as "one of the most prominent referees because of his style, courage, and judgment. He made the call regardless of the pressure, whom it involved, or where it was."

"Interestingly, none of these icon referees first worked in collegiate ball. The requirements then were simpler," says Nuñez. "You had to have mental stability, be in excellent condition, pass a rigid physical, and truly understand the game."

It was a two-ref system then. In 1988-89, the NBA permanently shifted to three-man crews.

Nuñez talked about the grind of the job. "It's not as bad as people think. You work about 12 games a month, maybe four in seven nights. You arrive in a city and rest all day. You'll probably do a lunch meeting with your crew, and arrive at the arena one-and-one-half hours before the game. Throughout the day, you program yourself to get ready for the game, looking at video tape. You have all day to focus, to work at it. We're supposed to be good. It's our only job."

In discussing the conditioning aspect with other retired NBA players, fans take for granted how physically taxing it is on referees to run with the players for seven miles a night. Remember, the players get to take a break on the bench and have a substitute come in. The referees don't get that luxury. Former Washington Bullet (now Wizards) Greg Ballard says today's NBA refs don't stay in the profession as long as their earlier generation counterparts. "You see guys getting out of this career much sooner with all the physical demand."

As a young referee, Nuñez remembers the struggles to learn every night, to earn the player's respect. "With today's technology, you have computers and six camera angles to review instant-replays. It's there for everyone to see. There is also an observer from the NBA at every game played. The electronic age spotlights everything now." Computers became part of the NBA referees' tool belts in the 1990's. "Everything became computerized, assignments, everything we did. Before that, we were sent informational bulletins in the mail. If something needed immediate attention, we got a phone call."

In the maiden years of the NBA, many referees had off-season jobs, "but you had to first get permission from the league to take that job," said Nuñez.

Other requirements of the job include stipulations of off-court behavior. "We can't (and don't) do interviews, and there's no fraternizing with players, coaches, or the teams," says Nuñez. "We don't travel on the same airplane or stay in the same hotel as them. We go to our own table at a restaurant, and after the game, go back to the hotel."

The NBA is serious about the conduct of its referees. All the professional leagues provide an anti-gambling seminar. The quickest way to get fired as an official is get involved in betting. Any image associated with gambling is a major integrity problem for professional sports.

As Nuñez pointed out, there were other lesser conditions back then. "There wasn't first class travel, just regular airlines for travel. Players even had to share a room in those early days. Now they have charter flights. Their medical attention is greatly improved now too. Back then, players had to play more while hurt. With only 18 NBA teams, you had to be tough to survive. Play wasn't dirtier, just physical."

Nuñez says he never had an object thrown at him in 30 years. "If you think about it, NBA security is very good. In comparison to others sports, the NFL officials are much more distantly removed from fans. It's baseball that lends itself to confrontation between umpires and managers, players or fans. That's where you'll get the rhubarbs." That and the National Hockey League, where fighting is far more a part of the sport.

From a compensation perspective, NBA and MLB officials are pretty close in earnings. These leagues seem to play leap frog on the pay scale.

Anyone who has a 35-year career is going to have several fond memories. For the final game Nuñez refereed, he was given the game ball and Michael Jordan autographed it. "It was a privilege to work through the eras of pro basketball that included Dr. J, Bird, Magic, and Jordan," says Nuñez. "They were all Hall of Famers!" Added Nuñez, "It was amazing how after I retired, that I was suddenly recognized for being a better referee. People started judging me more as a person."

These days, his son Tommy Nuñez, Jr., carries on the family tradition as a veteran NBA referee. There are three other father-son NBA referee legacies too; James Capers, Jr., Brian Forte, and Ron Garretson.

As busy as ever, Nuñez stays very civically involved with his Tommy Nuñez Scholarship and Youth Activities Foundation. Nuñez's foundation has been sponsoring and funding youth events and scholarships for many years. His National Hispanic Basketball Classic annual basketball tournament, played on Labor Day weekend, continues to raise money to help defray expenses for academic and athletic activities for economically disadvantaged and high-risk youth. He keeps busy with motivational speeches for school districts, juvenile detention centers, Indian reservations, and state and federal prisons. The message: "Stay positive, stay in school." Nuñez also helps instruct international basketball in Europe and conducts Phoenix-area clinics with his two sons. He is constantly giving back to the community.

Becoming an NBA referee is a lengthy process. With so many college-level referee positions out there, this is good from an opportunity standpoint. There are hundreds of colleges needing officials, but with all that competition to graduate to the NBA, imagine the difficulty in standing out. The best way to launch your dream of being an NBA referee is to start officiating at the youth league, move up to high school leagues, and then to college. Try to officiate as many games as possible. College level refereeing is not a pre-requisite.

Even then, you'll probably need an "in" to become an NBA referee. As usual, it is a 'who-you-know' business. If you aspire to referee at the college level, you need to attend offseason collegiate camps, many at the D 1 level.

The NBA typically wants you to have 10 to 14 years of experience. Then you submit a formal application to the NBA along with a detailed resumé and references. Then you must pass the NBA screening process and get invited to a summer identification camp after the NBA reviews resumes and contacts all references.

Nuñez admits there is some luck involved if you want to be a professional official. "Get involved in city ball, high school leagues, maybe junior college, or at the university level. There are also all kinds of Summer Leagues to be discovered. You just may get a recommendation from former officials or other people in sports. It's not a pre-requisite that you have to ref at the college level to get an NBA try-out, but once you are invited, you're on your own to prove yourself."

Still want to be a pro basketball referee? Here's the deal, says veteran collegiate ref Rick Showers: "Get in shape, know the rules, and go to camp. Listen to the veterans when they talk. And watch video."

To apply for the NBA, you have to go through Joe Borgia. Like father, like son, Joe Borgia is the son of the late Sid Borgia, a legendary referee who officiated in the NBA for 20 years, starting in 1946. Sid Borgia also was a supervisor of officials. As Vice President of Referee Operations, the younger Borgia is the NBA's Director of Officiating Programs and Development and is responsible for the administration of Referee Operations including recruiting.

Once the NBA identifies you, they invite you to work the Las Vegas Summer League, and the Los Angeles PRO Am league. The NBA Developmental League (D League) and the WNBA is another stepping stone into the NBA. "With the D League and the WNBA, there is more of a year-round opportunity for proving yourself," both Showers and Nuñez agree.

All of these games are evaluated and filmed, and you're tested throughout the year.

Referees in the Women's National Basketball Association (WNBA) earn about $500 per game for a 32-game season or a maximum of $16,000 annually.

At the beginning levels, you will likely need a flexible job that will allow for travel and games. There is even a publication called Referee Magazine. Take advantage of clinics in your area.

National Basketball Referees Association
P.O. Box 3522
Santa Monica, CA 90408
310-393-3522

Hockey Officials

If you like ice skating and don't mind getting hit by fast-flying players or a hundred-mile-per-hour puck, maybe becoming a National Hockey League official might not be too bad. They start at $115,000 and if they last 15 years, they move up to about $220,000 annually.

This is a job where you have to be in GREAT physical shape. If you think the puck is hard, try skating the length of the ice 400 times each game. All while eluding laser shots on goal and occasional flying fists.

Hockey officials are employed by the NHL, each working around 70 games a season. Because the job is so physically taxing, they don't have the longevity of other sports officials. For each game, there is a referee and two linesmen.

Here's something to consider about all football, basketball, and hockey officials. Unlike the athletes who occasionally get a resting period, these game officials don't have replacements. They are in action the whole game, always on the go.

On September 3, 1895 the first wholly professional football game was played between the Latrobe Athletic Association and the Jeannette Athletic Club. Latrobe won the contest 12–0. In 1897, the Latrobe Athletic Association paid all of its players for the whole season, becoming the first fully professional football team. In 1899, the Morgan Athletic Club, on the South Side of Chicago, was founded. This team later became the Chicago Cardinals and now is known as the Arizona Cardinals, making them the oldest continuously operating professional football team.

Chapter 11

Sports Medicine

The old medical adage was "just rub dirt on it and get back in there." Today's ever-growing specialization of athletic medicine provides a multitude of career opportunities that will allow a properly educated and trained individual to be associated with the sports industry.

The list of professional possibilities is extensive. This might seem like a directory outside a medical facility, but these medical positions are what today's teams require.

- Clinical medicine
- Exercise Physiology
- Orthopedics Kinesiology
- Physical Therapy
- Athletic Training
- Massage Therapy
- Sports Nutrition
- Psychology
- Athletic Training
- Cardiac/Pulmonary Rehabilitation
- Therapy Personal Training and Fitness Instruction
- Nutritionist/Sport Dietetics
- Occupational Therapy
- Podiatry

Educational requirements have become increasingly rigorous and vary among the many occupations. A sports doctor needs an M.D. D.O. and a specialized residency, but at the minimum, a career as a sports medical professional requires a degree from an accredited academic institution, state certification, and state licensure. Continued education is typically required, along with minimums for hours of supervised practice, especially if you want to advance to more technical specialties.

Coursework in a sports medical degree program may include:

- Cardiac Rehabilitative Therapy
- Orthopedic Radiology
- Physiotherapeutic Techniques
- Chiropractic Applications

- Musculoskeletal Injuries
- Nutrition
- Genetics and Sports Related Injuries

The range of salaries in the field of sports medicine varies as widely as the range of specialties. According to National Salary Data, trainers can earn as much as $43,000 per year, while sports medical doctor's salaries have been documented as high as $700,000 per year.

Orthopedist

At the core of sports medicine is the orthopedist, otherwise referred to as the Team Physician. These are the medical doctors that surgically keep your sports heroes in peak playing condition. The Team Physician is the cornerstone of the medical team and is available for duties that may involve orthopedic surgery or cardiac rehabilitation. They also oversee other health personnel. Their responsibilities include the clearing of players for return to action after an injury. They'll also work with the Certified Athletic Trainer (ATC) and the Student Athletic Trainer (STA).

A sport physician has a tough job. They need to get the injured athlete back to their peak performance level as soon as possible. Sometimes this is tough because the team doctor has to weigh not just the present but the future health of the player. The typical path for an orthopedist is to attend undergraduate school, and then medical school. Upon graduation, there will be a one-year internship, and then a four-year residency.

Dr. Richard Emerson

Dr. Richard Emerson is a renowned Doctor of Osteopathic Medicine in Phoenix who spent 17 years with the Phoenix Suns organization, first as their orthopedic consultant from 1983 to 1990, then as their Team Physician for the next 10 years. From the Walter Davis era through the Tom Chambers and Charles Barkley years, Dr. Emerson missed maybe four games.

Like all successful physicians and surgeons, Dr. Emerson has perfected his craft for five decades. He spent a year at the U.S. Air Force Medical Center in San Antonio, Texas, doing a surgical internship. During the Viet Nam war, Dr. Emerson was a military member in the US Air Force, spending a year as a flight surgeon in Da Nang, while earning several air medals during his tour. "I did a fair amount of orthopedic surgeries in Viet Nam. It was my responsibility to take care of the 421st Tactical F-1 Fighter squadron, just south of the demilitarized zone." Dr. Emerson's decorated duty as a weapons system operator also involved flying 60 combat missions, including five over Hanoi in North Viet Nam. "I flew as a 'back-seater' in an F-4 craft, which was used to battle Russian MIG's, plus drop bombs and napalm."

Following his military tour, Dr. Emerson started working in emergency and general surgery at Luke Air Force Base, followed by four years of continued orthopedic training in Phoenix. "In 1978, fellowships in sports medicine were just getting initiated in the U.S.," says Dr. Emerson. "A fellowship is where you focus on specializing in a certain field."

During his first year of private practice in 1978, Dr. Emerson established the much-acclaimed high school student-athlete sports physicals program. "We had some comprehensive programs then, examining 3,000 kids in a single year. I'd be attending games on Friday nights, conducting clinics during the day on Saturdays, and spend Saturday nights working Junior College football games."

In 1983, Dr. Emerson was in the right place at the right time. "Dr. Paul Steingard with the Phoenix Suns asked me to assist on a surgery on Rick Robey. Team General Manager Jerry Colangelo needed Robey's surgery done right away. It was Thanksgiving, but we operated anyway."

The following year, Suns All-Star Walter Davis was playing a pre-season game at the Forum in Los Angeles against the Lakers. The Olympic hockey team had played there the night before, and the ice under the court created a residue on the surface. Davis slipped, and tore his posterior cruciate ligament. After a knee scope, Dr. Emerson chose not to do surgery on Davis, rather to rehab the knee instead. "This went against the grain back then," said Dr. Emerson. "Davis ended up an All-Star that year, so the team's management was pleased with the result."

In the mid-1980's, most sports team doctors evolved from a generalist to orthopedic surgery training. "Today, there is no team doctor that isn't fellowship trained in orthopedics. Sports medicine is much more specialized today," says Dr. Emerson. "Orthopedics includes everything - bones, muscles, joints. Some of that will include sports injuries."

Dr. Emerson says orthopedics is your first step, followed by board certification. "I did my fellowship in sports medicine. I always knew I wanted to treat athletes. It was the late 1960's when the term 'sports medicine' became fashionable. Now you have medical doctors and doctors of osteopathic medicine. There's a lot of cross-over."

During his decade-long tenure as team doctor for the Suns, Dr. Emerson did surgeries on Dan Majerle, Kevin Johnson, and Charles Barkley, with his expert medical responsibilities growing to include the Arena Football League Arizona Rattlers, the WNBA Phoenix Mercury, and the NHL Phoenix Coyotes. In 2000, Dr. Emerson chose to step away and focus more on his private practice and his family. "It was time to step back," said Dr. Emerson. "It requires an enormous amount of time to stay current and on the cutting edge (no pun intended). There's a lot of pressure involved." Dr. Emerson performed five team surgeries that final season, including Tom Gugliotta, "one of the worst knee injuries I'd seen in any sport." Penny Hardaway was his last Suns surgery.

If it's a team doctor position you seek, Dr. Emerson suggests you get all the training you can. "Have patience and be willing to pay your dues. You're not going to come out of a medical program and get a job with a pro team or major college right away without necessary training. You need to affiliate with the right experts already doing it."

Physician and Sports Medicine   www.physsportsmed.com

Chiropractic

With all the physical wear and tear on athletes, there is a strong opportunity for those in the chiropractic field to be associated with sports teams.

The emphasis of manipulation is the primary treatment for Chiropractors. The D.C.'s focus is on the welfare of the nervous system. Other remedies to restore maximum functioning of the nervous system include use of water, light, massage, ultrasound, electric and heat therapy.

American Chiropractic Association   www.amerchiro.org

International Chiropractors Association   www.chiropractic.org

There are a lot of strange career paths that can lead to a job associated with sports, but this one takes the cake; actually, the pie. Dr. Roger Baker managed to secure the NBA's first position as a team chiropractor at a charity auction. I'm not sure if the bidding rhubarb was over apple, cherry or peach pie, but Dr. Baker found himself in competition with Phoenix Suns owner Jerry Colangelo for a year's worth of homemade pies. As is usually the case, Colangelo's generosity won out, but Dr. Baker didn't end up empty-handed. Dr. Baker and Colangelo got professionally acquainted, and it wasn't long before Dr. Baker was offered the position as the Suns' Team Chiropractor.

A sports career seemed a natural path for this Milwaukee native. "I can remember as a college student, attending the infamous 1967 NFL Championship 'Ice Bowl' playoff game between my Bart Starr-led Packers and the Dallas Cowboys," says Dr. Baker. "This was Vince Lombardi coaching against Tom Landry for the privilege of playing in the first-ever Super Bowl. The official temperature at game time was minus 15-degrees. The wind chill was minus 40-degrees." It was SO cold Lambeau Field's turf heating equipment malfunctioned. I'm sure hot chocolate or coffee outsold beer that day. "I was bundled up in a sleeping bag trying to stay warm," says Dr. Baker.

Dr. Baker has been a licensed chiropractor, since 1978. His position with the Suns evolved in the early 1990's. Since he was the NBA litmus test for this occupation, "no one knew how I should be compensated. I just told Colangelo I'd bill him by the number of players I worked on." That and a pair of front row seats. Some players would come to Dr. Baker's office for their adjustments while others got treated at the stadium. "Tom Chambers would always seem to be running late. I always made sure I reserved the seven-foot table for Tom. Even the Phoenix Gorilla required Dr. Baker's professional attention. "With the type of athletic performance the high-flying Gorilla provides, you can imagine the spinal problems this could create. I had to give the Gorilla more than a few back adjustments."

Some players required regular adjustments, others just when they were injured. "Dan Majerle played the game so physically, he was always playing with pain and injury." Some of Dr. Baker's other favorite NBA players included Kevin Johnson, Wayman Tisdale, and Tom Chambers. "With Chambers, the team whirlpool became known as the Tom Chambers Memorial Hot Tub," says Dr. Baker. "I also loved the 'sweater' wars I'd wage with [Suns coach] Cotton Fitzsimmons. We once showed up at the same event wearing the same sweater."

A typical game day for Dr. Baker would mean giving adjustments to five or six players, about five to ten minutes each. This would be separate from the physical therapy the trainers would provide. "A number of athletes typically play in discomfort. Pro sports are not for sissies. Trauma to their neck and lower back is an accumulation, especially with the mechanics of basketball. With all the constant jumping, there's a lot of pounding to their frame. A 30-year-old athlete is likely to be already arthritic from the excess wear and tear."

Dr. Baker also began treating hockey players. "Talk about tough, hockey players' bodies really take a pounding," says Dr. Baker. "That's also why the average life-span of an pro football career is just three to four years long."

Ironically, Dr. Baker stepped down from his position with the Suns in 1998 because of a back injury to himself. "I blew out two disks trying to catch a falling patient."

If the "pie" route doesn't provide the right recipe to your sports career, plan on eight years in school studying pathology, physiology, and anatomy, your basic M.D. college degree, followed by four academic years of Chiropractic College. This will include an internship in your last year.

Athletic Trainer

An athletic trainer is the medical umbilical cord to the athletes with their primary role to prevent injuries from occurring. When an injury does happen, the athletic trainer will evaluate the trouble and get proper medical treatment for the athlete.

This is a position that requires a major time commitment. Sports are now an around-the-clock year-long endeavor. During the season, the athletic trainer prepares players for practices and games, keeps records, attends every game and supervises rehabilitation in conjunction with a physician. They also administer physicals and drug tests. Wherever the team goes, so does the athletic trainer.

Once one season concludes and the bumps and bruises subside, it's not long before athletes start gearing up with a new conditioning program. Every endurance-pushing activity from cardiovascular to weight training to agility is accentuated. Whatever the weakness, athletic trainers will push their team to the limits.

Maybe the injury just requires heat treatments or a whirlpool. Maybe it's a twisted ankle that simply needs ice or a muscle strain that needs a massage.

A trusting relationship between the athletic trainer and athlete is a must. The coach relies on the athletic trainer to make sure athletes are physically ready. Sometimes athletic trainers are at odds with coaches because the player isn't ready to return to action.

Maybe you'll be the one to create the next breakthrough in athletic regimen. This is a wonderful position to consider if you are not gifted enough to be on the court or the playing field. Even high schools have athletic trainers. North Carolina made it a requisite in 1985 for athletic trainers to be on their staff. Many other states have since mandated the same.

Voluntary certification is available through the National Athletic Trainers Association (NATA) - www.nata.org

Sports Optometry

One of an athlete's critical skills is being able to see the ball, particularly for hitters in baseball and receivers in football. Imagine a quarterback having blurry vision trying to find a receiver on a deep pattern and only a pinpoint pass will keep the ball from being intercepted? Depth perception for basketball players, tennis players or golfers is also a dire part of their game. One of baseball's greatest hitters was Ted Williams. Williams had such superior vision, he could put pine tar on the barrel of his bat and once he hit the ball, he could tell you exactly where the smudge on the retrieved ball would be. Imagine all the time and expense put into equipment and training, yet proper eye care is just as crucial. With advanced laser technology, the value of vision has become an increasingly emphasized part of sports. Many pro athletes have taken advantage of laser technology to sharpen their eyesight.

Sports Massage Therapist

Athletes need to have their bodies finely tuned for their competitive field. All that physical pounding can't be dealt with by sitting in an ice bath after the game. They need the magic fingers of a sports massage therapist to give special attention to the part of their body that needs extra emphasis. Many teams now employ their own sports massage specialist to help their athletes maintain peak performance. This alleviates stress, promotes better circulation and assists achieving that sound mind-sound body overall goal.

American Massage Therapy Association   www.amtamassage.org

Sports Podiatry

A sports podiatrist (D.P.M.) works to treat and prevent foot injuries. No athlete can succeed, let alone perform without proper foot care. Any athlete with a stress fracture will concur. Since many athletes can have massive weight to support, this only adds to the stress and pounding subjected to their feet. If their personal "shock-absorbers" aren't up to the task, athletes' sports careers will be short-lived.

American Academy of Podiatric Sports Medicine   www.aapsm.org

Sports Nutrition

Fitness has gained major awareness in recent years, and nutrition has become an integral part of a team's preparation, with this dietary science becoming a crucial contributor to success. A sports nutritionist is the food coach, determining what foods go on the training table. A nutritionist will help with weight control, pregame meals, and vitamin and mineral supplementation. Some athletes need to pack on a few pounds, while others need to shed weight.

With such huge money at stake in sports, and such a short career time frame to achieve it, athletes themselves are always looking to gain that edge in performance. As such, some even employ the use of a personal sports nutritionist.

Certified Athletic Trainer

The Certified Athletic Trainer is responsible for care and prevention of athletic injury and serves as a liaison between the team physician, coaches, athletes, and parents. The ATC will administer first aid, initiate a treatment plan and protocol, design and implement rehab plans, and apply techniques that let the athlete regain physical activity.

The Student Athletic Trainer assists the ATC in helping treat injuries. The SAT also helps maintain and clean the athletic training facility, keep track of supplies and equipment, and assist in taping, wrapping, and changing dressings.

Some common sports injuries you might treat are concussions, muscle cramps, knee or ankle sprains, and shin splints.

Strength and Conditioning coach

This job involves playing more of a "behind the scenes" role. If you're going into this field, it is something you do because you love the work, sports, and being a part of a team. It is not the type of job you go into to earn high wages or gain recognition.

A sports conditioning coach works closely with athletic teams at professional, collegiate and high school levels, developing an effective training program in the areas of strength, speed, endurance, and power.

To get into this profession, you need to develop a background in and knowledge of athletics. A background in lifting and training techniques plays a key. If you've been a player, it gives you a better understanding how to train for a particular sport. It also gives you credibility and recognition, especially if you were a "star" athlete.

A degree in kinesiology, physical education, exercise, or bio-mechanics will help you train more effectively and is helpful in gaining access to sports settings. Sometimes, becoming a trainer happens because of whom you know, like the head coach.

Volunteer, get an internship, and/or get a graduate assistantship. These options will help you get the practical experience you need to be successful. It will let you see the life of a collegiate strength coach and help you decide whether you want to pursue this career choice. You will also learn the ropes from an expert. Don't forget the contacts that may evolve from this to land that next job.

The one thing you will need to do is get certified, if you're going to be a strength coach. There are various levels of certification.

Physical Therapist

A sports physical therapist is a highly trained health care professional that specializes in sports medicine. A PT helps restore and maintain maximum movement and functional ability for athletes. This may include treatment for debilitating injuries, or health problems caused by age or disease. Even non-contact sports like golf, swimming, or bowling can produce health issues and sideline an athlete. You might have to develop a rehab plan for anything from broken bones to muscle strains and everything in between, anything where movement and function are threatened.

Educationally, sports physical therapists need to study for a substantial amount of time before earning a license. Licensing regulations vary depending on the state. The average salary for an American PT is around $70,000, substantially more if you work for a pro sports team or major university.

Brooks Robinson (1966) and Carl Yastrzemski (1970) are the only players to be named baseball's All-Star MVP while playing for the losing team. There was no All-Star Game recognition for 'MVP' until 1962 with the Los Angeles Dodger's Maury Wills winning the inaugural award.

Chapter 12

How I Got Into Sports Without a Ticket

It's funny how you can look back in time and ask yourself, "If I hadn't done that, or gone there, would some notable direction in my life never have occurred?" I guess that's why I've always believed in destiny.

My amateur stats career really got ignited the day I went to my first NBA game. It's indelibly imprinted in my mind. November 15, 1969. The Philadelphia 76er's and All-Stars Archie Clark and Billy Cunningham were visiting the relatively new Seattle SuperSonics, led by player-coach and future Hall of Famer Lenny Wilkens.

The game was a birthday present from my parents. I was able to invite a bunch of friends to something as my guests, and this what I chose to do. I'm still not sure why, but what a fuse it lit.

When I was young, I had never shown much interest in sports, since I wasn't tall or athletically gifted. All the kids were bigger or better in baseball or basketball. I was too small (or too smart) to play football. My dad would hand me the sports page, but I'd reach for the comics.

The game couldn't have been any more entertaining. Clark led Philly with 34 points, and Cunningham lived up to his premier billing with 27 points, but this night belonged to Sonic center Bob Rule, a lefty, who torched Philly that night for a then-Seattle team record 49 points. Twenty-five of them came in one quarter. Talk about offense. Seattle won 146 to 136. The expansion-Sonics were only a 5 and 10 team (in just their third year of existence in the NBA), but I didn't care. A new NBA fan was born.

The excitement had me hooked and I couldn't wait to watch more games. Back then, television coverage was minimal, but when the original voice of the SuperSonics, Bob Blackburn, was on TV and/or radio calling the broadcast, I was glued.

In 1969, it was an exciting year in the NBA. Bill Russell, Wilt Chamberlain, Jerry West and "the Big O," Oscar Robertson, were just some of the headliners of the day. Elvin Hayes was the league's top rookie, leading the San Diego Rockets. My favorites were Baltimore's Earl "the Pearl" Monroe, and Connie Hawkins of Phoenix.

When I went to my first game, I got a game program, and in it was your own self-scoring sheet. Each player was noted with a row of 2's and 1's across the way. Fouls listed too. Three-point shots were only a part of the American Basketball Association then. At home, I started keeping score with these sheets. My dad would smile watching me track a player's points.

"Dad, Dick Snyder has 24 points! Jim Fox just set the Seattle team record with 30 rebounds -- in one game!" During the '60's, that was an average night for Chamberlain or Russell.

In recent years, I ran into Jim Fox, attending a Phoenix Suns game. The six-foot-eleven Fox was in the concession line with his grown son. I told him I remembered when he set that rebounding milestone and that it still stood as a franchise record. This was when Seattle still had their NBA franchise. Fox was pleased someone remembered. His son beamed with pride.

Back in the early 70's, the SuperSonics did a marketing cross-promotion with Bar S hot dogs and bacon. With each purchase came a coupon for a free Sonics game. The catch was you had to have an accompanying paying adult to get in. I ate a lot of hot dogs and bacon back then, just so I could get more Sonics coupons. Luckily we didn't eat kosher. My mom would faithfully buy Bar S, just so I could attend more games. My friend's parents would do the same.

With my teenage friends Pat Lamoureux, Rick Monzon and Mike York, I would politely approach some adult standing in the ticket line outside the Seattle Coliseum and ask if they wouldn't mind helping us get in for free with our hot dog or bacon coupon. "It won't cost you anything; we won't even sit near you."

Most people would accommodate us, and we ended up getting in free to nearly 30-plus Sonics games a year. Imagine accomplishing that today?

We were just 13, traveled to the games on a city bus, even on school nights, and felt like we practically had season tickets. After a while, all the ushers at the Coliseum recognized us. One of them liked us so well he'd let us slip in the press gate when no one was looking. Then he started working the ticket gate and would wave us in.

After one game, we found a box of old ticket stubs, so we helped ourselves. When we walked by good old Bob's entry gate, we'd hand him a stub from an old game, he'd tear it in half and hand us back both halves. If anyone was watching, no one would know. My friends and I felt like we owned the place. A few years later, I got my dad to buy a bottle of vodka, to give to Bob and show my gratitude for all the games he'd let me into. The bottle was polished off by halftime. So was our favorite usher, Bob.

After the games, we would hang out watching Bob Blackburn's post-game radio interview, hoping for a player autograph as they left the court. "Here comes Tom Meschery. Man, this guy is just dripping sweat." I know, because when he brushed against me, I got soaked. Then Rick and I would go around collecting left-behind programs. I needed more score sheets. Copy machines back then weren't an option, and carbon paper was messy. If need be, I'd pull out a ruler, and mark a bunch of 2's and 1's across a sheet of paper, but it didn't feel as official if I wasn't using the score sheet from a game program.

Learning the nuances of the various sports was something I was starting to become very interested in. In 1972, the *Seattle Post Intelligencer* sports page ran a weekly contest for the best sports question of the week. Typical prizes were a pair of tickets to a local sporting event. Why not write in? My question was: "In football, if a field goal kicker receives credit for the eight yards behind the line of scrimmage on the total distance of their kick, why was the punter's distance for a kick measured from the line of scrimmage only?" My inquiry was chosen and printed as the question of the week. The prize was a pair of tickets to watch Dan Fouts and the Oregon Ducks play at Husky Stadium against Washington and quarterback Sonny Sixkiller. It was Friday, the day before the game, and there were still no tickets in the mail. The columnist for the *P.I.* said he'd deliver them personally. When he arrived at my house with tickets, my Dad answered the door.

"Here are the tickets to tomorrow's game you've won, Mr. Capeloto."

My father told him, "No, the person who won the tickets is across the street playing football with his buddies."

The writer couldn't believe a little kid had won his trivia contest. My Dad took me to the game, my first football experience ever.

Two prolific college passers, Sonny Sixkiller and future NFL Hall of Famer Dan Fouts (class of 1993) matched up that day. The Ducks had opened the season 1 and 3. Oregon had first and goal as time was running out in the game. Four Fouts passes into the end zone all went for naught (although the last pass did look like pass interference by Calvin Jones), and Washington held on in an exciting finish, 23 to 17, their season-opening fifth win in a row.

Many years later, Sonny Sixkiller and I would share a broadcast booth, "Six" as an analyst for the Fox Northwest TV Channel, and me doing my stats thing.

My sports curiosity was growing. My passion for attending Sonics games continued through high school. At that time, Seattle was home to a Western Hockey League franchise, too. The Seattle Totems were just a step below the NHL and the action was fierce. Fights were prevalent every game. Soon I was attending 25-30 Totem games a year. Since it was also played at the Seattle Coliseum, the same ushers worked the games, including usher Bob, so these games became free to attend too.

Oh the fun we had badgering the players, especially in hockey. "Hey, Mad Dog Madigan, is your number seven your I.Q. or how many teeth you have left?" Looking back, it reminds me of the Paul Newman hockey classic, *Slap Shot.*

This all sounds like a trip down memory lane, but it served an unknowing purpose at the time. The itch of professional sports was ingraining itself in me for some later-in-life destiny. The door of opportunity was opening to a dominant part of my future life, and I had just walked through it. I just didn't know it at the time.

As a kid, not only was I practicing becoming a statistician, I had met the person who would later in life give me my first break in becoming a professional sports statistician, Bob Blackburn. If the Seattle Sonics had not left town to become the Oklahoma City Thunder, Bob's banner would still be hanging in the rafters of Key Arena with other retired Sonics heroes of the past.

To this day, I credit Bob Blackburn with the beginning of my sports hobby. Regrettably, Bob passed away in January 2010. Upon hearing the news, I called his wife Pat, and acknowledged how much Bob had influenced the past 36 years of my life. As one of Seattle's historical sportscasters, Bob influenced a lot of people's lives.

Seattle Seahawks ring-of-honor radio announcer, Pete Gross, would attest to that sentiment, as well. In the mid-1970's, Gross was already doing play-by-play for the University of Pacific in Stockton, California. In his spare time, Gross would drive to San Francisco and do stats for his friend and fellow broadcaster, Bob Blackburn. When Blackburn became aware that the NFL expansion Seahawks were looking for their first play-by-play radio announcer, he immediately gave his good buddy Pete a call. "Get your air check (audition tape) and send it to them right away!" Gross did, and succeeded in not only getting the job, but entertaining Seattle football fans for 17 seasons, before cancer took him away from us way too soon.

You just never know where your sports career will start. It might be keeping score at a little league game, or a YMCA basketball game. Maybe your high school needs scorekeeping help, or you can run the game clock. Perhaps, you're a coach for a youth team, or a referee.

In the process, you'll cross paths with a number of people with various sports connections, many who are sports fans just like you. Immerse yourself into the opportunity. Make yourself visible. Volunteer! Take initiative. Somewhere, someone will discover you. Perhaps you'll eventually end up sharing a courtside or press box seat.

Back to the Future

Currently, I am blessed to be able to hand-pick some NFL road games I want to work for the Seattle Seahawks radio team. Steve Raible (former Seahawk receiver) currently does play-by-play and NFL Hall-of-Fame quarterback Warren Moon (Class of 2006) is the analyst. Warren recently wrote his biography, *Never Give Up On Your Dream*, and he signed my copy saying "Enjoy the Journey." Boy, have I ever.

It was ironically at the University of Washington in 1975 where Warren Moon and I both began a separate journey. Strangely, we both share the same birth date, too, to the exact year.

As a sophomore, Warren was named the starting quarterback by Husky Head Coach Don James. Moon enjoyed a phenomenal and long career, his professional playing days lasting until he was 44 years old. His Washington football career honors included Pac 8 player of the year in 1977 and Rose Bowl MVP in 1978. In the Canadian Football League, he recorded six record-breaking seasons for Edmonton (including five Grey Cup Championships). Then Moon spent 17 more seasons (including nine Pro Bowls) in the NFL, with career stops at Houston, Minnesota, Seattle, and Kansas City. He finally hung up his cleats after the 2000 season. Combining his NFL and CFL stats, Moon's numbers are nearly unmatched in professional football history: 5,357 completions in 9,205 attempts for 70,553 yards and 435 touchdowns. His NFL passing yardage alone was nearly 50,000 yards. When he was elected into the Pro Football Hall of Fame in 2006, Moon became the first Canadian Football Hall of Famer, the first undrafted quarterback, and the first African-American quarterback to be so honored. Moon was elected in his first year of eligibility. And he went undrafted in the NFL? There should be scouts across the country that should have been fired for having blinders on.

I had just graduated from high school, and in early September 1975, even though college was not starting for another three weeks, I decided to take a walk on the large Husky campus to get oriented. I thought my initial major was going to be accounting because I always excelled in math. Calculating numbers quickly certainly comes in handy within my stats career. By chance, I happened across the Communications Building, so I walked in. To my surprise, a student radio station was in there. KCMU 90.3 FM, "Stick Us In Your Ear" was their slogan. I'd never seen a radio station before, so it caught my curiosity. Even though it was only a 10-watt station (most FM stations are 100,000 watts), it was still live radio. The nearby dorms could pick up the station, but the signal didn't go much farther.

The student who was on duty came out to talk with me. He asked if I was interested in helping out. I had no aspirations at that point of being a broadcaster. He said they could use help on their football crew and that they could use a spotter. A spotter got to sit in the Press Box, and get fed. "You get free lunch?" I was in. A few days later, KCMU's Sports Director, Steve Fimmel, gave me a call. Steve was a senior at Washington and did the student station's play-by-play. As a spotter, I would look across a prepared board that numerically listed all the players by position, offense and defense. It looked like a depth chart. Steve would use me as his extra set of eyes. Who made the tackle, which player caught the pass, who recovered the fumble? Another spotter had one team, I had the other. My (non-paid) job was to make the play-by-play guy sound like he was really on top of things, which is the same thing a stats guy does, except you're not tracking statistical numbers, you just point at the chart.

I attended every Husky football game my freshman year. For free. Most importantly at the time, I got fed twice a game, before the kickoff and at halftime.

Soon, I was assigned a weekly sportscast position. Once a week, I did a sports segment for KCMU, primarily reporting about Husky information, but other local sports news was included too. I was becoming a sportscaster. Certainly not what I expected to accomplish in college, but I was having a blast, gathering sports interviews, and attending games for free. The student station even had a pair of press passes to SuperSonic games. We'd sit high up in the unused Seattle Totem hockey broadcast booth during basketball games, talking into a cassette player and practicing play-by-play. We're talking way up in the rafters in the Bob Uecker seats. I was used to much closer free seats during my teens. This was definitely not in the front row.

In 1975, Boston Hall of Famer Bill Russell was the Sonics coach, and we'd even get to attend his post-game news conferences and go in the locker room for player interviews. This sports stuff sure beat doing algebra and trigonometry.

After lots of practice, I was eventually deemed reasonably capable of working at a basketball game. Lorenzo Romar, now the Husky head coach, started in the backcourt that season. Fimmel called the game. My job that night was to keep stats. Finally, I was assigned to do play-by-play, broadcasting games of the weaker opponents like Idaho State, or Seattle Pacific, a Division Three team. As a senior, Fimmel got the UCLA Bruins and the Seattle University Chieftains, Elgin Baylor's alma mater, among others. Senior privilege, but I didn't care (yet). It was thrilling to be part of the action. More importantly, I was gaining valuable practical experience as both a broadcaster and as a statistician.

Author as College Reporter Interviewing Lenny Wilkens

When I finally broadcast the games, I came to better understand what a play-by-play guy needed and when. This experience became invaluable. I learned the tempo of the broadcast: what to anticipate—and when to offer it to the announcer. These are two of the most critical attributes of a good statistician. If a foul just happened, you give the announcer the points and rebounds for the guy going to the line. Was the other player in foul trouble now? Was this going to cause a substitution?

Two trimesters under my freshman belt, I discovered that Fimmel was graduating early. The Sports Director position was now open. Here was a chance to really immerse myself. As Sports Director of the radio station, I'd get a chance to decide which football or basketball games I'd get to call as only a sophomore.

USC was coming to town. The Apple Cup against Washington State was a home game that season. I'd get to control assignment of the Sonics press passes, too, and still get into Sonics games for free. And I didn't need Bob the Usher anymore to get me in, though he still worked at the Coliseum for many more years. Thankfully, he never got busted for letting me in all those games. No more sneaking down to the courtside seats. Autographs? No problem. I'd have access to the locker room now.

Somewhat by default, I was named Sports Director of KCMU. A sophomore, Duncan Woodford, had out-interviewed me. After getting awarded the position, Duncan unexpectedly went to England for a year. Suddenly, the job was mine.

I was only a freshman, but I was getting to call 'live' play-by-play, just like the local Seattle sportscasting greats at that time. KIRO radio's Pete Gross, the original voice of the Seattle Seahawks (for 17 seasons), broadcast both pro and collegiate football and basketball games. KIRO at that time owned the Husky broadcast rights. Through a special arrangement with the University of Washington, KIRO let KCMU also do live play-by-play. Considering we were just students and only a 10-watt college station and KIRO could be heard over most of Western Washington, they weren't worried about the competition. We certainly appreciated their flexibility.

As a college student attending several Sonics games, I did a number of interviews with the Seattle players.

In 1976, Donald "Slick" Watts was a starter in the Sonics backcourt with "Downtown" Freddy Brown. Slick joined Seattle as an undrafted free agent in 1973. He quickly became a home-crowd favorite with his hustle and unbridled enthusiasm. Not being shy, I asked Slick if he'd join me as an analyst for our Washington collegiate broadcast. Slick  loved the spotlight and agreed. The crowd's reaction when he walked into Hec Edmundson Pavilion, the Husky's home court, decked out in a leather jump suit was practically a standing ovation. Here we were, just college students broadcasting for a 10-watt station, and Slick was our broadcast partner that night.

Before the game began, Pete Gross approached our broadcast table. With a devilish grin on his face, Pete said, "You don't mind if I borrow Slick for an interview at halftime, do you Glenn?"

"Sure, Pete, we can spare him for a few moments." I was hardly in a position to refuse.

I'll never forget the wry smile Pete gave me. I'm sure he respected my spunk for lining up professional athletes as analysts for our 10-watt broadcast.

Pete was great about helping me advance my announcing skills. I'd take air-checks (sample broadcasts) down to KIRO, and Pete would take time to critique them and offer pointers. I was also getting acquainted with other key sports figures in Seattle, KIRO TV's Wayne Cody, KOMO TV's Bruce King, and The Voice of the Sonics, Bob Blackburn.

Hopefully along the way, you'll also meet some professionals who will extend themselves to further your career, as I did with Pete, Bob, and these others. Again, take what opportunities that are offered. Because Pete saw me as ambitious, I later had the chance to be his statistician for some Sonics TV broadcasts in Portland and Phoenix.

As I entered my sophomore year at Washington, I was now in charge of the student sportscasts. My toughest challenge was learning how to pronounce Manu Tuiasosopo. When I wasn't doing play-by-play, I was doing stats and spotting, always practicing the craft. When my school and work schedule would allow, I also attended as many Sonics games as possible.

By this time, I was a recognizable face at the games, and I'd gotten to know Bob Blackburn personally. Bob had a large family with six children. At some point, he used all of them to be his courtside statisticians. There was always a Blackburn available to help out. But one night, Bob gave me a call and said he could use me for that night's game. It didn't take long to accept the invitation.

"I'll pay you $10, and if you work out, I'll give you $15 next time," said Bob. That was the going rate at the time.

Even today, the basketball stat form I still manually use is almost identical to Bob's back in the 70's. An X for a basket, an O for a miss, five across, start a new line. Fill in the circle for a made free throw, a circle with a dash through it for a missed foul shot. Bob added up the X's in his head on the fly, like a human calculator. If I missed something or messed up, he'd point it out on the fly, without missing a beat on his broadcast. Talk about multi-tasking.

"Downtown Freddie Brown for TWO! Brown now has 17 points tonight." No one could paint the picture of a game the way Bob did. You could just close your eyes and visualize the whole court. He almost lifted you out of your seat when describing a basket, as he said "TWO!" You knew it was big shot because you could hear the simultaneous crescendo of the crowd. (Three-pointers weren't implemented into the NBA until 1979.) Matter of fact, Bob used to get letters from fans that were blind, thanking him for helping them see the game through his broadcast.

Stat computers were still more than a decade away. During each timeout, I was to give Bob the ongoing shooting percentage for the quarter. No calculator available. Bob had his trusty book of baseball averages to calculate what percentage 6 divided by 13 was. I was now a professional statistician, because I got paid ten dollars. I couldn't wait to do it again.

Another way I got involved was with the SuperSonics, as a volunteer in their front office. Currently the President of the Golden State Warriors, Rick Welts was the Sonics Public Relations Director.

The Sonics PR department recorded a daily "Sonic Minute" that other radio stations in town would use during their sports reports, and I volunteered to do it for them. Before classes, I'd go to the Sonics' offices at 7 a.m. and write and record the latest goings on with the team. Back then, I'd record it into an old reel-to-reel tape player, (there weren't even cassette players then) that was then plugged into a designated phone jack for radio stations to tap into. What a thrill for me, to hear my Sonics report as part of Pete Gross' or Wayne Cody's radio sports report later in the day. After all these years, Welts and I still cross paths frequently.

This volunteer effort definitely helped my aspirations once I graduated from college. It contributed to the Sonics hiring me for their official stats crew during the 1980's. There's always something good that comes from applying yourself. In sports especially, it's a whom you know business.

My college experience provided me with many more exciting opportunities. I was able to attend the 1978 Rose Bowl on behalf of my student station. Washington upset Michigan 27-20, and Warren Moon was the MVP. As it only cost $40 for a side plane trip to Phoenix, where the Sonics played the Suns a few days earlier, I arranged with Pete Gross to work as his statistician for KIRO TV's road broadcast, earning $50 along the way. Bob Blackburn also helped me out. On the flight down, Bob introduced me to a couple college students who had won a free road trip with the Sonics through a radio promotion giveaway. The students generously offered to allow me to crash in their deluxe hotel room, while in Phoenix, saving me a lot of money. That night, Bob hosted them for dinner. He invited me along, too, if I agreed to do stats for free the next chance he needed me. No problem.

The next day, Bob also arranged for me to ride the Sonics team bus to the game. Head coach Lenny Wilkens wasn't familiar with me then, but he was gracious to allow it. Pete Gross did the TV broadcast, and I was by his side in Phoenix's Veteran's Memorial Coliseum. Back then, it was known as the Madhouse on McDowell. It was another signature moment in my evolving stats career. Now, I was doing road games, too. As someone who loves to travel, this was living the dream. Imagine hanging in the same hotel as Gus Williams and Dennis Johnson? This was the season Wilkens took over as head coach after the team opened the season 5 and 17. Wilkens went on to coach this Sonics team to the 1977-78 NBA finals against Washington's Bullets, losing in Game 7 at home.

Next, it was on to Pasadena, where I watched the Rose Bowl from the roof of the press box. I wasn't getting paid to attend, but once again, the experiences were priceless.

Another interesting chapter in my college sports career was related to Arizona State University, where my children, Chad and Amy, are currently students. Little did I know that in 1994, Tempe would eventually become home.

October 28th, 1978, the Sun Devils football team played at Husky stadium, and I called the play-by-play for KCMU that day. During the course of the game, legendary Arizona State head coach Frank Kush allegedly punched punter Kevin Rutledge in the mouth after a bad punt. From what I witnessed, Kush grabbed Rutledge by the face mask, lifted his helmet, and gave him an uppercut to the chin. I couldn't believe what I saw. I shared the experience over the air.

Within a few days of this broadcast, I started getting phone calls from various legal representatives in Arizona. Somewhere, somehow, someone had heard me broadcast (from my puny 10-watt station) that I witnessed and described Kush's punching incident over the air. Stenographers were now calling me for statements. Lawyers wanted an air-check of my broadcast. Wayne Cody, from local radio station KIRO, interviewed me about it. When we went to review the tapes, the comment wasn't on there. The board operator at KCMU must have stopped the recording at some point during the game. The air-check couldn't validate my comments. It felt like lawyers from both sides were playing tug-of-war with me. In mentioning this to Rick Welts, he advised me to play it straight.

"Don't be looking to accept any bribes for favorable testimony."

Even the local newspaper, *The Seattle Times*, ran a brief blurb on how I had slipped into some kind of Watergate time warp, since when I went to find the recording, "it was gone." Imagine being compared to President Nixon? The *Los Angeles Times* thought the *Seattle Times* article was so intriguing, they published it too. The L.A. blurb on the incident was listed right there next to a Johnny Carson story. I'd have never known about that piece, except that Bob Blackburn was in the L.A. airport heading home from a Sonics – Lakers game and picked up the paper while waiting for his flight. He gave it to me next time he saw me.

In September 1979, Rutledge filed a 1.1 million dollar lawsuit against Arizona State, accusing Kush and his staff of mental and physical harassment that forced him to transfer. Frank Kush was fired October 13, 1979. After two years, Kush was never found liable.

I never got subpoenaed to Phoenix. Naively, I was kind of hoping I would. Maybe I could have worked another road game. This is how your mind starts to work as a sports statistician. Road Trip!

In the spring of 1976, the Seattle Kingdome opened its doors to athletic competition. The Seattle Sounders soccer team played the New York Cosmos and the world-renowned soccer superstar Pele in front of 58,218 fans on April 25. In June of '76, Paul McCartney would perform the first-ever rock concert (sold out, of course). The Seattle Mariners were still a year away from their inaugural season.

Although now imploded, the Kingdome holds an amazing distinction. The Kingdome hosted the NFL Pro Bowl in 1977, the Major League Baseball All-Star Game in 1979, and the 1987 NBA All-Star Game, making it the only venue that has hosted all-star games for three major sports leagues. This is highly unlikely to be accomplished again, since most sports stadiums are built with the purpose of accommodating only a single sport.

In the spring of '76, the Husky varsity football team would square off against Washington alumni, a then-Husky tradition every year at the completion of Spring Ball. That year, they chose to hold the event on the fresh carpet of the newly minted Kingdome.

As the brand-new Sports Director at our student station, I wanted to accomplish something Big. With permission from faculty, we raised funds to pay for a broadcast line, and we got to announce this game. This was the first-ever football game broadcast from the Kingdome.

No other station (radio or TV) provided coverage. The one key player from the Alumni I remember most was Big Ben Davidson, one of the nastiest NFL players you'd ever encounter. Davidson's professional career as an Oakland Raider is well-chronicled. His reputation as a tough guy rivaled Dick Butkus of the Chicago Bears. In person, Ben was just a genuinely nice guy. He and his gravelly voice graciously did a pre-game interview with me on the field. What a thrill for a college freshman, broadcasting the first-ever football game from the Kingdome. How can you put a price on such fun and memorable experiences?

There's one other special college memory that stands out. As you've read, Bob Blackburn helped me immensely during my days at Washington. It was great when I finally had a chance to somewhat return the favor. Bob's son, Dave, had enrolled at Washington. Dave wanted to see if he had a few of the broadcasting genes his father had, so I added Dave to our KCMU sports staff. Soon Dave was joining me for Husky basketball broadcasts. Dave had played community college basketball and certainly knew his stuff. Plus, he had grown up listening to The Voice. First, Dave served as an analyst. Then he got a taste of doing play-by-play. Dave found out quickly he wasn't going to follow in his dad's footsteps. Just before his father passed away, Dave told me he fondly remembered this broadcasting experience between us, and how much respect it gave him for what his Dad had accomplished all these years. He mentioned it in his eulogy to his father.

My Fifteen Minutes of Fame

D 4   The Seattle Times   Friday, November 9, 1979

SPORTS PLUS

U.W. 'voice' has been there before

Sportscasts

Janine Gressel

Times staff reporter

LAST SEASON, the Huskies opened their football season against U.C.L.A. amidst the hub-bub of an A.B.C. network telecast and the debut of Bruce King on KOMO.

That morning, the real veteran Husky announcer, the fellow with more years behind the mike than any other now doing Husky sports, was preparing to leave for the stadium.

"My mom fixed me breakfast and, when I left, she said 'Do a good job, son, you're going up against Keith Jackson and Bruce King.'"

With that, Mrs. Capeloto's son, Glen, went to take his place behind the microphone for KCMU.

For five years, Glen has been the announcer for the Huskies on the University of Washington's student station. At only 10 watts, the KCMU signal is not going to blast listeners out of their chairs in Renton or Lynnwood, but Glen says his mom and dad get the station just fine way over in West Seattle.

GLEN TAKES his job seriously and, as he is about to do battle with the same biggies again in tomorrow's U.W.-U.S.C. broadcast, he has spent no little time and energy preparing a show worthy of a KOMO or an A.B.C. (KOMO-TV/4 will have the A.B.C. telecast at 1 p.m. KOMO Radio's pregame begins at 12:20 p.m.)

"I've prepared some 'Husky Flashbacks' in honor of the 20-year reunion of the Rose Bowl team and the Husky Hall of Fame inductions that are going on this weekend.

"They're sort of like the 'Olympic Moments' on TV — just a minute or two highlighting some person or accomplishment."

He talked to Joe Steele about doing the color commentary for the game, but Steele gave it a couple of day's thought and decided his wounded knee wasn't up to the exertion.

"I also called Ben Davidson," Glen said, "but he declined. He said he hasn't followed the team well enough — that he's not really a football fan!"

CAPELOTO IS also scurrying around trying to get taped interviews for his halftime show with some of the Husky celebrities in town for the festivities.

"I really geared up for this game," he said. "I started work on my spotting board early this week. After all, this may be my last chance to announce a really important game for the Huskies."

After five years (he "red-shirted" one season), Glen is finally going to graduate and go out into the big world.

He has one advantage. He already knows how it feels to compete with Keith Jackson and Bruce King.

N.F.L. '79, the N.B.C. pregame show, will be examining the Frank Kush situation and the N.C.A.A.'s probe of the Arizona State Football program at 9:30 a.m. Sunday, just before the coverage of the Seahawks-Browns game on KING-TV/5.

☆

AS THE KINGBOWL draws nearer (December 1), the various broadcast plans begin to jell.

Once again, Don James will provide the color commentary for the live coverage on the radio network. This year, since the broadcast has moved from KIRO to KOMO, Bob Rondeau will handle the play-by-play.

Being Part of the Action

After three-and-one-half decades of being a sports statistician, I continue to enjoy numerous opportunities, experiences, and add to some great memories.

My friend Doug Burkizer calls me Gump, after the famous Tom Hanks movie character, *Forrest Gump*. The nickname is in reference to all the interesting situations my sports career has put me in. Like when I found my way into the Arizona Diamondbacks locker room to hold the championship trophy after their exhilarating 2001 Game 7 win over the New York Yankees amidst all the spraying champagne.

In 1986, while traveling on business, I found myself in San Antonio. The Sonics were in town to play the Spurs. A quick call to Bob Blackburn, and guess what? I'm sitting court-side doing stats. At that time, the Sonics had new ownership, and the new owner also had just purchased KJR, giving them their own Seattle radio station. The new team owner understandably wanted the Sonics to be broadcast on their own airwaves; however, KIRO radio still held the contractual rights and they weren't willing to give the Sonics coverage up.

This Sonics broadcast tug-of-war became ugly, and Bob Blackburn became the victim in all this. Sonics ownership decided to play hardball with KIRO. The spat got very petty. Blackburn was told he'd have to do the broadcasts from the Seattle Coliseum's gondola, situated way up in the rafters where the old organ loft was. We're talking above the very last row of the upper section! Even though KIRO was the host station of the Sonics, they were also denied post-game interviews on the court. This was during home games and road games, both. Bob Blackburn interviewing the star of the game on the Seattle Coliseum floor was a tradition since the team's inception. Even when the game was over, a large number of home fans would always gather courtside to watch Bob chat with their home team heroes. It was a great way to connect the crowd with the players. Sometimes, it would even be a road player, or maybe a Sonic from the past.

With KIRO still maintaining their legal contract to broadcast the Sonics games, the Seattle players weren't allowed to join Bob for the post-game interview. KIRO had to send a reporter into the locker room, record an interview, and then deliver it to the engineer at the press table for delayed broadcast.

Such was the scenario when I did stats in San Antonio that day. After the game was over, Bob suddenly hands me a cassette recorder and microphone and says: "Glenn, you've been a broadcaster. Go in the locker room and interview a player for me." It had been four years since I had been on the air, but I was willing. After asking Seattle's Ricky Sobers a series of questions about the game, I gave the cassette to Bob, and, suddenly I was on the air back to Seattle conducting the post-game interview.

In 1987, as a member of the SuperSonics official stats crew, I enjoyed the privilege of sitting 'on' the floor adjacent to the photographers during the NBA All Star Game. The rosters of the teams that year included several current Hall of Famers. What an experience! The game was played in the Seattle Kingdome in front of a then-All Star game record of 34,275 fans. That attendance record didn't last long. The 1989 NBA All Star game in the Houston Astrodome attracted 44,735. The 2010 NBA All Star game at Dallas' Cowboy Stadium has set the current attendance standard with 108,713.

I also had the same vantage point the day before for, at the All Star Saturday festivities. This included the Slam Dunk competition, 3-point shooting contest, and Legends game, which allowed me to get the autograph of my idol, Pistol Pete Maravich and many other former stars. Michael Jordan just missed landing on me under the basket during his winning slam (versus finalist Dominique Wilkins) in an epic dunk-off at the Seattle Coliseum.

Prior to Saturday's Legends Game, I was collecting autographs. In the West's team locker room, coach-of-the-day Al Attles was diagramming some basic plays when participant Spencer Haywood tardily showed up for this exhibition game. Attles immediately wrote FINE across the chalkboard, and the rest of the players laughingly nodded in agreement. I'm not sure if Attles ever collected the fine from Haywood.

Before the All Star game, I was in the West locker room, watching the players prepare. Mostly, they spent the time kidding each other. A television was on, showing a highlight of Julius Erving doing a memorable wrap around under the basket lay-in against Kareem Abdul-Jabbar during the Philadelphia 76ers – Los Angeles Lakers 1980 Finals. The All-Stars in the locker room were razzing Jabbar for being schooled by Dr. J.

The ever-cool and usually reserved Jabbar responded: "I believe I was wearing 'the ring' at the end of that series." Immediate silence! Everyone shut up. No more picking on Kareem.

The 1986-87 season was also Dr. J's last, and the heyday for Magic Johnson, Larry Bird, Charles Barkley, Isaiah Thomas, Moses Malone and Michael Jordan. As a last-minute injury substitute for Ralph Sampson, Seattle Sonics star Tom Chambers stole the show and MVP honors with 34 points in the overtime win for the West, 154 to 149.

Tom Chambers now works for the Phoenix Suns as a TV analyst and in a Community Relations capacity. In 2008, I was in the Suns media room prior to working a game. It was early February, and the All Star game was coming up soon. I asked Chambers about the 1987 game and if he ever pulls out a tape to watch it.

"I don't have a tape of the game," he said.

Incredulous, I asked, "The league never gave a copy of the game to the MVP?"

"Never got one," Chambers replied.

To his shock, I told him I still had the game on video tape, "all the All-Star Saturday festivities, too."

Chamber's excitement level immediately elevated. "How much do you want for it?"

"I don't want anything for it," I responded. "I'd be happy to make you a DVD copy."

Chambers was so appreciative and excited he later took me out to lunch. Gump strikes again.

As I've heard from many sports announcers when they travel around the country, getting a decent statistician is a crap shoot. Many times, the host team will assign some young intern to the job. It may as well be a warm body. When I'm asked to work a game, I'll get introduced to the play-by-play guy and let him know I've been doing this since 1975.

The usual relieved response is, "Thank goodness, the last stat guy we had was miserable. He had NO clue what he was doing." Well, the same is true about some of the play-by-play announcers and game analysts. Some are much better than others, though they'd never admit it. Most are friendly, some are pompous.

By far, the BEST sportscaster I've ever worked with is the legendary and revered Vin Scully, the voice of the Los Angeles Dodgers since 1950. When I received my first call to sit beside this icon, I couldn't wait to tell people, "I get to work with Vin Scully!" This announcer was my hero and the main reason I was a lifelong Dodger fan! Scully has called just about every major sporting event there is. And now, I was getting a chance to work multiple series of games with him.

Not many people know or may remember this, but Scully was the original choice to do play-by-play for Monday Night Football. He turned the position down.

As great an announcer Scully is, he is an even nicer person. Ever-accommodating to the public, the gracious Scully will pose for photos and offer autographs without hesitation.

After each Dodger TV game I worked with Scully, he thanked me for doing a "good" job. Coming from him, that was high praise. Even after all these years as a statistician, I felt like I was auditioning. Since Scully incorporated into his broadcast nearly every note I passed along to him, I felt worthy. No one announces a game so smoothly or eloquently as Scully. It was an honor for me to work with him.

Our position in the Diamondback's press box is above the foul screen, directly behind home plate on the second level. We're open game to any foul balls that come rifling backwards. One game, a foul ball came screaming directly backwards. Thankfully, my head was up, and I saw it coming. From the trajectory, I could tell it wasn't going to hit me in the face, but it was going to be close. The baseball ricocheted off a heating vent just above me, grazed off my arm, and then bounced sideways off of Scully's shoulder. Vin never looked, never ducked, never even flinched, even when the ball hit him. He continued right on with his broadcast, smooth as can be. After the game, Scully autographed that ball for me, much to the chagrin of the fans down on the first level who wanted me to throw it back. Not a chance. Working with Scully was another item on my sports bucket list I was able to check off.

Another true gentleman in baseball is ESPN broadcaster, Jon Miller. I have always enjoyed Miller's impressions. He's the Rich Little of sports and does several impersonations, including a great Vin Scully. In 2003, Miller was working for the San Francisco Giants TV crew one night in Phoenix, and I was hired to work with him. We had met once before, at the 2001 World Series when Miller was calling the national radio broadcast. I doubt he remembered me, but he said he did. Again, I felt like I was auditioning, hoping to impress him enough that he'd refer me to ESPN. Miller was a lot of fun to work with and even gave me his best "Scully."

On July 25, 2010, Jon Miller was enshrined on this day for his broadcasting achievements. Miller's name will now join Vin Scully, Mel Allen, Red Barber, Curt Gowdy, Ernie Harwell, Joe Garagiola, Bob Uecker, Harry Kalas, Dave Niehaus, and many others in immortality in the Broadcast wing. I've had the honor of working with five of them. All class acts!

Speaking of bucket lists, meeting other iconic sports celebrities has been another benefit of doing this job. One of those was meeting my all-time favorite NFL football player, Joe "Willie" Namath.

The 1969 Super Bowl was the first football game I ever watched. Who can forget the New York Jets upsetting the Baltimore Colts for the AFL's first-ever championship over the NFL?

Besides doing my sports statistics work, which is my true passion, my primary employment since 1987 has been working as an account manager for various radio stations, selling advertising time and writing commercials. My station was conducting a grand opening appearance for a retirement community, and the new owner was a good friend of Joe Namath. Namath flew across the country from Florida to Phoenix to help out. There were hundreds of people that showed up, just to meet Namath. I was standing in line to get my picture taken with Namath, and I was next up. Joe politely says to me: "I'll be right with you."

While I was waiting there, holding my three footballs to get autographed, I said to Namath: "I don't get it, Joe. Just because a guy does one episode of the Brady Bunch, he thinks he's a big wheel."

Namath just cracked up. A real gentleman, he signed all my footballs, took a couple photos with me, and personally autographed a color glossy of him in his playing days with the Jets.

As great as that experience was, I've never been in more awe than when I got my photo taken with "The Greatest," Muhammad Ali. To me, this was like meeting the President.

Because of his Parkinson's disease, Ali couldn't speak, but he shook my hand, and as I told him what an honor it was for me to meet him, he looked me squarely in the eyes. What a highlight!

Another photograph I treasure is the one I got to take with Babe Ruth's daughter.

I was working a Spring Training game in Peoria, Arizona, and it was announced that Julia Ruth Stevens, who was still a big ambassador to baseball, was in attendance. The Bambino's daughter, wow! Talk about an umbilical cord back into baseball history. From the view of the television broadcast, I could roughly tell where she was located. It wasn't far from the press box. Even though I was working in the TV press booth, and the game was still going on, my camera and I sneaked out between innings, and found where she was seated. Not being shy, I politely approached her and told her I'd be truly honored to have a photograph with her. Julia Ruth Stevens was most gracious and accommodated me. Then, she asked me to sit with her. "Please, sit down young man, and join me."

How cool would that have been! Unfortunately, I had to get back to the broadcast booth, and hope they didn't fire me. When asked where I was, I told them I stepped out to use the bathroom.

"With a camera?"

Besides working the 2001 World Series, the most electric game I ever did stats for was the 2009 NFC Conference Championship game between the Philadelphia Eagles and the Arizona Cardinals. The Cardinals had never been to the Super Bowl, and the Phoenix area was upside down with anticipation. FOX TV had their A crew working, so I wasn't going to be hired by them. Westwood One's national radio broadcast traveled their top guys, too, including a statistician. Radio doesn't use a spotter. I was hell-bent on finding a way to get invited to work this historic game. Maybe Philadelphia radio would need a stats guy? I had worked for them a few years prior. Thankfully, they had the same producer. He remembered me and said they could use me. YES!

The game was amazing from a fan's and a statistician's perspective. Some games are so close there are no real discrepancies or story-lines. The yardage is close, time of possession is even, there's no real standout on offense to report about. Everything is almost equal. From a statistician's perspective, without significant disparities, you don't have as much to offer the announcers. Give me a 12-play drive, a time-consuming six-minute possession, something to pass along to the announcers.

For this NFC Title Game, it was an emotional roller coaster with huge story lines throughout. The Cardinals jumped all over the Eagles from the get-go, building a 24-6 half-time lead. Philly quarterback Donovan McNabb's first half QB rating was a microscopic 2.2. Generally, a quarterback with a 50 QB rating is considered having a horrendous game or season. This was for a Super Bowl berth. Not a great time to have your worst performance.

Philadelphia showed their mettle, returning from the break with 19 consecutive points of their own. With just 10:45 left in regulation time, Philadelphia finally led 25-24.

Cardinal's QB Kurt Warner to the rescue. Starting at the Cardinal 28-yard-line, Warner led his team on a clutch 72-yard, 14-play drive that consumed 7:52 off the clock. Warner's fifth consecutive completion during the game-winning rally was an eight yard TD pass to Tim Hightower (Warner's 4th TD of the day), resulting in the Cardinals being Super Bowl-bound for the first time. I can vividly recall setting my pencil down on my stat sheet with about three minutes to go. The 70,650 in attendance were going nuts. I could hardly hear the play-by-play announcer who was right next to me. The stadium never rocked louder. All I could think about was how lucky I was to be involved in this perhaps once-in-a-lifetime dramatic moment. I was just soaking it in. I can't ever recall stopping what I was doing to become a fan during a broadcast. At that moment, you couldn't help it.

Living the Dream

Once again, it's the Lakers battling the Celtics for the National Basketball Association championship. June 2010. Spero Dedes, the radio play-by-play announcer of the Los Angeles Lakers, is calling the game from Boston Garden. By the age of 30, Dedes had already worked play-by-play assignments for three of the four major U.S. networks. Still in his early 30's, this is Dedes' third straight NBA Finals.

Up until 2002, the Lakers faithful had known only one voice, THE legendary Chick Hearn! Hearn once broadcast 3,338 consecutive Lakers games from 1965 until 2001, without missing one Jerry West jumper, one Wilt Chamberlain rebound, one Kareem skyhook, or one Magic Johnson no-look pass.

Even then, it took a cardiac bypass surgery to sideline Chick. Chick Hearn, Lakers play-by-play announcer for 41 years! Hearn was a tough act to follow, to say the least. Chick was occasionally a tough guy to work with too. Working as his statistician for games in Seattle over the years, I once screwed up and accidentally noted free-throw totals for the wrong team. I caught my error early, but Chick proceeded to announce to Lakers land that his grandmother could do a better job. After the broadcast, I apologized for not being sharper, and he patted me on the back and said, "No, you did a fine job." I wonder if his grandmother ever kept stats for Chick. You learn early in your sports career to have thick skin and let it go.

Now Dedes is voicing the action back to L.A., as he had since 2005. The Lakers are once again battling Boston in arguably the most storied rivalry in all of sports.

Dating back to the 1947 NBA season, Boston and Los Angeles (formerly Minneapolis) have combined to win 32 league championships through the 2008-09 season. Which team would capture number 33?

Overall, these two teams have appeared in the NBA Finals a collective 52 times. The Celtics hold the all-time NBA record with 18 NBA titles; the Lakers are second with 16 coming into this finale. These teams have gone head-to-head for the coveted ring 12 times. Their franchises have 289 NBA Finals games between them. Chamberlain-Russell, West-Havlicek, Bird-Magic, all epic match-ups. No other pair of professional franchises comes close to this heated, historical rivalry. Just watch a highlight video involving Kurt Rambis' layup attempt defended by Kevin McHale if you disagree.

The New York Yankees have won a total of 27 World Series. If we're talking internationally, Real Madrid C.F. from Spain and S.L. Benifica from Portugal have won their respective soccer leagues 31 times each. But no pair of American pro teams has a rivalry like this.

Welcome to the world of a Sports Statistician. Research and preparation is only part of this position.

Now Dedes is calling the Finals once again. Boston defeated Los Angeles in 2008. The Lakers captured the trophy in 2009 against Orlando's Magic. Now it is Game 3; Lakers – Celtics (again). The 2010 NBA Finals!

"Pao Gasol grabs the rebound, Ahead to Fisher, Fisher across the time line, cross-court pass to Artest. The Lakers have made 8 of their last 9 shots, and are on an 18-4 run over the last 3:25."

Dedes couldn't possibly have mentally tabulated every one of those compelling details as the game proceeds. He's an excellent sportscaster. But no one has that kind of photographic memory. Not even his iconic predecessor, Chick Hearn. Dedes receives help.

"Nate Robinson with the steal, the Lakers' 15th turnover of the game."

He might have gotten that one from a stat monitor, but not likely during the course of a frenetic, fast-paced game, not a split second after it happened. The stat computer generally isn't that fast.

"Boston hasn't hit a field goal since 7:45 left in the third quarter. They're zero for their last seven shots."

Now a stat like that certainly didn't come from a computer. That's the value and importance of a good sports statistician. Someone who can actually influence what Dedes is telling his Lakers faithful back home about this pivotal championship playoff game. As he does so well, Spero provides the "what" that's going on, and along with analyst Mychal Thompson, a lot of the "why." An experienced statistician contributes a whole different dimension to the broadcast, reliably offering pertinent tidbits that complete a broadcast. It's kind of like being Magic Johnson. You didn't score the hoop, but you sure dished out a valuable assist.

Imagine being that guy, the statistician sitting right next to Spero, the one serving as sort of a maestro, courtside at the Celtics home court, no less. It's not in the original Boston Garden, where Wilt muscled with Russell, where Magic and Bird provided unbelievable battles for the ages, where "Havlicek stole the ball, Havlicek stole the ball" as we can still hear Boston radio legend Johnny Most's gravelly voice bellow out. That doesn't matter. This is still "the Gahden."

Dwayne Wade is courtside, looking dapper, wishing he was on the court, not beside it. Hall of Famer Julius Erving, Dr J. himself, is also a sideline spectator.

Former Presidential hopeful, Senator John Kerry is cheering in the stands, participating with his Massachusetts faithful. "Sir Charles," Charles Barkley is up in a suite working for the TV network, as is Lakers legend Magic Johnson. The NBA Finals are a happening.

The now silver-haired John Havlicek is in the stands, still revered as the hometown hero whose all-star motor was always operating at a mercurial level. Bob Cousy, the 1950's and 60's ball-handling magician of the Celtics, is sitting courtside like a shepherd still watching his flock. Cousy and superstar Celtic center Bill Russell earned so many title rings for Boston (11 championships from 1957-1969), they each ran out of fingers.

It doesn't get any better than this. Not even a Super Bowl or a World Series provides you with this kind of electricity, involvement or intimacy. You're actually sitting closer to the action than the players.

You could feel Red Auerbach's presence too. Outside the Garden, if you looked up in the Boston sky and saw a cloud overhead, you'd swear the plume had to be Auerbach's victory cigar, puffing smoke.

If Paul Revere were still alive, today he'd probably be riding through the streets of Boston screaming, "The Lakers are coming, the Lakers are coming!"

"Ray Allen has now missed all 13 shots tonight. Oh for six from three-point range. He's one short of an NBA Finals record."

No wonder Boston is losing. This is compelling stuff. Welcome to the excitement from the front row!

"The Celtics are mounting a comeback. They've made their last seven straight baskets."

Pertinent material! Were these shots the result of Lakers turnovers, or a series of missed Lakers shots? Was a key Lakers player on the bench because of foul trouble, thus triggering the Boston comeback? Was the Celtic bench providing an emotional lift? A good statistician is expected to help provide Dedes these insights and more, as it is happening, if not sooner.

One Boston fan told me he coughed up $1,400 per ticket for an end zone view of the court at the Garden. That's not for a season ticket, that's just one game. Dedes along with former Lakers star forward Mychal Thompson are both calling this highly intense action seated second row court-side, right on the center court stripe. So was I. Right there with them. This was my once-in-a-lifetime dream in the pulse of all this historical action. And I got paid to be there.

My admission to this gala sporting event was free, courtesy of being a professional sports statistician. For the Los Angeles fans back home, I'm a (silent) contributor to the excitement blaring from their radio.

Just a week prior to this 2010 NBA Championship, I'm working the NBA Western Conference Finals, sitting "in the Front Row," alongside Dedes, feeding him every trend-setting, gripping stat I can compile. This has been my professional hobby since 1975.

There are computers now available to provide the majority of the sports stats, but not all the numbers, and not as quickly. There's usually a crew of seven or so people that all pitch in to track various NBA-required statistical elements of the game. This is the Official Stat crew. They are hired by the team and responsible to the league.   I still track the games manually (and always have), every point, every rebound (offensive and defensive), shooting (game and individual – 2's and 3's), turnovers, fouls, free throws, and scoring runs down to the second. Biggest lead, bench scoring, ties, or lead changes, you name it. My unofficial method is in lieu of the task of several others combined.   When the computers go down or get behind because of corrections, and they often do, you still have to provide up-to-the-second information.   There are no lapses in the action.   The referees won't wait until the computers are back on-line. If a team hasn't had a field goal in the last 4:31, that's on me. No computer will provide me that information anyway.

Interestingly, when the referee and/or official crew needs verification of a particular play, sometimes they consult with me. Maybe an official is looking to put a few seconds back on the clock. "When did that last basket go in?" They'll confer with me. It is fun being part of the game.

It was game six, and the Lakers were looking to eliminate the Steve Nash-led Suns, and advance to the Finals to battle their long-time nemesis, the Boston Celtics. This is serious stuff. Before the game, I found out I couldn't even look like I was supporting the Lakers. I had worn a yellow polo shirt to the game which had dark blue stripes along the shoulders.   Then-Suns Vice President of Basketball of Operations, Dave Griffin, an 18-year Suns employee and long-time friend, approached me.

"What do you think you're doing? Did you not look in the mirror when you got dressed to come to the game? Are you crazy?"

My shirt apparently looked too much like Lakers colors and that just wouldn't do. Dave said, "Wait right here!"

Patiently, I waited courtside. Nearby was then-Suns General Manager, Steve Kerr, also a really nice guy. Steve also (kiddingly) questioned my loyalty. The color of my shirt reflected Lakers affinity in his mind too.

Griffin finally returned and tossed an orange T-shirt my way, and said, "Wear this!" Written across the front in bold letters, it said: "Beat L.A.!"

I told Dave, "Look, I'm sitting between two Lakers broadcasters, and it would be disrespectful to them."

I compromised, and walked a half mile back to my car in 100-degree heat to get another shirt. I was leaving after the game to go out of town and fortunately had another change of clothes.

Everyone was happy, except for the Suns after the game. In spite of an exciting Goran Dragic-led massive 4th quarter comeback, the Lakers eliminated Phoenix from the Western Conference Finals playoffs that night. Spero thanked me for doing a "great job" and slipped me a $100 bill for my night's work. That's good pay for a radio crew stats position. Much more than most radio guys pay. Plus I got an orange Beat L.A. T-shirt out of it, too. Not bad for a free front-row, on-the-floor, center-court view.

During the regular season, NBA fans in Phoenix have to pay more than $100,000 for their two sideline season tickets. It's no wonder I like this hobby.

"So Spero, I guess you'll want me there in Boston, courtside in the Garden, working the NBA Finals with you, right?"

Shockingly, he said; "Sure, Glenn, if you can make it."

I followed up with the obligatory: "Seriously?" He was serious. I know because I asked three times, "You're serious? You're TRULY serious? You're REALLY serious?"

When I finally accepted he wasn't pulling my leg, I told him I'd confirm with him within a couple days. Of course, that really meant at least mentioning it to my wife, Donna (she refers to herself as the sports widow), that I was going to Boston in a week for five days. When it comes to my sports travels, my wife is very accepting. After all these years, she just knows it's what I do, that it's part of my oxygen. It's part of my DNA.

Of course my two sons, Chad and Ryan, both immediately volunteered to go, but since Finals tickets weren't available, that ended the need for that conversation.

I couldn't believe it. I got to cross another item off my sports bucket list, working at an NBA Finals, in Boston no less. Against the Lakers!

I've also had the privilege of working for FOX TV as their 'official statistician' for the Phoenix-based games of the 2001 World Series. The official statistician is the back-up to the lead or talent statistician. The lead statistician is in a separate booth with the announcers. You interact with each other (and the TV control truck) via a headset. It's typical to have an official stats guy for television broadcasts, but certainly not radio.

In the 2001 World Series, the sentimental favorite New York Yankees were taking on the fledgling four-year-old Arizona Diamondbacks. With all the emotional wounds still very fresh coming from the 9-11 terrorist attack that year, all of America was still galvanizing, and that year's World Series was a patriotic-filled event. Monumentally, one of the most dramatic World Series ever played, too. I can still vividly remember when the Stealth airplane seemed to just hover above Bank One Ballpark stadium as a football field-sized American flag fluttered across the diamond. Security was on high alert. Soldiers could be seen walking sentry amongst the scaffolds in the ceiling of the ballpark roof. The flight path to the nearby Phoenix Sky Harbor airport runs adjacent to the ballpark, so whenever a plane nearly flew overhead, you couldn't help but gaze skyward with a little trepidation.

Out of concern another terrorist attack could be aimed at an international spectacle like a World Series, my wife actually had the audacity to suggest I might want to pass on working at this event. I told her, "No way! I'm not giving up a chance to work a World Series. I have life insurance. I'll risk it."

Especially for the games played in New York, security was on high alert. Fans entering Yankee Stadium had to pass through metal detectors. One thousand police officers were positioned throughout the stadium. Retired Arizona Diamondback outfielder Luis Gonzalez recently shared this interesting tidbit during a Phoenix radio interview about the players' experience with national security during the 2001 World Series. In spite of the recent 9-11 terrorist attacks in New York City, President George W. Bush agreed to throw out the ceremonial first pitch for Game 3 of the World Series home-opener at Yankee Stadium on October 30. Not since President Dwight Eisenhower in 1956 had the Commander in Chief done this honor. Prior to that, only three other sitting Presidents had ever thrown out the first pitch of a World Series, Franklin Roosevelt ('32 & '36), Calvin Coolidge ('24), and Woodrow Wilson ('15). It's safe to say, none of those Presidents had tossed out the first pitch under circumstances like President Bush.

Typically, a World Series game will utilize six umpires. When the President took the mound to the thunderous cheers of 57,000 plus fans, there was actually a seventh umpire on the field. In reality, the extra man in blue was secret service. The home plate umpire (for that ceremonial pitch) was also a secret service man. Who knew? The players did. Talk about pressure? After a prolonged thumbs-up to the crowd, President Bush wound up and threw a strike over the plate. The President walked off the field to patriotic chants of "U-S-A, U-S-A!"

Sometimes, working in a sports capacity offers you far more than you bargained for. Remember October 17, 1989, at 5:04 p.m.? Al Michaels was calling Game 3 of the Bay Area World Series, when an earthquake, (known as the Loma Prieta earthquake), 6.9 on the Richter scale, struck before the game even started. Sixty-seven lives were lost. Thousands were left homeless. There was an estimated Six billion dollars in property damage. So much for needing pitching counts or tabulating how many runners did they have in scoring position. Take cover! (The Oakland A's swept the San Francisco Giants in four games after a 10-day disruption in play. It was the first World Series in which the losing team never had the lead). There I go, being a statistician again.

Do you think, after surviving that evening, Michaels might have later said to himself, "Boy, do I believe in miracles!"?

It kind of felt that way for me during the 2001 World Series. I was always looking skyward, just in case.

The vantage point for my official stats position was directly above home plate for this World Series. There was not even a seat for me in the packed press box. I was right behind the public address announcer, Jeff Munn, standing the whole time. My compensation was $125 for each of those games, not huge, but the experience was priceless. A Cubs fan would die for any World Series at historic Wrigley Field. Considering the action-packed, non-stop drama of this seven-game series, and the world-wide attention it garnered because of the recent tragedies of the 9-11 attacks, this World Series will be remembered for its patriotic revitalization as much as its baseball history.

Fast forwarding back to the 2010 NBA Championships, now I got to experience being "in the front row" for an epic NBA Finals match-up.

Make no mistake. Being involved in many sports occupations is something you really have to have a passion for. It generally doesn't pay that well and is very time consuming. With all the time and commitment required, whether it's to be a traveling lead stats guy or many other sports-related positions, many will only get compensated maybe $350 to $500 for that whole weekend they just gave up. Not a ton of money for giving up two to three days of your free time. If you're a stats guy who gets hired free-lance by a local crewing company, a lot of times you make $75 to $100, sometimes up to $150 for that game. Other sports-related positions like cameraman or floor director don't pay much more and require a longer time commitment each day.

On any given Sunday in the fall, there are only 15 people in the whole country with a job as a lead stats guy for an NFL game. I was once one of those fortunate few in 2000, but the 9-11 attack caused some networks to economize and eliminate some traveling positions. Statisticians included. After that, an announcer who wanted to keep his 'personal' statistician had to pony up and pay for the statistician's airfare (probably out of accrued flight miles). That situation lasted just a couple years.

Your best shot at becoming some notable network announcer's personal stat guy is because they already know you. If a Marv Albert tells the network, "That's my guy," where Marv goes, you go. But how many Marv Albert's are out there?

One of my life's goals is to complete my sports bucket list. I just have to find a way to get an invite to a court-side seat at Staples Center for a celebrity-packed Lakers game, a game in New York's Madison Square Garden, a press-box view for a Super Bowl, and an Olympics. Bob Costas, need any help?

Oh, and work an NFL game in each city in the league. So far, I've worked games at 14 current stadiums and have (at least) visited seven others. I have 18 stadiums to go.

After All These Years

In January 2011, I got a chance to dust off the vocal chords and do play-by-play again. Arizona Christian University wanted the station I was employed with to broadcast some of their men's and women's basketball games. Because I was the only one at the station with any experience at this, I was nominated to do the games. It had only been 31 years since I last announced a game, no problem. Since it was my call to decide who would do stats for me, I hired my son Chad for the duty.

Talk about coming full circle. Not only was I getting to call the action again, my own son was following in my footsteps. Chad did a great job and has an obvious knack with numbers. He had already worked an NFL game for the Denver Broncos as a lead statistician the previous fall. Now he's gotten some basketball games under his belt. As he continues to gain more experience, the requests for him to work more games will start happening.

Nate, Nate, Nate. Do I have to explain the weak side defense again?

How do you expect to be an NBA coach someday, McMillan?

Through the years, you'll hear about a number of different freak injuries by athletes that force them to miss games. Pitcher Joel Zumaya strained his arm playing "Guitar Hero" on his PS2 and had to sit out three games. Race car driver Jimmie Johnson can win a Nextel Cup at 200 MPH, but he apparently can't stay put in a golf cart. He fell off it, breaking his left wrist.

During the 1985 NLCS, Vince Coleman was injured when the inattentive grounds crew at old Busch Stadium hit the speedster with the metal tarp cylinder as they were covering the field. That's what you get for stealing so many bases.

Chapter 13

The Globalization of TV Sports Coverage

If not for the advent of all sports network ESPN, there would probably be several thousand fewer sports-related positions available. And that's just at ESPN in the U.S. alone.

Not only has ESPN provided a multitude of job opportunities, it forced other networks to compete harder and really step up their game.

The resulting benefit was felt by many in the sports industry. Broadcast rights soared. Players got paid significantly higher contracts. The opportunities for announcers, analysts, columnists and sports writers also increased exponentially. Coaches now make astronomically more than their predecessors. It has all come with a price. Sports figures now live under an intense microscope, and not just the athletes. Every transgression gets the full-court press on media and fan coverage. Athletic celebrities like O.J. Simpson, Tiger Woods, Alex Rodriguez, and even announcers sometimes find it nearly impossible to maintain personal privacy.

The Cable revolution really got started in the 1970's with WTBS, Ted Turner's Atlanta-based Super Station. The Atlanta Braves were billed as America's Team. Move over Dallas Cowboys. Players suddenly became household names with the ever-evolving intense media time.

The Evolution of Televised Sports

May 17, 1939 - First Televised Sports Event: a baseball game between Columbia and Princeton

Aug. 26, 1939 - First Television Broadcast of a Pro Baseball Game - Cincinnati Reds vs. Brooklyn Dodgers. Red Barber was behind the mike.

Oct. 22, 1939 - First Television Broadcast of a Pro Football Game-Brooklyn Dodgers vs. Philadelphia Eagles

Feb. 25, 1940 - First Television Broadcast of a Hockey Game-New York Rangers vs. Montreal Canadiens

Feb. 28, 1940 - First Television Broadcast of a College Basketball Game - Fordham Univ. vs. Univ. of Pittsburgh

Oct. 3, 1951 - First Coast-to-Coast Television Broadcast of a Baseball Game- NY Giants vs. Brooklyn Dodgers, Game 3 of NL playoffs. Giants win on Bobby Thomson's homerun known as the "Shot Heard 'Round the World."- Ernie Harwell called the action.

Aug. 26, 1955 - First Color Television broadcast - Davis Cup match between Australia and the U.S. - NBC

Nov. 8, 1972 - First Sports Telecast by HBO - New York Rangers vs. Vancouver Canucks from Madison Square Garden.

The notable sports coverage I had available as a youth was NBC's Major League Game of the Week with Curt Gowdy and Tony Kubek, and ABC's Wide World of Sports. Who doesn't remember ABC's weekly show opening with "The Thrill of Victory, the Agony of Defeat"? That skier who crashed on the long jump must have experienced nightmares watching this weekly wipeout every Saturday.

Then Monday Night Football came on the scene in September 1970. Keith Jackson was the first play-by-play announcer that year, teaming up with Howard Cosell and "Dandy" Don Meredith as commentators. Did you know that Vin Scully was originally offered the position but declined? Scully told me he was perfectly content primarily doing Dodger broadcasts. ABC's Sports Producer Roone Arledge also courted Curt Gowdy, but Gowdy was unable to break his NBC Sports contract.

Though their network at the time had the lowest ratings, ABC was initially reluctant to enter this ground-breaking sports venture with the NFL. It was only after then-NFL Commissioner Pete Rozelle threatened to sign with the independent Hughes Sports Network (bankrolled by the reclusive Howard Hughes) did ABC finally sign a contract for the scheduled games.

Game One featured the New York Jets at the Cleveland Browns. The first sponsor of MNF was Marlboro Cigarettes. A fee of $65,000 for an ad minute proved a bargain, with 33-percent of the viewing audience tuning in.

By 1972, Frank Gifford was able to leave CBS and replaced Jackson as the play-by-play voice (Jackson continued as the premier voice of college football for 35 more years). The tandem of Gifford and Howard Cosell became MNF's announcing trademark. Johnny Pearson's composition entitled "Heavy Action" became Monday Night Football's musical signature. Gifford's MNF career would last until 1998, though his position as play-by-play ended in 1985. Al Michael's would succeed Gifford in this capacity starting in 1986.

What a phenomenon Monday Night Football created. Fans across America considered it a privilege to have their team showcased on Monday Night Football. If a player had a BIG game on MNF, what a boost it was for his career. Pro Bowls were the reward. There was just a certain mystique when it came to Monday Night Football. Anyone and anything associated with it was elevated to a higher level. Besides Michaels, Gifford and Cosell, a number of celebrated athletes have adorned the ABC

Monday Night Football Yellow Blazer. Joe Namath, Alex Karras, Dan Dierdorf, Fran Tarkenton, Boomer Esiason, Dan Fouts, and Dennis Miller.

It seems as if John Madden was a part of MNF forever, but it wasn't until 2002 that he teamed up with Al Michaels as a two-man announcing crew.

From 1977 through 1986, ABC also aired occasional games on Thursday and Sunday nights. These were billed by the network as Special Thursday Night/Sunday Night Editions of the landmark known as Monday Night Football.

There are countless moments in MNF history. One of the most remembered had nothing to do with the game or football in general. It occurred on December 8, 1980, during a match between the Miami Dolphins and New England Patriots, when Howard Cosell broke the news of famed Beatle John Lennon's assassination.

Even during a football broadcast, this horrific news crossed all journalistic boundaries and stunned a nationwide audience.

In 2006, after a 36-year run, ABC relinquished its Monday Night Football foothold. The NFL was switching its premier "game of the week" to NBC on Sunday nights. With the transition, and the continued perception as the 'game of the week' came Michaels and Madden. Heavy ABC financial losses and the opportunity for the NFL to showcase the Game of the Week at the end of their usual Sunday schedule dictated the move. Assuming the Monday night slot was ESPN.

It was 1979 when "Da Da Dunt, Da Da Dunt" began its pilgrimage into the American sports psyche. That's when the Entertainment and Sports Programming Network came on the scene. And with it, a significant piece of American sports culture was born.

The concept of 24-hour sports coverage was unheard of, especially on a tiny cable network. Would the masses possibly tune in to watch rodeos, tractor races, Australian Rules Football, and slow-pitch softball? Yet 2011 marked the 32nd anniversary of ESPN. Today, ESPN is a multibillion dollar business and a global force. As the most influential sports news entity around, nationally and internationally, ESPN has not only transformed sports on television, but journalistically too. Who can forget ESPN's coverage in 1994 of O.J. Simpson's historic murder trial? ESPN's monumental success and value certainly didn't need affirmation when the Walt Disney Company purchased them and ABC in 1995. According to an ESPN insider, Disney wasn't interested in ABC, just ESPN, but was forced to buy them both to consummate the deal.

Almost since its inception, the term "SportsCenter" is as recognized as a cell phone or a credit card. Announcers Keith Olbermann, Dan Patrick, and Bob Ley were the early pioneers that put ESPN on the map. Chris Berman's catch phrase "back, back, back, back" to describe a pending homerun is still mimicked in ballparks across the country.

It was August 16, 1978 when the notion of a 24-hour sports network was spawned by Bill Rasmussen and his son Scott. They both came up with the gutsy idea while snarled in traffic in Waterbury, Connecticut. Bill had just been released from his job as communications director and announcer for the New England Whalers, a semipro hockey team.

At that time, cable TV had not yet made its mass impact to the viewing public. Most people were lucky enough to have four or five channels to watch, and one of them was probably PBS. Today, ESPN broadcasts 65 sports 24 hours a day in 15 languages in more than 150 countries. Other ESPN spinoffs include ESPN 2, ESPN Classic (reruns of old games featuring legendary athletes), ESPNews, and ESPNU. Other offshoots include ESPN Radio, ESPN the Magazine, ESPN Deportes, and an acclaimed web site. Marketing offices exist in New York, Los Angeles, Chicago, Denver, Detroit, and Hong Kong.

Bristol, Connecticut, was and is the home base for this sports infotainment dynasty known as ESPN. It was initially chosen because property there at the time was cheap. The location was also chosen because it was equidistant between Boston and New York, just a two-hour drive either way. Small, crowded trailers marked the early days of the facilities. Annual paychecks of $20,000 were the beginning norm for upper producer positions. Getty Oil, through the influence of their executive Stuart Evey, was the initial financier in ESPN, making the 24-hour sports network possible with its ten million dollar beginning investment.

Friday, September 7, 1979, marked the first broadcast of Bill Rasmussen's all-sports network brainchild. Little could anyone have foreseen that day, that a sports-altering event was taking place.

Bob Pronovost would produce and direct the first broadcast. Budgets were tight, and the staff was short. Fifteen hour-plus days were as ordinary as people's having to multi-task before the term multi-task had even become common-place. Without indoor plumbing, outdoor portables served as bathrooms. Lee Leonard anchored the first broadcast, along with George Grande. Two million homes observed Day 1.

What was really being witnessed was a change forever in how other established networks, and ones yet to surface like the Turner Network and Fox Television, would have to significantly improve the way they journalistically provided their broadcast coverage of sports and news. No more settling for Walter Cronkite's signature catch phrase of "That's the way it is." TV viewing has never been the same.

In 1987, ESPN landed a contract to show NFL games on Sunday evenings. This turning point morphed ESPN from a smaller cable TV network into a marketing empire. It now reaches about 100 million U.S. viewers per month.

In 1984, ABC acquired ESPN from Getty Oil. ABC retained an 80 percent share and sold 20 percent to Nabisco. Nabisco later sold its 20 percent to the Hearst

Corporation. Twelve years and $19 billion dollars later, The Walt Disney Company bought ABC, Inc., and ESPN in 1996. The Hearst Corporation retained its 20 percent interest in ESPN. In 2008, Barron's Magazine indicated that ESPN alone represented more than 40 percent of Disney's entire value, an estimated $28 Billion Dollars. Present day, of the revenue generated by the Mighty Mouse monopoly, two-thirds is sourced to ESPN.

The impact and relevance of ESPN and CNN (founded by Ted Turner in 1980) continues to mushroom. As ESPN did with Sports, Cable News Network (CNN) was the first channel to provide 24-hour television news coverage and the first all-news television channel in the United States.

Just the fact that there are pay-television and cable channels is due in large part to these global wonders. How many other niche programs today are indebted to the trails blazed by ESPN and CNN? On the cable sports side, there's the Golf Channel and the Nascar Channel. Other sports-specific channels that have evolved include SPEED for auto racing, TVG Network for horse racing, and the Tennis Channel. The four major sports leagues have all just recently followed suit, forming their own networks and providing their own game coverage. The NBA Channel, the MLB Network, the NFL Network, and the NHL have all jumped on the pay-per-view bandwagon to seriously enhance their revenue sources. Where would CNBC, C Span, and the Weather Channel be without CNN's shrewd international foresight? How many foreign wars have we had a front row view of, courtesy of CNN?

How about the fans? Now because of direct broadcast satellite services, i.e. DirectTV and digital cable, it's possible for fans to watch virtually every game played by their favorite team.

Following suit now are the single-team cable networks. Examples are the YES Network (the New York Yankees) and NESN (Boston Red Sox). These aren't the first to exist. In the early 1980's, the Seattle SuperSonics offered the first paid subscription cable channel, called the Sonics Super Channel. Subscriptions couldn't carry the financial burden, and game attendance was being affected. Seattle was playing in the expansive Kingdome at that time, where a sell-out, save for an All Star or playoff game, became almost impossible. The Sonics Super Channel lasted for just a few years.

All of this competition and growth in the sports broadcasting industry has served to create a multitude of career opportunities for budding sports enthusiasts. Now there are several other sports channels around to provide career possibilities as well. The pay is still not great for the majority, but you're living your dream, and creating experiences and memories of a lifetime.

Salaries

Here's a sample of some of the positions posted at ESPN and their approximate compensation at the time of printing:

VP of Mobile Virtual Network Operations	$240,000
VP of International Development	$141,000
Marketing Manager	$60,000 - $137,500
Associate Marketing Manager	$60,000
Director of International Consumer Products	$130,000
Producer	$86,000 - $95,000
Technical Producer	$75,000
Coordinating Technical Director	$62,000
Senior Director	$140,000
Director	$112,000
Director of Programming	$95,000
Web Developer	$75,000
Operations Technician	$32,000
Vice President	$171,000
Feature Producer	$109,000
Account Executive	$93,000
Sales Assistant	$38,000
Senior Manager	$104,000
Production Assistant	$25,000
Project Manager	$92,000

Hourly Positions:

Production Assistant	$11.84
Operations Technician	$15.00
Assoc. Technical Producer	$21.00
Researcher	$17.00
Statistics Analyst	$17.00

It's encouraging to discover that ESPN provides its own tryout camp. If you want to audition for a career at ESPN, they have established a seven-month program to do so. This is ESPN's way of sifting through the national talent pool. Norby

Williamson went this free agent route to gain access to the ESPN family, and now, Williamson is the Executive Senior Vice President of Studio and Event Production at ESPN. His responsibility essentially encompasses nearly everything ESPN does.

ESPN certainly set an elevated standard for sports coverage, but one area in which early-on ESPN personality Keith Olbermann said they left themselves vulnerable as America's sports lone gathering place was in regional coverage. FOX TV's successful venture into regional college sports coverage confirmed this belief.

Pedro Gomez is a reporter for ESPN who primarily follows the big baseball stories around the country. Though he doesn't call Bristol, Connecticut, his work base, Gomez still occasionally wanders the hallowed halls at SportsCenter central. "I'm always shocked at how many young people are employed at ESPN."

FOX Television burst on the scene in 1986, initially as competition to the original 'Big 3' of ABC, CBS, and NBC. Besides its own success at a network level, Rupert Murdoch's FOX network also carved out its own significant sports niche, having wrestled away an NFC contract from CBS in 1993 with a four-year bid of $1.58 billion for the rights to the NFC. This was the first time CBS wasn't part of the NFL package since 1956. CBS did get back into the NFL picture, taking over the AFC rights from NBC. The boldness of FOX ushered in another elevated era in sports coverage. Shortly after, FOX added the NHL in 1994 (lasting until 1999), MLB in 1996, and NASCAR in 2001. FOX still retains those broadcast rights. Fox Sports has also been the exclusive broadcaster of the World Series since 2000.

Network TV and Cable Directory

ABC Sports
77 West 66th Street
New York, NY 10023
(212) 456-2186
www.abcsports.com

CBS Sports
51 W. 52nd Street
New York, NY 10019
(212) 975-4321
www.cbssports.com

NBC Sports
30 Rockefeller Plaza
New York, NY 10112
(212) 664-4444
www.nbc.com

CNN Sports
100 International Blvd.
1 CNN Center
Atlanta, GA 30303
(404) 827-1500
www.cnn.com/sports

ESPN
545 Middle Street
Bristol, CT 06010
(860) 766-2000
http://espn.go.com

Fox Sports Net Inc.
10201 West Pico Blvd #101-5
Los Angeles, CA 90064
(310) 369-6000
http://msn.foxsports.com

Turner Network Television
Sports
1050 Techwood Drive
Building 1000
Atlanta, GA 30318
(404) 827-1700
www.tnt.tv/sports

Regional Sports Coverage Offers Several Possibilities

Regional sports coverage has certainly proliferated throughout the country in the past couple decades. Even cities way down the list in TV market size are providing coverage that will provide sports-related opportunities for you.

It's quite likely your hometown's university or college provides at least radio broadcast coverage. Depending on market size or location, television is a strong possibility too. TV usually has need for a home statistician for football telecasts and many other freelance broadcast positions. They're unlikely to budget for traveling positions.

FOX Sports' coverage of professional and amateur sports now has evolved into 20 regional networks throughout the country. These FOX Sports Regional Networks, or simply Fox Sports Net (FSN), are a collection of cable TV regional sports networks throughout the United States.

These affiliates offer both professional and collegiate sports coverage you can maybe get involved in from a number of capacities.

FOX SPORTS NET

The current FOX Sports Net affiliates and the major teams they carry are:

FOX Sports Arizona - carries the Arizona Diamondbacks, Phoenix Coyotes, Phoenix Suns, Arizona State Sun Devils, and Arizona Wildcats.

FOX Sports Carolinas - carries the Carolina Hurricanes, Charlotte Bobcats, along with ACC collegiate football and basketball in North and South Carolina.

FOX Sports Detroit - carries the Detroit Tigers, Detroit Pistons and Detroit Red Wings.

FOX Sports Florida and Sun Sports - carries the Florida Marlins, Florida Panthers, Tampa Bay Rays, Orlando Magic, Miami Heat and Tampa Bay Lightning, plus local coverage of the Big East, Atlantic Sun, Conference USA, and Atlantic Coast.

FOX Sports Houston - carries the Houston Astros and Houston Rockets. It is also the home for the Houston Aeros (AHL), Houston Dynamo (MLS) plus Houston Cougars (NCAA) and Rice Owls (NCAA) coverage of the Conference USA athletic conference. It also features local Houston-area high school sports.

FOX Sports Indiana - carries the Indiana Pacers.

FOX Sports Kansas City - carries the Kansas City Royals. Big 12 Conference football from the University of Nebraska, University of Missouri, University of Kansas, and Kansas State University.

FOX Sports Midwest - carries the St. Louis Cardinals and St. Louis Blues. Also, the Missouri Valley Conference, the Missouri Tigers, St. Louis University Billikens, Kansas State Wildcats, and Nebraska Cornhuskers.

FOX Sports North - carries the Minnesota Twins, Minnesota Timberwolves and Minnesota Wild, along with the Universities of Minnesota, Wisconsin, Minnesota-Duluth, North Dakota and St. Cloud.

FSN Northwest (now ROOT Sports)- carries the Seattle Mariners, . Seattle Sounders FC, Seattle Storm (WNBA), and local coverage of the Pac 12, Western Athletic, Big Sky, West Coast and Mountain West, and WHL hockey.

FOX Sports Ohio - carries the Cleveland Cavaliers, Columbus Blue Jackets, and Cincinnati Reds.

FOX Sports Oklahoma - carries the Oklahoma City Thunder, the Oklahoma Sooners, the Oklahoma State Cowboys, and the Tulsa Shock.

FSN Pittsburgh - carries the Pittsburgh Pirates and Pittsburgh Penguins, Big East Basketball and the Atlantic 10.

Prime Ticket and FOX Sports West - carries the Los Angeles Dodgers, Anaheim Ducks, Los Angeles Clippers, Los Angeles Angels, Los Angeles Lakers, and Los Angeles Kings, along with USC, UCLA, the Pac 12, West Coast Conf., and Big West Conference, and MLS Soccer.

FSN Rocky Mountain - carries the Colorado Rockies

FOX Sports South and SportSouth - carries the Atlanta Braves, Atlanta Hawks, and Atlanta Thrashers, along with a variety of collegiate coverage.

FOX Sports Southwest - carries the Texas Rangers, Dallas Mavericks, San Antonio Spurs, and Dallas Stars, FC Dallas (MLS), San Antonio Silver Stars (WNBA), plus local coverage of the Southland, Big 12, and Conference USA

FOX Sports Tennessee - carries the Nashville Predators and Memphis Grizzlies.

FSN Utah - carries the Utah Jazz, along with the Big 12 Conference, Big Sky Conference, Western Athletic Conference, Conference USA, and Mountain West Conference

FOX Sports Wisconsin – primarily carries the Milwaukee Brewers and Milwaukee Bucks.

Comcast SportsNet

Another regional sports network is Comcast. Commencing in the 1990's, here is a list of the teams and areas Comcast Sports Net represents:

Comcast SportsNet California, based in Northern California with rights to the Sacramento Kings, Oakland Athletics, and San Jose Sharks games.

Comcast SportsNet Bay Area – serves as the San Francisco/Oakland/San Jose area with rights to the San Francisco Giants and Golden State Warriors games.

Comcast SportsNet Chicago – Their partnership includes the Chicago Cubs, Chicago White Sox, Chicago Blackhawks, and Chicago Bulls.

Comcast SportsNet Philadelphia. This took the place of SportsChannel Philadelphia, and includes rights to the Phillies, 76ers, and Flyers games.

Comcast SportsNet Northwest, based in Portland, Oregon, with rights to Portland Trail Blazers games.

Comcast SportsNet New England - Carries the Boston Celtics.

SportsNet New York, which is owned by the New York Mets, Time Warner, and Comcast. This launched in 2006.

Comcast/Charter Sports Southeast (CSS) is based in Atlanta, with sub-regional feeds available. Airs regional college and high school games and other sports.

Comcast SportsNet Washington is based in Washington, D.C. It includes rights to the Washington Wizards and Washington Capitals games. Also airs many DC United games.

Independent Regional Sports Networks

The following is a list of regional sports channels not part of a larger national network:

Altitude Sports and Entertainment, airs Colorado Avalanche hockey, Denver Nuggets basketball, Colorado Mammoth lacrosse, Colorado Rapids soccer, Colorado Springs Sky Sox minor league baseball, and other Denver and Rocky Mountain area sports.

BCSN, Buckeye Cable Sports Network operated for Toledo, Ohio.

Catch 47, Tampa Bay sports area network.

Channel 4 San Diego (4SD), with rights to San Diego Padres, Mountain West, and West Coast Conference games.

Comcast Television (Michigan) airs CCHA hockey games, Great Lakes Intercollegiate Athletic Conference football, Michigan High School Athletic Association games of several sports, college, and high school magazine shows. Also used for FOX Sports Detroit overflow games.

Cox Sports Television, is based in New Orleans and airs New Orleans Hornets basketball, New Orleans VooDoo arena football, and regional college action. (Louisiana, Texas, Florida and Arkansas).

ESPN Plus and Raycom Sports syndicate college football and college basketball games to over-the-air broadcast stations and some cable or satellite channels. Their games are also available on ESPN GamePlan and ESPN Full Court.

MSG Network or (MSG) – This was launched in 1969 as the first regional sports network in the United States and serves the New York City Metropolitan Area. Its new sister channel is MSG Plus. MSG and MSG Plus carry the New York Knicks, New York Rangers, New York Islanders, New Jersey Devils, Buffalo Sabres, New York Liberty, and Red Bull New York.

Metro Sports - A 24-hour sports network for Kansas City.

Mid-Atlantic Sports Network (MASN), co-owned by the Baltimore Orioles and Washington Nationals. MASN televises every available game of both teams (320 games annually). Also, official Network of the Baltimore Ravens, Georgetown Hoyas, George Mason Patriots, and UNC Wilmington Seahawks. Partnerships with Big South Conference, BB&T Classic. Regional provider of the Big East Game of the Week (football, men's basketball). Televises more than 520 live major sporting events annually.

New England Sports Network (NESN), which is owned by the Boston Red Sox (80%) and Boston Bruins (20%). Broadcasts Red Sox and Bruins games, the Beanpot, Boston College Basketball, Quinnipiac University athletics, and other live programming.

SportsTime Ohio (STO), is owned by the Cleveland Indians. (launched in 2006) Broadcasts 24 hours a day.

Time Warner Cable SportsNet, is operated by Time Warner Cable in the upstate New York cities of Rochester, Syracuse, Watertown, Binghamton, and Buffalo.

Yankees Entertainment and Sports (YES), which is owned by Yankee Global Enterprises LLC with 40% owned by Goldman Sachs. Carries the New York Yankees and New Jersey Nets.

Other notable Regional Sports TV Networks today include Versus and Raycom Sports.

Radio networks include Westwood One, Sports U.S.A., and Compass Media Sports.

How many ways can you name in which a runner can reach base without a hit?

Base on Balls

Obstruction (fielder's interference)

Hit by Pitch

Reach on Error

Fielder's Choice

Dropped 3rd Strike

Wild Pitch

Catcher interference

Chapter 14

To Work in Sports, Know Your Sports

What makes sports so special and enduring? It's the historical accomplishments that provide wonderful celebrations for people's lives. Perhaps you were witness to a no-hitter. Maybe you and your kids were there when your team won it all. Memories like these are photographic benchmarks to fans and families alike.

If you're going to be employed in sports, you better have a strong historic awareness. Here are three stories of individuals whose personal efforts left an indelible imprint in the sports world.

They Changed the Game

Pioneers of Modern Day Sports

Curt Flood

While Jackie Robinson is historically remembered and revered for breaking the color barrier of major league baseball in 1947, Curt Flood should be remembered for paying a heavy financial and emotional price to pave the way for the economic rights of future ballplayers. By challenging baseball's reserve clause, Flood lost money, coaching jobs after his All Star playing-days, and his shot at the Hall of Fame. More than a century after this country abolished slavery, major league baseball owners were still practicing it, so Flood's challenging of professional baseball's Reserve Clause in 1970 was socially relevant too. Flood's defiance of MLB's servitude policy legally forced baseball to weigh its orderly tradition and history against freedom, change, and capitalism.

Flood was a three-time MLB All-Star and seven-time Gold Glove center fielder, hitting more than .300 six times during his 15-year major league career. Flood spent 12 seasons in a St Louis Cardinals uniform, starting in 1958. After the 1969 season, St Louis attempted to trade the then 31-year-old Flood to the Philadelphia Phillies. Baseball's infamous 'reserve clause,' bound a player to his team for perpetuity as part of their standard player's contract. One year at a time, ballplayers were treated like a piece of property, with freedom as a professional athlete completely restricted.

Flood did not want to live in Philadelphia, a city he viewed as racist. Remember, the 1960's was a decade in which the United States experienced one big dissent after another, with American citizens dedicated to change. The U.S. was heavily embroiled in the Viet Nam war; President John Kennedy was assassinated (1963); the southern part of the United States were marching for civil rights, with Dr. Martin Luther King being gunned down (1968); and JFK's brother, then-Presidential candidate Robert Kennedy, also was murdered two months later (1968). If ever there was a 20th century decade in United States history in which civil rights protests and campus gripes were the primary thesis, the 1960's rated right up there. In the 20 - year Viet Nam war (1955-1975), 58,159 brave American soldiers died fighting for freedom, while back home, accomplished athletes were still hypocritically being denied their professional freedom. So Flood's anti-establishment challenge of MLB's reserve clause certainly suited the theme of the times.

In a December 24, 1969, letter to Baseball Commissioner Bowie Kuhn, Flood demanded that the commissioner declare him a free agent:

"After twelve years in the major leagues, I do not feel I am a piece of property to be bought and sold irrespective of my wishes. I believe that any system which produces that result violates my basic rights as a citizen and is inconsistent with the laws of the United States and of the several States.

It is my desire to play baseball in 1970, and I am capable of playing. I have received a contract offer from the Philadelphia club, but I believe I have the right to consider offers from other clubs before making any decision. I, therefore, request that you make it known to all Major League clubs my feelings in this matter, and advise them of my availability for the 1970 season."

On January 16, 1970, Flood pursued his playing freedom in the case known as Flood v. Kuhn (Commissioner Bowie Kuhn). Flood sat out the entire 1970 season. He stood to make about $100,000 that season. MLB's Players Association financially stood behind Flood's $1-million dollar lawsuit, and former U.S. Supreme Court Justice Arthur Goldberg represented Flood. Over the course of two-and-one-half years, the case proceeded from district court to circuit court and finally climbed to the U.S. Supreme Court. Former players Jackie Robinson and Hank Greenberg testified on Flood's behalf, as did former owner Bill Veeck. Not one current player testified or attended the proceedings, probably fearing repercussion and blacklisting from baseball's establishment.

Arthur Goldberg argued that the reserve clause depressed wages and limited players to one team for life. Predictably, MLB owners cried blasphemy. Major League Baseball's counsel countered that Commissioner Kuhn acted in the way he did "for the tradition and sanctity of the game." The Supreme Court eventually ruled 5 – 3 in favor of major league baseball, upholding their exemption from antitrust statutes. For now, baseball's supremacy over of ballplayers would remain intact.

In many respects, the arguments by baseball's representation in the early 1970's did foretell the future if free agency was allowed. "The richest teams would monopolize all the great talent and win all the championships. The best players would change teams every year in search of the best offer." Nostradamus couldn't have forecast it any better. Forty years later, that paints baseball's current landscape exactly. You can understand why today's sports fans yearn for the good old days when players stayed with one team their whole career.

The reserve clause decision only delayed the inevitable. Baseball's sacrilege tradition of hot dogs and Cracker Jacks was soon to change, and America's pastime would never be the same. Though Flood lost his challenge, the dispute served a far bigger purpose when in 1975, pitchers Andy Messersmith and Dave McNally fought for their professional baseball freedom. Arbitrator Peter Seitz ruled that since Messersmith and McNally played for one season without a contract, they could become free agents, thus striking down the reserve clause and creating the dawn of widespread free agency.

Salaries soon skyrocketed. In 1976, player salaries were about eight times that of the average working American. Within two decades, ballplayer's wages exploded to 50 times higher than the average American wage. Baseball's biggest wage earner in 2010 was New York's Alex Rodriguez with a player salary of $33 million dollars, along with four million more in endorsements. That only placed him fifth overall on the list of highest earning athletes. Golf claims the top two spots. Tiger Woods, despite off-the-course transgressions and resulting lost endorsements, still pulled in more than $90 million, and Phil Mickelson earned more than $61 million dollars in winnings and endorsements. Boxer Floyd Mayweather Jr. was number three in earnings at $60 million, and LeBron James was fourth with a 2010 paycheck adding up to nearly $46 million.

Philadelphia eventually traded Flood's rights to the Washington Senators in 1971, where Flood played just 13 games under Ted Williams before ending his career. Flood died of throat cancer in 1997 at the age of 59. Dozens of former ballplayers paid tribute.

So many professional athletes benefitted from Flood's social legacy and fight for injustice, yet it still seems today's ballplayers who have made multiple millions don't acknowledge where their riches evolved from.

I can't help but wonder that at a time when civil unrest was sweeping the country, if the case might have turned out differently had a white player challenged this premise of involuntary servitude. The Supreme Court's ruling certainly mirrored society's social resistance at the time.

Though denied his dream of being enshrined in Cooperstown, in the history of sports labor agreements, Curt Flood is a Hall of Famer.

Ann Meyers Drysdale - The Queen of Sports

Ann Meyers Drysdale

Perhaps the most accomplished and distinguished woman in the sports world today is Ann Meyers Drysdale. Meyers Drysdale has been a standout in everything she has done from being a Hall-of-Fame basketball player to award-winning sports journalist and now sports management. When it comes to sports and life, Meyers Drysdale has batted 1.000.

As an athlete, Meyers Drysdale broke new ground in women's and men's basketball. I include men's basketball on her resumé because in 1979, Meyers Drysdale became the first female to ever sign a contract with an NBA team, the Indianapolis Pacers. She received a $50,000 no-cut contract and participated in three-day tryouts, but was not chosen for the final squad.

Throughout her all-star basketball career, Ann was a pioneer, and one of the most talented women to have ever played the game. When she was refused on her endeavor to play for her high school's boys team (not for lack of talent), Ann instead became the first player to be part of the U.S. National team while still in high school.

Says Ann: "It turned out to be a blessing, but it was frustrating. The boy's high school coach involved admitted to me later in life that because the precedent of a girl playing varsity boys basketball was just so new, no one knew how to handle the situation. Not the coaches, not the parents of the other male players. How would the locker room be handled?"

After leading her high school girls' teams to an 80-5 record, Ann became the first woman to be signed to a four-year athletic scholarship in college, at UCLA (1976-1979). While a Bruin, she was the first four-time All-American basketball player (male or female). She also accomplished another first by becoming the only player (male or female) in school history to record a quadruple-double (20 points, 14 rebounds, 10 assists and 10 steals).

Between 1975 and 1979, Meyers Drysdale won the Gold Medal at the '75 Pan American games, was a silver-medalist Olympian in '76, and took home another world championship gold medal at the FIBA World Championship for Women in '79.

The late 70's also included Meyers Drysdale being the first woman player drafted by the Women's Professional Basketball League (WBL) in 1978.

Among her many athletic honors, Meyers Drysdale was enshrined in 1993 in the Naismith Memorial Basketball Hall of Fame in Springfield, Massachusetts as the first woman inductee. In 2007, Ann was one of only three women players included in the inaugural class of inductees into the FIBA [International Basketball Federation] Hall of Fame, and other than Bill Russell and Dean Smith, the only American player. Meyers Drysdale also joined Kareem Abdul-Jabbar, Bill Walton, and Denise Curry in 1990 as one of the first four basketball players to have their numbers retired by UCLA.

For an encore to her athletic accomplishments, Ann has served as a network TV sports analyst for ESPN, CBS, NBC, ABC and FOX for nearly 30 years.

Still not finished, Meyers Drysdale is currently the President and General Manager for the WNBA's Phoenix Mercury and Vice President of the Phoenix Suns. When you discuss her lengthy, trailblazing career, it might be simplest to sum it up as been there, done that, since it seems there's nothing she hasn't accomplished. Therefore, what better individual to offer perspective on a career in sports, be it as a participant, part of the media, or in management, than Ann Meyers Drysdale. Even her late husband, Don Drysdale, was a Hall of Fame (1984) all-star pitcher for the Los Angeles Dodgers and a long-time sports broadcaster for ABC and several MLB teams.

When Meyers Drysdale was offered her three-day tryout with the NBA Indiana Pacers in 1979, Ann didn't do it as a publicity stunt, nor did then-Pacer owner Sam Nassi at the time. Ann has never bought into the you-can't-do-that theory. She'd already been denied certain opportunities, like denial to play for the boys' varsity, but she's never backed down. She had just been drafted #1 by the fledgling Women's Basketball League in 1979, but didn't want to forfeit her amateur status. Meyers Drysdale's had intentions of playing in the Olympics again in 1980.

As it turned out, Meyers Drysdale wouldn't have had her opportunity to play in the 1980 Moscow Olympics because President Jimmy Carter prevented U.S. Olympians from participating as a political protest of the Soviet's war in Afghanistan. Other countries that joined the boycott included Japan, West Germany, China, the Philippines, and Canada. The United Kingdom and France supported the boycott but let their athletes decide whether to participate. As a result, the United Kingdom and France sent a much smaller delegation of athletes than usual. Overall, 65 countries did not participate, despite being invited. Only 80 nations participated. In 1984, Russia and 13 other Eastern Bloc countries reciprocated by boycotting the 1984 Los Angeles Olympics.

Thankfully, Meyers Drysdale had already decided that once the NBA came knocking, she was not going to pass on the chance to compete with the boys again. Ann was dead set on playing in the NBA, not because she was a woman, but for her abilities. Even prior to the three-day rookie free agent tryout camp, Ann felt disrespect and resistance. Pacer's coach Bob "Slick" Leonard paid her a visit in California in an attempt to talk her out of trying out. Others in the Pacer organization attempted to talk her out of it too. Ann knew Leonard had already made up his mind about her chances of getting invited to training camp, but she wasn't going to give him the satisfaction. Besides, it was the owner's idea and decision to let her proceed. As she expected, when the camp was over, Meyers Drysdale was cut, even though she felt she'd earned a shot to advance, at least to training camp.

"There were just too many intangibles they couldn't or didn't know how to deal with," Ann said. The ribbing she'd take, concerns from wives and girlfriends, the dealing with male egos because "you let some girl beat you," and gee, where will she shower? "I could have always used the hotel shower. Besides, I have five brothers," she said grinning.

The country club was closed to females. It still is in most sports.

"Danica Patrick still faces a double standard for being a female race car driver. Women jockeys still face a similar stigma. Do you think the horse really knows, or cares whether it's a man or woman on board? Does a race car have gender bias? When Michelle Wie has competed against men, does the golf club care who's swinging it? Either you're good enough to compete, or you're not." As it turns out, 1980 saw Meyers Drysdale become the first woman to broadcast an NBA game as an analyst for Pacers TV and radio. Ann also worked in their PR department.

Meyers Drysdale says society has grown a long way toward gender equity in sports, but it has a long way to go. "More fathers and husbands are getting involved with supporting and coaching their daughters. More women can get athletic scholarships." On the college level, thousands of new women's athletic teams have been created since Congress approved Title IX of the Education Amendments of 1972, the federal law that prohibited sex discrimination at schools receiving federal money. But while the number of women's collegiate teams has doubled to almost 8,000, the proportion of women who coach these teams has actually been declining. "The Title IX money is being used to pay men, rather than the women who used to get most of the coaching jobs."

It wasn't just on the playing court Meyers Drysdale experienced condescending and prejudicial attitudes. In 1981, she took a job for KGMB radio in Hawaii as an analyst for University of Hawaii's men's basketball. Right off the bat, she had three strikes against her. She was white, she was female, and she was replacing someone locally. Hate letters welcomed her to the Islands.

Adversity and discrimination still exist. They come in biases the form of age, gender, appearance, and race. As a broadcaster, Meyers Drysdale experienced it because she didn't have long hair. Says Ann: "The look the networks want to display also includes the length of a female's nails, and whether she's pretty enough," Ann says. "Do you think Howard Cosell would have been hired for his looks? Most times, sports knowledge or experience isn't enough for a woman. That's why they're relegated to positions like sideline reporting."

There's even non-acceptance to a broadcast having more than one female voice to listen to. "Male viewers or listeners have difficulty with the pitch of a woman's voice. They can tolerate one high-pitched voice in a broadcast, but two is considered too many. One voice is not considered 'low' enough." Again, the double standard exists for women.

Meyers Drysdale has never backed down from a challenge. Her family wouldn't allow it. "Growing up with five brothers and five sisters, you don't get a lot of pity. My parents were both very hard workers. Their work ethic was contagious. Education was expected. Academics were important. We couldn't play sports until all our homework was done."

Growing up, Ann usually competed against her brothers and their buddies. Ann said she viewed her older sister Patty as an even better athlete than she was. For all her family's athletic achievements, it was fascinating to find out they never grew up with a hoop at their house.

One brother, Dave, preceded Ann to UCLA and was also an All-American basketball player under legendary coach John Wooden. Drafted by the Lakers, Dave was part of the famous trade with the Milwaukee Bucks that brought Kareem Abdul-Jabbar to Los Angeles.

Looking back, Ann felt that the publicity from being famous siblings at UCLA was a stimulus for women's athletics at the time. Dave was a senior on Wooden's final UCLA team in 1975. That season culminated in yet another Bruin NCAA men's basketball national championship. (UCLA won 10 national titles in 12 years under Coach Wooden). Ann was a starring frosh. It made for great PR and human interest.

As a broadcaster, Meyers Drysdale has also hit several home runs, but not before she learned to climb out of her shell. Before college, Ann said many previous interviews of her athletic accomplishments were answered with one-word responses or a shrug of the shoulders or a nod of the head. It was her broadcast professor at UCLA which helped give her confidence for public speaking.

"If you remember, UCLA All American Bill Walton spoke with a stutter in his college and early professional days. Once Walton overcame his speech impediment, he became an accomplished sports analyst." Meyers Drysdale affectionately refers to the revered Coach Wooden as "Papa" and remembers their humorous discussion about Walton's ascension to broadcasting. "At first you couldn't get Bill Walton to properly speak," said Wooden. "Now you can't get him to stop talking."

Meyers Drysdale says she has always been proud to represent her country. In the Pan Am games in 1979, she was the first woman to ever carry the U.S. flag into international competition. Because her team won the gold medal, the women basketball squad was going to get the privilege of staying in the hotel, rather than the sports village. Unfortunately, Bobby Knight created an international incident while coaching the men's squad and the opportunity was scuttled. "Back then, when women represented our country, we didn't get the same support or consideration as men," says Ann.

For today's aspiring women, be it sports or otherwise, Meyers Drysdale suggests hard work and passion. "Love what you're doing! Certainly credibility helps, but be adaptable and love your product. You never know when you meet someone, what they can do for you down the road."

In Meyers Drysdale's case, athletics trained her for life. "Sports is life! You learn how to communicate, to work as a team, to develop fundamentals and leadership skills. Just like a front office, it's a team effort. You work with the coaches and players, and that instills that winning attitude of working hard. Like athletics, it continues that competitive edge. Failing is not failing. Winning is not final. Success is about courage. It's an ongoing test. You've got to fail to succeed."

Meyers Drysdale also questions the naysayers about women athletes and the WNBA's ability to survive 15 years already. "Why are the critics so mad at us? The NBA struggled in its infancy years too. NBA franchises folded or were moved to other cities just like our league."

Overall, Meyers Drysdale says it's about the game of life. "Anything is possible! You've just got to ask. Teachers, coaches, they all touch your lives. Learn from that. Put yourself out there and others will too. We're all a role model. What character do you have when no one is looking? Character is who you are. Reputation is what others perceive you to be." In the case of Ann Meyers Drysdale, she excels at both.

Spencer Haywood

Spencer Haywood had a decorated basketball career, but it seems as if he has remained cloaked in anonymity for nearly 30 years. He was LeBron James before there was a LeBron James, a man-child among boys on the basketball court. Haywood soared above the rim before Dr. J and David "Skywalker" Thompson. As they say today, he had game. Yet if it wasn't for Spencer Haywood, a who's who of NBA Hall of Famers and All-Stars like Michael Jordan, Magic Johnson, Bob McAdoo, and Isiah Thomas and even players that went directly to the NBA from high school like Moses Malone, Darryl Dawkins, Shawn Kemp, LeBron James, and Dwight Howard would not have had early entry into professional basketball.

Spencer Haywood began achieving his basketball fame as a teenager. After averaging 28.2 points and 22.1 rebounds per game for Trinidad State Junior College in Colorado for the 1967-68 season, Haywood earned his place onto the Olympic

Spencer Haywood
From the lens of George Kalinsky

basketball team as the youngest player ever to don the red, white, and blue for America's basketball team. Since basketball had been invented in America, this particular international competition had been heavily balanced in the favor of the U.S. since its first Olympic competition in 1936. Historically, the U.S. team had won every Olympic basketball Gold Medal through 1964. But politics and social upheaval in the U.S. was rearing its ugly influence even before this 1968 Olympics. Already, black basketball players' participation at Division One schools had increased, inspired in part by the monumental 1966 NCAA Basketball Championship victory by Texas Western College over the University of Kentucky. For that title tilt, Texas Western coach Don Haskins fielded an all-black starting lineup. Coach Adolph Rupp's entire Kentucky team was white. Dr. Harry Edwards, who has been at the forefront of Race and Sports in America for 40 years, organized the Olympic Project for Human Rights in 1967 to protest racism in sport as well as racial segregation in the United States and throughout the world. At that time, Dr. Edwards was a professor at San Jose State and 1968 was already dotted with social upheaval in America, with Martin Luther King, Jr.'s assassination and the emergence of the Black Panther Party. There were riots going on in major cities like Detroit and Los Angeles. In Mexico City, just ten days before the start of the Olympics, Mexico security forces massacred hundreds of students occupying the National University.

As another protest to social injustice and racial inequities of the day, some of the nation's top amateur hoopsters, including Lew Alcindor, Wes Unseld, and Elvin Hayes, boycotted playing for the U.S.A. national Olympic team in '68. Just about anyone who witnessed the 1968 games in Mexico City can vividly remember the black gloves Tommy Smith and John Carlos wore in protest from the medals victory podium, one of the more enduring and poignant images in Olympics history. One of the basic principles of the Olympic Games that politics play no part whatsoever in them had been violated, and Avery Brundage, President of the International Olympic Committee, stripped Carlos and Smith of their medals and had them removed from the Olympic Village.

Asked his view about this, Spencer Haywood said, "Smith and Carlos were just making a statement to blacks only. It was a little power salute. Because of the black boycott, we weren't even supposed to be there. Then they were ostracized for their protest. America turned their back on them for years." Olympic Boxer George Foreman took the opposite political route. After beating a Russian for the Heavyweight Gold, Foreman walked around with a small American flag.

Meanwhile, back on the hardwoods, it was left to Haywood, along with Jo Jo White, Charlie Scott, and others to maintain the tradition of international dominance by the U.S. Olympic basketball team. Usually the clear-cut favorite in this Olympic event, this amateur basketball squad wore a heavy torch of responsibility against the favored Russians.

Haywood would lead the 1968 Olympic basketball team to Gold, setting a U.S.A. field goal percentage record of .719 and an average of 16.1 points in Mexico

City. "I also set records for the most rebounds in the history of the Olympics and blocked shots," Haywood recalled. He did all this as a 19-year-old. The U.S. team went undefeated at 9 and 0.

For his sophomore year of college, Haywood transferred to Division One University of Detroit and led the NCAA in rebounding with a 21.5 average per game while scoring 32.1 points per game during the 1968-69 season. He was voted first-team All-America alongside LSU's Pete Maravich (44.2 points per game), Niagra's Calvin Murphy (33.1 college career average), Purdue's Rick Mount (33.3 pt. avg.), and UCLA's Lew Alcindor (26.2 pt. average). Now that's a serious Dream Team.

Haywood might have stuck around for another two collegiate seasons; however, Haywood says a pre-arranged understanding with the University of Detroit that Spencer's high school coach and legal guardian, Will Robinson [Spencer referred to him as his father], would be hired as the team's next coach fell through. Will Robinson would go on to become the nation's first black coach in NCAA Division One basketball, coaching Illinois State (and Doug Collins) from 1970-1975. Haywood said, "I was lied to! The University of Detroit reneged on the deal, so that's when I decided to advance to professional basketball." There was another reason too. "My mother was still picking cotton in the Mississippi delta, sun up to sun down, for just $2 a day. My family needed my financial support."

Haywood was simply too good to spend four years on the college level anyway. Because of his age, the NBA wouldn't yet have him, so Haywood signed a 6-year, $1.9 million deal with the ABA's Denver Rockets for the 1969-70 season. "The General Manager of the Indiana Pacers, Mark Storm [father of national broadcaster Hannah Storm], explained the acceptance of an underclassman like me as 'promotional relief,' saying I was given a chance to play pro basketball because we are all former sons of slave owners, and this is our way of reparation," says Haywood.

His ABA rookie season clearly validated Haywood's supreme skills and quickly silenced the doubters that a 20-year-old could hold his own among the pros. If Haywood didn't break the laws of gravity, he was certainly slow to obey them. Haywood was simultaneously named Rookie-of-the-Year and the youngest player ever named Most Valuable Player at only 20 years old, leading the fledgling league in scoring at 30.0 points per game and rebounding at 19.5 rebounds per game. For good measure, Haywood also won the ABA's 1970 All-Star Game MVP with a strong 23 point, 19 rebound and 7 blocked shot performance for the West team. Considering that this All Star game boasted players the likes of Rick Barry, Mel Daniels, and Louie Dampier, Haywood had clearly established himself as one of the game's greatest players, regardless of the competition or his youth. No one in the history of sports had monopolized all these honors by just 20 years of age.

Haywood's association with the ABA wouldn't last long. Haywood's attorney, Al Ross called Spencer's ABA contract fraudulent and a farce. Only $400,000 of the $1.9 million was actually guaranteed. The rest of its so-called six-year value was predicated upon an anticipated 30-percent return from Wall Street, "and I'd only start receiving the money between the age of 50 and 70," said Haywood. So Haywood again felt he had been misled and taken advantage of. "We tried to renegotiate, but that failed."

With the NBA vehemently trying to quash the upstart American Basketball Association and the ABA battling for relevance, the competition for talent was fierce. This was a period when the NBA was also expanding, having just added teams in Portland, Cleveland, and Buffalo in 1970, thus their need for more quality and star players. It was at this time that Phoenix won a coin flip over the Seattle SuperSonics for the rights to sign Connie Hawkins, a New York City playground legend. The Hawk had been barred from the NCAA in 1961 for alleged involvement in a point-shaving scandal while a freshman at the University of Iowa. How could this have occurred since freshman weren't allowed to play varsity ball by the NCAA? It was alleged that Hawkins had introduced other players to a man convicted of fixing games. Hawkins was never charged or arrested, but was expelled from college anyway. It was 1969 before the NBA finally accepted Hawkins into their league (along with a $1.3 million dollar settlement). When the Suns got Hawkins, Haywood says maverick Sonics owner Sam Schulman was told by the NBA he was first in line for the next assigned superstar player. "No one realized it would be me," Haywood said. "The league would have preferred it had been Los Angeles. Lakers owner Jack Kent Cooke even spoke to me, saying if I couldn't play for a year until my college class graduated, he'd still pay me anyway." (Can you imagine a lineup that featured Wilt Chamberlain, Elgin Baylor, Jerry West and Spencer Haywood?)

Subsequently, Spencer Haywood was signed out of the rival American Basketball Association in 1970 by the fledgling Seattle SuperSonics for six years at $1.5 million dollars. The National Basketball Association, which still required a player to wait until his college class had graduated, screamed foul, threatening to veto the contract and implement various retaliatory sanctions against the SuperSonics. Haywood and Schulman chose to challenge the NBA's eligibility rules and filed an anti-trust suit against the league (Haywood v. National Basketball Association).

Lenny Wilkens was Seattle's head coach that season. "When Spencer was brought to the team, Schulman told me what they were trying to accomplish and was confident they would prevail," Wilkens said. "I tried to encourage Spencer to focus on the game and not on the rhetoric going on. Spencer's teammates liked him, accepted him, and supported him, but it was still tough on him. Spencer would play a game, then another injunction gets delivered just before game time, and he'd have to sit out. He'd play a game or two, then he couldn't play again. It really bothered him. As his coach, I'd try to keep his spirits up, reminding him we were going to beat this and not worry about the distractions."

Schulman's financial support was part of the reason Haywood signed with Seattle. Wilkens recalls that Schulman said he was going to go all the way to get this done, promising he would pay whatever it cost. Another motivation for Haywood's accepting the Sonics' offer was that his brother Joe had served at Fort Lewis near Seattle on his way to the Vietnam War and had given Seattle glowing reviews, telling his sibling it was a city with no racism.

Golden State Warriors President and COO, Rick Welts was a teenage ball boy for Seattle at the time and had a front court view to Haywood's Sonics debut. As Welts vividly remembers, "I still recall the buzz and anticipation in the crowd. The rest of the team was already on the court warming up. Everyone was excitedly waiting for Haywood to make his appearance. As a four-year-old franchise, this was Seattle's first real superstar. When he came out of the tunnel, the crowd was electrified. Then he hit his first warm-up shot and everyone went nuts."

As a youth, I was at that first game, too, and I can also picture Haywood draining that first patent fade away shot from the foul line. The fledgling Sonics were now on the NBA map.

"Having Haywood really created a buzz," said Wilkens. "Everyone had heard about him and he didn't disappoint. Haywood was an incredible athlete and truly lived up to the billing. He could do all kinds of things with the basketball. People were excited to see his talent."

Haywood's challenge went all the way to the U.S. Supreme Court. Haywood's legal team argued that the conduct of the NBA was a "group boycott" and a violation of the Sherman Antitrust Act. The central issue was whether the NBA draft policy was a restraint on trade and therefore illegal in accordance with the Sherman Act? An injunction was issued in Haywood's favor stating, "If Haywood is unable to continue to play professional basketball for Seattle, he will suffer irreparable injury in that a substantial part of his playing career will have been dissipated, his physical condition, skills and coordination will deteriorate from lack of high-level competition, and his public acceptance as a super star will diminish to the detriment of his career." Remember, this court case was going on at the same time Curt Flood was challenging major league baseball's reserve clause.

Spencer Haywood
From the lens of
George Kalinsky

Lenny Wilkens began his NBA career in St. Louis with the Hawks in 1960 while Flood was still a Cardinal fan favorite and knew him well. "Here, Haywood was going through his legal challenges at the same time Flood was legally challenging baseball's reserve clause. Flood ended up being blackballed; he went through hell. He never got his playing form back. I was worried about the same thing happening to Spencer," Wilkens said.

While his case was being resolved in court, Haywood continued to play for Seattle on court, getting booed in several hostile NBA arenas around the country. There were times he played only after an announcement was made that the game was being played under protest. "This happened frequently but that's what we went through as a team," said Wilkens. One Public Address Announcer in Cincinnati had the audacity to tell the crowd, "There is an illegal player on the court" during a pre-game introduction of Haywood. As a young teenager, I remember hearing Sonics broadcaster Bob Blackburn announce that introduction during one of Seattle's games. Haywood said, "I remember Wilt (Chamberlain) telling me once, 'I'm glad it was you, and not me.'"

Besides being his coach, Wilkens was still a player and could certainly relate. "A lot of guys were happy to see someone challenging the establishment but glad it wasn't them."

Some basketball fans were in an uproar because they thought Haywood was trying to destroy the college game. While Haywood was suing the NBA, he was simultaneously being sued by the ABA for breach of contract with the Denver Rockets. In addition, the NCAA and the University of Detroit were also suing Haywood for leaving college to go to the ABA, claiming that Haywood's departure caused the university millions for him not playing his junior and senior years there. "The NCAA was worried that this ruling could destroy things and affect future recruiting," said Haywood.

Wilkens said Haywood's attempt to change the status quo on pro basketball's early entry rule had nothing to do with college basketball's future. "The University of Detroit was just being selfish. At that time, there weren't that many college players that could step into the pros. There have been a few capable of making the jump, but not enough to impact college basketball."

"It was like I was playing under probation," said Haywood. "All the time, I was being booed on the court, and constantly being served with injunctions to not play."

Some opposing veteran NBA players were no more welcoming, viewing Haywood's far-reaching youth movement against the NBA's customary college rule as a threat to their future job security. No one wanted a bunch of "kids" pilfering their professional

Haywood Defending Phil Jackson
From the lens of George Kalinsky

livelihood and paychecks. On the court, Haywood was brutalized without consequence, getting elbowed in the midsection, getting clothes-lined coming off picks, and losing some of his teeth from wild elbows. Players regularly took physical liberty on Haywood, trying to break his will. The referees swallowed their whistles, letting the flagrant stuff against Haywood go without a foul call, probably figuring they were doing their league a favor, especially with the ABA trying to carve out their professional basketball niche. And so it went. For Haywood, there was no recess from the bodily abuse on the court, and for a long time, there was no mental recess from the other court.

"Some of the abuse was obvious," said Wilkens. Wilkens also likened some of this to what a lot of rookies experience. "Veterans are always going to try and knock a rookie down. I went through it in St Louis as a rookie. Players, even on my own team tried to beat the hell out of me, to get me to quit at the beginning. They wanted to see if I could take it."

"Even when checking into the team hotel," Haywood said, "I'd go to my room and there'd be a couple thugs waiting near my door with a photographer. They would punch me in the gut, kick me, and do anything they could do to provoke a fight. They were trying to bait me into an altercation, so I'd get arrested and kicked out of the league. It was malicious back then, and yet I couldn't fight back."

Haywood's Sonics roommate in 1970 was Garfield Heard, a starting rookie forward for Seattle that year out of Oklahoma. Heard remembered that "Haywood took a lot of abuse that year; someone was always doing everything they could to get Spencer thrown in jail. But he wouldn't retaliate. He handled everything very well. I can recall players who'd threaten not to play if Haywood was on the court, but eventually they still did. Even the officials had it out for him. There were also times 'Woody' was threatened to be physically removed from the basketball court. He didn't know from one game to the next whether the courts would allow him to play. Will he play, won't he play. The league clearly wanted him out." Heard remembers the emotional abuse from the players, too. "Some key star players wouldn't even talk to Haywood." "You've got to take your hat off to Spencer," added Wilkens. "I know my coaching staff backed him all the way, as did his teammates."

Haywood's spirit and the SuperSonics' determination would not be deterred. Through it all, Welts said he remembers the 21-year-old Haywood remaining "very poised, while still playing at a very high level." Wilkens concurred. "He handled himself very well. No other player had to go through that kind of stuff."

Haywood played only 33 games during the 1970-71 season with Seattle, starting, stopping and starting again with each temporary injunction as the case moved through the court system. He spent more than one game sitting outside on the team bus after being told he had to leave the locker room, if and when he was allowed to enter the arena at all.

As his coach, Wilkens was concerned about Haywood getting consistent playing time. Haywood says, "I had to stand out in the snow sometimes, 'off' the stadium property grounds. I never seemed to have refuge, not even while playing. I was constantly called the N-word, and glass bottles were thrown at me. I was raw meat, with imprints still on my forehead to this day because of going around picks and getting elbowed. Players were allowed to do anything they wanted. Brutal punches thrown my way, and the refs looked the other way. I still have a lot of scars. I spent a lot of days crying."

Haywood remembers one time when he was simply warming up for a game in Chicago. "I was alone on one end of the court, and Chet Walker was shooting at the opposite end by himself. Walker somehow tweaked his ankle, and the next day, the Bulls sued me for $600K, blaming me for being a distraction. This was thrown out as a frivolous case."

Wilkens remembers the shenanigans too. "Teams would start the game late, try to figure out a way to get him out of the game. Whatever they thought they could do to distract him," said Wilkens.

After a series of appeals, Haywood v. National Basketball Association in 1971 resulted in a U.S. Supreme Court decision that ruled, 7–2, against the National Basketball Association. Haywood had successfully slam-dunked the NBA's age barrier. His case caused a shockwave through every city in the league, and forever changed the face of the NBA. Shortly after this landmark judgment, the NBA eventually agreed to settle out of court. Haywood says "The settlement with Sam Schulman was pennies on the dollar. Haywood personally received no financial damages. "I just wanted to play." Seattle's legal team incurred $3 million in expenses. Even after all this drama subsided, the very next year, the NBA expansion Buffalo Braves drafted Haywood in 1972, claiming he should now be eligible since his college class had just graduated. Once again, Seattle received a favorable decision regarding Haywood's playing rights. The NBA ruled that Seattle already held the contractual rights to Haywood.

Gar Heard feels that Haywood's victory in court definitely cleared the path for other ABA players to cross-over to the NBA. "Guys like John Brisker and Jim McDaniel soon signed with Seattle. Other ABA players could now switch too." The NBA and the ABA started playing a series of exhibition games after the Haywood ruling, with the ABA holding its own against the so-called superior league. "The Haywood case had a major influence on the NBA and ABA finally merging in 1976," says Heard.

The two leagues might have merged right then and there, except that NBA All-Star Oscar Robertson filed a law suit against the NBA that prevented unification of the two competing leagues from happening for six more years. The NBA owners saw the financial writing on the wall, and actually voted in 1970 to indeed merge with the ABA. However, the NBA Players Association filed an April 1970 lawsuit on antitrust grounds, claiming the ABA's existence resulted in increased salaries for players in both leagues. The Robertson suit wasn't resolved until 1976, making it impossible for the merger to happen while this case was pending.

In the meantime, Haywood was no longer shackled by his lawsuit and was finally free to play full time for Seattle. The next two seasons, Haywood made the All-NBA first team twice, setting forever Sonics records of 29.2 points and 13.4 rebounds per game in 1973-74. He played in four NBA All-Star games, scoring 23 points and snaring 11 rebounds in the 1974 contest (finishing second to Bob Lanier for MVP honors).

Haywood had gone from Public Enemy No. 1 to a sought-after celebrity. I can remember a TV appearance he made on 'The Dating Game.' In 1973, Haywood said a salesman approached him to promote a new shoe line. "The guy was operating out of the back of his car, and offered me half ownership of his company if I'd help endorse his sneaker. I told him I didn't need to be compensated and did it for nothing. We were all in the Pacific Northwest and I just wanted him to do well." Turns out, the shoe salesman was named Phil Knight, originator of the NIKE sports empire. "When Phil offered me that opportunity, Phil didn't even have a factory at that time. I still have a copy of that 1973 NIKE poster," says Haywood. "I don't think he's going to give me half now."

Overall, during his five seasons with Seattle, Haywood averaged 24.9 points per game and 12.1 rebounds per game. He also played for New York, New Orleans, Los Angeles and Washington, playing 14 pro seasons for six teams. He retired in 1983.

Haywood Controlling the Boards
From the lens of George Kalinsky

Besides paving the way for Haywood to play for Seattle, the Supreme Court's "early entry" verdict forever altered the structure of the amateur draft for pro sports and for future underclassmen to enter the league without four years of college under their belts. The NBA changed its rules to allow for "hardship entry" into the draft if a collegiate player could prove that the income from playing in the NBA was necessary to his family. The Haywood Rule became known as the hardship rule.

Alvan Adams was part of the reason this charade was dropped in 1976. Adams was a junior at Oklahoma and filed for early entry. Since Adams' father was a wealthy oilman, the NBA questioned Alvan's hardship status. Says Adams, "My father wouldn't sign their forms, saying it was my son applying for the league's employment, not me. Alvan's the one without the money."

The league revised its code so that all underclassmen were allowed into the draft. Thanks to Woody, teenagers would no longer be turned away from playing professional basketball. Like ESPN's trend-setting impact on cable television, it marked the beginning of the modern sports era from the business side. The San Francisco Warrior's Phil Chenier was the first to benefit from the new rule.

Though he was a dominating player in his day, Haywood is not yet in the Naismith Basketball Hall of Fame. "The NBA always told me I'd pay a price for the irreparable damage the league felt my lawsuit caused. This is just another way of the league getting back at me," Haywood said.

Haywood's #24 Jersey was ultimately retired by the SuperSonics during a halftime ceremony on February 26, 2007. Wilkens was in Seattle's front office at that time and pushed for Haywood's Sonics acknowledgement. "Haywood was certainly deserving of the honor," said Wilkens. Finally, at the 2010 All Star Game in Dallas, Haywood was honored by the NBA, but even this didn't seem like enough to pacify Haywood. "My portion of the ceremony only lasted one minute. In spite of more than four hours of broadcast coverage, not once did TV mention it or show it over the air. That was the biggest dagger. To this day, I'm still paying the price."

Today's NBA descendants don't seem to identify Haywood's place in hoops history and appreciate the opportunity and financial windfall he made possible for them. Haywood jump-started plenty of NBA careers. Twenty-one of the 24 All Star game participants in 2010 came into the league under the landmark off-the-court regulation Haywood changed forty years earlier. They were all instant millionaires due to Haywood's pioneering efforts. Yet when it comes to recognition of Haywood's contribution to their paychecks, the silence is deafening.

Haywood says it's already arranged that he'll eventually get into the NBA Hall of Fame in 2012 for his playing accomplishments and contributions to the game. "It's a done deal. I'll be going in as a Knick." I asked why not as a Sonic, where he experienced his best NBA years? "Because the Sonics franchise doesn't exist anymore," replied Haywood. Personally, I debate the NBA's logic. If Oscar Robertson wasn't already a Hall of Famer, would the Big O go in as a Sacramento King, since the Cincinnati Royals are defunct?

Like Curt Flood did for Major League Baseball free agency, Haywood pioneered legal precedence as the NBA's original early-entry player. Like Jackie Robinson, he courageously endured and survived the taunts to challenge the NBA status quo, yet he's still waiting for his rightful place in basketball history for his impact on the sport.

Wilkens says today's players should be reminded of player's contributions like Haywood's. "The Players Association should go into the archives and do a documentary on Haywood. He paved the way for them. How often do you hear about

Curt Flood? These guys are why pro sports have evolved the way they have. Flood and Haywood opened those doors."

Although he achieved stardom for the Seattle SuperSonics, and never donned a Portland uniform, Haywood hopes to be recognized and remembered as a "trailblazer."

Football's Early Foundation

I don't imagine that when Walter Camp invented American football in 1878, the terms Blitz, Bomb, Coffin Corner Kick, Cover Three, and Bubble Screen came to mind. Dime Coverage wasn't yet a strategy, and a Face Mask hadn't been invented yet, nor had Helmets. A Hook and Ladder still was a term applied to the fire department. A Pistol Formation meant execution of another kind. A Pocket was something to hold change, and a Sack was intended to hold your lunch. Division was an arithmetic term. Football has come a long way.

The game of American Football as we know it today reportedly dates back to the nineteenth century. There is some evidence to support that the ancient Greeks played a version of football they called harpaston. This game supposedly took place on a rectangular field with goal lines on both ends. There were two teams of equal number, divided by a center line. The game began by throwing the harpaston or handball into the air. The object of the game was to pass, kick, or run the ball past the opposing team's goal line.

The history of American football can be traced to early versions of rugby, with both games having their origin in varieties of football played in the United Kingdom in the mid-19th century. Walter Camp, considered the Father of American Football, initiated important rule changes that developed and distinguished the American game. Among these were the line of scrimmage, the snap from center to quarterback, and the down and distance. These rule adoptions revolutionized the game. In 1888, tackling below the waist was allowed, and in 1889, the officials were given whistles and stopwatches.

During the first half of the 20th century, collegiate football grew in popularity. Bowl games were created to bolster the attractiveness of the college game.

Like rugby, football was a mob game in its infancy. Collisions often led to serious injuries and sometimes even death. The situation came to a head in 1905 when there were 19 fatalities nationwide. President Theodore Roosevelt threatened to shut the game down if drastic changes were not made. This led to the formation of the Intercollegiate Athletic Association of the United States (later to become the NCAA), in an effort to make the game safer. In 1906, to open up the game and reduce injury, the forward pass was introduced. This became a big step towards the evolution of the modern game. It was Amos Alonzo Stagg who introduced innovations such as the huddle, the tackling dummy, and the pre-snap shift.

NFL Divisions (team's founding date)

AFC NORTH

Baltimore Ravens(1996)

Cincinnati Bengals (1968)

Cleveland Browns (1946)

Pittsburgh Steelers (1933)

AFC SOUTH

Houston Texans   (2002)

Indianapolis Colts(1944)

Jacksonville Jaguars (1995)

Tennessee Titans (1960)

AFC EAST

Buffalo Bills (1960)

Miami Dolphins (1966)

New England Patriots (1960)

New York Jets (1960)

AFC WEST

Denver Broncos (1960)

Kansas City Chiefs (1960)

Oakland Raiders (1960)

San Diego Chargers (1960)

NFC NORTH

Chicago Bears (1920)

Detroit Lions (1930)

Green Bay Packers (1921)

Minnesota Vikings (1961)

NFC SOUTH

Atlanta Falcons (1966)

Carolina Panthers (1995)

New Orleans Saints (1967)

Tampa Bay Buccaneers (1976)

NFC EAST

Dallas Cowboys (1960)

New York Giants (1925)

Philadelphia Eagles (1933)

Washington Redskins (1932)

NFC WEST

Arizona Cardinals (1920)

San Francisco 49ers (1946)

Seattle Seahawks (1976)

St. Louis Rams (1937)

Scoring and penalty rule changes continued. Field goals were lowered to three points in 1909. In 1912, touchdowns were raised to six points. In 1914, there was now a roughing-the-passer penalty.

In the early 20th century, early star players like Jim Thorpe, Bronko Nagurski, and Red Grange helped the NFL become successful. From 1930 to 1958, football became more of a regional sport, with numerous college football conferences coming into prominence. Growth also occurred in the passing game. Part of this occurred when the circumference of the ball was shrunk, making it easier to grip and throw. In 1934, the rules committee also removed two major penalties. One was for a loss of five yards for a second incomplete pass in any series. Another was a loss of downs and a loss of possession for an incomplete pass in the end zone.

In 1920, the American Professional Football Association was formed. Two years later, the league changed its moniker to the National Football League.

The introduction of the Heisman Trophy in 1953, awarded by New York City's Downtown Athletic Club, recognized the nation's most outstanding college football player. It remains a highly coveted award in American sports. Jay Berwanger, a halfback from the University of Chicago was the first recipient, and subsequently the first-ever NFL draft pick in 1936.

Television coverage has played a major part in the proliferation of football, more so in the professional ranks. There was enormous TV success with the NFL's 1958 title game, giving pro football a big boost of popularity. This resulted in the NFL becoming a trendy national phenomenon, with college football maintaining its solid regional ties. From another perspective on the popular growth of college football, in 1940 there were only five bowl games (Rose, Orange, Sugar, Sun, and Cotton). Now there are 35 bowl games.

The growth of football didn't come without challenges. The American Football League (AFL), a viable alternative to the NFL, began play in 1960. Competition for players brought on the pressure for the NFL to merge the two leagues. University of Alabama passer Joe Namath rejected the NFL to play for the New York Jets. Namath became the face of the AFL during the 1960's. In 1966, the AFL forced a partial merger with the NFL, with the two leagues agreeing to have a common draft and play in a common, season-ending championship game, initially known as the AFL-NFL World Championship. Two years later, the game's name was changed to the Super Bowl. In 1970, the two leagues merged to form a new 26-team league. The merger resulted in the NFL sharing gate and broadcasting revenues between home and visiting teams.

With the growth of college football's appeal came more television coverage. Starting in 1952, the NCAA claimed and negotiated all TV broadcast rights for its member institutions. In 1984, several schools brought suit against the NCAA under the Sherman Antitrust Act to negotiate their own TV deals. The Supreme Court ruled against the NCAA. Schools can now negotiate their own deals.

In the early stages of the game of football, a pig's bladder was inflated and used as the ball. By comparison, today's football is an inflated rubber bladder enclosed in a pebble-grained leather cover or cowhide. This material is used because it is both durable and easily tanned.

Basketball – Past to the Present

Who knew when James Naismith invented the game of basket ball in 1891, that it would become a multi-billion dollar sport? Naismith was asked by the YMCA to invent a new but non-rowdy indoor game that could be played during the cold winter.

The first game was primitively played using a soccer ball and two mounted peach baskets. Teams played nine against nine. Naismith instituted 13 original rules. Though basketball's popularity would soon spread across the nation, it would take more than another half-century before basketball became recognized as an entertaining and legitimate professional sport.

Formal professional basketball leagues were initiated in 1898, with six teams taking part in the first National Basketball League. This league lasted for six seasons. In 1906, metal hoops, nets, and boards were introduced. The soccer ball was replaced by a Spalding ball, similar to the one used today. Some teams enclosed their court with chicken-wire to speed up the game and keep the ball in play. Media in the day referred to players as "cagers." Most court's dimensions were about two-thirds the size of today's NBA version.

Other local leagues were soon formed, and regional undertakings expanded Naismith's novel sport. Throughout the Northeast, the style of play differed as much as the rules they tolerated. Shooting was restricted to the two-handed set shot and layups. Passing was to be the focus. When Naismith handed down his original 13 rules, dribbling was nowhere to be found. Since extreme violence among players was typical with gladiator-like shoving and head-butting the norm, players who were ensnared with the ball by defenders would fumble or drop it away. Part of this was out of self-preservation. The man with the ball was like a running back scampering for his life. Thus, the innovation of dribbling came to be. It truly was a cage match. Other advances of the time were the pick-and-roll and the bounce pass. The jump shot wouldn't become part of basketball's fabric until the 1940's, and the dunk didn't become a consistent part of the game until the 1960's.

By 1910, regional basketball proliferated, with numerous pro leagues connected by railroad lines. Players jumped from team to team, offering their services to the highest bidder. Some participants were listed on as many as five different rosters at a time. Professional basketball continued on into the 1920's like a barn-storming circus, going town to town. Teams would play more than a hundred games a year. Included were the original New York Celtics (founded in 1914; the Boston Celtics weren't founded until 1946) with players required to sign a contract to play with them.

In an effort to nationalize the game, the American Basketball League was founded in 1925. Player contracts became exclusive. Harsh fines were instituted for dirty play. The league eventually tumbled in the early 1930's due to the Great Depression.

In 1936, basketball finally became an Olympic sport, being included in the Berlin Olympic Games. The games were played on an outdoor clay court, with the United States winning the inaugural gold medal and Canada finishing second.

In 1946, another national league was established, the Basketball Association of America. It was formed by a group of hockey team owners looking to fill their empty arena when their hockey teams were on the road. Their strategy of controlling major-market cities forced a merger with their then-rival National Basketball League, thus leading to the formation of the National Basketball Association in 1949. Now the East

Coast big-city teams would compete with Midwest-market talent and pro basketball would have a definitive set of regulations.

The Harlem Globetrotters have been a basketball treasure for decades. They began in the late 1920's as six players touring the Midwest during the dead of winter in an unheated Model-T Ford. The Trotters hardly earned enough to pay for gas to get to the next town. By the 1950's, Abe Saperstein's creation was an international hit, with the team living up to its moniker of Globetrotters by playing on multiple continents before record-setting throngs. The Trotters even defeated the reigning-champion, George Mikan-led Minneapolis Lakers, in both 1948 and 1949. The Trotters soon contributed to the social integration of the new NBA in 1950, when the league selected African-American players Chuck Cooper (first to be drafted) and Earl Lloyd (first to play an NBA game) in that year's draft.

A major contributor to the modernization of the game was George Mikan. The 6'10" Mikan made the big man position fashionable in the 1940's and 1950's. He was clearly basketball's best player of his era, with hook shots that were nearly unstoppable. Goaltending in both college and pro basketball was prohibited because of him. The NBA also legislated that the lane was widened (from six to twelve feet) so future giants couldn't post up under the basket without incurring a three-second violation. In order to counter Mikan's dominance, teams would stall to win games; however this resulted in the NBA's initially stalling in garnering TV coverage and fan support. This boring strategy of teams killing the clock once they got the lead resulted in very low-scoring games and lots of fouls to get the ball back.

In 1954, the NBA mercifully adopted the shot clock, which forced teams to shoot within 24 seconds. This was the creation of Danny Biasone, the owner of the Syracuse Nationals. This rule adoption rescued the NBA and revolutionized the game with a faster pace, more possessions, and a more electrifying game.

Another superstar big man from 1954 to 1965 was the Hawks' (St. Louis/Atlanta) Bob Pettit, who made the All-Star team all 11 of his seasons in the NBA. Pettit was also a two-time MVP.

What do Wilt Chamberlain, Elgin Baylor, Jerry West, Oscar Robertson, and many other NBA players from 1957-1969 have in common? They all had to learn to live with defeat, thanks to the juggernaut dynasty known as the Boston Celtics, who won the championship 11 times. Talk about four-leaf-clover luck, even perennial All-Star Bob Cousy fell into the Celtics' laps in the 1950 dispersal draft from the Chicago Stags. The Celtics had the Midas touch. Only Chamberlain's 1967 Philadelphia 76ers managed to wrestle the title away (once).

Another notable social event occurred in the NBA during this 12-year stretch. Basketball became fully integrated with Bill Russell's taking on the basketball role of Jackie Robinson. Unlike baseball, where an individual could make an impact regardless of the racial slurs and humiliation, African American basketball players of the 1950's endured an additional kind of prejudice. Their slight was getting neglected on the court, often getting ignored on offense. It was OK for them to bust-ass while playing defense or getting rebounds, but getting their touches on offense was mostly taboo. Thanks to Russell, Wilt, Baylor, Robertson, Lenny Wilkens, and many others, African Americans became a vital part of the NBA. The 1964-65 Celtics were the first NBA team to start an all-black lineup. Russell was the first African American MVP. Thanks to these timely superstars, the social climate of the NBA changed.

You can't look back at basketball history without noting the goliath contributions of Wilt Chamberlain. Chamberlain joined the Philadelphia Warriors in 1959. His rookie year, he averaged 37.6 points and 27 rebounds. Nicknamed the Big Dipper (as well as several other monikers), Chamberlain was the petrifying, super-human gold standard of the new NBA. Unstoppable, he averaged more than 50 points one season and scored 100 points in a single game. His one undeniable nemesis was Bill Russell. Their epic battles were the face of the NBA during the 1960's.

Other players of this era who seemed to defy kryptonite were Jerry West, Oscar Robertson, and Elgin Baylor. Praised for his "Mr. Clutch" reputation, it's West's silhouette that adorns the NBA logo. In the 1965 Western Division finals playoffs against the Baltimore Bullets, West averaged an NBA-record 46.3 points. The "Big O" averaged a triple-double for an entire season, finishing with 181 in his career. The high-scoring Baylor averaged nearly 35 points a game over a three-year stretch and is credited for acrobatically re-shaping the game. Nothing could stop these superstars.

The landscape of the NBA in the 1970's is mostly remembered for Lew Alcindor's (Kareem Abdul-Jabbar) massive impression on the league and also for player versus league litigation that changed the sport (professionally and collegiately) forever. The merger with the rival American Basketball Association in 1976 was the culmination of two lawsuits.

Seattle's Spencer Haywood sued the NBA in 1970 just for the privilege to play in the league. It didn't matter that Haywood had already played a year professionally in the ABA. The NBA technically still viewed him as an underclassman. The 21-year-old Haywood won his lawsuit, with the U.S. Supreme court ruling that Haywood's situation was a hardship case and that he should have the right to support his family. This landmark ruling opened the door for many future superstars to enter the league before graduating from college.

The NBA and ABA would have merged in 1970, except that the Oscar Robertson class-action lawsuit against the NBA was still pending. The 1970 Robertson suit mostly targeted the reserve clause, which allowed teams to extend a player's contract in perpetuity. With the rival ABA willing to considerably up the ante of player's contracts in a bidding war, the NBA viewed this as a major threat to basketball's financial structure. The NBA players felt the reserve clause restricted their mobility to join the higher-paying ABA. Pro baseball's Curt Flood was simultaneously suing major league baseball for the same reason but he was going solo without his fellow player's support. As president of the National Basketball Player's

Association, Robertson had union backing. This case remained unresolved for six years. The NBA finally settled in 1976, awarding $4.5 million in damages to the plaintiffs for lost wages.

In 1976, the NBA and the rival league finally merged. With the absorption of four surviving ABA teams came a changed image of the game, not necessarily for the better. Some of the ABA's former high-flying dynamic athletes, sky-walkers like Julius Erving, Spencer Haywood, and David Thompson, and already established NBA scoring machines like Pistol Pete Maravich, Nate Archibald, and Bob McAdoo provided a new flair for the fans.

If there was a dominant 70's team, it was the New York Knicks, with self-less players like Walt Frazier, Willis Reed, Bill Bradley, and Dave DeBusschere. Reed's gimpy-kneed walk into Madison Square Garden for Game 7 of the 1970 Finals against Chamberlain and the Lakers is a poignant moment in NBA lore. Reed wasn't supposed to play but willed himself into action, despite a damaged knee. The late 1970's in the NBA is also remembered for the sullied reputation created by drugs and the dearth of dynasties, caused in part by free agency. Fans frowned on what the league had become, a violent sport with uninhibited athletes who had been bestowed with massive amounts of cash. The beauty of the team-oriented blue-collar sport seemed gone, replaced by singular achievement. Never mind the talent explosion, the fan-base was withering away. But with the late-decade birth of ESPN and the 1979 addition of two game-changing superstars, a league revival was just around the corner.

The NBA got its much-needed make-over during the 1980's, primarily thanks to Boston's Larry Bird and Los Angeles' Magic Johnson. The Celtics and Lakers teams garnered eight of the decade's championships, regenerating a fierce rivalry from the 1960's. The 1980's also saw a major influx of new stars led by Michael Jordan, Akeem Olajuwon, the irrepressible Charles Barkley, Dominique Wilkens, Karl Malone, Isiah Thomas, and Scottie Pippen.

Thanks to the evolution of ESPN, cable TV, and regional sports coverage, national TV networks were now forced to compete harder for the attention of sports fans. The NBA suddenly attracted wide-spread popularity. Broadcast rights, ratings, revenue, and player paychecks soared. The league swiftly had a new personality. Bird, Magic, and Jordan gave it a new energy. It's hard to say which player had more pure will to win.

The three-point shot had just entered the NBA in 1979. Bird seemed to make it his personal domain, winning the All-Star 3-point shootout competition in its first three years.

Though the NBA had already begun to go vertical in the 1970's, 1980's players like Michael Jordan and Dominique Wilkins re-crafted elevation to new heights. Known as "His Airness," Jordan's vicious, tongue-wagging dunks became stuff of legend. So did his consistent scoring exploits. Not to be outdone, Wilkins was a nightly highlight film.

While the Detroit Pistons completed the 1980's with back-to-back titles, the Chicago Bulls were just warming up for their run at six titles in the 1990's. The Houston Rockets managed to grab the brass ring in '94 and '95, but an asterisk should probably be attached to their title accomplishment. Those were the two years Jordan chose to temporarily retire from the NBA, taking a hiatus to take a swing at playing pro baseball. Serving as bookends to the Rocket's two championships were two three-peats by the Bulls. Jordan was the Finals MVP in four of the six Bulls titles.

As they had during the Magic Johnson and Abdul-Jabbar era of the 80's, the Lakers re-established their dominance in the new century, winning four championships. Three of those titles were behind the soap opera tandem of Shaquille O'Neal and Kobe Bryant. These two competing teammates grabbed headlines by dominating on the court and having a contentious relationship outside the stadium. The San Antonio Spurs also managed to grab three titles behind Tim Duncan.

The first decade of the 21st century also served as a renaissance of fast-break basketball. Led by two-time MVP Steve Nash, every time they grabbed a defensive rebound, the run-and-gun Phoenix Suns played like dragsters shot from cannons. The Suns saga of speed became the standard for other fast-break teams and served to reinvigorate the NBA. The draft class of 2003 provided a new infusion of stars with LeBron James, Dwayne Wade, and Chris Bosh joining the NBA.

As we enter the second decade of the 2000's, now they're all teammates in Miami.

Who is the only person to officiate All-Star games in both Major League Baseball and the NBA?

Jake O'Donnell holds this distinction, working as a major league umpire from 1968 to 1971, and as an NBA referee for 28 years from 1967 to 1995.

Here's my subjective view of some of the greatest NBA players by position.

Center

Bill Russell was a supreme defensive player and team leader of the Boston Celtics. During his career the Celtics, he won 11 NBA championships in his 13 years of playing.

Wilt Chamberlain was the most physically imposing and athletic of all centers. One season he averaged 50 points and 25 rebounds a game. Of course, he is also famous for scoring 100 points in a single game.

Point Guard

Magic Johnson At 6' 9", he was the tallest guard to ever play in the NBA. Johnson would often get triple doubles in games: over 10 points, assists, and rebounds.

Oscar Robertson Known as the BIG O, Roberson averaged a triple double for a whole season.

Shooting Guard

Michael Jordan has been called the greatest basketball player ever. The 6' 6" shooting guard had tremendous leaping ability, allowing him to make freakish dunks over his opponents. He was extremely quick and a defensive leader in steals. He was a true competitor.

Jerry West was a 6' 4" guard for the Los Angeles Lakers. He was known as "Mr. Clutch" because he would especially excel during crunch-time in a game. The silhouette of the NBA logo is a caricature of West.

Forward

Larry Bird could do anything on a basketball court with a dead-eye shot and a court vision never before seen for a player at his position. Bird was one of the NBA's greatest clutch players.

Julius Erving "Dr. J" was a prolific scorer and acrobat on the court. When driving the lane, he was almost unstoppable when going in for a dunk.

50 Greatest NBA Players of All Time

Kareem Abdul-Jabbar	James Worthy	Nate Archibald
Karl Malone	Moses Malone	Paul Arizin
Pete Maravich	Charles Barkley	Kevin McHale
Rick Barry	Elgin Baylor	George Mikan
Earl Monroe	Dave Bing	Larry Bird
Hakeem Olajuwon	Wilt Chamberlain	Shaquille O'Neal
Bob Cousy	Robert Parish	Dave Cowens
Bob Pettit	Billy Cunningham	Scottie Pippen
Dave DeBusschere	Willis Reed	Oscar Robertson
Clyde Drexler	Julius Erving	David Robinson
Patrick Ewing	Bill Russell	Walt Frazier
Dolph Shayes	George Gervin	Bill Sharman
Hal Greer	John Stockton	Isiah Thomas
John Havlicek	Elvin Hayes	Nate Thurmond
Magic Johnson	Wes Unseld	Sam Jones
Bill Walton	Michael Jordan	Jerry Lucas
Lenny Wilkens	Jerry West	

Baseball's Infancy

Baseball has a history that goes back to even the colonial days. In 1791 in Pittsfield, Massachusetts, baseball was referenced in a town ordinance that banned the playing of the game within 80 yards of the town meeting house. "Base ball" was also referenced as a game that was a Saturday ritual in 1823 on the then-outskirts of New York City (an area today known as Greenwich Village).

The New York Knickerbockers weren't always a basketball team. In September 1845, a social club for the upper middle classes of New York City formed an amateur baseball team. This is the first team recognized to play under modern rules. In earlier versions of baseball rules, a fielder could simply throw the ball at a runner and he'd be out. The Knickerbocker Rules changed this tactic. Plugging the runner was prohibited. Now, fielders were required to tag the runner or force the runner out. Apparently, this helped alleviate all the arguments and fist-fights that ensued.

The first competitive game played under the Knickerbocker rules was June 19, 1846. In Hoboken, New Jersey, the New York Nine trounced the Knickerbockers 23 to 1. The rules caught on, and this version of baseball became known as the New York Game.

Through 1855, New York newspapers at the time still covered cricket more than baseball. In 1857, the National Association of Base Ball Players was formed to govern baseball and establish a championship. Sixteen teams formed this initial organization. The NABBP received a boost from the Civil War. By 1865, there were almost 100 clubs, and by 1867, more than 400 teams, stretching all the way to California and Louisiana. This helped create a more unified national version of baseball.

Rules to that point did not allow professional play. That changed in 1869. It was then, that the Cincinnati Red Stockings in Ohio became the first professional club of the NABBP. They dissolved after two years and moved to Boston, creating the Boston Red Stockings in 1871. Another club of the day was the Chicago White Stockings. They won the championship in 1870, and later became the Chicago Cubs. The Cubs are the oldest team in American organized sports. Interesting how the two oldest and most historic ball parks that still exist today in the major leagues are Boston's Fenway Park (open since 1912) and Chicago's Wrigley Field (the Cub's home since 1916). The National Association of Base Ball Players lasted 12 years as the governing body of amateur leagues. The Brooklyn Atlantics became the first true dynasty in the sport, winning the championship seven of those seasons.

Interestingly, the Great Chicago Fire of 1871 had an impact on the forming of a major league. The Chicago White Stockings' home field and most of their equipment had been destroyed by the fire, forcing the team to withdraw from the amateur league while the city recovered. They returned to National Association play in 1874. In the meantime, the Boston Red Stockings dominated play. Boston also hoarded many of the game's premier players, including those under contract. Contract-jumping ended up causing an organized attempt toward a more ethical league. The result was the organized formation of the National Base Ball League in 1876. The establishment of the current American League came in 1901.

The National League clubs now had the ability to enforce player contracts, thus preventing players from jumping to higher-paying clubs. With the focus on the teams rather than the players now, teams were forced to play all their games. Once out of the running for a league championship, some teams had been forfeiting scheduled games. This had been a frequent occurrence. Gambling on games was also a problem for the new professional league. Worried about credibility, the new National League made a conscious effort to reduce gambling and avoid the doubt it created on the validity of their game.

As previously noted, organized amateur baseball received a big boost of popularity during the Civil War. There were no race restrictions. Now that the National League was formed, teams in the 1880's chose to have a gentlemen's agreement to exclude non-white players from professional baseball. For the African-American players who were already in the league, they were unceremoniously dropped. Moses Fleetwood Walker, the actual first African-American to play professional baseball, along with his brother Welday Walker, was dumped from his major league roster. An unknown number of African-Americans continued to play in the major leagues by passing themselves off as Indians, or South or Central Americans. The Cuban Giants became the first professional black baseball club in 1885. In the early 1920s, New York Giants' manager John McGraw slipped a black player, Charlie Grant, into his lineup (reportedly by passing him off to the front office as an Indian). The Reserve Clause, which now restricted players from free movement to other clubs caused the early years of the National League a lot of headaches and challenges. One result was the formation of several competitive leagues. None survived, though the American Association did last ten years (1881-1891). Its tolerance of selling alcohol to spectators did give it the moniker as the "beer and whiskey" league. The National League and the American Association champions did meet in a postseason championship series for a number of years. Not quite the World Series, but almost.

One league that did manage to stick around was the Western League. The Western League began play in 1894 with teams in Detroit, Indianapolis, Milwaukee, Minneapolis, Kansas City, Grand Rapids, Sioux City, and Toledo. For the 1900 season, the league changed its name to the American League. Several teams were moved to larger, strategic cities with the intent of challenging the National League. In 1901, the American League began operation as a major league.

This off-the-field competition between the two major leagues caused a barrage of legal disputes over contract breaking. Other remaining independent leagues, feeling the financial repercussion of the National and American League's bidding war for players, eventually sold players to the more affluent leagues in order to maintain their survival.

After 1902, the National and American Leagues decided to cease cross-raiding the other leagues' rosters. This also reinforced the power of the clubs over the players, with the reserve clause keeping players a slave to their teams. In essence, ball players had become a commodity.

Other results of this agreement were the formal arrangement of a World Series between the two league champions. In 1903, Boston's American League team won the first World Series. The agreement also quelled the possibility of any more rebellions from independent leagues. Though they didn't want to acknowledge the National and American Leagues as superior, the Independent leagues had basically become the minor leagues.

1900 to 1919 – the Dead Ball Era

In the first two decades of the 20th Century, baseball was much more aggressive and violent than today. Inside pitching was the norm. Ty Cobb would steal a base with spikes flying. The Dead Ball era was so-named because of the dominance of pitchers like Cy Young, Christy Mathewson, Walter Johnson, and Grover Cleveland Alexander. It was also a result of the thriftiness of the owners who didn't want to pay the then hefty sum of $3.00 per baseball. Back in the early part of the 1900's, that would equate to nearly $80 a ball today. If there was a foul ball, security guards at the ballpark would retrieve the balls hit into the crowd. It was common for one ball to make its way through an entire game. Only lost balls got replaced. Is this what helped Cy Young win an unthinkable 511 games in his 22-year career? Rick Honeycutt wouldn't have needed a thumb tack to scuff up the ball. Imagine what renowned spit-baller Gaylord Perry could have done with an out-of-shape ball scarred with mud and grass. Perry intimidated and irritated hitters by the mere gesture of somehow doctoring the ball. Opposing managers would go ballistic if Perry even grazed the bill of his cap. Back in the early 1900's, Perry would have been salivating over not having to salivate the ball.

I once crossed paths with Perry at a North Carolina airport, long after his 314-win, 22-season major league career was complete. Perry was the first pitcher to have been named the Cy Young award winner in both the National League and American League. Perry was famous for doctoring the baseball. His favorite trick pitch was the old Puffball, where he would load up on rosin so that a puff of white smoke would release while he threw his pitches. I had previously met Perry during a 1998 Harmon Killebrew charity golf tournament in Phoenix, and at that time, he had kindly autographed baseballs for my three kids. I walked over to thank him. We got to talking about contemporary power pitchers like Randy Johnson. I asked Perry how blazing his fast ball was during his prime.

"Glenn, it's not the velocity of the ball," said Perry. "It's the location of the pitch. I used to bring it 94 miles an hour, but movement and location is really the key."

Somewhere during the conversation, I must have forgotten diplomacy and responded: "And maybe a little saliva?"

The gracious and good-natured Perry broke into a big mischievous grin. Looking skyward with his hand on his chin, acting like he'd given the matter deep consideration, Perry innocently replied: "Not that I recall."

Despite the dominance of pitchers during the dead ball era, some superstar hitters did make their mark in baseball lore. Home runs weren't plentiful, but there were great players during this generation. Shortstop Honus Wagner (the Flying Dutchman) primarily with the Pittsburgh Pirates is considered to be one of the best to ever play shortstop. Wagner won eight batting titles during his 20-year career (tied for first with Tony Gwynn). The Georgia Peach, Ty Cobb, collected a career batting average of .366.

Attendance in the beginning of the century would average around 3,200. But baseball's popularity was growing. By 1909, fan support nearly doubled to more than 5,800. Larger stadiums were built or existing grounds were enlarged, ballparks like Ebbets Field in Brooklyn, Tiger Stadium in Detroit, the Polo Grounds in Manhattan, Boston's Fenway Park, and Comiskey Park and Wrigley Field in Chicago.

Only Fenway Park and Wrigley Field still exist today. With no television or radio coverage, fans had no other choice but to go to the ballpark. In 1909, the average industrial worker in America made $594 a year and worked a 52-hour week. A Model T Ford cost $850, and a cross-country trip by car took 56 days. The price of admission to a baseball game then ranged from about 25 cents for the bleachers to $2 for a box seat.

Concerned about the lack of offense, baseball did make a number of adjustments to the rules in 1920. The result was more of an advantage by the hitters. The largest parks brought the outfield fences closer. The size, shape, and construction of the ball had to meet stricter guidelines, too, which caused the ball to travel further.

The Negro Leagues and Racial Integration

In 1920, the Negro National League was founded by a former ballplayer, Rube Foster. The Eastern Colored League was established in 1923. The Great Depression eventually caused them to fold.

It was from 1942 to 1948 that the Negro League World Series was revived, but 1948 marked the end of the Negro Leagues, with financial difficulties ending their existence. Change for the white-only major leagues was already on the horizon.

The major league's color-barring practice lasted until April 15, 1947, when Jackie Robinson became the first modern era African-American player for the Brooklyn Dodgers. Larry Doby soon joined the American League's Cleveland Indians in July of 1947. In 1948, Roy Campanella joined Robinson in Brooklyn. Satchel Paige, who had pitched more than 2,400 innings in the Negro Leagues, sometimes two and three games a day, joined Doby in 1948. When nearly all pitchers his age have already hung up their cleats, Paige was just beginning his major league career at the young age of 42. He continued to play baseball until he was at 59. His ERA in the Major Leagues was 3.29. Paige played for the Indians, St. Louis Browns and Kansas City Athletics from 1948-1965.

The 50-year plus color barrier that had existed since the evolution of professional baseball was finally broken, but it would still take a number of years before baseball became fully integrated. It wasn't until 1959 that the Boston Red Sox became the final major league baseball team to integrate.

Latin American players also benefitted from the integration of baseball. In 1951, two Chicago White Sox, Venezuelan-born Chico Carrasquel and Cuban-born (and black) Minnie Miñoso, became the first Hispanic All-Stars.

Frank Robinson was the 1956 Rookie of the Year with the Cincinnati Reds. In 1975, Robinson became the first African American manager in the major leagues, serving as the Cleveland Indian's player-manager.

The integration of baseball was not restricted to just American soil. In the 1950's, Japan was also adjusting to the ghettoization of ball players. Wally Yonamine was of Japanese lineage, but was not welcome in Japan's baseball world. That's because Yonamine was a Japanese American. Only six years after the devastating attacks on Hiroshima and Nagasaki, Yonamine became the Japanese equivalent of Jackie Robinson, becoming the first U.S. professional baseball player to play in Japan.

Yonamine's baseball beginning was despised. His style of play was aggressive. Yonamine's sacrifice bunts and yelling at the umps was not appreciated. Japanese fans had not experienced this kind of baseball. Yonamine dodged rocks, verbal abuse and even the Japanese mafia, but his in-your-face flair finally won over his detractors. Yonamine led the Yomiuri Giants to eight pennants, and along the way, he was a three-time batting champion. In 1957, he was the league's MVP. Yonamine became wildly popular and was eventually honored by the Emperor. He later managed several

Japanese teams. When compared to Jackie Robinson, Yonamine dismissed the association, saying the African-American ballplayer had it much rougher being accepted.

In 1920, doctoring baseballs was outlawed, but it was a single player that altered baseball history. In 1919, Boston Red Sox owner Harry Frazee sold George Herman Ruth to the New York Yankees. Ruth had begun his major league career in 1914 as a left-handed pitcher for the Red Sox. His bat was too valuable to leave on the bench between starts, so Boston converted him to the outfield.

In Ruth's first season as a Yankee (1920), "The Bambino" belted an unheard of 54 home runs. The following year, Ruth hit 59 dingers. Later, 1927 saw the Sultan of Swat go yard 60 times. Power-hitters dominated the 1920's and 1930's, with sluggers like Jimmie Foxx, Lou Gehrig, Hack Wilson, and Hank Greenberg. Team themes like "Murder's Row" and the "Gashouse Gang" gave baseball a new identity that proved very popular with its fans.

Baseball's growth and awareness also evolved from its first electronic media coverage. August 5, 1921 marked the first radio broadcast of a baseball game. Pittsburgh's KDKA announced the game from Forbes Field, with Harold Arlin behind the microphone for the Phillies-Pirates matchup.

The Great Depression threw baseball a curveball with average attendance dropping below 5,000.

It was 1933 when the Mid-season Classic, pitting each league's greatest players in an exhibition game, was introduced. Fittingly, Babe Ruth hit the All-Star game's first home run.

Three years later, 1936 saw the creation of the Baseball Hall of Fame with five players initially inducted. This first lineup included Honus Wagner, Christy Mathewson, Ty Cobb, Walter Johnson and Babe Ruth. Upstate New York's Cooperstown is the home for baseball's hallowed history. It formally opened in 1939. It's not easy to find, but this quaint destination is a MUST for all baseball fans. Be sure you mapquest it first.

World War II

The war years saw many patriotic players join the armed forces. Boston's hitting great Ted Williams joined the military as a fighter pilot in 1942 for World War II and was recalled in 1952 for 39 more combat missions during Korean War. Williams still managed to hit .406 in 1941. No one has achieved this lofty batting accomplishment since. Williams didn't even earn the league MVP that season. He was overshadowed by Joe DiMaggio, who also missed major league time starting in 1943 to serve his country for two years. DiMaggio had a 56-game hitting streak to earn 1941 Most Valuable honors in the American League.

Cleveland Hall-of-Fame pitcher Bob Feller also gave up four years of his career for America's freedom.

On December 8, 1941, Feller enlisted in the Navy, volunteering immediately for combat service while becoming the first Major League Baseball player to do so following the attack on Pearl Harbor on December 7. Feller served as Gun Captain aboard the USS Alabama.

The founding of the All-American Girls Professional Baseball League took place in 1943. It lasted for 11 seasons. Tom Hanks and Geena Davis helped tell the story of the war-time ladies' league in the 1992 movie, *A League of Their Own*.

After World War II, baseball attendance increased to nearly 15,000 per game and kept on growing. With two New York National League teams relocating to the West Coast in 1958, baseball's expansion in the 1960's, combined with the increase of regular season games from 154 to 162, attendance records continued to be set.

Henry Aaron

Here's an intriguing and true war story that even Hammerin' Hank might not know about himself. In the early 1950's, Henry Aaron was a promising minor leaguer in the Milwaukee Braves system but had just been drafted to serve his country. Little did Aaron know that the Army doctor who conducted his military physical would turn out to be his guardian angel.

Dr. Marvin B. Wolf was drafted into the army in 1952 and sent to 5th Army in Milwaukee to be a medical examiner of new recruits. Dr. Wolf was an avid baseball fan, often watching a game on TV while listening to another contest on the radio. It was Dr. Wolf who drew the responsibility of Aaron's health assessment to join the military. Mind you, the Korean War was going on at the time. If inducted, Aaron would have likely gone off to war and lost at least two years from his baseball career. What if something tragic had happened to Henry? Fortunately, it never came to be. Somehow, Dr. Wolf thought there "might" be something wrong with Aaron's knee. Dr. Wolf rejected him for military service, allowing Aaron to continue his baseball career uninterrupted, and the rest is history. Aaron went on to play 22 years as one of baseball's all-time greatest players with that questionable knee.

Had Aaron been inducted into the military, he likely wouldn't have passed Babe Ruth's home run milestone. How is it that Dr. Wolf didn't deem a young, great athlete like Aaron physically fit to serve his country? Dr. Wolf's son, William Wolf, has his opinion on the matter direct from the source. "My Dad was such a huge baseball fan, he didn't want to disrupt Hank's blossoming baseball career." From this first-hand story, you can draw your own conclusions as to Aaron's fitness or lack thereof to pass the army physical. I'm sure other baseball fans will give Dr. Marvin Wolf a pass for his military medical review of Henry Aaron.

Relocation and Expansion

It was 1958 when the Brooklyn Dodgers headed to Los Angeles, and the rival New York Giants landed in San Francisco. Three years later, the American League expanded to Anaheim to create the California Angels and to the nation's capital to form the Washington Senators. This was major league baseball's first expansion in over 70 years. Expansion was soon on the fast track with the 1962 National League addition of the Houston Colt .45's and the New York Mets. The Athletics left Kansas City in 1968 to become the Oakland A's. Kansas City soon was back in the big leagues, with the Royals joining the Seattle Pilots as American League expansion teams in 1969. The Pilots didn't fly in Seattle very long. After just one season of playing in the Seattle Rainiers' Pacific Coast League Triple-A ballpark known as Sick's Stadium, the underfinanced Pilot's ownership group lost the team to a car dealer from Milwaukee named Bud Selig, who acquired the team in bankruptcy court. The 1969 Pilots became the 1970 Milwaukee Brewers. Selig has been officially serving as baseball's commissioner since 1998. Two other teams joined the National League in 1969, the San Diego Padres and the Montreal Expos.

It was 1972 when the Dallas market absorbed the Washington Senators, becoming the Texas Rangers.

Still sore over losing their Pilots in 1970, Seattle, King County, and the State of Washington sued the American League for $32 million dollars on breach of contract and anti-trust grounds. After six years of litigation, the ensuing settlement resulted in another Seattle expansion team known as the Mariners. The Toronto Blue Jays also entered the American League that year in 1977.

It wasn't until 1993 before baseball expanded again. That was the year the National League added Denver's Colorado Rockies and the Miami area was awarded the Florida Marlins.

In 1998, each league added another team, with the Tampa Bay Devil Rays joining the American League, and the Arizona Diamondbacks setting up shop in Phoenix as a National League franchise. To create an equal number of teams within each league, Milwaukee's Brewers switched to the National League in 1994. The National League remains at 16 teams, and the American League remains at 14.

Baseball Divisions (Team's Founding Date)

American League

West
Seattle Mariners (1977)
Los Angeles Angels of Anaheim (1961)
Texas Rangers (1961 as Wash. Senators)
Oakland A's (1901 as Philadelphia Athletics)

National League

West
Arizona Diamondbacks (1998)
Los Angeles Dodgers (1883 as Brooklyn Atlantics)
Colorado Rockies (1993)
San Francisco Giants (1883 as New York Gothams)
San Diego Padres (1969)

Central
Detroit Tigers (1894)
Minnesota Twins (1894 as Kansas City Blues)
Cleveland Indians (1894-Grand Rapids Rustlers)
Chicago White Sox (1894 as Sioux City)
Kansas City Royals (1969)

East
Baltimore Orioles (1894 as Milwaukee Brewers)
Toronto Blue Jays (1977)
New York Yankees (1901 as Baltimore Orioles)
Tampa Bay Rays (1998)
Boston Red Sox (1901)

Central
Cincinnati Reds (1890)
St Louis Cardinals (1882 as St L. Brown Stockings)
Houston Astros (1962 as Colt 45's)
Chicago Cubs (1870 as Chicago White Stockings)
Pittsburgh Pirates (1882 as Allegheny)
Milwaukee Brewers (1969 as AL Seattle Pilots)

East
Philadelphia Phillies (1883)
Wash. Nationals (1969 as Montreal Expos
New York Mets (1962)
Miami Marlins (1993)
Atlanta Braves (1871 as Boston Red Stockings)

> The Philadelphia Phillies are the oldest continuous, one-name, one-city franchise in all of professional American sports, dating to 1883.

Baseball, Forever Tainted by the Steroid Era

If ever there were a sport that is all about statistics, it is baseball. Baseball's glorious and long, traditional history cannot be viewed without using numbers to compare teams, players and eras. The fans, management, the players, their agents, everyone is obsessed with the numbers. Even casual fans get their fix by reading the box scores every morning.

If you question the influence of statistics in baseball, just look at the scoreboards of professional ballparks across the country. At Chase Field in Phoenix, a player's entire season is listed for all to see: every hit, at-bat, strikeout, double, RBI, stolen base, etc. This display exists at nearly all MLB stadiums. Pitch counts are up there on a scoreboard, too, along with how fast the last pitch was. Want to know how many strikeouts a pitcher has. It'll also be up there, probably sponsored by a local convenience store. Even the YES Network, which broadcasts NY Yankee games, started exhibiting ongoing pitch counts in the upper corner of the screen where you see the display of the current score and the mini diamond showing which bases have runners on board.

My son, Chad, learned how to read at a very early age, just so he could see how his hometown Sonics or Mariners did the night before. During the 1996 Seattle-Chicago NBA Finals, Chad (then age 5) said to me: "Dad, Hersey Hawkins shouldn't be covering Scottie Pippen, he's going to get posted up." As they say, the apple doesn't fall far from the tree. Then it's: "Dad, Griffey hit another homer, and Edgar Martinez was 3 for 4 with 4 RBI's." This was a preschooler. It saved me a lot of time reading the sports page.

It's such an injustice that the steroid disgrace placed a permanent stain on the game, and that career accomplishments by players from yesteryear will be overshadowed by players who artificially achieved their place in baseball history through performance-enhancing drugs. Who was truly the best home run hitter of all time? Now it's a discussion based on opinion only, not mere feats. Sadly, baseball's hallowed history will always have a blemish now.

Many baseball purists blame the lure of big contracts for pushing players to perform beyond their ability via performance-enhancing drugs. Former New York Yankee and Seattle Pilot Jim Bouton's groundbreaking tell-all book about his 1969 season in Seattle, *Ball Four*, acknowledged that amphetamines (a pep pill referred to as greenies) were in widespread use at least in the 1960's. Conditioning wasn't nearly as much a focus back then. With a 162-game season and tiring travel schedules, players needed a pick me up. Back then, there was no backlash from the fans.

Today is a new sports era, with greatly enhanced compensation for athletes courtesy of free agency, global media coverage, and exorbitant TV network contracts. Monumental performance translated into big bucks, so some players turned to more modern performance enhancing drugs, like Ephedra and improved steroids. Among other effects, Ephedra (a Chinese herb) speeds up the heart. Some consider it a weight-loss short-cut, so overweight athletes would take advantage of it. In 2003, Steve Bechler of the Baltimore Orioles was one who took Ephedra to lose weight. Bechler collapsed while pitching and died. Soon Ephedra was banned.

Though then-baseball commissioner Fay Vincent tried to ensure the prohibition of illegal substances during the early 1990's, MLB did not enforce nor emphasize it. Bud Selig became baseball's official commissioner in 1998 (he'd been unofficially handling the duties without the formal title since 1992). Major league baseball endured a strike in 1994 (the labor dispute cancelled that year's World Series and along the way, nearly 950 games). Baseball needed all the positive publicity it could assemble to regain fan support. Albeit artificially, the 1998 home run race between St Louis' Mark McGwire and the Chicago Cubs' Sammy Sosa gave baseball the fan stimulus package it needed, with McGwire socking 70 home runs, and Sosa going yard for 66.

Not to be outdone, 2001 saw Barry Bonds go herculean for 73 HR's, but Bonds late-career sprint for the all-time home run record provoked a backlash over steroids. Steroids increase a person's testosterone level, enabling a person to body-build more easily. Some athletes used steroids because it drastically shortens rehab time from injury, or so they claim. The main advantage is an increase in endurance and strength. Until he stopped playing in 2007 (rather until no team wanted his baggage anymore), Bonds went on to set baseball's all-time home run record with 762, surpassing Henry Aaron's honorable career achievement of 755. Because of speculation over his use of Performance Enhancing Drugs, Bonds' records never received the acclaim of his baseball predecessors. Part of this is due to Bonds' poor relationship with the media and some fans. Additionally in 2001, during his single season record home run chase, the 9/11 terrorist attacks dominated the national spotlight.

During the height of ESPN's blanket coverage of Bonds' controversial alleged steroid use and his pursuit of Hank Aaron's all-time home run record, Pedro Gomez was assigned full time to shadow Bonds' every move. Gomez's assignment went on for nearly three years.

Gomez is a voting member for Cooperstown's revered Hall of Fame, and he says he feels in the majority of the other ballot casters. "I never did and never will vote for Barry Bonds, Mark McGwire, Rafael Palmeiro, or Juan Gonzalez. These guys were first-ballot ballplayers. They have stained the game," says Gomez. "These players (and others) have hurt themselves more than the game. I am not in the minority on that opinion either. I have spoken with several current Hall of Famers regarding worthiness of those accused of (and of those who have belatedly admitted) steroid use. One notable HOF member said if any of those players ever get in, he will never attend ceremonies again. Personally, I don't think the steroid cheaters will ever get the necessary 75-percent vote to get voted into Cooperstown."

"The abusers got the fame, they got the dollars, they got the statistical numbers, but they will never get the final piece of the puzzle, enshrinement in the Hall," Gomez added. "Sadly, we will never truthfully know what their place in baseball history is."

Baseball has been criticized for turning a blind eye to its drug problems. MLB certainly indirectly benefited from steroid use during their post-1994 strike era when their battle for fan and media attention was more a priority.

Barry Bonds is still a central figure in baseball's steroid scandal. In 2007, Bonds was indicted on charges of perjury and obstruction of justice. He was accused of lying to the grand jury during the government's investigation of BALCO (Bay Area Laboratory Co-operative), a controversial sports medicine/nutrition center in Burlingame, California. Bonds testified he never knowingly took any illegal steroids. The trial concluded April 13, 2011, with Bonds being found guilty of one count of obstruction of justice.

Baseball's drug policies have since become much stricter, yet many consider it window dressing to what needs to take place. In 2006, Commissioner Selig tasked former United States Senator George J. Mitchell to lead an investigation into the use of performance-enhancing drugs in Major League Baseball, and December 13, 2007, the 409-page Mitchell Report was released. In his report, Sen. Mitchell outlined a long list of recommendations for the Commissioner to consider. Selig responded by hailing the report a Call to Action. The report described the use of anabolic steroids and human growth hormone (HGH) in MLB and assessed the effectiveness of the MLB Joint Drug Prevention and Treatment Program. The report includes names of 89 MLB players who are alleged to have used steroids or drugs. MLB's current agreement with the MLB

Players Association regarding performance-enhancing steroids became effective in 2003, and expired in 2011.

Jim Bouton was quoted in the *New York Times* about his thoughts of the Mitchell report. "Because the Players Association and the owners dragged their feet for so many years on the issue of performance-enhancing drugs, they need to take a big leap forward. Not only for the integrity of the game and the health of its players, but also for the health of athletes everywhere that aspire to play in the big leagues."

Bouton had his own suggestions on the steps major league baseball needs to take: "Avoid a continual race with the chemists. Baseball needs to ban performance-enhancing drugs not yet invented. Take annual blood samples from the players and keep them for future reference. If a new PED is discovered, these samples could be re-tested, with guilty players paying the price." And that price? "Give offenders a lifetime ban from baseball! Far more games have been illegally impacted by drugs than gambling. Players have made a conscious decision to cheat. One strike and you're out!"

Sadly, you can't put the toothpaste back in the tube. What were once considered hallowed records in America's favorite pastime are now a matter of subjective public opinion and fodder for debate between sports fans and media experts. Maybe baseball can somehow apply Sabermetrics, which is defined as "the search for objective knowledge about baseball." In the meantime, baseball's records are destined to be a matter of public opinion and defined by which era they were accomplished in. I feel sorry for the kids who grew up in this black-eye, steroid era of baseball. The games may as well have been contended on their play station games. That way, the accomplishments are just as real, even for those who did play the game with integrity.

Meanwhile, America's pastime continues, and the potential of triple-crown possibilities and Cy Young candidates keep the ballparks full. The fans still know who their favorite stars are. Dads still bring their family to a ballpark with the kids toting their gloves with the hope a batting practice home run ball might find its way into their mitt.

> The Atlanta Braves and Chicago Cubs are the National League's two remaining charter franchises. Atlanta was founded in Boston, Massachusetts, in 1871 as the Boston Red Stockings.

Women's Growth in Sports

Today's females are just as impassioned about sports as their male counterparts. Women now compete professionally and as amateurs in nearly every major sport with broad acceptance throughout the world. In a few instances, such as tennis and figure skating, women rival or exceed their male counterparts in popularity. The future for women's involvement in sports is bright, but women still have a long way to go before they truly invade "the good old boys club."

Current involvement of women in sports is a far cry from their delicate beginnings. The evolution of women's athletic participation over the past 150 years is a mirrored reflection of change in modern society. The 19th amendment in 1920, which addressed the women's suffrage movement and gave women the right to vote, also resulted in modest gains for women in sports and intercollegiate competition. The social conscience of America continued to change in the 1950's and 1960's. With the push for Civil Rights and the passage of the Civil Rights Act of 1964, both minorities and women received a boost in status. Female participation in sports was rising dramatically toward gender parity. Then in 1972, the most important piece of legislation for women in sport was passed: Title IX became law.

Title IX, the Educational Amendment Act, stated that "federal money could not be given to public school programs that discriminated against girls." Schools were forced to have equal men's and women's sports, equal scholarship funds, and equal equipment, marking the beginning of modern sport.

Before Title IX, only one of 27 girls participated in high school sports. Today, that ratio is one of every three girls plays on a high school team.

For most of history, athletic competition has been regarded as an exclusively masculine affair. Some of this was due to a relative lack of public interest in female athletics. Prior to 1870, activities for women were recreational rather than sport-specific in nature. Female participation was something more to be fashionable. Activities like horseback riding, showboating and swimming were for pleasure, not competition. Women were encouraged 'not' to exert themselves. Society deemed a woman's physiology as the top reason for limiting their participation in athletics.

As female athleticism rose, certain sports were deemed suitable. One womanly sport that was popular was croquet, which allowed women and men to play together. But women still remained locked in society's corset prison. Social change eventually came about through dress reform. As the bicycle became an acceptable form of exercise, women were allowed to 'adjust' their attire accordingly.

Let's take a chronological look back at the historical evolution of women in sports.

- 776 B.C. - The first Olympics are held in ancient Greece. Women are excluded, so they compete every four years in their own Games of Hera, to honor the Greek goddess who ruled over women and the earth.

- 396 B.C. - Kyniska, a Spartian princess, wins an Olympic chariot race, but is barred from collecting her prize in person.

- 1552 - Mary, Queen of Scots (1542-87), an avid golfer, coins the term "caddy" by calling her assistants cadets. It is during her reign that the famous golf course at St. Andrews is built.

- 1811 - On January 9, the first known women's golf tournament is held at Musselburgh Golf Club, Scotland, among the town fishwives.
- 1866 - Vassar College fields the first two women's amateur baseball teams.
- 1867 - St. Andrew's in Scotland is the first golf club to allow ladies.
- 1872 - Mills College in Oakland, California establishes women's baseball teams.
- 1875 - The "Blondes" and "Brunettes" play their first match In Springfield, Illinois on Sept. 11. Newspapers heralded the event as the "first game of baseball ever played in public for gate money between feminine ball-tossers."
- 1876 - Nell Saunders defeated Rose Harland in the first United States women's boxing match, receiving a silver butter dish as a prize.
- 1883 - The first baseball "Ladies Day" is held on June 16 by the NY Giants, where both escorted and unescorted women are allowed into the park for free.
- 1884 - Women's singles tennis competition is added to Wimbledon. Maud Watson wins in both 1884 and '85.
- 1885 - Annie Oakley (Phoebe Ann Moses, 1860-1926), 25, is the sharp-shooting star of the Buffalo Bill Wild West Show. She could hit a moving target while riding a galloping horse; hit a dime in mid-air; and regularly shot a cigarette from her husband's lips.
- 1886 - The first known women's lacrosse game is played.
- 1887 - Indoor baseball (the forerunner of softball) was invented by George Hancock at the Farragut Boat Club on Chicago's South Side. The first game was played on Thanksgiving Day. The basic equipment included a huge 17-inch ball and a stick-like bat. No gloves were worn, and the catcher wore no mask. It quickly became the indoor winter sport of choice for boys and girls in the area.
- 1890 - A women's baseball club plays a game against the Danville, Illinois Browns before 2,000 fans on Sunday, June 8. As the women leave town in carriages for Covington, Indiana, they are arrested and fined a total of $100 for disturbing the peace by playing baseball on Sunday in violation of the local "Blue Laws." The men's team members are also arrested.
- 1892 - Hessie Donahue, who donned a loose blouse, bloomers and boxing gloves and sparred a few rounds as part of a vaudeville act, knocks out legendary heavyweight champion John L. Sullivan for over a minute after he accidentally landed a real blow on her during the act.
- 1896 - The first women's intercollegiate basketball championship is played between Stanford and the University of California at Berkeley. Stanford wins 2-1 on April 4 before a crowd of 700 women.
- 1896 - At the first modern Olympics in Athens, a woman is barred from the official race.
- 1900 - The first 19 women to compete in the modern Olympic Games in Paris, France, play in just three sports: tennis, golf, and croquet.
- 1900 The first women's ice hockey league is organized.

- 1904 - Amanda Clement, just 16 years old, becomes the first female umpire to officiate a men's baseball game in Iowa for pay.

- 1908 - The national anthem of baseball, Take Me Out to the Ball Game, is written about a young girl's love of the game.

- 1910 - Australia's Annette Kellerman is arrested for swimming in Boston Harbor in an "indecent" one-piece swimsuit for exposing her legs.

- 1911 - Helene Britton becomes the first woman owner of a major league team, the St. Louis Cardinals, from 1911 to 1917.

- 1914 - The American Olympic Committee formally opposes women's athletic competition in the Olympics. The only exception is the floor exercise, where women are required to wear long skirts.

- 1914 - Women's basketball rules change to allow half-court play. Full court play for women doesn't come in until the 1970's.

- 1915 - In a stunt, aviator Ruth Law drops a grapefruit from her plane for Brooklyn Dodger outfielder Casey Stengel to catch. Having forgotten to take the baseball into the plane with her, she makes a last minute substitution.

- 1916 - 100 women compete in the first "Championship of the World" bowling tournament. The total purse was $222.

- 1918 - Eleanora Sears (a great-great-granddaughter of Thomas Jefferson, born in 1881) accumulates 240 trophies during her athletic career. She demonstrated that women could play men's games and was a prime liberator of women in sports.

- 1923 – Twenty-two percent of US colleges have varsity sports teams for women.

- 1928 - Sonja Henie (1912-69) wins the first of three consecutive Olympic gold medals (1932 and 1936) in figure skating. This inspires thousands of young women to take up figure skating.

- 1928 - The Summer Olympic Games open gymnastics and five track and field events to women.

- 1931 - Baseball Commissioner Judge Kenesaw Mountain Landis bans women from professional baseball after 17-year-old pitcher Virne Beatrice "Jackie" Mitchell strikes out Babe Ruth and Lou Gehrig in an exhibition game for the Chattanooga Lookouts. Landis voids Mitchell's contract, saying baseball is "too strenuous" for women.

- 1932 - Two black American women, Louise Stokes and Tidye Pickett qualify for the Olympic Games in Los Angeles, but are not allowed to compete.

- 1933 - Pope Pius XI condemns women who attend boxing matches.

- 1943 - Phillip K. Wrigley, owner of the Chicago Cubs, establishes the All-American Girls Softball League, the forerunner of the All-American Girls Baseball League (AAGBL).

- 1946 - Mary Garber starts writing about sports full time in 1946, covering athletics in North Carolina. She is believed to be the first female staff sports reporter at a daily paper.

- 1949 - Wilson Sporting Goods agrees to sponsor the Ladies Professional Golf Association (LPGA).

- 1953 - International basketball competition begins for women, with the U.S.A. women's basketball team winning the gold medal in the World Championships.

- 1963 - The LPGA championship tournament is televised for the first time.

- 1965 - Donna De Varona, a 1964 Olympic swimmer, becomes the first woman sports broadcaster on national TV for ABC.

- 1966 - Roberta Gibb of the U.S. becomes the first woman to finish the Boston Marathon.

- 1968 - The Olympic Committee conducts gender tests for the first time in international sports at the Winter Games in Grenoble, France.

- 1970 - Diana Crump becomes the first woman to ride in the Kentucky Derby aboard Fathom on May 2.

- 1971 - The five-player, full-court game and the 30-second shot clock is introduced to women's basketball.

- 1972 - Congress passes Title IX of the Education Amendments of 1972. "No person in the United States shall, on the basis of sex, be excluded from participation in, be denied the benefits of, or be subject to discrimination under any education program or activities receiving Federal financial assistance." When President Nixon signs the act on July 23 about 31,000 women are involved in college sports; spending on athletic scholarships for women is less than $100,000; and the average number of women's teams at a college is 2.1.

- 1973 - Billie Jean King wins the battle-of-the-sexes tennis match against Bobby Riggs

- 1974 - Little League Baseball admits girls (after losing a lawsuit).

- 1974 - Chris Evert becomes the first female athlete to earn $1 million in her career.

- 1975 - Title IX goes into effect

- 1976 - Ann Meyers becomes the first female recipient of a full athletic scholarship at UCLA. She became the only player (male or female) in school history to record a quadruple-double (20 points, 14 rebounds, 10 assists and 10 steals).

- 1977- Mary Shane, the first woman to be hired by MLB as TV play-by-play commentator for the Chicago White Sox.

- 1977 - Lucy Harris becomes the first woman to be drafted by an NBA team (New Orleans Jazz).

- 1978 - Ann Meyers signs a contract to try out for the Indiana Pacers, the first woman to sign a contract with an NBA team.

- 1978 - Melissa Ludtke of Sports Illustrated files a lawsuit; a US District Court judge rules that male and female reporters should have the same access to athletes, even if it means entering locker rooms while athletes are dressing.

- 1980 - A total of 233 women compete in the Winter Olympic Games in Lake Placid – up from 21 that competed there in 1932.

- 1982 - The Supreme Court rules that Title IX covers coaches and other employees as well as students.

- 1984 - Victoria Roche becomes the first girl to play in the Little League World Series in Williamsport, PA.

- 1985 - Lynette Woodward (a member of the **gold**-medal winning Olympic basketball team in 1984) and Jackie White become the first **women to** play for the Harlem Globetrotters.

- 1986 - Nancy Lieberman-Cline becomes the **first woman** to play in a men's professional basketball league when she joins the USBL's Springfield Fame.

- 1987 - Gayle Sierens becomes the first woman to do a play-by-play for a National Football League game, Kansas City vs. Seattle on December 27.

- 1992 - *A League of Their Own*, a movie by director Penny Marshall about the first year of the All American Girls Professional Baseball League, was a box office hit, due in large part to the many women who went to see female sports role models on the screen.

- 1992 - The first two women are inducted into the Basketball Hall of Fame.

- 1994 - Ground is broken for the Women's Basketball Hall of Fame in Knoxville, Tennessee, the first sports hall of fame devoted solely to women's athletics.

- 1996 - 2.4 million girls play high school sports, including 819 football players, 1,164 wrestlers, and 1,471 ice hockey players.

- 1997 - The inaugural Women's National Basketball Association season begins on June 21.

It's not just on the playing surface that women have made inroads into sports. Another frontier where women have penetrated what was once man's sole domain is in the sports broadcast arena. Women and sports television were not considered a good match. Sport was predominantly followed by guys, and men just didn't readily accept women as sports experts. They wanted to listen to male commentary when it came to following their favorite teams. One recent study said that women's sports get only 8-percent of all print and television coverage.

Since the mid-1960's, there have been many pioneers in women's sport broadcasting and other sports media. Though they were still overshadowed by men, Donna DeVarona and Jane Chastain performed exceptionally. DeVarona, a 1964 Olympics swimmer made her TV debut in 1965. She was just 17 years old. Women who were knowledgeable in sports were becoming more acceptable as the feminist movement progressed. Yet there were still territories that seemed impenetrable. The press box was treated like a fraternity, and the locker rooms were still considered out of bounds.

Jane Chastain started her sportscasting career in the mid 1960's and was the first woman to work for a large network (CBS). She is also thought to be the first woman to do play-by-play.

By the mid 1970's, other women made their mark. Jayne Kennedy, Phyllis George, Lesley Visser, and Gayle Gardner became recognizable names.

In the mid 70's, Phyllis George, a former Miss America, worked with CBS on the pre-game show for the NFL. Replacing George was Jayne Kennedy. Neither woman was hired for their football knowledge, but they provided a feminine element to a male-dominated broadcast. They were still considered a novelty.

Gayle Gardner provided a role model for aspiring women sportscasters. She was the first female sports anchor to appear weekly on a major network. Gardner was qualified and respected as a sportscaster, hired for her skills and knowledge. On Aug. 3, 1993, Gardner was the first woman to do TV play-by-play of a baseball game for KNGN-TV in Denver. It was the Colorado Rockies vs. the Cincinnati Reds.

Lesley Visser, who currently works for ESPN and ABC Sports, became the first female NFL beat writer in 1976. Working for CBS, Visser was the first woman to work a Super Bowl sideline in 1995. In 2006, she was elected into the Football Hall of Fame. Visser says, "The three most important things for a sportscaster are knowledge of the game, a passion for sports and the profession, and the stamina to get past the struggles." She considers play-by-play as a great hole in the marketplace. "It's something women should be able to aspire to." The problem is, there isn't a minor league for women who have these aspirations. It's much tougher for females to get their start in the business.

Jeannie Morris didn't have problems getting into the field of sports as a reporter. But as a woman, she was not allowed the same facilities as the men. Morris was assigned to cover the Minnesota Vikings vs. the Chicago Bears at the Metropolitan Stadium in Minnesota in the early 70's. Because Morris was a female, she was not permitted to work in the press box. Morris ended up reporting the game seated above the box -- outside in a blizzard. Even when women were allowed access to the press box, female reporters weren't provided with bathrooms. They had to find a distant, inconvenient facility with the spectators.

In 1977, Mary Shane became the first woman to be hired by major league baseball as the new TV play-by-play commentator for the Chicago White Sox.

Suzyn Waldman was the first radio beat reporter to cover the New York Yankees and the New York Knicks. Waldman was also the first female announcer on a nationally televised baseball broadcast, and the first woman to do play-by-play for the Yankees.

In 1987, Gayle Sierens became the first woman to do a play-by-play for a National Football League game. It was Kansas City vs. Seattle on December 27.

Sherry Davis became the first woman public address announcer in major league baseball in 1993, working for the San Francisco Giants.

Linda Cohn is currently working for ESPN. ESPN was the first national network to hire women for anchor positions, and is considered the best among television networks for hiring women for sportscasting positions.

In 1989, CNN followed ESPN's lead, adding Hannah Storm as a sports anchor. Other names to make their sportscasting mark were Sally Jenkins, Ann Meyers Drysdale, and Robin Roberts. Roberts covered the 1992 Men's NCAA Final Four, and

Meyers Drysdale covered the 1992 NCAA Women's Final Four. As former star basketball players, both were able to use their practical knowledge during their broadcast. Women were finally being given the credibility they deserved and recognized for their expertise.

Pam Ward is another successful trend-setter, joining ESPN in 1996 as an ESPN News anchor. Ward now serves as a play-by-play commentator on college football and men's and women's college basketball, including Final Four telecasts. Ward has served as studio host for WNBA telecasts, and also hosted NBA Today, NBA 2Night, NHL 2Night, NFL Tonight and for ESPN Radio, the NFL on ESPN Radio, and major league baseball pre- and post-game shows.

On November 22, 2000, Ward became the first woman to work play-by-play on a Division I college football game when she called ESPN2's telecast of Bowling Green at Toledo. That same year she called the Division III Championship and the Motor City Bowl for the networks. Beginning in 2001, Ward called her first full season of college football. Move over Marv Albert.

Women sportscasters and reporters of today have become more skilled now. They've had to. They are still greatly outnumbered by men. There is still an imbalance of compensation and prestige. Along with that, women still have to determine balance in their lives. Do they want to invest time into their career more than they want to have a marriage and children? It's a tough choice when so much travel is required.

The starring roles still belong to the men. Today, NFL shows have gone back to males only with former male athletes getting hired as commentators.

The locker room is still considered a private sanctuary, but it's been a long time since female sports reporters broke the gender line to conduct interviews in men's locker rooms. There're still the occasional catcalls from the players, but for the most part, a woman in the men's locker room is old news.

Paola Boivin is a veteran sports columnist and reporter for the *Arizona Republic*. She grew up in Chicago and developed her sports interest early in life going to White Sox games with her father. "My dad was a diehard baseball fan and after working a long day, going to the games was his refuge. I learned early how much hardworking blue collar guys appreciated sports. That fostered my love for sports. I was always a good writer, too, so being a sportswriter seemed like a natural marriage for my career."

After attending the University of Illinois, Boivin returned to Chicago, where she began stringing for the *Chicago Tribune* covering high school games. While searching for her next career opportunity, Boivin and a friend relocated to California, accepting a job in Beverly Hills with a telephone service company. Further professional aspirations led Boivin to accept a job at a small town daily in Camarillo, California.

It was there, Boivin experienced breaking the gender line the hard way. In the 1980's, Boivin was assigned to cover a Dodgers game against the St. Louis Cardinals. She went into the Cardinals clubhouse to interview Terry Pendleton, who was from the same area where she worked in Southern California.

This was Boivin's first visit in a clubhouse. Suddenly, she felt something hit her in the back of the head. An unhappy player had thrown his jock at her out of anger she was in there. Following a lewd comment directed at her, Boivin jetted out of the clubhouse. The player she was interviewing, Pendleton, immediately came out and apologized on behalf of his idiot teammate. This was downright harassment in the workplace. "Since," Boivin says, "teams have done a much better job of educating players about how to treat all reporters fairly and equally. The face of media has certainly changed."

Women's privilege to enter the locker room had already been formally challenged in 1978, when Melissa Ludtke filed a suit on her behalf for being kept out of the locker room during a major league baseball World Series. One year later, the courts ruled in Ludtke's favor. The courts said Major League Baseball violated the 14th Amendment Equal Protection Clause, which relates back to harassment in the workplace. This precedent-setting case became known as the Melissa Ludtke Rule. How about when the situation is reversed, when male reporters go into the female locker room after a WNBA game? Boivin confirms the league does allow it. "And the female athletes are much more welcoming because the women's leagues are starved and appreciative for the media attention and recognition."

The next stop on Boivin's career path was the *Los Angeles Daily News* where, in the early 1990's, she was fortunate enough to be assigned UCLA football and basketball and the NFL's L.A. Rams. "I was willing to do anything and cover whatever I was asked. It paid to be knowledgeable about nearly every sport," says Boivin.

Since 1994, Boivin has called Phoenix home, currently representing the *Arizona Republic* as a columnist. "I remember my first assignment. I interviewed a 12-year-old, snot-nosed croquet champion. Talk about becoming versatile."

For blossoming beat writers, Boivin says you can't be singularly focused on sports. It pays to be well-rounded beyond just sports knowledge. "A lot of sports figures get arrested. You need to understand the court process too. You need to know more than just X's and O's."

Boivin also recommends you "Read, read, read. It's important to be yourself and develop your own style. It will translate better."

I asked Boivin if she felt she was a flag bearer being a female sports writer. "It never crossed my mind. When I do my day-to-day job, I work hard to be responsible and accurate. I'm not naïve. I know people look at me with a critical eye and judge me as a female writer. You should see some of the emails I still get weekly pertaining to my gender."

Another area in sports where women are certainly outnumbered by men is in sports management. Women breaking into sports management are still a minority, with rare successful exceptions like Ann Meyers Drysdale, or Val Ackerman, who after historically becoming the first president of the WNBA in 1996, became the first female president of U.S.A. Basketball in 2005.

The inequity against women in sports still clearly exists. From a player's perspective, salaries are nowhere near comparable either. Veteran players in the WNBA with 0-2 years of service will make about $36,570 for the three-month summer season. Veteran women will make more, but nowhere close to their male counterparts. That's why stars like Diana Taurasi and Sue Bird go overseas during the non-WNBA season. They get substantially higher compensation in Russia and Europe. The WNBA's maximum salary cap in 2011 was $852,000. A WNBA champion player receives a bonus of $10,500 for winning the title. WNBA earnings are strictly regulated, right down to $5,000 for a Sportsmanship Award. In the NBA, Kobe Bryant alone currently makes around $25 million a season (not counting endorsements), which is 30 times one WNBA team's total, and two-and-one-half times the combined salary total of all 12 teams in the WNBA.

What about the effect of Title IX? Proof of its impact can somewhat be told by statistics. Before Title IX, at the high school level boys outnumbered girls in sports at more than 10 to 1 (under 300,000 girls as compared to 3.6 million boys.) Fast forward to 35 years later -- and at the high school level, the 4.3 million boys playing sports are almost matched by the over 3 million girls involved in athletics. Though Title IX has helped equal the playing field, in some ways it's worked in reverse, with many men taking coaching jobs once held by women (now that there's pay involved). In some ways, this has created even more imbalance. I guess equality works both ways.

The principal author of Title IX was U.S. House Representative Patsy Mink, from Hawaii. When Mink passed away in 2002, Title IX was renamed the Patsy T. Mink Equal Opportunity in Education Act, for her contributions toward equal rights in this country.

There was a recent study conducted by the John Curley Center for Sports Journalism at Penn State. Their findings: Out of 775 sports information director positions from universities throughout the country, only 14-percent were held by women. This study also concluded that in newspaper sports departments, only nine-percent were female supervisors.

In other off-the-field opportunities, women are finding careers at universities, at sporting events, and for teams that need marketing, sales, and other management positions, both in men's and women's professional sports. There is still a double standard, but the playing surface has been leveling for years. With today's abundance of sports coverage on TV, there are more prospects for women than ever.

Many gender biases still remain, like the myth that women shouldn't be on management teams if they haven't played the sport. This mostly applies to football.

The reality is, women have to prove themselves more than men do, especially in sports. To infiltrate the male-dominated sports industry has taken and will take years for women to accomplish. Triumphs are being made, but ever so slowly.

Here are some places you might contact for career assistance:

Association for Women in Sports Media
3899 N. Front Street
Harrisburg, PA 17110
(717) 703-3086

The Online Sports Career Center is a resource of sports-related career opportunities and a resume bank for potential employers within the many segments of the Sports and Recreation Industries. Go to: Onlinesports.com

There is also a networking group called WISE, for Women in Sports and Events.

Women in Sports and Events
244 Fifth Avenue
Suite #2087
New York, NY 10001
(212) 726-8282

Here's where WISE has various Chapters:

- Atlanta
- Bay Area
- Boston
- Chicago
- Cleveland
- Los Angeles
- NYC Metro
- Washington DC

If it's coaching you crave, another sports-related web site is: Coachingjobs.com

Back in 1997, Violet Palmer became the first woman to officiate an NBA game. Matter of fact, Palmer was the first female to referee a major men's sport at any top professional level. Talk about breaking the glass ceiling.

Palmer broke into the NBA as one of two female referees. Dee Kantner was the other.

Kanter is currently the head of the WNBA officials. To makes things spooky for players and officials, Palmer's first NBA assignment occurred in 1997, on Halloween night in Vancouver, British Columbia. The matchup was a game between the

Vancouver Grizzlies and the Dallas Mavericks. Players initially didn't know what to make of this. Were they in for a trick or treat?

Currently, Palmer is still the only woman among the NBA's 58-member officiating staff. Going into the 2010-2011 season, she is now entering her 14th season of officiating in the NBA. Palmer has now officiated hundreds of NBA games and was one-third of the officiating crew for the December 19, 2006, Knicks-Nuggets Brawl. All 10 players were ejected that night. In 2001, she established Violet Palmer's Official Camp to train youths in the art of refereeing. The training ground for other referees with NBA aspirations is working in the NBA Development League and the WNBA.

A typical schedule for NBA referees is about 55-70 games a season, and about 10 games a month. Because of her tireless work ethic, Palmer keeps up with both the players and her peers. By keeping up with film work and becoming a student of the game, she's mastering her own profession. Palmer is recognized as a solid official.

Administration is another area where women can make in-roads in the sports world. Such was the case for Susan Webner, currently the Manager for Minor League Administration for the Arizona Diamondbacks.

Webner grew up in Phoenix, but went across the country to attend the University of Pennsylvania where she majored in business. While in high school, she was very interested in sports, competing yearly in tennis and swimming. While at Penn, Webner accomplished two primary things related to sports, working as a photographer for the school's paper, *The Daily Pennsylvanian*, and functioning as a statistician for the student radio station's football and basketball broadcasts. She also pre-taped interviews with other Ivy League and non-conference coaches.

"It was about mid-way through college that I decided to pursue a career in sports," says Webner. "My first sports internship was in Philadelphia, working for the Comcast U.S. Indoor Men's Tennis Tournament. I even wore a mascot outfit, a giant tennis ball called 'Top Spin.' I got another break when a college friend who had gotten a job with the Phillies, asked me to also apply. I sent my resume and thankfully, the Phillies front office had a lot of University of Pennsylvania alumni. The Penn basketball head coach, Fran Dunphy, also lent an assist with a referral call."

Webner spent the 1996 season interning for the Phillies with "no guarantee for future employment." Her baseball duties included season ticket and group sales at then-Veterans Stadium, which also played home to the NFL's Eagles. "I then applied for an internship with the Eagles but was told I was over-qualified," says Webner. "The Eagles eventually offered me a full-time position in Penthouse Suite Operations, which meant I was now working every event at Veterans Stadium."

Webner had already been plotting a return to her native Arizona. "In 1995, while I was with the Phillies, the National League had awarded a franchise to Phoenix. My friend Felisa Israel, a Phoenix Suns employee, referred my resume to the

Diamondbacks sales department. One-and-a-half-years later, out of the blue, the D-backs gave me a call. I couldn't believe they kept my resume that long! Three weeks later, I accepted a position with them, selling season and group tickets again."

Webner's degree was in marketing, so when the D-backs started up their DiamondBackers Fan Loyalty program in 1999, she spearheaded the effort. Her success led to dual duty with the Phoenix Suns' Fans First version, as their two front offices then worked in conjunction with each other.

Heading into the 2001 season, Webner gravitated to the PR department, working in media relations. This magical D-backs season resulted in a World Series win and a lot of additional responsibility. "That was the season Gonzo (Luis Gonzalez) hit 57 home runs. I was editing the media guide and handling playoff credentials for major league baseball. It was something different every day for the next five years," said Webner.

Webner's organization skills didn't go unnoticed. She was drafted by director of player development A.J. Hinch in 2006 to work in his department, a position she has happily held ever since.

Webner's current tasks are varied. Among her many responsibilities, she handles player payroll for the minor leaguers not on the 40-man roster, visas for all foreign players, contracts for all minor league staff, and expense reports for roving instructors. Add to that flight and hotel arrangements, spring training coordination, and catering, and lots of budgeting. It is Webner's job to make sure people are where they are supposed to be to start the season.

Webner is a great example of someone who carved out her own niche in sports and was willing to pay her dues. Her advice is to widen your net. "You don't have to start your career at a major league-level or some other pro team. You have the minor leagues, the Olympics, ESPN; maybe it's working for Rawlings [baseball's glove company] or a sponsoring advertiser like Gatorade. You just never know what an internship or beginning position could lead to. I'm fortunate because I love what I do every day! When you do get an opportunity, be prepared and put some thought into it."

Women's Sports Foundation	www.womenssportsfoundation.org
Women in Sports Career	www.womensportscareers.com
Association for Women in Sports Media	www.awsmonline.org

Records Are Meant To Be Broken, But Not These

Part of the allure of sports is the potential to witness records being established and/or broken. As a broadcaster, radio or TV crew member, team employee, or fan, you're fortunate when you can say: "I was there when so and so hit four home runs in one game, or when what's his name broke the scoring record." What I'd give to feel the electricity of witnessing a no-hitter in person.

Here's a list of records that shouldn't ever be broken – even with the use of performance enhancing drugs.

Joe DiMaggio's 56-Game Hit Streak

This is arguably one of the greatest achievements in baseball history.

DiMaggio's unwavering performance was accomplished within a single season. "The Streak" began May 15, 1941, against the Chicago White Sox. The Cleveland Indians finally ended the Yankee Clipper's record run on July 17. During his hitting tear, DiMaggio hit .408, along with 15 home runs, and 55 RBI's. During this unmatched accomplishment, "Joltin' Joe" managed 91 hits in 223 at-bats, and 22 multi-hit games. Considering there was also a World War going on at the time, DiMaggio's hitting streak was an inspiration during troubled times. Amazingly, DiMaggio went on to hit in another 17 straight games after the streak was broken. In 1978, Pete Rose came closest with a 44-game hit streak. Rose holds another distinction. He holds the all-time career hit mark with 4,256. That is also a record unlikely to ever be approached.

In 1887, Denny Lyons of the Philadelphia Athletics (American Association) had a 52-game hitting streak. That was the year the major leagues adopted a new rule which counted walks as hits. This rule lasted only one season. Lyons' streak included two games in which his only "hits" were walks. In 1968, MLB ruled that walks in 1887 would not be counted as hits.

Nolan Ryan's Career Strikeout Record

I don't imagine anyone will even come close to the 5,714 K's accomplished by the "Ryan Express." As great and lengthy a career that the "Big Unit" Randy Johnson had, he came up short with 4,875 strikeouts.

Rocky Marciano's String of Victories

The Rock's string of victories in the heavyweight division, 49-0 still stands after 50 years. To put this in perspective, a twenty-year-old would have to win five title matches a year for the first five years of his career just to be 25 – 0. No one fights that many matches these days in a single year. Then, with two title fights a year, he would have to go undefeated for yet another 12 years. With all the prize money paid these days, no boxer is going to bother boxing that often and that long. Within the boxing arena, a couple other records that appear unapproachable are Julio Cesar Chavez's 89 consecutive wins and Archie Moore's 141 knockouts.

Wilt Chamberlain's 100 Point Game

Most NBA teams struggle to collectively score 100 points. Wilt also scored 78, 73 (twice), and 72. Kobe Bryant did manage to come somewhat close with an 81-point effort against Toronto in 2006.

Here are a few other goliath Chamberlain accomplishments that are astounding:

- Chamberlain never fouled out of a game

- In his first NBA season in 1959, Chamberlain averaged 37.6 points and 27 rebounds

- The 'Stilt' averaged 50.4 points per game in 1961-62. This included forty-five 50 point games that season. For good measure, Wilt scored 42 points and hauled in 24 rebounds in the 1962 All-Star game.

- The Big Dipper averaged 22.9 rebounds for his career, including 11 rebounding titles. His single game high is 55 rebounds.

- Wilt holds 72 official NBA records, 63 by himself

Chicago Bulls Season Record of 72 Wins

The most attainable record might be the NBA Chicago Bulls' record for wins in a season (72). Michael Jordan and Scottie Pippen led the way during this 1995-96 accomplishment.

Los Angeles Lakers NBA Record Of 33 Straight Wins

Jerry West and Wilt Chamberlain led this onslaught in 1971. Between November 5, 1971, and January 7, 1972, the Lakers were invincible. Interestingly, they finally lost a game to the Milwaukee Bucks, led by up and coming superstar Lew Alcindor (Kareem Abdul-Jabbar).

Cy Young's 511 Career Wins

Young's career total occurred over 22 seasons. That's averaging more than 23 victories a year EVERY season! It's unlikely we may ever even see a 300-game winner again, with 5-man rotations and all the late-game pitching specialists that exist today. A pitcher would have to achieve 15 seasons with 20 victories in each to come close to 300 wins. Imagine having 20-plus victories a year for more than 25 seasons, Young did.

Wayne Gretzky 200 Points in one Season

Gretzky is the only NHL player to total over 200 points in one season—a feat he accomplished four times. During 20 NHL campaigns, Gretzky scored an imposing 3,239 points (playoffs included). Toss in 50 hat tricks, and 61 NHL records when he retired in 1999, and you can see why he was simply known as the "Great One."

UCLA's 88-Game Win Streak and
7 Straight NCAA Basketball Titles

Here's another pair of records that won't happen again. Hard to believe they ever did. Directed by the coaching exploits of the "Wizard of Westwood," John Wooden, the Bruins ruled college basketball from 1964-1975. Along the way, players like Lew Alcindor and Bill Walton helped lead UCLA to 10 national titles in 12 years. UCLA experienced four perfect undefeated seasons (1964, 1967, 1972, and 1973.) The 88-game regular season winning streak came during 1971-1974. John Wooden was UCLA's coach from 1948-1975, culminating his coaching career with another NCAA title.

UConn's 90-Game Win Streak

Imagine defying gravity for three years. The University of Connecticut Women Huskies did just that, exceeding their UCLA male counterparts with 90 straight victories. The last time the women Huskies lost occurred April 6, 2008, when they fell to Stanford, 82-73, in the national semifinals. Since, their average margin of victory had been an astounding 33 points per game. In the second half of all those 90 victories combined, the U Conn Huskies trailed for a collective total of only 13 minutes, 21 seconds. Ten of those minutes came in a single contest against number two rated Baylor. Besides the Harlem Globetrotters, they were the only invincible team in basketball. On December 30, 2010, the U Conn Huskies gals were finally conquered. Ironically, by the last team that defeated them, Stanford, 71-59.

Byron Nelson's 11 Straight PGA Wins

If golfers get 2 or 3 straight wins, they are considered on fire. Byron Nelson must have been scorching in 1945 when he won 18 tournaments, including 11 straight. Nelson's PGA career was relatively brief, lasting just 11 years. He retired at age 34 to be a rancher.

Stan Musial, a 24-time All-Star selection played with the St Louis Cardinals his entire career (1941-1963). Considered to be the steadiest hitter of his era, "Stan the Man" validated this by achieving a distinct record never likely to be duplicated. Musial compiled 3,630 career hits (4th all-time). Unbelievably, he attained 1,815 of the hits playing at home, and equaled that with 1,815 base knocks on the road. That's as consistent as it gets.

Chapter 15

Directories – Where to Look For Your Start

Professional Sports

National Football League

National Football League
280 Park Avenue, 15th Floor
New York, NY 10017
(212) 450-2000

NFL Players Association
1133 20th St., N.W.
Washington, DC 20036
(202) 756-9100

National Football Conference
NFC West

Arizona Cardinals	www.azcardinals.com	(602) 379-0101
Seattle Seahawks	www.seahawks.com	(425) 203-8000
San Francisco 49ers	www.49ers.com	(408) 562-4949
Saint Louis Rams	www.stlouisrams.com	(314) 982-7267

NFC North

Detroit Lions	www.detroitlions.com	(313) 216-4000
Green Bay Packers	www.packers.com	(920) 569-7500
Minnesota Vikings	www.vikings.com	(952) 828-6500
Chicago Bears	www.chicagobears.com	(847) 295-9657

NFC South

Atlanta Falcons	www.atlantafalcons.com	(770) 965-3115
New Orleans Saints	www.neworleanssaints.com	(504) 731-1799
Carolina Panthers	www.panthers.com	(704) 358-7000
Tampa Bay Buccaneers	www.buccaneers.com	(813) 870-2700

NFC East

Dallas Cowboys	www.dallascowboys.com	(972) 556-9959
New York Giants	www.giants.com	(201) 935-8111
Philadelphia Eagles	www.philadelphiaeagles.com	(215) 463-2500
Washington Redskins	www.redskins.com	(703) 726-7000

American Football Conference
AFC West

San Diego Chargers	www.chargers.com	(858) 874-4500
Denver Broncos	www.denverbroncos.com	(303) 649-9000
Kansas City Chiefs	www.kcchiefs.com	(816) 920-9300
Oakland Raiders	www.raiders.com	(510) 864-5000

AFC North

Baltimore Ravens	www.baltimoreravens.com	(410) 701-4000
Cincinnati Bengals	www.bengals.com	(513) 621-3550
Cleveland Browns	www.clevelandbrowns.com	(440) 891-5000
Pittsburgh Steelers	www.steelers.com	(412) 432-7800

AFC South

Houston Texans	www.houstontexans.com	(832) 667-2004
Indianapolis Colts	www.colts.com	(317) 297-2658
Jacksonville Jaguars	www.jaguars.com	(904) 633-6000
Tennessee Titans	www.titansonline.com	(615) 565-4000

AFC East

Buffalo Bills	www.buffalobills.com	(716) 648-1800
Miami Dolphins	www.miamidolphins.com	(954) 452-7010
New England Patriots	www.patriots.com	(508) 543-8200
New York Jets	www.newyorkjets.com	(973) 549-4687

National Basketball Association

Nat. Basketball Association
Olympic Tower, 645 Fifth Avenue
New York, NY 10022
(212) 407-8000

Nat. Basketball Players Association
310 Lenox Avenue
New York, NY 10027
(212) 655-0880

Eastern Conference

Atlantic Division
Boston Celtics	www.celtics.com	(617) 854-8000
New York Knicks	www.nyknicks.com	(212) 465-6471
Toronto Raptors	www.raptors.com	(416) 815-5600
Philadelphia 76ers	www.sixers.com	(215) 339-7666
New Jersey Nets	www.njnets.com	(201) 935-8888

Central Division
Cleveland Cavaliers	www.cavs.com	(216) 420-2260
Chicago Bulls	www.bulls.com	(312) 455-4000
Detroit Pistons	www.pistons.com	(248) 377-3260
Indiana Pacers	www.pacers.com	(317) 917-2599
Milwaukee Bucks	www.bucks.com	(414) 227-0500

Southeast Division
Miami Heat	www.heat.com	(786) 777-4328
Orlando Magic	www.orlandomagic.com	(407) 916-2400
Wash. Wizards	www.washingtonwizards.com	(202) 661-5000
Charlotte Bobcats	www.bobcats.com	(704) 688-7600
Atlanta Hawks	www.hawks.com	(404) 878-3800

Western Conference

Northwest Division
Denver Nuggets	www.nuggets.com	(303) 405-1100
Okla. City Thunder	www.thunder.nba.com	(405) 429-7900
Utah Jazz	www.utahjazz.com	(801) 325-2500
Portland Trailblazers	www.trailblazers.com	(503) 234-9291
Minnesota Timberwolves	www.timberwolves.com	(612) 673-1600

Pacific Division
Phoenix Suns	www.suns.com	(602) 379-7900
Los Angeles Clippers	www.clippers.com	(310) 862-6000
Golden State Warriors	www.warriors.com	(510) 986-2200
Los Angeles Lakers	www.lakers.com	(310) 420-6106
Sacramento Kings	www.kings.com	(916) 455-4647

Southwest Division

Dallas Mavericks	www.mavs.com	(214) 665-4660
San Antonio Spurs	www.spurs.com	(210) 444-5500
Houston Rockets	www.rockets.com	(713) 758-7200
New Orleans Hornets	www.hornets.com	(504) 593-4700
Memphis Grizzlies	www.grizzlies.com	(901) 205-1234

Women's National Basketball Association

Eastern Conference

Atlanta Dream	www.AtlantaDream.net	(404) 693-5181
Connecticut Sun	www.ConnecticutSun.com	(860) 862-4000
Chicago Sky	www.chicagosky.net	(312) 828-9550
Indiana Fever	www.feverbasketball.com	(317) 917-2500
New York Liberty	www.nyliberty.com	(212) 465-6256
Washington Mystics	www.WashingtonMystics.com	(202) 527-7540

Western Conference

Phoenix Mercury	www.phoenixmercury.com	(602) 514-8333
Los Angeles Sparks	www.lasparks.com	(213) 929-1300
Minnesota Lynx	www.lynxbasketball.com	(612) 673-1600
San Antonio Silver Stars	www.SASilverstars.com	(210) 444-5000
Seattle Storm	www.stormbasketball.com	(206) 217-WNBA
Tulsa Shock	www.tulsashock.net	(918) 949-9700

Major League Baseball

Major League Baseball
245 Park Avenue, 31st Floor
New York, NY 10167
(212) 931-7800

MLB Players Association
12 E. 49th Street
New York, NY 10017
(212) 826-0808

American League

West

Seattle Mariners	www.mariners.com	(206) 346-4000
Los Angeles Angels	www.angelsbaseball.com	(714) 940-2000
Texas Rangers	www.texasrangers.com	(817) 273-5222
Oakland A's	www.oaklandathletics.com	(510) 638-4900

Central

Detroit Tigers	www.tigers.com	(313) 471-2000
Minnesota Twins	www.twinsbaseball.com	(612) 659-3400
Cleveland Indians	www.indians.com	(216) 420-4200
Chicago White Sox	www.whitesox.com	(312) 674-1000
Kansas City Royals	www.royals.com	(816) 921-8000

East

Boston Red Sox	www.redsox.com	(617) 267-9440
Toronto Blue Jays	www.bluejays.com	(416) 341-1000
New York Yankees	www.yankees.com	(718) 293-4300
Tampa Bay Rays	www.raysbaseball.com	(727) 825-3137
Baltimore Orioles	www.orioles.com	(410) 685-9800

National League

West

Arizona Diamondback	www.dbacks.com	(602) 462-6500
Los Angeles Dodgers	www.dodgers.com	(323) 224-1500
Colorado Rockies	www.ColoradoRockies.com	(303) 292-0200
San Francisco Giants	www.sfgiants.com	(415) 972-2000
San Diego Padres	www.padres.com	(619) 795-5000

Central

Cincinnati Reds	www.reds.com	(513) 765-7000
St Louis Cardinals	www.cardinals.com	(314) 345-9600
Houston Astros	www.astros.com	(713) 259-8000
Chicago Cubs	www.cubs.com	(773) 404-2827
Pittsburgh Pirates	www.pirates.com	(412) 323-5000
Milwaukee Brewers	www.brewers.com	(414) 902-4400

East

Philadelphia Phillies	www.phillies.com	(215) 463-6000
Washington Nationals	www.nationals.com	(202) 349-0400
Atlanta Braves	www.braves.com	(404) 522-7630
New York Mets	www.mets.com	(718) 507-6387
Miami Marlins	www.marlins.com	(305) 626-7400

Minor League Baseball (www.web.minorleaguebaseball.com)

League Name - Level (# of teams)

International League - AAA (14)	international.league.milb.com
Pacific Coast League - AAA (16)	web.minorleaguebaseball.com
Eastern League - AA (12)	eastern.league.milb.com
Southern League - AA (10)	southern.league.milb.com
Texas League - AA (8)	web.minorleaguebaseball.com/index.jsp?sid=l109
California League - A* (10)	california.league.milb.com
Carolina League - A* (8)	carolina.league.milb.com
Florida State League - A* (12)	web.minorleaguebaseball.com/index.jsp?=l123
Midwest League - A (16)	midwest.league.milb.com
South Atlantic - A (14)	web.minorleaguebaseball.com/index.jsp?sid=l116
New York-Penn League - A** (14)	www.minorleaguebaseball.com/index.jsp?sid=l127
Northwest League - A** (8)	northwest.league.milb.com/index.jsp?sid=l126
Appalachian League - Rookie (10)	appalachian.league.milb.com/index.jsp?sid=l120
Pioneer League - Rookie (8)	www.pioneerleague.com
Arizona League - Rookie (14)	mlb.mlb.com/mlb/events/afl/index.jsp
Gulf Coast League – Rookie (15)	web.minorleaguebaseball.com/index.jsp?sid=l124

    * = Advanced

    ** = Short Season

National Hockey League

National Hockey League
1185 Avenue of the Americas, 12th Floor
New York, NY 10036
(212) 789-2000

NHL Players Association
20 Bay Street, Suite 1700
Toronto, Ontario, Canada, M5J 2N8
(416) 313-2300

Western Conference

Northwest
Vancouver Canucks	www.canucks.nhl.com	(604) 899-7400
Calgary Flames	www.flames.nhl.com	(403) 777-2177
Minnesota Wild	www.wild.nhl.com	(651) 602-6000
Colorado Avalanche	www.avalanche.nhl.com	(303) 405-1100
Edmonton Oilers	www.oilers.nhl.com	(780) 414-4000

Pacific
Phoenix Coyotes	www.coyotes.nhl.com	(623) 772-3200
San Jose Sharks	www.sharks.nhl.com	(408) 287-7070
Anaheim Ducks	www.ducks.nhl.com	(714) 704-2700
Los Angeles Kings	www.kings.nhl.com	(213) 742-7100
Dallas Stars	www.stars.nhl.com	(214) 387-5500

Central
Detroit Red Wings	www.redwings.nhl.com	(313) 396-7444
Chicago Blackhawks	www.blackhawks.nhl.com	(312) 455-7000
Nashville Predators	www.predators.nhl.com	(615) 770-2000
Columbus Blue Jackets	www.bluejackets.nhl.com	(614) 246-4625
St Louis Blues	www.blues.nhl.com	(314) 622-2500

Eastern Conference

Atlantic
Philadelphia Flyers	www.flyers.nhl.com	(215) 465-4500
Pittsburgh Penguins	www.penguins.nhl.com	(412) 642-1300
New York Rangers	www.rangers.nhl.com	(212) 465-6000
New York Islanders	www.islanders.nhl.com	(516) 501-6700
New Jersey Devils	www.devils.nhl.com	(973) 757-6100

Northeast

Boston Bruins	www.bruins.nhl.com	(617) 624-1900
Buffalo Sabres	www.sabres.nhl.com	(716) 855-4100
Montreal Canadiens	www.canadiens.nhl.com	(514) 932-2582
Toronto Maple Leafs	www.mapleleafs.nhl.com	(416) 815-5400
Ottawa Senators	www.senators.nhl.com	(613) 599-0250

Southeast

Washington Capitals	www.capitals.nhl.com	(202) 266-2277
Tampa Bay Lightning	www.lightning.nhl.com	(813) 301-6600
Carolina Hurricanes	www.hurricanes.nhl.com	(919) 467-7825
Winnipeg Jets	www.jets.nhl.com	(204) 987-7825
Florida Panthers	www.panthers.nhl.com	(954) 835-7000

College Directories

Universities and colleges are a great source of opportunities to break into the sports world. Here is a list of Division I institutions, listed alphabetically by state, team nickname, location, and conferences. Also noted is a web site that will help direct you to the Sports Information Office. It's the University's sports information office that you should get close to. Volunteer internships are generally welcome.

ALABAMA

Univ. of Alabama Crimson Tide	Tuscaloosa	Southeastern	www.rolltide.com
Alabama A & M Bulldogs	Normal	Southwestern Athletic	www.aamusports.com
Alabama State Univ. Hornets	Montgomery	Southwestern Athletic	www.bamastatesports.com
Auburn University Tigers	Auburn	Southeastern	www.auburntigers.cstv.com
Jacksonville St. Univ. Gamecocks	Jacksonville	Ohio Valley	www.jsugamecocksports.com
Samford University Bulldogs	Homewood	Southern	www.samfordsports.cstv.com
Univ. of South Alabama Jaguars	Mobile	Sun Belt	www.usajaguars.com
Troy University Trojans	Troy	Sun Belt	www.troytrojans.com
U. Alabama Birmingham Blazers	Birmingham	Conference U.S.A.	www.uabsports.cstv.com

ARIZONA

Univ. of Arizona Wildcats	Tucson	Pac 12	www.arizonawildcats.com
Arizona State Univ. Sun Devils	Tempe	Pac 12	www.thesundevils.cstv.com
N. Arizona Univ. Lumberjacks	Flagstaff	Big Sky	www.nauathletics.com

ARKANSAS

Univ. of Arkansas Razorbacks	Fayetteville	Southeastern	www.arkansasrazorbacks.com
U. of Arkansas Little Rock Trojans	Little Rock	Sun Belt	www.ualrtrojans.com
Arkansas-Pine Bluff U. Lions	Pine Bluff	Southwestern Athletic	www.uapblionsroar.com
Arkansas St Univ. Red Wolves	Jonesboro	Sun Belt	www.astateredwolves.com
U. of Central Arkansas Bears	Conway	Southland	www.uca.edu/athletics

CALIFORNIA

Cal Poly-SLO Mustangs	San Luis Obispo	Big West	www.calpolymustangs.com
Bakersfield Roadrunners	Bakersfield	Independent	www.gorunners.com
Cal State Fullerton Titans	Fullerton	Big West	www.fullertontitans.com
Cal St Northridge Matadors	Northridge	Big West	www.gomatadors.cstv.com
California Golden Bears	Berkeley	Pac 12	www.calbears.com
Fresno State Bulldogs	Fresno	Western Athletic	www.gobulldogs.com
Long Beach State 49er's	Long Beach	Big West	www.longbeachstate.com
Loyola Marymount Lions	Los Angeles	West Coast	www.lmulions.com/sports
Univ. of Pacific Tigers	Stockton	Big West	www.pacifictigers.cstv.com
Pepperdine Univ. Waves	Malibu	West Coast	www.pepperdinesports.com
Sacramento St. Hornets	Sacramento	Big Sky	www.hornetsports.com

Saint Mary's Gaels	Moraga	West Coast	www.smcgaels.cstv.com
San Diego Toreros	San Diego	West Coast	www.usdtoreros.cstv.com
San Diego State Aztecs	San Diego	Mountain West	www.goaztecs.cstv.com
San Francisco Dons	San Francisco	West Coast	www.usfdons.com
San Jose State Spartans	San Jose	Western Athletic	www.sjsuspartans.com
Santa Clara Broncos	Santa Clara	West Coast	www.santaclarabroncos.com
Univ. of Stanford Cardinal	Palo Alto	Pac 12	www.gostanford.com
U. of Cal Davis Aggies	Davis	Big West	www.ucdavisaggies.com
U. of Cal Irvine Anteaters	Irvine	Big West	www.ucirvinesports.com
U. C. Riverside Highlanders	Riverside	Big West	www.ucr.edu/athletics.com
U. C. Santa Barbara Gauchos	Santa Barbara	Big West	www.ucsbgauchose.cstv.com
U.C.L.A. Bruins	Los Angeles	Pac 12	www.uclabruins.com
U. S. C. Trojans	Los Angeles	Pac 12	www.usctrojans.com

COLORADO

Air Force Falcons	Colo. Springs	Mountain West	www.goairforcefalcons.com
Colorado Buffaloes	Boulder	Pac 12	www.cubuffs.com
Colorado State Rams	Ft. Collins	Mountain West	www.csurams.com
University of Denver Pioneers	Denver	Sun Belt	www.denverpioneers.com
Northern Colorado U. Bears	Greeley	Big Sky	www.uncbears.com

CONNECTICUT

Central Conn. St. Univ. Devils	New Britain	Northeast	www.ccsubluedevils.com
University of Connecticut Huskies	Storrs	Big East	www.uconnhuskis.com
Fairfield University Stags	Fairfield	Metro Atlantic Athletic	www.fairfieldstags.com
University of Hartford Hawks	W. Hartford	America East	www.new.hartfordhawks.com
University of Quinnipiac Bobcats	Hamden	Northeast	www.quinnipiacbobcats.com
Sacred Heart University Pioneers	Fairfield	Northeast	www.sacredheartpioneers.com
Yale University Bulldogs	New Haven	Ivy League	www.yalebulldogs.com

DELAWARE

U. of Delaware Fightin' Blue Hens	Newark	Colonial Athletic	www.bluehens.com
Delaware St. University Hornets	Dover	Mid-Eastern Athletic	www.dsuhornets.com

DISTRICT OF COLUMBIA (Washington D.C.)

American University Eagles	Washington	Patriot League	www.aueagles.com
George Washington U. Colonials	Washington	Atlantic 10	www.gwsports.com
Georgetown University Hoyas	Washington	Big East	www.guhoyas.com
Howard University Bison	Washington	Mid-Eastern Athletic	www.howard-bison.com

FLORIDA

Bethune-Cookman Wildcats	Daytona Beach	Mid-Eastern Athletic.	www.b-cuathletics.com
Florida International Panthers	Miami	Sun Belt	www.fiusports.com
University of Florida Gators	Gainesville	Southeastern	www.gatorzone.com
Florida A & M Rattlers	Tallahassee	Mid-Eastern Athletic	www.famurattlersports.com

Florida Atlantic Univ. Owls	Boca Raton	Sun Belt	www.fausports.com
Florida Gulf Coast Univ. Eagles	Fort Myers	Atlantic Sun	www.fgcuathletics.com
Florida State University Seminoles	Tallahassee	Atlantic Coast	www.seminoles.com
Jacksonville University Dolphins	Jacksonville	Atlantic Sun	www.judolphins.com
University of Miami Hurricanes	Coral Gables	Atlantic Coast	www.hurricanesports.cstv.com
Univ. of North Florida Ospreys	Jacksonville	Atlantic Sun	www.unfospreys.com
University of South Florida Bulls	Tampa	Big East	www.gousfbulls.com
Stetson University Hatters	DeLand	Atlantic Sun	www.gohatters.com
Univ. of Central Florida Knights	Orlando	Conference U.S.A.	www.ucfathletics.cstv.com

GEORGIA

University of Georgia Bulldogs	Athens	Southeastern	www.georgiadogs.com
Georgia Southern Univ. Eagles	Statesboro	Southern	www.georgiasoutherneagles.com
Georgia State Univ. Panthers	Atlanta	Colonial Athletic Assn	www.georgiastatesports.com
Georgia Tech Yellow Jackets	Atlanta	Atlantic Coast	www.ramblinwreck.cstv.com
Kennesaw State Owls	Kennesaw	Atlantic Sun	www.ksuowls.com
Mercer University Bears	Macon	Atlantic Sun	www.mercerbears.com
Savannah State Univ. Tigers	Savannah	Independent	www.ssuathletics.com

HAWAII

Univ. of Hawaii Rainbow Warriors	Honolulu	Western Athletic	www.hawaiiathletics.com

IDAHO

Boise State University Broncos	Boise	Mountain West	www.broncosports.com
University of Idaho Vandals	Moscow	Western Athletic	www.govandals.com
Idaho State University Bengals	Pocatello	Big Sky	www.isubengals.com

ILLINOIS

Bradley University Braves	Peoria	Missouri Valley	www.bubraves.com
Chicago State University Cougars	Chicago	Great West	www.gocsucougars.com
DePaul University Demons	Chicago	Big East	www.depaulbluedemons.com
Eastern Illinois Univ. Panthers	Charleston	Ohio Valley Conf	www.eiupanthers.com
University of Illinois Fighting Illini	Champaign	Big 10	www.fightingillini.com
Illinois State University Redbirds	Normal	Missouri Valley	www.goredbirds.com
Loyola University Ramblers	Chicago	Horizon League	www.loyolarambers.cstv.com
Northern Illinois Univ. Huskies	DeKalb	Mid-American	www.niuhuskies.com
Northwestern University Wildcats	Evanston	Big 10	www.nusports.cstv.com
Southern Illinois Salukis	Carbondale	Missouri Valley	www.siusalukis.cstv.com
SIU- Edwardsville Cougars	Edwardsville	Ohio Valley	www.siuecougars.com
U. of Illinois at Chicago Flames	Chicago	Horizon League	www.uicflames.com
Western Illinois Leathernecks	Macomb	Mid-American	www.goleathernecks.com

INDIANA

Ball State Cardinals	Muncie	Mid-American	www.ballstatesports.com
Butler University Bulldogs	Indianapolis	Horizon League	www.butlersports.com
Univ. of Evansville Purple Aces	Evansville	Missouri Valley	www.gopurpleaces.com

Indiana University Hoosiers	Bloomington	Big 10	www.iuhoosiers.cstv.com
Indiana State Sycamores	Terre Haute	Missouri Valley	www.gosycamores.com
Indiana U-Purdue U-Ft Wayne	Indianapolis	Summit League	www.ipfw.edu
Notre Dame Fighting Irish	Notre Dame	Independent	www.und.com
Purdue Boilermakers	West Lafayette	Big 10	www.purduesports.com
Valparaiso Crusaders	Valparaiso	Horizon League	www.valpoathletics.com

IOWA

Drake University Bulldogs	Des Moines	Missouri Valley	www.drakebulldogs.org
Iowa Hawkeyes	Iowa City	Big 10	www.hawkeyesports.com
Iowa State Cyclones	Ames	Big 12	www.cyclones.com
Northern Iowa Panthers	Cedar Falls	Missouri Valley	www.unipanthers.com

KANSAS

Kansas Jayhawks	Lawrence	Big 12	www.kuathletics.com
Kansas State Wildcats	Manhattan	Big 12	www.kstatesports.com
Wichita State Shockers	Wichita	Missouri Valley	www.goshockers.com

KENTUCKY

Eastern Kentucky Colonels	Richmond	Ohio Valley	www.ekusports.com
Kentucky Wildcats	Lexington	Southeastern	www.ukathletics.com
Louisville Cardinals	Louisville	Big East	www.uoflsports.com
Morehead State Eagles	Morehead	Ohio Valley	www.msueagles.com
Murray State University Racers	Murray	Ohio Valley	www.goracers.com
Western Kentucky Hilltoppers	Bowling Green	Sun Belt	www.wkusports.com

LOUISIANA

Centenary College of Louisiana	Shreveport	Summit League	www.gocentenary.com
Grambling State University	Grambling	Southwestern Athletic	www.gsutigers.com
U. of LA Lafayette Ragin' Cajuns	Lafayette	Sun Belt	www.ragincajuns.com
U. of LA at Monroe Warhawks	Monroe	Sun Belt	www.ulmathletics.com
Louisiana Tech Bulldogs	Ruston	Western Athletic	www.latechsports.com
L S U Tigers	Baton Rouge	Southeastern	www.lsusports.net
McNeese State Cowboys	Lake Charles	Southland	www.mcneesesports.com
Nicholls State Colonels	Thibodaux	Southland	www.geauxcolonels.cstv.com
Northwestern St Univ Demons	Natchitoches	Southland	www.nsudemons.com
S. E. Louisiana University Lions	Hammond	Southland	www.lionsports.net
Southern University Jags	Baton Rouge	Southwestern Athletic	www.gojagsports.cstv.com
Tulane University Green Wave	New Orleans	Conference U.S.A.	www.tulanegreenwave.com

MAINE

| University of Maine Black Bears | Orono | America East | www.goblackbears.com |

MARYLAND

Coppin State University Eagles	Baltimore	Mid-Eastern Athletic	www.coppinstatesports.com
Loyola U. Maryland Greyhounds	Baltimore	Metro Atlantic Athletic	www.loyolagreyhounds.com
Maryland Terrapins	College Park	Atlantic Coast	www.umterps.com
Morgan State University Bears	Baltimore	Mid-Eastern Athletic	www.morganstatebears.com
Mount St Mary's Mountaineers	Emmitsburg	Northeast	www.mountathletics.com
Navy Midshipmen	Annapolis	Patriot League	www.navysports.com
Towson University Tigers	Towson	Colonial Athletic Assn	www.towsontigers.com
U. of MD Baltimore Co. Retrievers	Catonsville	America East	www.umbcretrievers.com
U. of MD Eastern Shore Hawks	Princess Anne	Mid-Eastern	www.umeshawks.com

MASSACHUSETTS

Boston College Eagles	Chestnut Hill	Atlantic Coast	www.bceagles.cstv.com
Boston University Terriers	Boston	America East	www.goterriers.com
Harvard University Crimson	Cambridge	Ivy League	www.gocrimson.com
Holy Cross Crusaders	Worcester	Patriot League	www.goholycross.com
U. of Massachusetts Minutemen	Amherst	Atlantic 10	www.umassathletics.com
Northeastern Huskies	Boston	Colonial Athletic	www.gonu.com

MICHIGAN

Central Michigan Chippewas	Mt Pleasant	Mid-American	www.cmuchippewas.com
Detroit University Titans	Detroit	Horizon League	www.detroittitans.com
Eastern Michigan Eagles	Ypsilanti	Mid-American	www.emueagles.com
Univ of Michigan Wolverines	Ann Arbor	Big 10	www.mgoblue.com
Michigan State Spartans	East Lansing	Big 10	www.msuspartans.com
Oakland University Grizzlies	Rochester	Summit League	www.ougrizzlies.com
Western Michigan Broncos	Kalamazoo	Mid-American	www.wmubroncos.com

MINNESOTA

Minnesota Golden Gophers	Minn/St. Paul	Big 10	www.gophersports.com

MISSISSIPPI

Alcorn State University Braves	Lorman	Southwestern Athletic	www.alcornsports.com
Jackson State Tigers	Jackson	Southwestern Athletic	www.jsutigers.cstv.com
Mississippi State Bulldogs	Starkville	Southeastern	www.mstateathletics.com
Mississippi Valley St. Delta Devils	Itta Bena	Southwestern Athletic	www.mvsu.edu/athletics
University of Mississippi Rebels	Oxford	Southeastern	www.olemisssports.com
Southern Miss Golden Eagles	Hattiesburg	Conference U.S.A.	www.southernmiss.cstv.com

MISSOURI

University of Missouri Tigers	Columbia	Big 12	www.mutigers.com
Missouri State Univ. Bears	Springfield	Missouri Valley	www.missouristatebears.com
St. Louis Billikens	St. Louis	Atlantic 10	www.slubillikens.com
Southeast Missouri St. Redhawks	Cape Girardeau	Ohio Valley	www.gosoutheast.cstv.com
U. of MO – Kansas City Kangaroos	Kansas City	Summit League	www.umckkangaroos.com

MONTANA

Montana Grizzlies	Missoula	Big Sky	www.montanagrizzlies.com
Montana State Bobcats	Bozeman	Big Sky	www.msubobcats.com

NEBRASKA

Creighton University Bluejays	Omaha	Missouri Valley	www.gocreighton.com
Nebraska Cornhuskers	Lincoln	Big 10	www.huskers.com

NEVADA

Nevada Wolfpack	Reno	Western Athletic	www.nevadawolfpack.com
U. of NV Las Vegas Rebels	Las Vegas	Mountain West	www.unlvrebels.com

NEW HAMPSHIRE

Dartmouth College	Hanover	Ivy League	www.dartmouthsports.com
New Hampshire Wildcats	Durham	America East	www.unhwildcats.com

NEW JERSEY

Fairleigh Dickinson Knights	Hackensack	Northeast	www.fduknights.com
Monmouth University Hawks	W. Long Branch	Northeast	www.gomuhawks.com
New Jersey Tech Highlanders	Newark	Great West	www.njithighlanders.com
Princeton Tigers	Princeton	Ivy League	www.goprincetontigers.com
Rider University Broncs	Lawrenceville	Metro Atlantic Athletic	www.gobroncs.com
Rutgers University Knights	New Brunswick	Big East	www.scarletknights.com
St Peter's College Peacocks	Jersey City	Metro Atlantic Athletic	www.spc.edu/athletics
Seton Hall Pirates	South Orange	Big East	www.shupirates.com

NEW MEXICO

New Mexico Lobos	Albuquerque	Mountain West	www.golobos.com
New Mexico State Aggies	Las Cruces	Western Athletic	www.nmstatesports.com

NEW YORK

Albany State Univ. Great Danes	Albany	America East	www.ualbanysports.com
Army Black Knights	West Point	Patriot League	www.goarmysports.com
Binghampton Univ. Bearcats	Vestal	America East	www.bubearcats.com
Buffalo State University Bulls	Buffalo	Mid-American	www.buffalostateathletics.com
Canisius College Golden Griffins	Buffalo	Metro Atlantic Athletic	www.gogriffs.com
Colgate University Raiders	Hamilton	Patriot League	www.gocolgateraiders.com
Columbia University Lions	New York	Ivy League	www.gocolumbialions.com
Cornell University Big Red	Ithaca	Ivy League	www.cornellbigred.com
Fordham University Rams	Bronx	Atlantic 10	www.fordhamsports.com
Hofstra University Pride	Hempstead	Colonial Athletic Assn.	www.gohofstra.com
Iona College Gaels	New Rochelle	Metro Atlantic Athletic	www.icgaels.com
Long Island University Blackbirds	Brooklyn	Northeast	www.liuathletics.com
Manhattan College Jaspers	Riverdale	Metro Atlantic Athletic	www.gojaspers.com
Marist College Red Foxes	Poughkeepsie	Metro Atlantic Athletic	www.goredfoxes.cstv.com

Niagara University Purple Eagles	Lewiston	Metro Atlantic Athletic	www.purpleeagles.com
St. Bonaventure Univ. Bonnies	Olean	Atlantic 10	www.gobonnies.com
St. Francis College Terriers	Brooklyn	Northeast	www.sfcathletics.com
St. John's University Red Storm	Jamaica	Big East	www.redstormsports.com
Siena College Saints	Loudonville	Metro Atlantic Athletic	www.sienasaints.com
Stony Brook Univ. Seawolves	Stony Brook	America East	www.goseawolves.org
Syracuse University Orange	Syracuse	Big East	www.suathletics.com
Wagner College Seahawks	Staten Island	Northeast	www.wagnerathletics.com

NORTH CAROLINA

Appalachian St. Mountaineers	Boone	Southern	www.goasu.com
Campbell Univ. Fighting Camels	Buies Creek	Atlantic Sun	www.gocamels.com
U. of N. Carolina Charlotte 49ers	Charlotte	Atlantic 10	www.charlotte49ers.com
Davidson College Wildcats	Davidson	Southern	www.davidsonwildcats.com
Duke University Blue Devils	Durham	Atlantic Coast	www.goduke.com
East Carolina University Pirates	Greenville	Conference U.S.A.	www.ecupirates.com
Elon University Phoenix	Elon	Southern Conference	www.elonphoenix.com
Gardner-Webb Runnin' Bulldogs	Boiling Springs	Big South	www.gwusports.com
High Point University Panthers	High Point	Big South	www.highpointpanthers.com
North Carolina Tar Heels	Chapel Hill	Atlantic Coast	www.tarheelblue.cstv.com
North Carolina A & T Aggies	Greensboro	Mid-Eastern Atlantic	www.ncataggies.com
N. Carolina Central Univ. Eagles	Durham	Mid-Eastern Athl.	www.nccueaglepride.cstv.com
North Carolina State Wolfpack	Raleigh	Atlantic Coast	www.gopack.com
UNC Asheville Bulldogs	Asheville	Big South	www.uncabulldogs.com
UNC Greensboro Spartans	Greensboro	Southern	www.uncgspartans.com
UNC Wilmington Seahawks	Wilmington	Colonial Athletic Assn.	www.uncwsports.com
Wake Forest Demon Deacons	Winston-Salem	Atlantic Coast	www.wakeforestsports.cstv.com
Western Carolina Catamounts	Cullowhee	Southern	www.catamountsports.com

NORTH DAKOTA

U. of North Dakota Fighting Sioux	Grand Forks	Great West	www.fightingsioux.com
N. Dakota State Univ. Bison	Fargo	The Summit League	www.gobison.com

OHIO

Akron University Zips	Akron	Mid-American	www.gozips.com
Bowling Green University Falcons	Bowling Green	Mid-American	www.bgsufalcons.com
University of Cincinnati Bearcats	Cincinnati	Big East	www.gobearcats.com
Cleveland State Univ. Vikings	Cleveland	Horizon League	www.csuvikings.com
Dayton University Flyers	Dayton	Atlantic 10	www.daytonflyers.com
Kent State Univ. Golden Flashes	Kent	Mid-American	www.kentstatesports.com
Miami University RedHawks	Oxford	Mid-American	www.muredhawks.com
Ohio University Bobcats	Athens	Mid-American	www.ohiobobcats.com
Ohio State University Buckeyes	Columbus	Big 10	www.ohiostatebuckeyes.com
Toledo University Rockets	Toledo	Mid-American	www.utrockets.com
Wright St. University Raiders	Fairborn	Horizon League	www.wsuraiders.com
Xavier University Musketeers	Cincinnati	Atlantic 10	www.goxavier.com

Youngstown St Univ. Penguins	Youngstown	Horizon League	www.ysusports.com

OKLAHOMA

Oklahoma Sooners	Norman	Big 12	www.soonersports.com
Oklahoma State Cowboys	Stillwater	Big 12	www.okstate.com
Oral Roberts U. Golden Eagles	Tulsa	The Summit League	www.orugoldeneagles.com
Tulsa University Hurricane	Tulsa	Conference U.S.A.	www.tulsahurricane.com

OREGON

Oregon Ducks	Eugene	Pac 12	www.goducks.com
Oregon State Beavers	Corvallis	Pac 12	www.osubeavers.com
Portland University Pilots	Portland	West Coast	www.portlandpilots.com
Portland St University Vikings	Portland	Big Sky	www.goviks.com

PENNSYLVANIA

Bucknell University Bison	Lewisburg	Patriot League	www.bucknellbison.com
Drexel University Dragons	Philadelphia	Colonial Athletic Assn	www.drexeldragons.com
Duquesne University Dukes	Pittsburgh	Atlantic 10	www.goduquesne.com
La Salle University Explorers	Philadelphia	Atlantic 10	www.goexplorers.com
Lafayette College Leopards	Easton	Patriot League	www.goleopards.com
Lehigh Univ. Mountain Hawks	Bethlehem	Patriot League	www.lehighsports.com
Univ. of Pennsylvania Quakers	Philadelphia	Ivy League	www.pennathletics.com
Penn State Univ. Nittany Lions	State College	Big 10	www.gopsusports.com
Pittsburgh University Panthers	Pittsburgh	Big East	www.pittsburghpanthers.com
Robert Morris Univ. Colonials	Moon Township	Northeast	www.rmucolonials.com
St. Francis Univ. Red Flash	Loretto	Northeast	www.sfcathletics.com
St. Joseph's Univ. Hawks	Philadelphia	Atlantic 10	www.sjuhawks.com
Temple University Owls	Philadelphia	Atlantic 10	www.owlsports.com
Villanova University Wildcats	Radnor Township	Big East	www.villanova.com

RHODE ISLAND

Brown University Bears	Providence	Ivy League	www.brownbears.com
Bryant University Bulldogs	Smithfield	Northeast	www.bryantbulldogs.com
Providence College Friars	Providence	Big East	www.friars.com
Rhode Island Univ. Rams	Kingston	Atlantic 10	www.gorhody.com

SOUTH CAROLINA

Charleston Southern U Buccaneers	Charleston	Big South	www.csusports.com
The Citadel Bulldogs	Charleston	Southern	www.citidelsports.com
Clemson University Tigers	Clemson	Atlantic Coast	www.clemsontigers.cstv.com
Coastal Carolina U. Chanticleers	Conway	Big South	www.goccusports.com
College of Charleston Cougars	Charleston	Southern	www.cofcsports.com
Furman University Paladins	Greenville	Southern	www.furmanpaladins.com
Presbyterian College Blue Hose	Clinton	Big South	www.gobluehose.com
South Carolina Gamecocks	Columbia	Southeastern	www.gamecocksonline.cstv.com

South Carolina State Bulldogs	Orangeburg	Mid-Eastern Athletic	www.scsuathletics.com
South Carolina Upstate Spartans	Spartanburg	Atlantic Sun	www.upstatespartans.com
Winthrop University Eagles	Rock Hill	Big South	www.winthropeagles.com
Wofford College Terriers	Spartanburg	Southern	www.woffordterriers.com

SOUTH DAKOTA

South Dakota University Coyotes	Vermillion	The Summit League	www.usdcoyotes.com
South Dakota St. Univ. Jackrabbits	Brookings	The Summit League	www.gojacks.com

TENNESSEE

Austin Peay St. Univ. Governors	Clarksville	Ohio Valley	www.letsgopeay.com
Belmont University Bruins	Nashville	Atlantic Sun	www.belmontbruins.cstv.com
U of Tennessee Chattanooga Mocs	Chattanooga	Southern	www.gomocs.com
E. Tennessee St. U. Buccaneers	Johnson City	Atlantic Sun	www.etsubucs.com
Lipscomb University Bisons	Nashville	Atlantic Sun	www.lipscombsports.com
Memphis University Tigers	Memphis	Conference U.S.A.	www.gotigersgo.com
Middle Tennessee St. Blue Raiders	Murfreesboro	Sun Belt	www.goblueraiders.com
Tennessee Volunteers	Knoxville	Southern	www.utsports.com
Tennessee-Martin Skyhawks	Martin	Ohio Valley	www.utmsports.com
Tennessee St. U. Tigers	Nashville	Ohio Valley	www.tsutigers.com
Tennessee Tech Golden Eagles	Cookeville	Ohio Valley	www.ttusports.com
Vanderbilt Univ. Commodores	Nashville	Southern	www.vucommodores.cstv.com

TEXAS

Baylor University Bears	Waco	Big 12	www.baylorbears.com
Houston University Cougars	Houston	Conference U.S.A.	www.uhcougars.com
Houston Baptist Huskies	Houston	Great West	www.hbuhuskies.com
Lamar University Cardinals	Beaumont	Southland	www.lamarcardinals.com
U. of North Texas Mean Green	Denton	Sun Belt	www.meangreensports.com
Prairie View A & M Panthers	Prairie View	Southwestern Athletic	www.pvamu.edu
Rice University Owls	Houston	Conference U.S.A.	www.riceowls.com
Sam Houston St. Bearkats	Huntsville	Southland	www.gobearkats.com
Southern Methodist Mustangs	University Park	Conference U.S.A.	www.smumustangs.cstv.com
Stephen F Austin Lumberjacks	Nacogdoches	Southland	www.sfajacks.cstv.com
Texas Christian Horned Frogs	Fort Worth	Mountain West	www.gofrogs.cstv.com
Texas Longhorns	Austin	Big 12	www.texassports.com
Texas A & M Aggies	College Station	Big 12	www.aggieathletics.com
Tex A&M–Corpus Christi Islanders	Corpus Christi	Southland	www.goislanders.com
Texas Southern U. Tigers	Houston	Southwestern Athletic	www.tsu.edu
Texas State Bobcats	San Marcos	Southland Conference	www.txstatebobcats.com
Texas Tech Red Raiders	Lubbock	Big 12	www.texastech.com
UT Arlington Mavericks	Arlington	Southland	www.utamavs.com
UT San Antonio Roadrunners	San Antonio	Southland	www.goutsa.com
UT El Paso Miners	El Paso	Conference USA	www.utepathletics.cstv.com
UT Pan American Broncs	Edinburg	Great West	www.utpabroncs.com

UTAH

Brigham Young Univ. Cougars	Provo	Mountain West	www.byucougars.com
Southern Utah Thunderbirds	Cedar City	The Summit League	www.suutbirds.com
Utah Utes	Salt Lake City	Pac 12	www.utahutes.cstv.com
Utah State Aggies	Logan	Western Athletic	www.utahstateaggies.com
Utah Valley Univ. Wolverines	Orem	Great West	www.wolverinegreen.com
Weber State Univ. Wildcats	Ogden	Big Sky	www.weberstatesports.com

VERMONT

Vermont Univ. Catamounts	Burlington	America East	www.uvmathletics.com

VIRGINIA

George Mason Univ. Patriots	Fairfax	Colonial Athletic	www.gomason.cstv.com
Hampton Univ. Pirates	Hampton	Mid-Eastern Athletic	www.hamptonpirates.com
James Madison Univ. Dukes	Harrisonburg	Colonia Athletic	www.jmusports.com
Liberty University Flames	Lynchburg	Big South	www.libertyflames.com
Longwood Univ. Lancers	Farmville	Independent	www.longwoodlancers.com
Norfolk St. Univ. Spartans	Norfolk	Mid-Eastern Athletic	www.nsuspartans.com
Old Dominion Univ. Monarchs	Norfolk	Colonial Athletic Assn	www.odusports.com
Radford University Highlanders	Radford	Big South	www.ruhighlanders.com
Richmond Univ. Spiders	Richmond	Atlantic 10	www.richmondspiders.com
Virginia Cavaliers	Charlottesville	Atlantic Coast	www.virginiasports.com
Virginia Commonwealth Rams	Richmond	Colonial Athletic	www.vcuathletics.com
Virginia Tech Hokies	Blacksburg	Atlantic Coast	www.hokiesports.com
Virginia Military Institute Keydets	Lexington	Big South	www.vmikeydets.com
William & Mary Tribe	Williamsburg	Colonial Athletic Assn	www.tribeathletics.com

WASHINGTON

Eastern Washington Univ. Eagles	Cheney	Big Sky	www.goeags.com
Gonzaga University Bulldogs	Spokane	West Coast	www.gozags.com
Seattle University Redhawks	Seattle	Independent	www.goseattleu.com
Washington Huskies	Seattle	Pac 12	www.gohuskies.com
Washington State Cougars	Pullman	Pac 12	www.wsucougars.com

WEST VIRGINIA

Marshall Univ Thundering Herd	Huntington	Conference USA	www.herdzone.cstv.com
West Virginia Mountaineers	Morgantown	Big East	www.westvirgina.rivals.com

WISCONSIN

Marquette Univ Golden Eagles	Milwaukee	Big East	www.gomarquette.com
U-Wisc. Milwaukee Panthers	Milwaukee	Horizon League	www.uwmpanthers.cstv.com
U-Wisc Green Bay Phoenix	Green Bay	Horizon League	www.greenbayphoenix.com
Wisconsin Badgers	Madison	Big 10	www.uwbadgers.com

WYOMING

Wyoming University Cowboys	Laramie	Mountain West	www.wyomingathletics.com

College Conferences (by TV market size)

Atlantic Coast Conference
Boston College (7)
Georgia Tech (8)
Maryland (9)
University of Miami (16)
Duke (28)
North Carolina (28)
N C State (28)
Clemson (36)
Wake Forest (46)
Virginia Tech (67)
Florida State (108)
Virginia (181)

Big East
Rutgers (1)
South Florida (13)
Pittsburgh (22)
West Virginia (22)
Connecticut (29)
Cincinnati (33)
Louisville (48)
Syracuse (80)

Big Ten
Northwestern (3)
Michigan (11)
Minnesota (15)
Indiana (26)
Ohio State (32)
Illinois (84)
Wisconsin (85)
Iowa (87)
Penn State (99)
Nebraska (104)
Michigan State (112)
Purdue (189)

Big 12
Kansas (31)
Oklahoma (45)
Oklahoma State (45)
Texas (51)
Iowa State (71)
Baylor(95)
Texas A & M (95)
Missouri (137)
Kansas State (139)
Texas Tech (148)

Pac 12
U C L A (2)
U S C (2)
California (6)
Stanford (6)
Arizona State (12)
Washington (14)
Colorado (18)
Arizona (68)
Washington State (77)
Oregon (120)
Oregon State (120)

Southeast
Georgia (8)
Vanderbilt (30)
Alabama (40)
Mississippi (47)
Tennessee (58)
Kentucky (64)
South Carolina (81)
L S U (94)
Arkansas (102)
Auburn (128)
Mississippi State (133)
Florida (162)

INDEPENDENT
Notre Dame (89)

College Ruling Bodies

National Collegiate Athletic Association
700 W. Washington Street
Indianapolis, IN 46206-6222
(317) 917-6222
www.ncaa.org

College Sports Information Directors of America
University of North Alabama
UNA-Box 5038
Florence, AL 35632
www.CoSIDA.com

What Sport Do You Want To Get Involved In?

Archery	Hunting
Badminton	Lacrosse
Baseball	Martial Arts
Basketball	Media Coverage
Betting	Motorsports
Boating	Olympic
Bowling	Paintball
Boxing	Roller Derby
Climbing	Rugby
Coaching	Scuba Diving
Cricket	Shooting
Cycling	Skateboarding
Disabled	Skating
Equestrian	Snowboarding
Extreme Sports	Soccer
Fencing	Squash
Field Hockey	Strength Sports
Fishing	Table Tennis
Football	Tennis
Golf	Track & Field
Gymnastics	Volleyball
Handball	Water Sports
Hockey	Wrestling

In Appreciation

There are numerous people who have shared and contributed valuable time, resourceful information, and wonderful career advice that I am indebted to. Without their professional assistance and encouragement, this book could have never been developed. I am forever grateful.

Steve Raible	**Spencer Haywood**	**Lenny Wilkens**
Warren Moon	**Paula Boivin**	**Susan Webner**
Pedro Gomez	**John Olson**	**Rick Showers**
Jerry Colangelo	**Tommy Nuñez**	**David Griffin**
Rick Welts	**Brian O'Connell**	**Todd Dreyer**
Gary Bender	**Amy Kelso**	**Ralph Kelso**
Vince Kozar	**Ed Cunningham**	**Jerry Heck**
Doug Tammaro	**Michael McDonald**	**Pat Zipfel**
Garfield Heard	**Lon Babby**	**Dr. Roger Baker**
Dr. Richard Emerson	**Ed Olsen**	**Jessica Webb**
Ann Meyers Drysdale	**Paul Coro**	**Clare Farnsworth**
Spero Dedes	**George Tanner**	**Alvan Adams**
Mychal Thompson	**Andre Benavidez**	**Matt Patterson**
Bob Rondeau	**Mrs. Bob Blackburn**	**Dave Blackburn**
Jimmy Walker	**Randy Policar**	**John James**
Ron Wolfley	**Eddie Johnson**	**Bill Wolf**
Allen Campbell	**Marc St. Yves**	**Harvey Shank**

A special thanks to my outstanding editor, Cherie Tucker, from Grammar Works in Seattle! Mike Sankey and Mark Sankey of BRB Publications in Tempe, Arizona have been a god-send to me for their guidance, expertise and support in getting the book prepared for printing. Robin Fox and Associates in Scottsdale, Arizona did an outstanding and creative job in designing the book cover. Lane 'the Big Dog' Davidson from Tempe was invaluable in preparing and upgrading my photographs. A sincere shout-out also goes to Lance Simkins in Phoenix for providing the cover photo. Last but not least, thanks to my brother Dave and all my teenage friends, Pat Lamoureux, Bob Besaw, Mike York, Rick Monzon, Chris Mickelson, Mike Hay, Gene Rousseau and Randy Kirlin for joining me for so many SuperSonics games. All those good times set the foundation for this book.

I appreciate your taking the time to read this book. Hope you learned something valuable from it.

Good luck in your endeavors!

Glenn Capeloto

Photo Permission: Seattle Mariners